Houghton
Mifflin
Harcourt

Volume 2

W0008367

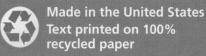

Made in the United States
Text printed on 100%
recycled paper

Houghton
Mifflin
Harcourt

Dear Students and Families,

Welcome to **Go Math!**, Grade 4! In this exciting mathematics program, there are hands-on activities to do and real-world problems to solve. Best of all, you will write your ideas and answers right in your book. In **Go Math!**, writing and drawing on the pages helps you think deeply about what you are learning, and you will really understand math!

By the way, all of the pages in your **Go Math!** book are made using recycled paper. We wanted you to know that you can Go Green with **Go Math!**

Sincerely,

The Authors

Made in the United States
Text printed on 100% recycled paper

Authors

Juli K. Dixon, Ph.D.
Professor, Mathematics Education
University of Central Florida
Orlando, Florida

Edward B. Burger, Ph.D.
President, Southwestern University
Georgetown, Texas

Steven J. Leinwand
Principal Research Analyst
American Institutes for
    Research (AIR)
Washington, D.C.

Contributor

Rena Petrello
Professor, Mathematics
Moorpark College
Moorpark, CA

Matthew R. Larson, Ph.D.
K-12 Curriculum Specialist for
    Mathematics
Lincoln Public Schools
Lincoln, Nebraska

Martha E. Sandoval-Martinez
Math Instructor
El Camino College
Torrance, California

English Language
Learners Consultant

Elizabeth Jiménez
CEO, GEMAS Consulting
Professional Expert on English
    Learner Education
Bilingual Education and
    Dual Language
Pomona, California

VOLUME 1
Place Value and Operations with Whole Numbers

 Critical Area Developing understanding and fluency with multi-digit multiplication, and developing understanding of dividing to find quotients involving multi-digit dividends

(1) Place Value, Addition, and Subtraction to One Million   **3**

Domain Number and Operations in Base Ten
COMMON CORE STATE STANDARDS 4.NBT.A.1, 4.NBT.A.2, 4.NBT.A.3, 4.NBT.B.4

GO DIGITAL

Go online! Your math lessons are interactive. Use *i*Tools, Animated Math Models, the Multimedia eGlossary, and more.

Chapter 1 Overview

In this chapter, you will explore and discover answers to the following **Essential Questions**:

- How can you use place value to compare, add, subtract, and estimate with whole numbers?
- How do you compare and order whole numbers?
- What are some strategies you can use to round whole numbers?
- How is adding and subtracting 5- and 6-digit numbers similar to adding and subtracting 3-digit numbers?

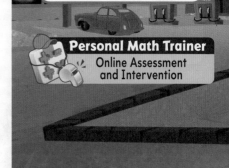

Personal Math Trainer
Online Assessment and Intervention

Chapter 2 Overview

In this chapter, you will explore and discover answers to the following **Essential Questions**:

• What strategies can you use to multiply by 1-digit numbers?
• How can you use models to multiply a multi-digit number by a 1-digit number?
• How can you use estimation to check your answer?
• How does the partial products strategy use place value?

Practice and Homework

Lesson Check and Spiral Review in every lesson

Chapter 3 Overview

In this chapter, you will explore and discover answers to the following **Essential Questions**:

• What strategies can you use to multiply 2-digit numbers?
• How can you use place value to multiply 2-digit numbers?
• How can you choose the best method to multiply 2-digit numbers?

© Houghton Mifflin Harcourt Publishing Company

4 Divide by 1-Digit Numbers   195

Domains Operations and Algebraic Thinking
Number and Operations in Base Ten
COMMON CORE STATE STANDARDS 4.OA.A.3, 4.NBT.B.6

Chapter 4 Overview

In this chapter, you will explore and discover answers to the following **Essential Questions**:

- How can you divide by 1-digit numbers?
- How can you use remainders in division problems?
- How can you estimate quotients?
- How can you model division with a 1-digit divisor?

Chapter 5 Overview

In this chapter, you will explore and discover answers to the following **Essential Questions**:

- How can you find factors and multiples, and how can you generate and describe number patterns?
- How can you use models or lists to find factors?
- How can you create a number pattern?

5 Factors, Multiples, and Patterns 277

Domain Operations and Algebraic Thinking

COMMON CORE STATE STANDARDS 4.OA.B.4, 4.OA.C.5

VOLUME 2

Fractions and Decimals

 Critical Area Developing an understanding of fraction equivalence, addition and subtraction of fractions with like denominators, and multiplication of fractions by whole numbers

6 Fraction Equivalence and Comparison   **325**

Domain Number and Operations–Fractions
COMMON CORE STATE STANDARDS 4.NF.A.1, 4.NF.A.2

7 Add and Subtract Fractions   **383**

Domain Number and Operations–Fractions
COMMON CORE STATE STANDARDS 4.NF.B.3a, 4.NF.B.3b, 4.NF.B.3c, 4.NF.B.3d

Critical Area

GO DIGITAL

Go online! Your math lessons are interactive. Use *i*Tools, Animated Math Models, the Multimedia eGlossary, and more.

Chapter 6 Overview

Essential Questions:
- What strategies can you use to compare fractions and write equivalent fractions?
- What models can help you compare and order fractions?
- How can you find equivalent fractions?
- How can you solve problems that involve fractions?

Chapter 7 Overview

Essential Questions:
- How do you add or subtract fractions that have the same denominator?
- Why do you add or subtract the numerators and not the denominators?
- Why do you rename mixed numbers when adding or subtracting fractions?
- How do you know that your sum or difference is reasonable?

8 Multiply Fractions by Whole Numbers 453

Domain Number and Operations–Fractions
COMMON CORE STATE STANDARDS 4.NF.B.4a, 4.NF.B.4b, 4.NF.B.4c

9 Relate Fractions and Decimals 493

Domains Number and Operations–Fractions
Measurement and Data
COMMON CORE STATE STANDARDS 4.NF.C.5, 4.NF.C.6, 4.NF.C.7, 4.MD.A.2

Geometry, Measurement, and Data

Critical Area

Common Core **Critical Area** Understanding that geometric figures can be analyzed and classified based on their properties, such as having parallel sides, perpendicular sides, particular angle measures, and symmetry

Real World Project Landscape Architects 546

10 Two-Dimensional Figures 547

Domains Operations and Algebraic Thinking
Geometry

COMMON CORE STATE STANDARDS 4.OA.C.5, 4.G.A.1, 4.G.A.2, 4.G.A.3

✓ Show What You Know 547
Vocabulary Builder 548
Chapter Vocabulary Cards
Vocabulary Game 548A
1 Lines, Rays, and Angles 549
2 Classify Triangles by Angles 555
3 Parallel Lines and Perpendicular Lines 561
4 Classify Quadrilaterals 567
✓ Mid-Chapter Checkpoint 573
5 Line Symmetry 575
6 Find and Draw Lines of Symmetry 581
7 **Problem Solving** • Shape Patterns 587
✓ Chapter 10 Review/Test 593

11 Angles 599

Domain Measurement and Data

COMMON CORE STATE STANDARDS 4.MD.C.5a, 4.MD.C.5b, 4.MD.C.6, 4.MD.C.7

✓ Show What You Know 599
Vocabulary Builder 600
Chapter Vocabulary Cards
Vocabulary Game 600A
1 **Investigate** • Angles and Fractional Parts of a Circle 601
2 Degrees 607
3 Measure and Draw Angles 613
✓ Mid-Chapter Checkpoint 619
4 **Investigate** • Join and Separate Angles 621
5 **Problem Solving** • Unknown Angle Measures 627
✓ Chapter 11 Review/Test 633

GO DIGITAL

Go online! Your math lessons are interactive. Use *i*Tools, Animated Math Models, the Multimedia eGlossary, and more.

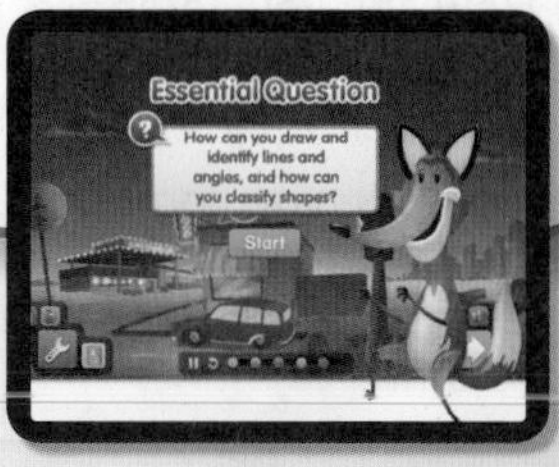

Chapter 10 Overview

Essential Questions:

- How can you draw and identify lines and angles, and how can you classify shapes?
- What are the building blocks of geometry?
- How can you classify triangles and quadrilaterals?
- How do you recognize symmetry in a polygon?

Chapter 11 Overview

Essential Questions:

- How can you measure angles and solve problems involving angle measures?
- How can you use fractions and degrees to understand angle measures?
- How can you use a protractor to measure and classify angles?
- How can equations help you find the measurement of an angle?

Critical Area # Fractions and Decimals

Common Core

CRITICAL AREA Developing an understanding of fraction equivalence, addition and subtraction of fractions with like denominators, and multiplication of fractions by whole numbers

A *luthier,* or guitar maker, at his workshop

Building Custom Guitars

Do you play the guitar, or would you like to learn how to play one? The guitar size you need depends on your height to the nearest inch and on *scale length*. Scale length is the distance from the *bridge* of the guitar to the *nut*.

Get Started

WRITE ▸ *Math*

Order the guitar sizes from the least size to the greatest size, and complete the table.

Important Facts

Guitar Sizes for Students			
Age of Player	Height of Player (to nearest inch)	Scale Length (shortest to longest, in inches)	Size of Guitar
4–6	3 feet 3 inches to 3 feet 9 inches	19	
6–8	3 feet 10 inches to 4 feet 5 inches	20.5	
8–11	4 feet 6 inches to 4 feet 11 inches	22.75	
11–Adult	5 feet or taller	25.5	

Size of Guitar: $\frac{1}{2}$ size, $\frac{4}{4}$ size, $\frac{1}{4}$ size, $\frac{3}{4}$ size

Adults play $\frac{4}{4}$-size guitars. You can see that guitars also come in $\frac{3}{4}$, $\frac{1}{2}$, and $\frac{1}{4}$ sizes. Figure out which size guitar you would need according to your height and the scale length for each size guitar. Use the Important Facts to decide. **Explain** your thinking.

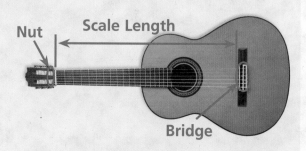

Nut   Scale Length

Bridge

_____

_____

Completed by _____

 Show What You Know

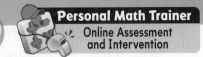

Personal Math Trainer
Online Assessment
and Intervention

Check your understanding of important skills.

Name _____

▶ **Part of a Whole** **Write a fraction for the shaded part.** (3.NF.A.1)

1. _____   2. _____   3. _____

▶ **Name the Shaded Part** **Write a fraction for the shaded part.** (3.NF.A.1)

4. _____   5. _____   6. 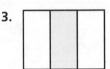 _____

▶ **Compare Parts of a Whole** **Color the fraction strips to show the fractions. Circle the greater fraction.** (3.NF.A.3d)

7. $\frac{1}{2}$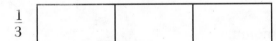

$\frac{1}{3}$

8. $\frac{1}{5}$

$\frac{1}{3}$

 **Math in the Real World**

Earth's surface is covered by more than 57 million square miles of land. The table shows about how much of Earth's land surface each continent covers. Which continent covers the greatest part of Earth's land surface?

Continent	Part of Land Surface
Asia	$\frac{3}{10}$
Africa	$\frac{1}{5}$
Antarctica	$\frac{9}{100}$
Australia	$\frac{6}{100}$
Europe	$\frac{7}{100}$
North America	$\frac{1}{6}$
South America	$\frac{1}{8}$

Vocabulary Builder

▶ **Visualize It** •

Complete the flow map by using the words with a ✓.

Whole Numbers and Fractions

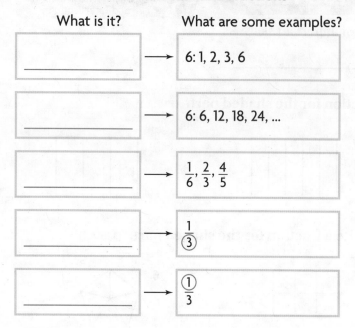

What is it?   What are some examples?

6: 1, 2, 3, 6

6: 6, 12, 18, 24, ...

$\frac{1}{6}, \frac{2}{3}, \frac{4}{5}$

$\frac{1}{③}$

$\frac{①}{3}$

Review Words

common multiple

✓ denominator

✓ factor

✓ fraction

✓ multiple

✓ numerator

Preview Words

benchmark

common denominator

equivalent fractions

simplest form

▶ **Understand Vocabulary** •

Complete the sentences by using preview words.

1. A fraction is in _____ if the numerator and denominator have only 1 as a common factor.

2. _____ name the same amount.

3. A _____ is a common multiple of two or more denominators.

4. A _____ is a known size or amount that helps you understand a different size or amount.

GO DIGITAL
• Interactive Student Edition
• Multimedia eGlossary

Chapter 6 Vocabulary

benchmark

punto de referencia

6

common denominator

denominador común

9

denominator

denominador

22

equivalent fractions

fracciones equivalentes

29

fraction

fracción

36

multiple

múltiplo

55

numerator

numerador

56

simplest form

mínima expresión

84

A common multiple of two or more denominators

Example: Some common denominators for $\frac{1}{4}$ and $\frac{5}{6}$ are 12, 24, and 36.

A known size or amount that helps you understand a different size or amount

You can use $\frac{1}{2}$ as a benchmark to help you compare fractions.

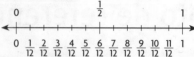

Two or more fractions that name the same amount

Example: $\frac{3}{4}$ and $\frac{6}{8}$ name the same amount.

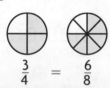

$$\frac{3}{4} = \frac{6}{8}$$

The number below the bar in a fraction that tells how many equal parts are in the whole or in the group

Example: $\frac{3}{4}$ ← denominator

The product of a number and a counting number is called a multiple of the number

Example:

$$\begin{array}{cccc} 3 & 3 & 3 & 3 \\ \times\,1 & \times\,2 & \times\,3 & \times\,4 \\ \hline 3 & 6 & 9 & 12 \end{array}$$

← counting numbers
← multiples of 3

A number that names a part of a whole or part of a group

Example:

$\frac{1}{3}$

A fraction is in simplest form when the numerator and denominator have only 1 as a common factor

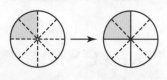

$$\frac{2}{8} = \frac{1}{4}$$

↑ simplest form

The number above the bar in a fraction that tells how many parts of the whole or group are being considered

Example: $\frac{1}{5}$ ← numerator

Going to San Francisco

For 2 to 4 players

Materials

- 3 of one color per player: red, blue, green, and yellow playing pieces
- 1 number cube

How to Play

1. Put your 3 playing pieces in the START circle of the same color.

2. To get a playing piece out of START, you must toss a 6.
   - If you toss a 6, move 1 of your playing pieces to the same-colored circle on the path.
   - If you do not toss a 6, wait until your next turn.

3. Once you have a playing piece on the path, toss the number cube to take a turn. Move the playing piece that many tan spaces. You must get all three of your playing pieces on the path.

4. If you land on a space with a question, answer it. If you are correct, move ahead 1 space.

5. To reach FINISH, you must move your playing piece up the path that is the same color as your playing piece. The first player to get all three playing pieces on FINISH wins.

Word Box

benchmark

common denominator

denominator

equivalent fractions

fraction

multiple

numerator

simplest form

CALIFORNIA

START

Explain how you know that $\frac{2}{6}$ is in simplest form.

How do you know when a fraction is in simplest form?

FINISH

What is a fraction?

What are equivalent fractions?

How can you find a fraction that is equivalent to $\frac{1}{3}$?

Why are $\frac{1}{2}$ and $\frac{2}{4}$ equivalent fractions?

START

What is the difference between a multiple and common multiple?

Explain the relationship between a common multiple and a common denominator.

START

What is the meaning of common denominator?

What is the simplest form of a fraction?

FINISH

How do you find the common denominator of $\frac{2}{3}$ and $\frac{3}{5}$?

What is a multiple?

What is a benchmark?

How are benchmarks used to compare fractions?

In a fraction, what does the numerator represent?

In a fraction, what does the denominator represent?

START

The Write Way

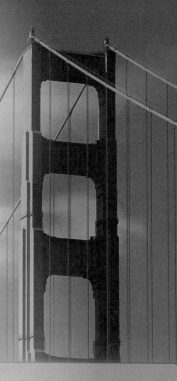

Reflect

Explain how to find the common denominator for $\frac{2}{3}$ and $\frac{1}{4}$.

• Work with a partner to explain and illustrate two ways to find equivalent fractions. Use a separate piece of paper for your drawing.

• Write about all the different ways you can show 25.

• Summarize how you would order the fractions $\frac{2}{3}$, $\frac{7}{8}$, and $\frac{4}{5}$, including any "false starts" or "dead ends."

Equivalent Fractions

Essential Question How can you use models to show equivalent fractions?

Common Core
Number and Operations—
Fractions—4.NF.A.1
MATHEMATICAL PRACTICES
MP4, MP5, MP7

Investigate

Materials ■ color pencils

Joe cut a pan of lasagna into third-size pieces. He kept $\frac{1}{3}$ and gave the rest away. Joe will not eat his part all at once. How can he cut his part into smaller, equal-size pieces?

A. Draw on the model to show how Joe could cut his part of the lasagna into 2 equal pieces.

You can rename these 2 equal pieces as a fraction of the original pan of lasagna.

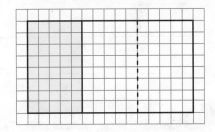

Suppose Joe had cut the original pan of lasagna into equal pieces of this size.

How many pieces would there be? _____

What fraction of the pan is 1 piece? _____

What fraction of the pan is 2 pieces? _____

You can rename $\frac{1}{3}$ as _____.

B. Now draw on the model to show how Joe could cut his part of the lasagna into 4 equal pieces.

You can rename these 4 equal pieces as a fraction of the original pan of lasagna.

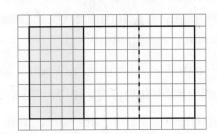

Suppose Joe had cut the original pan of lasagna into equal pieces of this size.

How many pieces would there be? _____

What fraction of the pan is 1 piece? _____

What fraction of the pan is 4 pieces? _____

You can rename $\frac{1}{3}$ as _____.

C. Fractions that name the same amount are **equivalent fractions**. Write the equivalent fractions.

$$\frac{1}{3} = \frac{}{} = \frac{}{}$$

Draw Conclusions

1. Compare the models for $\frac{1}{3}$ and $\frac{2}{6}$. How does the number of parts relate to the sizes of the parts?

_____

_____

2. Describe how the numerators are related and how the denominators are related in $\frac{1}{3} = \frac{2}{6}$.

_____

_____

_____

3. **THINK SMARTER** Does $\frac{1}{3} = \frac{3}{9}$? Explain.

_____

_____

Make Connections

Savannah has $\frac{2}{4}$ yard of ribbon, and Isabel has $\frac{3}{8}$ yard of ribbon. How can you determine whether Savannah and Isabel have the same length of ribbon?

The equal sign ($=$) and not equal to sign ($\neq$) show whether fractions are equivalent.

Tell whether $\frac{2}{4}$ and $\frac{3}{8}$ are equivalent. Write $=$ or $\neq$.

STEP 1 Shade the amount of ribbon Savannah has.

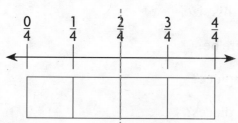

STEP 2 Shade the amount of ribbon Isabel has.

Think: $\frac{2}{4}$ yard is not the same amount as $\frac{3}{8}$ yard.

So, $\frac{2}{4}$ ◯ $\frac{3}{8}$.

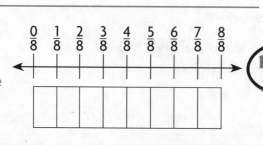

Math Talk

MATHEMATICAL PRACTICES ④

Use Models How could you use a model to show that $\frac{4}{8} = \frac{1}{2}$?

328

Share and Show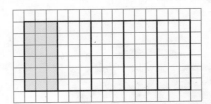

Use the model to write an equivalent fraction.

1.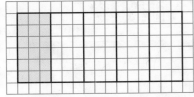

$$\frac{1}{5} \qquad = \qquad \underline{\hspace{2cm}}$$

2.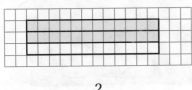

$$\frac{2}{3} \qquad = \qquad \underline{\hspace{2cm}}$$

Tell whether the fractions are equivalent. Write = or ≠.

3. $\frac{1}{6} \bigcirc \frac{2}{12}$

4. $\frac{2}{5} \bigcirc \frac{6}{10}$

5. $\frac{4}{12} \bigcirc \frac{1}{3}$

6. $\frac{5}{8} \bigcirc \frac{2}{4}$

7. $\frac{5}{6} \bigcirc \frac{10}{12}$

8. $\frac{1}{2} \bigcirc \frac{5}{10}$

Problem Solving • Applications

9. **GO DEEPER** Manny used 8 tenth-size parts to model $\frac{8}{10}$. Ana used fewer parts to model an equivalent fraction. How does the size of a part in Ana's model compare to the size of a tenth-size part? What size part did Ana use?

_____

_____

_____

10. **MATHEMATICAL PRACTICE ⑤ Use a Concrete Model** How many eighth-size parts do you need to model $\frac{3}{4}$? Explain.

_____

_____

_____

What's the Error?

11. **THINK SMARTER** Ben brought two pizzas to a party. He says that since $\frac{1}{4}$ of each pizza is left, the same amount of each pizza is left. What is his error?

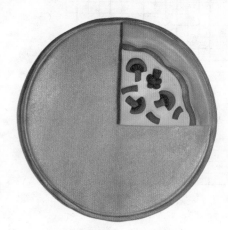

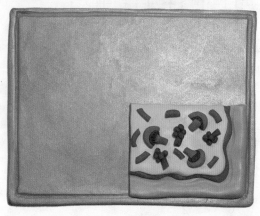

Draw models of 2 pizzas with a different number of equal pieces. Use shading to show $\frac{1}{4}$ of each pizza.

Describe Ben's error.

12. **THINK SMARTER** For numbers 12a–12d, tell whether the fractions are equivalent by selecting the correct symbol.

12a. $\frac{3}{15}$ $\begin{array}{c} = \\ \neq \end{array}$ $\frac{1}{6}$

12b. $\frac{3}{4}$ $\begin{array}{c} = \\ \neq \end{array}$ $\frac{16}{20}$

12c. $\frac{2}{3}$ $\begin{array}{c} = \\ \neq \end{array}$ $\frac{8}{12}$

12d. $\frac{8}{10}$ $\begin{array}{c} = \\ \neq \end{array}$ $\frac{4}{5}$

Equivalent Fractions

Common Core

COMMON CORE STANDARD—4.NF.A.1
Extend understanding of fraction equivalence and ordering.

Use the model to write an equivalent fraction.

1.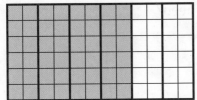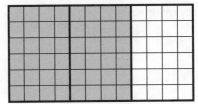

$\frac{4}{6}$ = $\frac{2}{3}$

2.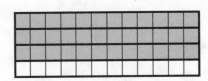

$\frac{3}{4}$ =   _____

Tell whether the fractions are equivalent. Write = or ≠.

3. $\frac{8}{10} \bigcirc \frac{4}{5}$ 4. $\frac{1}{2} \bigcirc \frac{7}{12}$ 5. $\frac{3}{4} \bigcirc \frac{8}{12}$ 6. $\frac{2}{3} \bigcirc \frac{4}{6}$

Problem Solving

7. Jamal finished $\frac{5}{6}$ of his homework. Margaret finished $\frac{3}{4}$ of her homework, and Steve finished $\frac{10}{12}$ of his homework. Which two students finished the same amount of homework?

8. Sophia's vegetable garden is divided into 12 equal sections. She plants carrots in 8 of the sections. Write two fractions that are equivalent to the part of Sophia's garden that is planted with carrots.

9. **WRITE** ▸*Math* Draw a model to show a fraction that is equivalent to $\frac{1}{3}$ and a fraction that is not equivalent to $\frac{1}{3}$.

Lesson Check

1. A rectangle is divided into 8 equal parts. Two parts are shaded. What fraction is equivalent to the shaded area of the rectangle?

2. Jeff uses 3 fifth-size strips to model $\frac{3}{5}$. He wants to use tenth-size strips to model an equivalent fraction. How many tenth-size strips will he need?

Spiral Review

3. Cassidy places 40 stamps on each of 8 album pages. How many stamps does she place?

4. Maria and 3 friends have 1,200 soccer cards. If they share the soccer cards equally, how many will each person receive?

5. Six groups of students sell 162 balloons at the school carnival. There are 3 students in each group. If each student sells the same number of balloons, how many balloons does each student sell?

6. Four students each made a list of prime numbers.

    Eric: 5, 7, 17, 23
    Maya: 3, 5, 13, 17
    Bella: 2, 3, 17, 19
    Jordan: 7, 11, 13, 21

    Who made an error and included a composite number? Write the composite number from his or her list.

FOR MORE PRACTICE
GO TO THE
Personal Math Trainer

Name _____

Generate Equivalent Fractions

Essential Question How can you use multiplication to find equivalent fractions?

Common Core — **Number and Operations— Fractions—4.NF.A.1**
MATHEMATICAL PRACTICES
MP4, MP7, MP8

Unlock the Problem Real World

Sara needs $\frac{3}{4}$ cup of dish soap to make homemade bubble solution. Her measuring cup is divided into eighths. What fraction of the measuring cup should Sara fill with dish soap?

> • Is an eighth-size part of a measuring cup bigger or smaller than a fourth-size part?
>
> _____

Find how many eighths are in $\frac{3}{4}$.

STEP 1 Compare fourths and eighths.

Shade to model $\frac{1}{4}$.
Use fourth-size parts.

1 part

Shade to model $\frac{1}{4}$.
Use eighth-size parts.

2 parts

You need _____ eighth-size parts to make 1 fourth-size part.

STEP 2 Find how many eighths you need to make 3 fourths.

Shade to model $\frac{3}{4}$.
Use fourth-size parts.

3 parts

Shade to model $\frac{3}{4}$.
Use eighth-size parts.

6 parts

You needed 2 eighth-size parts to make 1 fourth-size part.

So, you need _____ eighth-size parts to make 3 fourth-size parts.

So, Sara should fill $\frac{\boxed{}}{8}$ of the measuring cup with dish soap.

MATHEMATICAL PRACTICES ④

Interpret a Result Explain how you knew the number of eighth-size parts you needed to make 1 fourth-size part.

1. Explain why 6 eighth-size parts is the same amount as 3 fourth-size parts.

🔑 Example — Write four fractions that are equivalent to $\frac{1}{2}$.

MODEL	WRITE EQUIVALENT FRACTIONS	RELATE EQUIVALENT FRACTIONS
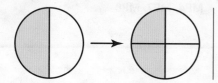	$\frac{1}{2} = \frac{2}{4}$	$\frac{1 \times 2}{2 \times 2} = \frac{2}{4}$
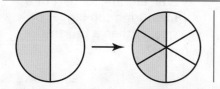	$\frac{1}{2} = \frac{\square}{6}$	$\frac{1 \times \square}{2 \times 3} = \frac{\square}{6}$
	$\frac{1}{2} = \frac{\square}{\square}$	$\frac{1 \times \square}{2 \times \square} = \frac{\square}{\square}$
	$\frac{1}{2} = \frac{\square}{\square}$	$\frac{1 \times \square}{2 \times \square} = \frac{\square}{\square}$

So, $\frac{1}{2} = \frac{2}{4} = \frac{\square}{6} = \frac{\square}{\square} = \frac{\square}{\square}$.

2. Look at the model that shows $\frac{1}{2} = \frac{3}{6}$. How does the number of parts in the whole affect the number of parts that are shaded? Explain.

_____

_____

3. Explain how you can use multiplication to write a fraction that is equivalent to $\frac{3}{5}$.

_____

_____

_____

4. Are $\frac{2}{3}$ and $\frac{6}{8}$ equivalent? Explain.

_____

_____

Name _____

1. Complete the table below.

MODEL	WRITE EQUIVALENT FRACTIONS	RELATE EQUIVALENT FRACTIONS
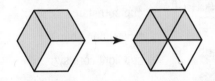	$\dfrac{2}{3} = \dfrac{4}{6}$	$\dfrac{2 \times \square}{3 \times \square} = \dfrac{\square}{\square}$
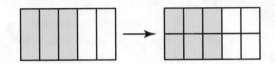	$\dfrac{3}{5} = \dfrac{6}{10}$	$\dfrac{3 \times \square}{5 \times \square} = \dfrac{\square}{\square}$
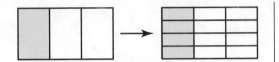	$\dfrac{1}{3} = \dfrac{4}{12}$	$\dfrac{1 \times \square}{3 \times \square} = \dfrac{\square}{\square}$

> **Math Talk** MATHEMATICAL PRACTICES ②
>
> **Reason Abstractly** Can you multiply the numerator and denominator of a fraction by 0? Explain.

Write two equivalent fractions.

✓ **2.** $\dfrac{4}{5}$

$\dfrac{4}{5} = \dfrac{4 \times \square}{5 \times \square} = \dfrac{\square}{\square}$

$\dfrac{4}{5} = \dfrac{4 \times \square}{5 \times \square} = \dfrac{\square}{\square}$

$\dfrac{4}{5} = \dfrac{\square}{\square} = \dfrac{\square}{\square}$

✓ **3.** $\dfrac{2}{4}$

$\dfrac{2}{4} = \dfrac{2 \times \square}{4 \times \square} = \dfrac{\square}{\square}$

$\dfrac{2}{4} = \dfrac{2 \times \square}{4 \times \square} = \dfrac{\square}{\square}$

$\dfrac{2}{4} = \dfrac{\square}{\square} = \dfrac{\square}{\square}$

Write two equivalent fractions.

4. $\dfrac{3}{6}$

$\dfrac{3}{6} = \dfrac{\square}{\square} = \dfrac{\square}{\square}$

5. $\dfrac{3}{10}$

$\dfrac{3}{10} = \dfrac{\square}{\square} = \dfrac{\square}{\square}$

6. $\dfrac{2}{5}$

$\dfrac{2}{5} = \dfrac{\square}{\square} = \dfrac{\square}{\square}$

Tell whether the fractions are equivalent. Write = or ≠.

7. $\dfrac{5}{6} \bigcirc \dfrac{10}{18}$

8. $\dfrac{4}{5} \bigcirc \dfrac{8}{10}$

9. $\dfrac{1}{5} \bigcirc \dfrac{4}{10}$

10. $\dfrac{1}{4} \bigcirc \dfrac{2}{8}$

Problem Solving • Applications (Real World)

Use the recipe for 11–12.

11. [THINK SMARTER] Kim says the amount of flour in the recipe can be expressed as a fraction. Is she correct? Explain.

_____

_____

_____

Face Paint Recipe
$\frac{2}{8}$ cup cornstarch
1 tablespoon flour
$\frac{9}{12}$ cup light corn syrup
$\frac{1}{4}$ cup water
$\frac{1}{2}$ teaspoon food coloring

12. [GO DEEPER] How could you use a $\frac{1}{8}$-cup measuring cup to measure the light corn syrup?

_____

_____

_____

13. [MATHEMATICAL PRACTICE 5] **Communicate** Explain using words how you know a fraction is equivalent to another fraction.

_____

_____

_____

_____

Show Your Work

14. [THINK SMARTER] Kyle drank $\frac{2}{3}$ cup of apple juice. Fill in each box with a number from the list to generate equivalent fractions for $\frac{2}{3}$. Not all numbers will be used.

$$\frac{2}{3} = \frac{\square}{6} = \frac{12}{\square} = \frac{\square}{\square}$$

2	4	6	8
12	15	16	18

Generate Equivalent Fractions

Common Core

COMMON CORE STANDARD—4.NF.A.1
Extend understanding of fraction equivalence and ordering.

Write two equivalent fractions for each.

1. $\frac{1}{3}$

$$\frac{1 \times 2}{3 \times 2} = \frac{2}{6}$$

$$\frac{1 \times 4}{3 \times 4} = \frac{4}{12}$$

2. $\frac{2}{3}$

_____

_____

3. $\frac{1}{2}$

_____

_____

4. $\frac{4}{5}$

_____

_____

Tell whether the fractions are equivalent.
Write = or ≠.

5. $\frac{1}{4} \bigcirc \frac{3}{12}$

6. $\frac{4}{5} \bigcirc \frac{5}{10}$

7. $\frac{3}{8} \bigcirc \frac{2}{6}$

8. $\frac{3}{4} \bigcirc \frac{6}{8}$

9. $\frac{5}{6} \bigcirc \frac{10}{12}$

10. $\frac{6}{12} \bigcirc \frac{5}{8}$

11. $\frac{2}{5} \bigcirc \frac{4}{10}$

12. $\frac{2}{4} \bigcirc \frac{3}{12}$

Problem Solving ·Real· World

13. Jan has a 12-ounce milkshake. Four ounces in the milkshake are vanilla, and the rest is chocolate. What are two equivalent fractions that represent the fraction of the milkshake that is vanilla?

_____

14. Kareem lives $\frac{4}{10}$ of a mile from the mall. Write two equivalent fractions that show what fraction of a mile Kareem lives from the mall.

_____

15. **WRITE** ▸Math Explain how you can determine if $\frac{1}{3}$ and $\frac{4}{12}$ are equivalent fractions.

_____

_____

Lesson Check (4.NF.A.1)

1. Jessie colored a poster. She colored $\frac{2}{5}$ of the poster red. Write a fraction that is equivalent to $\frac{2}{5}$.

2. Marcus makes a punch that is $\frac{1}{4}$ cranberry juice. Write two fractions that are equivalent to $\frac{1}{4}$.

Spiral Review (4.OA.A.3, 4.OA.C.5, 4.NBT.B.5)

3. An electronics store sells a large flat screen television for $1,699. Last month, the store sold 8 of these television sets. About how much money did the televisions sell for?

4. Matthew has 18 sets of baseball cards. Each set has 12 cards. About how many baseball cards does Matthew have?

5. Diana had 41 stickers. She put them in 7 equal groups. She put as many as possible in each group. She gave the leftover stickers to her sister. How many stickers did Diana give to her sister?

6. Christopher wrote the number pattern below. The first term is 8.

    8, 6, 9, 7, 10, ...

    What is a rule for the pattern?

FOR MORE PRACTICE
GO TO THE
Personal Math Trainer

Name _____

Simplest Form

Essential Question How can you write a fraction as an equivalent fraction in simplest form?

 Common Core Number and Operations—Fractions—4.NF.A.1

MATHEMATICAL PRACTICES
MP4, MP6, MP7

Unlock the Problem

Vicki made a fruit tart and cut it into 6 equal pieces. Vicki, Silvia, and Elena each took 2 pieces of the tart home. Vicki says she and each of her friends took $\frac{1}{3}$ of the tart home. Is Vicki correct?

🔑 Activity

Materials ■ color pencils

STEP 1 Use a blue pencil to shade the pieces Vicki took home.

_____

STEP 2 Use a red pencil to shade the pieces Silvia took home.

_____

STEP 3 Use a yellow pencil to shade the pieces Elena took home.

- Into how many pieces was the tart cut?

_____

- How many pieces did each girl take?

_____

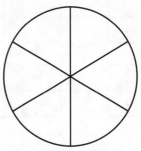

The tart is divided into _____ equal-size pieces. The 3 colors on the model show how to combine sixth-size pieces to make

_____ equal third-size pieces.

So, Vicki is correct. Vicki, Silvia, and Elena each took —— of the tart home.

 Math Talk

MATHEMATICAL PRACTICES ④

Interpret a Result
Compare the models for $\frac{2}{6}$ and $\frac{1}{3}$. Explain how the sizes of the parts are related.

- What if Vicki took 3 pieces of the tart home and Elena took 3 pieces of the tart home. How could you combine the pieces to write a fraction that represents the part each friend took home? Explain.

_____

_____

_____

Simplest Form A fraction is in **simplest form** when you can represent it using as few equal parts of a whole as possible. You need to describe the part you have in equal-size parts. If you can't describe the part you have using fewer parts, then you cannot simplify the fraction.

🔑 One Way Use models to write an equivalent fraction in simplest form.

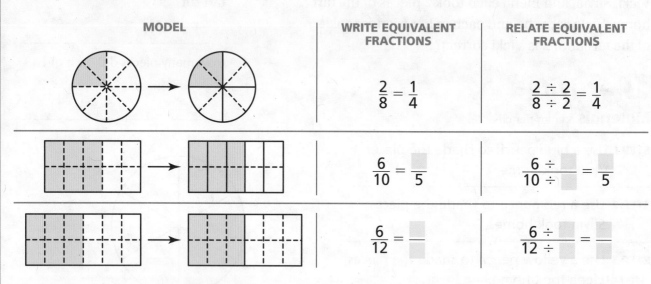

MODEL	WRITE EQUIVALENT FRACTIONS	RELATE EQUIVALENT FRACTIONS
	$\frac{2}{8} = \frac{1}{4}$	$\frac{2 \div 2}{8 \div 2} = \frac{1}{4}$
	$\frac{6}{10} = \frac{\blacksquare}{5}$	$\frac{6 \div \blacksquare}{10 \div \blacksquare} = \frac{\blacksquare}{5}$
	$\frac{6}{12} = \frac{\blacksquare}{\blacksquare}$	$\frac{6 \div \blacksquare}{12 \div \blacksquare} = \frac{\blacksquare}{\blacksquare}$

To simplify $\frac{6}{10}$, you can combine tenth-size parts into equal groups with 2 parts each.

So, $\frac{6}{10} = \frac{6 \div \blacksquare}{10 \div \blacksquare} = \frac{\blacksquare}{\blacksquare}$.

🔑 Another Way Use common factors to write $\frac{6}{10}$ in simplest form.

A fraction is in simplest form when 1 is the only factor that the numerator and denominator have in common. The parts of the whole cannot be combined into fewer equal-size parts to show the same fraction.

STEP 1 List the factors of the numerator and denominator. Circle common factors.

Factors of 6: _____, _____, _____, _____

Factors of 10: _____, _____, _____, _____

STEP 2 Divide the numerator and denominator by a common factor greater than 1.

$\frac{6}{10} = \frac{6 \div \blacksquare}{10 \div \blacksquare} = \frac{\blacksquare}{\blacksquare}$

Since 1 is the only factor that 3 and 5 have in common, _____ is written in simplest form.

340

© Houghton Mifflin Harcourt Publishing Company

Name _____

1. Write $\frac{8}{10}$ in simplest form.

$$\frac{8}{10} = \frac{8 \div \boxed{}}{10 \div \boxed{}} = \boxed{}$$

Write the fraction in simplest form.

2. $\frac{6}{12}$

3. $\frac{2}{10}$

4. $\frac{6}{8}$

5. $\frac{4}{6}$

On Your Own

Write the fraction in simplest form.

6. $\frac{9}{12}$

7. $\frac{4}{8}$

8. $\frac{10}{12}$

9. $\frac{20}{100}$

> **Math Talk**
>
> **MATHEMATICAL PRACTICES 6**
>
> **Explain** how you know a fraction is in simplest form.

Tell whether the fraction is in simplest form.
Write *yes* or *no*.

10. $\frac{2}{8}$

11. $\frac{9}{12}$

12. $\frac{5}{6}$

13. $\frac{4}{10}$

14. **GO DEEPER** There are 18 students in Jacob's homeroom. Six students bring their lunch to school. The rest eat lunch in the cafeteria. In simplest form, what fraction of students eat lunch in the cafeteria?

_____

Problem Solving • Applications

Use the map for 15–16.

15. **MATHEMATICAL PRACTICE (7) Identify Relationships** What fraction of the states in the southwest region share a border with Mexico? Is this fraction in simplest form?

_____

16. **THINK SMARTER** **What's the Question?**
$\frac{1}{3}$ of the states in this region are on the Gulf of Mexico.

_____

_____

Regions of the United States

☐ Northeast
☐ Southeast
☐ Middle West
☐ Southwest
☐ West

17. **GO DEEPER** Pete says that to write $\frac{4}{6}$ as $\frac{2}{3}$, you combine pieces, but to write $\frac{4}{6}$ as $\frac{8}{12}$, you break apart pieces. Does this make sense? Explain.

_____

_____

_____

WRITE ▸ *Math*
Show Your Work

18. **THINK SMARTER ➕** In Michelle's homeroom, $\frac{9}{15}$ of the students ride the bus to school, $\frac{4}{12}$ get a car ride, and $\frac{2}{30}$ walk to school. For numbers 18a–18c, select True or False for each statement.

Personal Math Trainer

18a. In simplest form, $\frac{3}{5}$ of the students ride the bus to school.　　○ True　　○ False

18b. In simplest form, $\frac{1}{4}$ of the students get a car ride to school.　　○ True　　○ False

18c. In simplest form, $\frac{1}{15}$ of the students walk to school.　　○ True　　○ False

Simplest Form

COMMON CORE STANDARD—4.NF.A.1
Extend understanding of fraction equivalence and ordering.

Write the fraction in simplest form.

1. $\frac{6}{10}$

$\frac{6}{10} = \frac{6 \div 2}{10 \div 2} = \frac{3}{5}$

2. $\frac{6}{8}$

_____

3. $\frac{5}{5}$

_____

4. $\frac{8}{12}$

_____

5. $\frac{100}{100}$

_____

6. $\frac{2}{6}$

7. $\frac{2}{8}$

8. $\frac{4}{10}$

Tell whether the fractions are equivalent.
Write = or ≠.

9. $\frac{6}{12} \bigcirc \frac{1}{12}$

10. $\frac{3}{4} \bigcirc \frac{5}{6}$

11. $\frac{6}{10} \bigcirc \frac{3}{5}$

12. $\frac{3}{12} \bigcirc \frac{1}{3}$

Problem Solving · Real World

13. At Memorial Hospital, 9 of the 12 babies born on Tuesday were boys. In simplest form, what fraction of the babies born on Tuesday were boys?

_____

14. Cristina uses a ruler to measure the length of her math textbook. She says that the book is $\frac{4}{10}$ meter long. Is her measurement in simplest form? If not, what is the length of the book in simplest form?

_____

15. **WRITE** ▸*Math* Explain using words or drawings how to write $\frac{6}{9}$ in simplest form.

_____

_____

_____

Lesson Check (4.NF.A.1)

1. Six out of the 12 members of the school choir are boys. In simplest form, what fraction of the choir is boys?

2. Write $\frac{10}{12}$ in simplest form.

Spiral Review (4.OA.A.3, 4.OA.B.4, 4.NBT.B.5, 4.NF.A.1)

3. Each of the 23 students in Ms. Evans' class raised $45 for the school by selling coupon books. How much money did the class raise?

4. List two common factors of 36 and 48.

5. Bart uses $\frac{3}{12}$ cup milk to make muffins. Write a fraction that is equivalent to $\frac{3}{12}$.

6. Ashley bought 4 packages of juice boxes. There are 6 juice boxes in each package. She gave 2 juice boxes to each of 3 friends. How many juice boxes does Ashley have left?

FOR MORE PRACTICE
GO TO THE
Personal Math Trainer

Name _____

Common Denominators

Essential Question How can you write a pair of fractions as fractions with a common denominator?

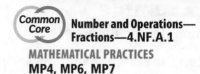

Common Core Number and Operations—Fractions—4.NF.A.1
MATHEMATICAL PRACTICES
MP4, MP6, MP7

Unlock the Problem

Martin has two rectangles that are the same size. One rectangle is cut into $\frac{1}{2}$-size parts. The other rectangle is cut into $\frac{1}{3}$-size parts. He wants to cut the rectangles so they have the same size parts. How can he cut each rectangle?

A **common denominator** is a common multiple of the denominators of two or more fractions. Fractions with common denominators represent wholes cut into the same number of parts.

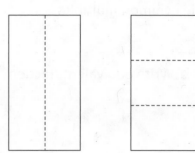

Activity Use paper folding and shading.

Materials ■ 2 sheets of paper

Find a common denominator for $\frac{1}{2}$ and $\frac{1}{3}$.

STEP 1

Model the rectangle cut into $\frac{1}{2}$-size parts. Fold one sheet of paper in half. Draw a line on the fold.

_____

STEP 2

Model the rectangle cut into $\frac{1}{3}$-size parts. Fold the other sheet of paper into thirds. Draw lines on the folds.

_____

STEP 3

Fold each sheet of paper so that both sheets have the same number of parts. Draw lines on the folds. How many equal

parts does each sheet of paper have? _____

STEP 4

Draw a picture of your sheets of paper to show how many parts each rectangle could have.

So, each rectangle could be cut into _____ parts.

MATHEMATICAL PRACTICES ④

Use Models How did the models help you find the common denominator for $\frac{1}{2}$ and $\frac{1}{3}$?

Example Write $\frac{4}{5}$ and $\frac{1}{2}$ as a pair of fractions with common denominators.

You can use common multiples to find a common denominator. List multiples of each denominator. A common multiple can be used as a common denominator.

STEP 1 List multiples of 5 and 2. Circle common multiples.

5:     5,   10,   _____, _____, _____, _____

2:     _____, _____, _____, _____, _____, _____

STEP 2 Write equivalent fractions.

$$\frac{4}{5} = \frac{4 \times \boxed{}}{5 \times \boxed{}} = \frac{\boxed{}}{10}$$

$$\frac{1}{2} = \frac{1 \times \boxed{}}{2 \times \boxed{}} = \frac{\boxed{}}{10}$$

Choose a denominator that is a common multiple of 5 and 2.

You can write $\frac{4}{5}$ and $\frac{1}{2}$ as _____ and _____ .

> ⚠ **ERROR Alert**
>
> Remember that when you multiply the denominator by a factor, you must multiply the numerator by the same factor to write an equivalent fraction.

1. Are $\frac{4}{5}$ and $\frac{1}{2}$ equivalent? Explain.

_____

_____

_____

2. Describe another way you could tell whether $\frac{4}{5}$ and $\frac{1}{2}$ are equivalent.

_____

_____

_____

 **Share and Show**

1. Find a common denominator for $\frac{1}{3}$ and $\frac{1}{12}$ by dividing each whole into the same number of equal parts. Use the models to help.

common denominator: _____

$\frac{1}{3}$

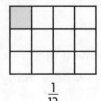
$\frac{1}{12}$

Name _____

Write the pair of fractions as a pair of fractions with a common denominator.

2. $\frac{1}{2}$ and $\frac{1}{4}$

3. $\frac{3}{4}$ and $\frac{5}{8}$

4. $\frac{1}{3}$ and $\frac{1}{4}$

5. $\frac{4}{12}$ and $\frac{5}{8}$

MATHEMATICAL PRACTICES ⑥

Explain how using a model or listing multiples helps you find a common denominator.

On Your Own

Write the pair of fractions as a pair of fractions with a common denominator.

6. $\frac{1}{4}$ and $\frac{5}{6}$

7. $\frac{3}{5}$ and $\frac{4}{10}$

Tell whether the fractions are equivalent. Write = or ≠.

8. $\frac{3}{4} \bigcirc \frac{1}{2}$

9. $\frac{3}{4} \bigcirc \frac{6}{8}$

10. $\frac{1}{2} \bigcirc \frac{4}{8}$

11. $\frac{6}{8} \bigcirc \frac{4}{8}$

12. **GO DEEPER** Jerry has two same-size circles divided into the same number of equal parts. One circle has $\frac{3}{4}$ of the parts shaded, and the other has $\frac{2}{3}$ of the parts shaded. His sister says the least number of pieces each circle could be divided into is 7. Is his sister correct? Explain.

_____

_____

Problem Solving • Applications

13. **GO DEEPER** Carrie has a red streamer that is $\frac{3}{4}$ yard long and a blue streamer that is $\frac{5}{6}$ yard long. She says the streamers are the same length. Does this make sense? Explain.

_____

_____

_____

_____

14. **THINK SMARTER** Leah has two same-size rectangles divided into the same number of equal parts. One rectangle has $\frac{1}{3}$ of the parts shaded, and the other has $\frac{2}{5}$ of the parts shaded. What is the least number of parts into which both rectangles could be divided?

_____

15. **MATHEMATICAL PRACTICE 6** Julian says a common denominator for $\frac{3}{4}$ and $\frac{2}{5}$ is 9. What is Julian's error? **Explain**.

WRITE ▸ *Math*
Show Your Work

_____

_____

_____

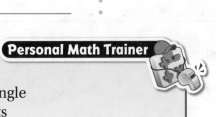 **Personal Math Trainer**

16. **THINK SMARTER +** Miguel has two same-size rectangles divided into the same number of equal parts. One rectangle has $\frac{3}{4}$ of the parts shaded, and the other has $\frac{5}{8}$ of the parts shaded.

Into how many parts could each rectangle be divided? Show your work by sketching the rectangles.

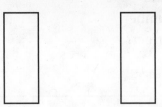

Common Denominators

Common Core COMMON CORE STANDARD—4.NF.A.1
Extend understanding of fraction equivalence and ordering.

Write the pair of fractions as a pair of fractions with a common denominator.

1. $\frac{2}{3}$ and $\frac{3}{4}$

Think: Find a common multiple.
3: 3, 6, 9, ⑫ 15
4: 4, 8, ⑫ 16, 20

$\frac{8}{12}, \frac{9}{12}$

2. $\frac{1}{4}$ and $\frac{2}{3}$

3. $\frac{3}{10}$ and $\frac{1}{2}$

4. $\frac{3}{5}$ and $\frac{3}{4}$

5. $\frac{2}{4}$ and $\frac{7}{8}$

6. $\frac{2}{3}$ and $\frac{5}{12}$

7. $\frac{1}{4}$ and $\frac{1}{6}$

Tell whether the fractions are equivalent. Write = or ≠.

8. $\frac{1}{2} \bigcirc \frac{2}{5}$

9. $\frac{1}{2} \bigcirc \frac{3}{6}$

10. $\frac{3}{4} \bigcirc \frac{5}{6}$

11. $\frac{6}{10} \bigcirc \frac{3}{5}$

Problem Solving Real World

12. Adam drew two same size rectangles and divided them into the same number of equal parts. He shaded $\frac{1}{3}$ of one rectangle and $\frac{1}{4}$ of the other rectangle. What is the least number of parts into which both rectangles could be divided?

13. Mera painted equal sections of her bedroom wall to make a pattern. She painted $\frac{2}{5}$ of the wall white and $\frac{1}{2}$ of the wall lavender. Write an equivalent fraction for each fraction using a common denominator.

14. **WRITE** ▸*Math* How are a common denominator and a common multiple alike and different?

Lesson Check (4.NF.A.1)

1. Write a common denominator for $\frac{1}{4}$ and $\frac{5}{6}$.

2. Two fractions have a common denominator of 8. What could the two fractions be?

Spiral Review (4.NBT.A.2, 4.NBT.B.5, 4.NBT.B.6, 4.NF.A.1)

3. What number is 100,000 more than seven hundred two thousand, eighty-three?

4. Aiden baked 8 dozen muffins. How many total muffins did he bake?

5. On a bulletin board, the principal, Ms. Gomez, put 115 photos of the fourth-grade students in her school. She put the photos in 5 equal rows. How many photos did she put in each row?

6. Judy uses 12 tiles to make a mosaic. Eight of the tiles are blue. What fraction, in simplest form, represents the tiles that are blue?

FOR MORE PRACTICE GO TO THE Personal Math Trainer

Name _____

Problem Solving • Find Equivalent Fractions

Essential Question How can you use the strategy *make a table* to solve problems using equivalent fractions?

 Number and Operations— Fractions—4.NF.A.1
MATHEMATICAL PRACTICES
MP1, MP4, MP6

Unlock the Problem

Anaya is planting a flower garden. The garden will have no more than 12 equal sections. $\frac{3}{4}$ of the garden will have daisies. What other fractions could represent the part of the garden that will have daisies?

Read the Problem

What do I need to find?	**What information do I need to use?**	**How will I use the information?**
_____ that could represent the part of the garden that will have daisies	_____ of the garden will have daisies. The garden will not have more than _____ equal sections.	I can make a _____ to find _____ fractions to solve the problem.

Solve the Problem

I can make a table and draw models to find equivalent fractions.

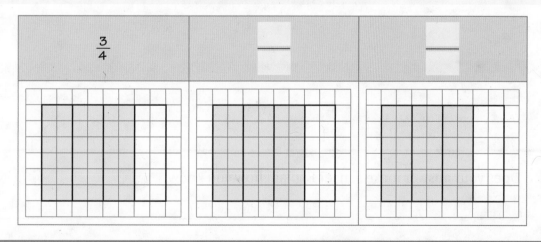

$$\frac{3}{4}$$

1. What other fractions could represent the part of the garden that will have daisies? Explain. _____

_____

_____

Math Talk
MATHEMATICAL PRACTICES ④

Interpret a Result
Compare the models of the equivalent fractions. How does the number of parts relate to the size of the parts?

❶ Try Another Problem

Two friends are knitting scarves. Each scarf has 3 rectangles, and $\frac{2}{3}$ of the rectangles have stripes. If the friends are making 10 scarves, how many rectangles do they need? How many rectangles will have stripes?

Read the Problem

What do I need to find?	What information do I need to use?	How will I use the information?

Solve the Problem

2. Does your answer make sense? Explain how you know.

_____

_____

_____

Math Talk

MATHEMATICAL PRACTICES ❶

Analyze What other strategy could you have used and why?

Name _____

Share and Show

Unlock the Problem
✓ Use the Problem Solving Mathboard.
✓ Underline important facts.
✓ Choose a strategy you know.

1. Keisha is helping plan a race route for a 10-kilometer charity run. The committee wants to set up the following things along the course.

> **Viewing areas:** At the end of each half of the course
>
> **Water stations:** At the end of each fifth of the course
>
> **Distance markers:** At the end of each tenth of the course

Which locations have more than one thing located there?

First, make a table to organize the information.

	Number of Locations	First Location	All the Locations
Viewing Areas	2	$\frac{1}{2}$	$\frac{1}{2}$
Water Stations	5	$\frac{1}{5}$	$\frac{1}{5}$
Distance Markers	10	$\frac{1}{10}$	$\frac{1}{10}$

Next, identify a relationship. Use a common denominator, and find equivalent fractions.

Finally, identify the locations at which more than one thing will be set up. Circle the locations.

_____

_____

2. **THINK SMARTER** What if distance markers will also be placed at the end of every fourth of the course? Will any of those markers be set up at the same location as another distance marker, a water station,

or a viewing area? Explain. _____

_____

_____

3. Fifty-six students signed up to volunteer for the race. There were 4 equal groups of students, and each group had a different task.

How many students were in each group? _____

On Your Own

4. THINK SMARTER A baker cut a pie in half. He cut each half into 3 equal pieces and each piece into 2 equal slices. He sold 6 slices. What fraction of the pie did the baker sell?

_____

5. GO DEEPER Andy cut a tuna sandwich and a chicken sandwich into a total of 15 same-size pieces. He cut the tuna sandwich into 9 more pieces than the chicken sandwich. Andy ate 8 pieces of the tuna sandwich. What fraction of the tuna sandwich did he eat?

WRITE ▸ Math
Show Your Work

_____

6. MATHEMATICAL PRACTICE ⑥ Luke threw balls into these buckets at a carnival. The number on the bucket gives the number of points for each throw. What is the least number of throws needed to score exactly 100 points? **Explain**.

_____

_____

_____

7. THINK SMARTER Victoria arranges flowers in vases at her restaurant. In each arrangement, $\frac{2}{3}$ of the flowers are yellow. What other fractions can represent the part of the flowers that are yellow? Shade the models to show your work.

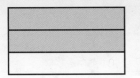

$\frac{2}{3}$ $\frac{}{12}$ $\frac{}{}$

Name _____

Problem Solving • Find Equivalent Fractions

Common Core
COMMON CORE STANDARD—4.NF.A.1
Extend understanding of fraction equivalence and ordering.

Solve each problem.

1. Miranda is braiding her hair. Then she will attach beads to the braid. She wants $\frac{1}{3}$ of the beads to be red. If the greatest number of beads that will fit on the braid is 12, what other fractions could represent the part of the beads that are red?

$\frac{2}{6}, \frac{3}{9}, \frac{4}{12}$

2. Ms. Groves has trays of paints for students in her art class. Each tray has 5 colors. One of the colors is purple. What fraction of the colors in 20 trays is purple?

_____

3. Miguel is making an obstacle course for field day. At the end of every sixth of the course, there is a tire. At the end of every third of the course, there is a cone. At the end of every half of the course, there is a hurdle. At which locations of the course will people need to go through more than one obstacle?

_____

4. **WRITE** ▸*Math* Draw and compare models of $\frac{3}{4}$ of a pizza pie and $\frac{6}{8}$ of a same-size pie.

_____

_____

_____

Lesson Check (4.NF.A.1)

1. A used bookstore will trade 2 of its books for 3 of yours. If Val brings in 18 books to trade, how many books can she get from the store?

_____

2. Every $\frac{1}{2}$ hour Naomi stretches her neck; every $\frac{1}{3}$ hour she stretches her legs; and every $\frac{1}{6}$ hour she stretches her arms. Which parts of her body will Naomi stretch when $\frac{2}{3}$ of an hour has passed?

_____

Spiral Review (4.OA.B.4, 4.NBT.B.4, 4.NBT.B.6, 4.NF.A.1)

3. At the beginning of the year, the Wong family car had been driven 14,539 miles. At the end of the year, their car had been driven 21,844 miles. How many miles did the Wong family drive their car during that year?

_____

4. Widget Company made 3,600 widgets in 4 hours. They made the same number of widgets each hour. How many widgets did the company make in one hour?

_____

5. Tyler is thinking of a number that is divisible by 2 and by 3. Write another number by which Tyler's number must also be divisible.

_____

6. Jessica drew a circle divided into 8 equal parts. She shaded 6 of the parts. What fraction is equivalent to the part of the circle that is shaded?

_____

FOR MORE PRACTICE
GO TO THE
Personal Math Trainer

Name _____

 **Mid-Chapter Checkpoint**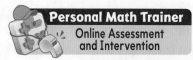

Personal Math Trainer
Online Assessment
and Intervention

Vocabulary

Choose the best term from the box.

Vocabulary
common denominator
equivalent fractions
factor

1. _____ name the same amount. (p. 327)

2. A _____ is a common multiple of
two or more denominators. (p. 345)

Concepts and Skills

Write two equivalent fractions. (4.NF.A.1)

3. $\frac{2}{5}$ = _____ = _____

4. $\frac{1}{3}$ = _____ = _____

5. $\frac{3}{4}$ = _____ = _____

Tell whether the fractions are equivalent. Write = or ≠. (4.NF.A.1)

6. $\frac{2}{3} \bigcirc \frac{4}{12}$

7. $\frac{5}{6} \bigcirc \frac{10}{12}$

8. $\frac{1}{4} \bigcirc \frac{4}{8}$

Write the fraction in simplest form. (4.NF.A.1)

9. $\frac{6}{8}$

10. $\frac{25}{100}$

11. $\frac{8}{10}$

**Write the pair of fractions as a pair of fractions with a
common denominator.** (4.NF.A.1)

12. $\frac{3}{10}$ and $\frac{2}{5}$

13. $\frac{1}{3}$ and $\frac{3}{4}$

14. Sam needs $\frac{5}{6}$ cup mashed bananas and $\frac{3}{4}$ cup mashed strawberries for a recipe. He wants to find whether he needs more bananas or more strawberries. How can he write $\frac{5}{6}$ and $\frac{3}{4}$ as a pair of fractions with a common denominator? (4.NF.A.1)

15. Karen will divide her garden into equal parts. She will plant corn in $\frac{8}{12}$ of the garden. What is the fewest number of parts she can divide her garden into? (4.NF.A.1)

16. **GO DEEPER** Olivia is making scarves. Each scarf will have 5 rectangles, and $\frac{2}{5}$ of the rectangles will be purple. How many purple rectangles does she need for 3 scarves? (4.NF.A.1)

17. Paul needs to buy $\frac{5}{8}$ pound of peanuts. The scale at the store measures parts of a pound in sixteenths. What measure is equivalent to $\frac{5}{8}$ pound? (4.NF.A.1)

Compare Fractions Using Benchmarks

Essential Question How can you use benchmarks to compare fractions?

Common Core Number and Operations—
Fractions—4.NF.A.2
MATHEMATICAL PRACTICES
MP2, MP6, MP7

 Unlock the Problem Real World

David made a popcorn snack. He mixed $\frac{5}{8}$ gallon of popcorn with $\frac{1}{2}$ gallon of dried apple rings. Did he use more dried apple rings or more popcorn?

 **Activity** Compare $\frac{5}{8}$ and $\frac{1}{2}$.

Materials ■ fraction strips

Use fraction strips to compare $\frac{5}{8}$ and $\frac{1}{2}$. Record on the model below.

$\frac{1}{2}$	$\frac{1}{2}$	$\frac{1}{2}$

$\frac{5}{8}$	$\frac{1}{8}$	$\frac{1}{8}$	$\frac{1}{8}$	$\frac{1}{8}$	$\frac{1}{8}$	$\frac{1}{8}$	$\frac{1}{8}$	$\frac{1}{8}$

$\frac{5}{8}$ ◯ $\frac{1}{2}$

So, David used more _____ .

Math Talk

MATHEMATICAL PRACTICES ⑦

Look for Structure How are the number of eighth-size parts in $\frac{5}{8}$ related to the number of eighth-size parts you need to make $\frac{1}{2}$?

1. Write five fractions equivalent to $\frac{1}{2}$. What is the relationship between the numerator and the denominator of fractions equivalent to $\frac{1}{2}$?

_____

_____

2. How many eighths are equivalent to $\frac{1}{2}$?

_____

3. How can you compare $\frac{5}{8}$ and $\frac{1}{2}$ without using a model?

_____

_____

Benchmarks A **benchmark** is a known size or amount that helps you understand a different size or amount. You can use $\frac{1}{2}$ as a benchmark to help you compare fractions.

🔑 Example Use benchmarks to compare fractions.

A family hiked the same mountain trail. Evie and her father hiked $\frac{5}{12}$ of the trail before they stopped for lunch. Jill and her mother hiked $\frac{9}{10}$ of the trail before they stopped for lunch. Who hiked farther before lunch?

Compare $\frac{5}{12}$ and $\frac{9}{10}$ to the benchmark $\frac{1}{2}$.

STEP 1 Compare $\frac{5}{12}$ to $\frac{1}{2}$.

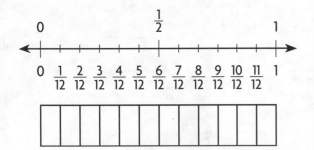

Think: Shade $\frac{5}{12}$.

$\frac{5}{12}$ ◯ $\frac{1}{2}$

STEP 2 Compare $\frac{9}{10}$ to $\frac{1}{2}$.

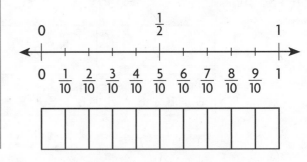

Think: Shade $\frac{9}{10}$.

$\frac{9}{10}$ ◯ $\frac{1}{2}$

Since $\frac{5}{12}$ is _____ than $\frac{1}{2}$ and $\frac{9}{10}$ is _____ than $\frac{1}{2}$, you know that $\frac{5}{12}$ ◯ $\frac{9}{10}$.

So, _____ hiked farther before lunch.

4. Explain how you can tell $\frac{5}{12}$ is less than $\frac{1}{2}$ without using a model.

   _____

   _____

5. Explain how you can tell $\frac{7}{10}$ is greater than $\frac{1}{2}$ without using a model.

   _____

   _____

Name _____

1. Compare $\frac{2}{5}$ and $\frac{1}{8}$. Write < or >.

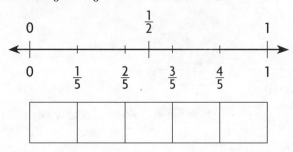

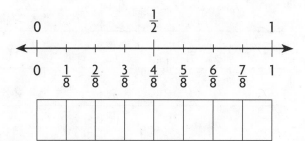

$\frac{2}{5}$ ◯ $\frac{1}{8}$

Compare. Write < or >.

2. $\frac{1}{2}$ ◯ $\frac{4}{6}$

3. $\frac{3}{10}$ ◯ $\frac{1}{2}$

4. $\frac{11}{12}$ ◯ $\frac{4}{8}$

5. $\frac{5}{8}$ ◯ $\frac{2}{5}$

On Your Own

MATHEMATICAL PRACTICES ⑥

Compare How do you know $\frac{1}{3} < \frac{1}{2}$?

Compare. Write < or >.

6. $\frac{8}{10}$ ◯ $\frac{3}{8}$

7. $\frac{1}{3}$ ◯ $\frac{7}{12}$

8. $\frac{2}{6}$ ◯ $\frac{7}{8}$

9. $\frac{4}{8}$ ◯ $\frac{2}{10}$

MATHEMATICAL PRACTICE ② **Reason Quantitatively** **Algebra** Find a numerator that makes the statement true.

10. $\frac{2}{4} < \frac{\Box}{6}$

11. $\frac{8}{10} > \frac{\Box}{8}$

12. $\frac{10}{12} > \frac{\Box}{4}$

13. $\frac{2}{5} < \frac{\Box}{10}$

14. When two fractions are between 0 and $\frac{1}{2}$, how do you know which fraction is greater? Explain.

15. **GO DEEPER** If you know that $\frac{2}{6} < \frac{1}{2}$ and $\frac{3}{4} > \frac{1}{2}$, what do you know about $\frac{2}{6}$ and $\frac{3}{4}$?

16. **GO DEEPER** Sandra has ribbons that are $\frac{3}{4}$ yard, $\frac{2}{6}$ yard, $\frac{1}{5}$ yard, and $\frac{4}{7}$ yard long. She needs to use the ribbon longer than $\frac{2}{3}$ yard to make a bow. Which length of ribbon could she use for the bow?

Problem Solving · Applications

17. **THINK SMARTER** Saundra ran $\frac{7}{12}$ of a mile. Lamar ran $\frac{3}{4}$ of a mile. Who ran farther? Explain.

_____

_____

_____

_____

WRITE *Math* · **Show Your Work**

18. **What's the Question?** Selena ran farther than Manny.

_____

_____

19. **GO DEEPER** Chloe made a small pan of ziti and a small pan of lasagna. She cut the ziti into 8 equal parts and the lasagna into 9 equal parts. Her family ate $\frac{2}{3}$ of the lasagna. If her family ate more lasagna than ziti, what fraction of the ziti could have been eaten?

_____

20. **THINK SMARTER** James, Ella, and Ryan biked around Eagle Lake. James biked $\frac{2}{10}$ of the distance in an hour. Ella biked $\frac{4}{8}$ of the distance in an hour. Ryan biked $\frac{2}{5}$ of the distance in an hour. Compare the distances biked by each person by matching the statements to the correct symbol. Each symbol may be used more than once or not at all.

$\frac{2}{10}$ ● $\frac{4}{8}$ • • =

$\frac{4}{8}$ ● $\frac{2}{5}$ • • <

$\frac{2}{10}$ ● $\frac{2}{5}$ • • >

Name _____

Compare Fractions Using Benchmarks

Common Core

COMMON CORE STANDARD—4.NF.A.2
Extending understanding of fraction equivalence and ordering.

Compare. Write < or >.

1. $\frac{1}{8}$ $\boxed{<}$ $\frac{6}{10}$

   Think: $\frac{1}{8}$ is less than $\frac{1}{2}$.

   $\frac{6}{10}$ is more than $\frac{1}{2}$.

2. $\frac{4}{12}$ $\bigcirc$ $\frac{4}{6}$

3. $\frac{2}{8}$ $\bigcirc$ $\frac{1}{2}$

4. $\frac{3}{5}$ $\bigcirc$ $\frac{3}{3}$

5. $\frac{7}{8}$ $\bigcirc$ $\frac{5}{10}$

6. $\frac{9}{12}$ $\bigcirc$ $\frac{1}{3}$

7. $\frac{4}{6}$ $\bigcirc$ $\frac{7}{8}$

8. $\frac{2}{4}$ $\bigcirc$ $\frac{2}{3}$

9. $\frac{3}{5}$ $\bigcirc$ $\frac{1}{4}$

10. $\frac{6}{10}$ $\bigcirc$ $\frac{2}{5}$

11. $\frac{1}{8}$ $\bigcirc$ $\frac{2}{10}$

12. $\frac{2}{3}$ $\bigcirc$ $\frac{5}{12}$

Problem Solving · Real World

13. Erika ran $\frac{3}{8}$ mile. Maria ran $\frac{3}{4}$ mile. Who ran farther?

14. Carlos finished $\frac{1}{3}$ of his art project on Monday. Tyler finished $\frac{1}{2}$ of his art project on Monday. Who finished more of his art project on Monday?

_____

15. **WRITE** ▸*Math* Explain a strategy you could use to compare $\frac{2}{6}$ and $\frac{5}{8}$.

_____

_____

_____

Lesson Check (4.NF.A.2)

1. What symbol makes the statement true?

   $$\frac{4}{6} \bigcirc \frac{3}{8}$$

2. Write a fraction, less than 1, with a demoninator of 6 that is greater than $\frac{3}{4}$.

   _____

Spiral Review (4.OA.A.3, 4.OA.B.4, 4.NBT.B.6)

3. Abigail is putting tiles on a table top. She needs 48 tiles for each of 8 rows. Each row will have 6 white tiles. The rest of the tiles will be purple. How many purple tiles will she need?

   _____

4. Each school bus going on the field trip holds 36 students and 4 adults. There are 6 filled buses on the field trip. How many people are going on the field trip?

   _____

5. Noah wants to display his 72 collector's flags. He is going to put 6 flags in each row. How many rows of flags will he have in his display?

   _____

6. Julian wrote this number pattern on the board:

   3, 10, 17, 24, 31, 38.

   Which of the numbers in Julian's pattern are composite numbers?

   _____

FOR MORE PRACTICE
GO TO THE
Personal Math Trainer

Name _____

Compare Fractions

Essential Question How can you compare fractions?

 Common Core Number and Operations—
Fractions—4.NF.A.2

MATHEMATICAL PRACTICES
MP2, MP3, MP6

Unlock the Problem Real World

Every year, Avery's school has a fair. This year, $\frac{3}{8}$ of the booths had face painting and $\frac{1}{4}$ of the booths had sand art. Were there more booths with face painting or sand art?

Compare $\frac{3}{8}$ and $\frac{1}{4}$.

One Way Use a common denominator.

When two fractions have the same denominator, they have equal-size parts. You can compare the number of parts.

THINK	MODEL AND RECORD
Think: 8 is a multiple of both 4 and 8. Use 8 as a common denominator.	Shade the model. Then compare.

$$\frac{1}{4} = \frac{1 \times \boxed{}}{4 \times \boxed{}} = \frac{\boxed{}}{8}$$

$\frac{3}{8}$ already has 8 as a denominator.

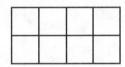

$\frac{3}{8}$ ◯ $\frac{2}{8}$

Another Way Use a common numerator.

When two fractions have the same numerator, they represent the same number of parts. You can compare the size of the parts.

THINK	MODEL AND RECORD
Think: 3 is a multiple of both 3 and 1. Use 3 as a common numerator.	Shade the model. Then compare.

$\frac{3}{8}$ already has 3 as a numerator.

$$\frac{1}{4} = \frac{1 \times \boxed{}}{4 \times \boxed{}} = \frac{3}{\boxed{}}$$

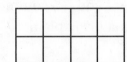

$\frac{3}{8}$ ◯ $\frac{3}{12}$

Since $\frac{3}{8}$ ◯ $\frac{1}{4}$, there were more booths with _____.

 Math Talk

MATHEMATICAL PRACTICES ②

Reason Abstractly Why can you not use $\frac{1}{2}$ as a benchmark to compare $\frac{3}{8}$ and $\frac{1}{4}$?

Try This! **Compare the fractions. Explain your reasoning.**

A $\frac{3}{4}$ ◯ $\frac{1}{3}$

_____

_____

_____

_____

B $\frac{3}{5}$ ◯ $\frac{3}{8}$

_____

_____

_____

_____

C $\frac{3}{4}$ ◯ $\frac{7}{8}$

_____

_____

_____

_____

D $\frac{4}{5}$ ◯ $\frac{2}{3}$

_____

_____

_____

_____

1. Which would you use to compare $\frac{11}{12}$ and $\frac{5}{6}$, a common numerator or a common denominator? Explain.

_____

_____

2. Can you use simplest form to compare $\frac{8}{10}$ and $\frac{3}{5}$? Explain.

_____

_____

Name _____

1. Compare $\frac{2}{5}$ and $\frac{1}{10}$.

   Think: Use _____ as a common denominator.

   $\frac{2}{5} = \frac{ \times }{ \times } = \frac{}{}$

   $\frac{1}{10}$

   Think: 4 tenth-size parts ◯ 1 tenth-size part.

   $\frac{2}{5}$ ◯ $\frac{1}{10}$

2. Compare $\frac{6}{10}$ and $\frac{3}{4}$.

   Think: Use _____ as a common numerator.

   $\frac{6}{10}$

   $\frac{3}{4} = \frac{ \times }{ \times } = \frac{}{}$

   Think: A tenth-size part ◯ an eighth-size part.

   $\frac{6}{10}$ ◯ $\frac{3}{4}$

Compare. Write <, >, or =.

✓ 3. $\frac{7}{8}$ ◯ $\frac{2}{8}$

✓ 4. $\frac{5}{12}$ ◯ $\frac{3}{6}$

5. $\frac{4}{10}$ ◯ $\frac{4}{6}$

6. $\frac{6}{12}$ ◯ $\frac{2}{4}$

Math Talk

MATHEMATICAL PRACTICES ②

Use Reasoning How can using a common numerator or a common denominator help you compare fractions?

On Your Own

Compare. Write <, >, or =.

7. $\frac{1}{3}$ ◯ $\frac{1}{4}$

8. $\frac{4}{5}$ ◯ $\frac{8}{10}$

9. $\frac{3}{4}$ ◯ $\frac{2}{6}$

10. $\frac{1}{2}$ ◯ $\frac{5}{8}$

MATHEMATICAL PRACTICE ② **Reason Quantitatively** **Algebra** **Find a number that makes the statement true.**

11. $\frac{1}{2} > \frac{}{3}$

12. $\frac{3}{10} < \frac{}{5}$

13. $\frac{5}{12} < \frac{}{3}$

14. $\frac{2}{3} > \frac{4}{}$

15. **GO DEEPER** Students cut a pepperoni pizza into 12 equal slices and ate 5 slices. They cut a veggie pizza into 6 equal slices and ate 4 slices. Use fractions to compare the amounts of each pizza that were eaten.

_____

Unlock the Problem Real World

16. THINK SMARTER Jerry is making a strawberry smoothie. Which measure is greatest, the amount of milk, cottage cheese, or strawberries?

Strawberry Smoothie
3 ice cubes
$\frac{3}{4}$ cup milk
$\frac{2}{6}$ cup cottage cheese
$\frac{8}{12}$ cup strawberries
$\frac{1}{4}$ teaspoon vanilla
$\frac{1}{8}$ teaspoon sugar

a. What do you need to find?

_____

b. How will you find the answer?

_____

_____

c. Show your work.

d. Jerry needs more _____ than the other two ingredients.

17. GO DEEPER Angie, Blake, Carlos, and Daisy went running. Angie ran $\frac{1}{3}$ mile, Blake ran $\frac{3}{5}$ mile, Carlos ran $\frac{7}{10}$ mile, and Daisy ran $\frac{1}{2}$ mile. Which runner ran the shortest distance? Who ran the greatest distance?

_____

18. THINK SMARTER Elaine bought $\frac{5}{8}$ pound of potato salad and $\frac{4}{6}$ pound of macaroni salad for a picnic. Use the numbers to compare the amounts of potato salad and macaroni salad Elaine bought.

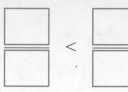

4

5

6

8

Compare Fractions

Common Core

COMMON CORE STANDARD—4.NF.A.2
Extend understanding of fraction equivalence and ordering.

Compare. Write <, >, or =.

1. $\dfrac{3}{4}$ $<$ $\dfrac{5}{6}$

   Think: 12 is a common denominator.

   $\dfrac{3}{4} = \dfrac{3 \times 3}{4 \times 3} = \dfrac{9}{12}$

   $\dfrac{5}{6} = \dfrac{5 \times 2}{6 \times 2} = \dfrac{10}{12}$

   $\dfrac{9}{12} < \dfrac{10}{12}$

2. $\dfrac{1}{5}$ $\bigcirc$ $\dfrac{2}{10}$

3. $\dfrac{2}{4}$ $\bigcirc$ $\dfrac{2}{5}$

4. $\dfrac{3}{5}$ $\bigcirc$ $\dfrac{7}{10}$

5. $\dfrac{4}{12}$ $\bigcirc$ $\dfrac{1}{6}$

6. $\dfrac{2}{6}$ $\bigcirc$ $\dfrac{1}{3}$

7. $\dfrac{1}{3}$ $\bigcirc$ $\dfrac{2}{4}$

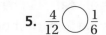

Problem Solving · Real World

8. A recipe uses $\dfrac{2}{3}$ cup of flour and $\dfrac{5}{8}$ cup of blueberries. Is there more flour or more blueberries in the recipe?

9. Peggy completed $\dfrac{5}{6}$ of the math homework and Al completed $\dfrac{4}{5}$ of the math homework. Did Peggy or Al complete more of the math homework?

10. **WRITE** ▸ *Math* Give an example of fractions that you would compare by finding common denominators, and an example of fractions you would compare by finding common numerators.

_____

_____

Lesson Check (4.NF.A.2)

1. Pedro fills a glass $\frac{2}{4}$ full with orange juice. Write a fraction with a denominator of 6 that is greater than $\frac{2}{4}$.

2. Today Ian wants to run less than $\frac{7}{12}$ mile. Write a fraction with a denominator of 4 to respresent a distance that is less than $\frac{7}{12}$ mile.

_____

_____

Spiral Review (4.OA.B.4, 4.NBT.A.1, 4.NBT.B.5, 4.NF.A.1)

3. Ms. Davis traveled 372,645 miles last year on business. What is the value of 6 in 372,645?

4. One section of an auditorium has 12 rows of seats. Each row has 13 seats. What is the total number of seats in that section?

_____

_____

5. Sam has 12 black-and-white photos and 18 color photos. He wants to put the photos in equal rows so each row has either black-and-white photos only or color photos only. In how many rows can Sam arrange the photos?

6. The teacher writes $\frac{10}{12}$ on the board. Write this fraction in simplest form.

_____

_____

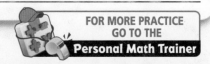

FOR MORE PRACTICE
GO TO THE
Personal Math Trainer

Name _____

Compare and Order Fractions

Essential Question How can you order fractions?

 Common Core **Number and Operations—Fractions—4.NF.A.2**

MATHEMATICAL PRACTICES
MP2, MP4, MP6

⚷ Unlock the Problem Real World

Jody has equal-size bins for the recycling center. She filled $\frac{3}{5}$ of a bin with plastics, $\frac{1}{12}$ of a bin with paper, and $\frac{9}{10}$ of a bin with glass. Which bin is the most full?

- Underline what you need to find.
- Circle the fractions you will compare.

🔑 Example 1 Locate and label $\frac{3}{5}$, $\frac{1}{12}$, and $\frac{9}{10}$ on the number line.

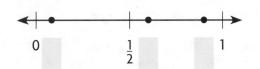

Math Idea

Sometimes it is not reasonable to find the exact location of a point on a number line. Benchmarks can help you find approximate locations.

STEP 1 Compare each fraction to $\frac{1}{2}$.

$\frac{3}{5} \bigcirc \frac{1}{2}$ $\frac{1}{12} \bigcirc \frac{1}{2}$ $\frac{9}{10} \bigcirc \frac{1}{2}$

_____ and _____ are both greater than $\frac{1}{2}$.

_____ is less than $\frac{1}{2}$.

Label $\frac{1}{12}$ on the number line above.

STEP 2 Compare $\frac{3}{5}$ and $\frac{9}{10}$.

Think: Use 10 as a common denominator.

$$\frac{3}{5} = \frac{ \times }{ \times } = \frac{}{}$$

Since $\frac{6}{10} \bigcirc \frac{9}{10}$, you know that $\frac{3}{5} \bigcirc \frac{9}{10}$.

Label $\frac{3}{5}$ and $\frac{9}{10}$ on the number line above.

The fraction the greatest distance from 0 has the greatest value.

The fraction with the greatest value is _____.

So, the bin with _____ is the most full.

Math Talk MATHEMATICAL PRACTICES ④

Use Models How do you know you located $\frac{3}{5}$ on the number line correctly?

- Compare the distance between $\frac{3}{5}$ and 0 and the distance between $\frac{9}{10}$ and 0. What can you conclude about the relationship between $\frac{3}{5}$ and $\frac{9}{10}$? Explain.

_____

_____

🔑 Example 2 Write $\frac{7}{10}$, $\frac{1}{3}$, $\frac{7}{12}$, and $\frac{8}{10}$ in order from least to greatest.

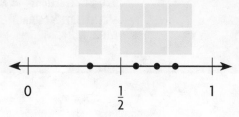

STEP 1 Compare each fraction to $\frac{1}{2}$.

List fractions that are less than $\frac{1}{2}$: _____

List fractions that are greater than $\frac{1}{2}$: _____

The fraction with the least value is _____.

Locate and label $\frac{1}{3}$ on the number line above.

_____

STEP 2 Compare $\frac{7}{10}$ to $\frac{7}{12}$ and $\frac{8}{10}$.

Think: $\frac{7}{10}$ and $\frac{7}{12}$ have a common numerator.

$$\frac{7}{10} \bigcirc \frac{7}{12}$$

Think: $\frac{7}{10}$ and $\frac{8}{10}$ have a common denominator.

$$\frac{7}{10} \bigcirc \frac{8}{10}$$

Locate and label $\frac{7}{10}$, $\frac{7}{12}$, and $\frac{8}{10}$ on the number line above.

The fractions in order from least to greatest are _____.

So, _____ < _____ < _____ < _____.

Try This! Write $\frac{3}{4}$, $\frac{3}{6}$, $\frac{1}{3}$, and $\frac{2}{12}$ in order from least to greatest.

_____ < _____ < _____ < _____

Name _____

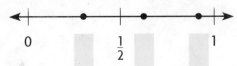

1. Locate and label points on the number line to help you write $\frac{3}{10}$, $\frac{11}{12}$, and $\frac{5}{8}$ in order from least to greatest.

0      $\frac{1}{2}$ 1

_____

Write the fraction with the greatest value.

2. $\frac{7}{10}$, $\frac{1}{5}$, $\frac{9}{10}$

3. $\frac{5}{6}$, $\frac{7}{12}$, $\frac{7}{10}$

4. $\frac{2}{8}$, $\frac{1}{8}$, $\frac{2}{4}$, $\frac{2}{6}$

Write the fractions in order from least to greatest.

5. $\frac{1}{4}$, $\frac{3}{6}$, $\frac{1}{8}$

6. $\frac{3}{5}$, $\frac{2}{3}$, $\frac{3}{10}$, $\frac{4}{5}$

7. $\frac{3}{4}$, $\frac{7}{12}$, $\frac{5}{12}$

MATHEMATICAL PRACTICES ②

Use Reasoning How can benchmarks help you order fractions?

On Your Own

Write the fractions in order from least to greatest.

8. $\frac{2}{5}$, $\frac{1}{3}$, $\frac{5}{6}$

9. $\frac{4}{8}$, $\frac{5}{12}$, $\frac{1}{6}$

10. $\frac{7}{100}$, $\frac{9}{10}$, $\frac{4}{5}$

MATHEMATICAL PRACTICE ② **Reason Quantitatively** **Algebra** Write a numerator that makes the statement true.

11. $\frac{1}{2} < \frac{}{10} < \frac{4}{5}$

12. $\frac{1}{4} < \frac{5}{12} < \frac{}{6}$

13. $\frac{}{8} < \frac{3}{4} < \frac{7}{8}$

Unlock the Problem

14. THINK SMARTER Nancy, Lionel, and Mavis ran in a 5-kilometer race. The table shows their finish times. In what order did Nancy, Lionel, and Mavis finish the race?

a. What do you need to find?

_____

_____

b. What information do you need to solve the problem?

_____

_____

c. What information is not necessary?

_____

d. How will you solve the problem?

_____

_____

Finish line

5-Kilometer Race Results	
Name	**Time**
Nancy	$\frac{2}{3}$ hour
Lionel	$\frac{7}{12}$ hour
Mavis	$\frac{3}{4}$ hour

e. Show the steps to solve the problem.

f. Complete the sentences.

The runner who finished first is _____.

The runner who finished second is _____.

The runner who finished third is _____.

15. GO DEEPER Alma used 3 beads to make a necklace. The lengths of the beads are $\frac{5}{6}$ inch, $\frac{5}{12}$ inch, and $\frac{1}{3}$ inch. What are the lengths in order from shortest to longest?

_____

16. THINK SMARTER Victor has his grandmother's recipe for making mixed nuts.

$\frac{3}{4}$ cup pecans	$\frac{2}{12}$ cup peanuts
$\frac{1}{2}$ cup almonds	$\frac{7}{8}$ cup walnuts

Order the ingredients used in the recipe from least to greatest.

_____

Compare and Order Fractions

Common Core **COMMON CORE STANDARD—4.NF.A.2**
Extend understanding of fraction equivalence and ordering.

Write the fractions in order from least to greatest.

1. $\frac{5}{8}$, $\frac{2}{12}$, $\frac{8}{10}$

   Use benchmarks and a number line.

   Think: $\frac{5}{8}$ is close to $\frac{1}{2}$. $\frac{2}{12}$ is close to 0.

   $\frac{8}{10}$ is close to 1.

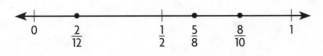

$$\frac{2}{12} < \frac{5}{8} < \frac{8}{10}$$

2. $\frac{1}{5}$, $\frac{2}{3}$, $\frac{5}{8}$

   _____

3. $\frac{1}{2}$, $\frac{2}{5}$, $\frac{6}{10}$

4. $\frac{4}{6}$, $\frac{7}{12}$, $\frac{5}{10}$

5. $\frac{1}{4}$, $\frac{5}{8}$, $\frac{1}{2}$

_____   _____   _____

Problem Solving · Real World

6. Amy's math notebook weighs $\frac{1}{2}$ pound, her science notebook weighs $\frac{7}{8}$ pound, and her history notebook weighs $\frac{3}{4}$ pound. What are the weights in order from lightest to heaviest?

   _____

   _____

7. Carl has three picture frames. The thicknesses of the frames are $\frac{4}{5}$ inch, $\frac{3}{12}$ inch, and $\frac{5}{6}$ inch. What are the thicknesses in order from least to greatest?

   _____

   _____

8. **WRITE** ▸ *Math* How is ordering fractions on a number line similar to and different from ordering whole numbers on a number line?

   _____

   _____

Lesson Check (4.NF.A.2)

1. Juan's three math quizzes this week took him $\frac{1}{3}$ hour, $\frac{4}{6}$ hour, and $\frac{1}{5}$ hour to complete. List the lengths of time in order from least to greatest.

2. On three days last week, Maria ran $\frac{3}{4}$ mile, $\frac{7}{8}$ mile, and $\frac{3}{5}$ mile. List the distances in order from least to greatest.

Spiral Review (4.OA.B.4, 4.NBT.B.5, 4.NBT.B.6, 4.NF.A.1)

3. Santiago collects 435 cents in nickels. How many nickels does he collect?

4. Lisa has three classes that each last 50 minutes. What is the total number of minutes of the three classes?

5. Alicia wrote these numbers: 2, 9, 15, 21. Which of Alicia's numbers is NOT a composite number?

6. Mrs. Carmel serves $\frac{6}{8}$ of a loaf of bread with dinner. Write a fraction with a denominator of 4 that is equivalent to $\frac{6}{8}$.

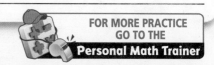

FOR MORE PRACTICE
GO TO THE
Personal Math Trainer

Name _____

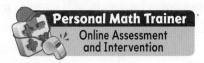
1. For numbers 1a–1d, tell whether the fractions are equivalent by selecting the correct symbol.

   1a. $\frac{4}{16}$ □ (=, ≠) $\frac{1}{4}$

   1c. $\frac{5}{6}$ □ (=, ≠) $\frac{25}{30}$

   1b. $\frac{3}{5}$ □ (=, ≠) $\frac{12}{15}$

   1d. $\frac{6}{10}$ □ (=, ≠) $\frac{5}{8}$

2. Juan's mother gave him a recipe for trail mix.

$\frac{3}{4}$ cup cereal	$\frac{2}{3}$ cup almonds
$\frac{1}{4}$ cup peanuts	$\frac{1}{2}$ cup raisins

   Order the ingredients used in the recipe from least to greatest.

   ☐   ☐   ☐   ☐

3. Taylor cuts $\frac{1}{5}$ sheet of construction paper for an arts and crafts project. Write $\frac{1}{5}$ as an equivalent fraction with the denominators shown.

   ☐ /10   ☐ /15   ☐ /25   ☐ /40

4. A mechanic has sockets with the sizes shown below. Write each fraction in the correct box.

   $\frac{7}{8}$ in. $\frac{3}{16}$ in. $\frac{1}{4}$ in. $\frac{3}{8}$ in. $\frac{4}{8}$ in. $\frac{11}{16}$ in.

less than $\frac{1}{2}$ in.	equal to $\frac{1}{2}$ in.	greater than $\frac{1}{2}$ in.

GO DIGITAL   Assessment Options
Chapter Test

5. Darcy bought $\frac{1}{2}$ pound of cheese and $\frac{3}{4}$ pound of hamburger for a barbecue. Use the numbers to compare the amounts of cheese and hamburger Darcy bought.

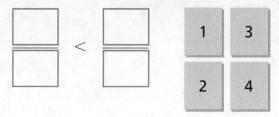

6. Brad is practicing the piano. He spends $\frac{1}{4}$ hour practicing scales and $\frac{1}{3}$ hour practicing the song for his recital. For numbers 6a–6c, select Yes or No to tell whether each of the following is a true statement.

6a. 12 is a common denominator of $\frac{1}{4}$ and $\frac{1}{3}$. ○ Yes ○ No

6b. The amount of time spent practicing scales can be rewritten as $\frac{3}{12}$. ○ Yes ○ No

6c. The amount of time spent practicing the song for the recital can be rewritten as $\frac{6}{12}$. ○ Yes ○ No

7. In the school chorus, $\frac{4}{24}$ of the students are fourth graders. In simplest form, what fraction of the students in the school chorus are fourth graders?

_____ of the students

8. Which pairs of fractions are equivalent? Mark all that apply.

○ $\frac{8}{12}$ and $\frac{2}{3}$ ○ $\frac{4}{5}$ and $\frac{12}{16}$

○ $\frac{3}{4}$ and $\frac{20}{28}$ ○ $\frac{7}{10}$ and $\frac{21}{30}$

9. Sam worked on his science fair project for $\frac{1}{4}$ hour on Friday and $\frac{1}{2}$ hour on Saturday. What are four common denominators for the fractions? Explain your reasoning.

Name _____

10. Morita works in a florist shop and makes flower arrangements. She puts 10 flowers in each vase, and $\frac{2}{10}$ of the flowers are daisies.

Part A

If Morita makes 4 arrangements, how many daisies does she need? Show how you can check your answer.

_____ daisies

Part B

Last weekend, Morita used 10 daisies to make flower arrangements. How many flowers other than daisies did she use to make the arrangements? Explain your reasoning.

_____ other flowers

11. **THINK SMARTER +** In Mary's homeroom, $\frac{10}{28}$ of the students have a cat, $\frac{6}{12}$ have a dog, and $\frac{2}{14}$ have a pet bird. For numbers 11a–11c, select True or False for each statement.

Personal Math Trainer

11a. In simplest form, $\frac{5}{14}$ of the students have a cat.   ○ True   ○ False

11b. In simplest form, $\frac{2}{4}$ of the students have a dog.   ○ True   ○ False

11c. In simplest form, $\frac{1}{7}$ of the students have a pet bird.   ○ True   ○ False

12. Regina, Courtney, and Ellen hiked around Bear Pond. Regina hiked $\frac{7}{10}$ of the distance in an hour. Courtney hiked $\frac{3}{6}$ of the distance in an hour. Ellen hiked $\frac{3}{8}$ of the distance in an hour. Compare the distances hiked by each person by matching the statements to the correct symbol. Each symbol may be used more than once or not at all.

$\frac{7}{10} \quad \bigcirc \quad \frac{3}{6}$ •   • <

$\frac{3}{8} \quad \bigcirc \quad \frac{3}{6}$ •   • >

$\frac{7}{10} \quad \bigcirc \quad \frac{3}{8}$ •   • =

13. Ramon is having some friends over after a baseball game. Ramon's job is to make a vegetable dip. The ingredients for the recipe are given.

Ingredients in Vegetable Dip	
$\frac{3}{4}$ cup parsley	$\frac{5}{8}$ cup buttermilk
$\frac{1}{3}$ cup dill	$\frac{1}{2}$ cup cream cheese
$\frac{6}{8}$ cup scallions	$\frac{1}{16}$ cup lemon juice

Part A

Which ingredient does Ramon use the greater amount of, buttermilk or cream cheese? Explain how you found your answer.

Part B

Ramon says that he needs the same amount of two different ingredients. Is he correct? Support your answer with information from the problem.

© Houghton Mifflin Harcourt Publishing Company

Name _____

14. Sandy is ordering bread rolls for her party. She wants $\frac{3}{5}$ of the rolls to be whole wheat. What other fractions can represent the part of the rolls that will be whole wheat? Shade the models to show your work.

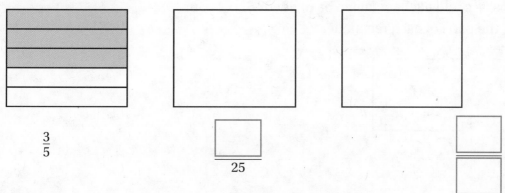

$\frac{3}{5}$ 25

15. Angel has $\frac{4}{8}$ yard of ribbon and Lynn has $\frac{3}{4}$ yard of ribbon. Do Angel and Lynn have the same amount of ribbon? Shade the model to show how you found your answer. Explain your reasoning.

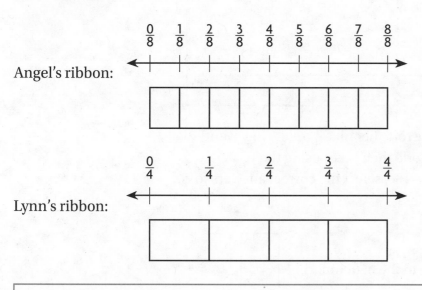

Angel's ribbon:

Lynn's ribbon:

16. Ella used $\frac{1}{4}$ yard of red ribbon. Fill in each box with a number from the list to show equivalent fractions for $\frac{1}{4}$. Not all numbers will be used.

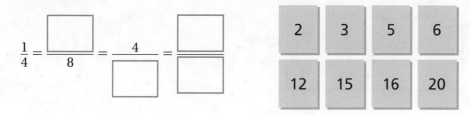

$\frac{1}{4} = \frac{\boxed{}}{8} = \frac{4}{\boxed{}} = \frac{\boxed{}}{\boxed{}}$

| 2 | 3 | 5 | 6 |
| 12 | 15 | 16 | 20 |

17. 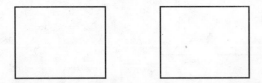 Frank has two same-size rectangles divided into the same number of equal parts. One rectangle has $\frac{3}{4}$ of the parts shaded, and the other has $\frac{1}{3}$ of the parts shaded.

Part A

Into how many parts could each rectangle be divided? Show your work by drawing the parts of each rectangle.

Part B

Is there more than one possible answer to Part A? If so, did you find the least number of parts into which both rectangles could be divided? Explain your reasoning.

18. Suki rode her bike $\frac{4}{5}$ mile. Claire rode her bike $\frac{1}{3}$ mile. They want to compare how far they each rode their bikes using the benchmark $\frac{1}{2}$. For numbers 18a–18c, select the correct answers to describe how to solve the problem.

18a. Compare Suki's distance to the benchmark: $\frac{4}{5}$ $\boxed{\begin{array}{c} < \\ > \\ = \end{array}}$ $\frac{1}{2}$.

18b. Compare Claire's distance to the benchmark: $\frac{1}{3}$ $\boxed{\begin{array}{c} < \\ > \\ = \end{array}}$ $\frac{1}{2}$.

18c. Suki rode her bike $\boxed{\begin{array}{c} \text{a longer distance than} \\ \text{the same distance as} \\ \text{a shorter distance than} \end{array}}$ Claire.

Add and Subtract Fractions

✔ Show What You Know

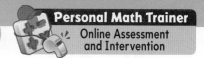 Personal Math Trainer
Online Assessment and Intervention

Check your understanding of important skills.

Name _____

▶ **Fractions Equal to 1** **Write the fraction that names the whole.** (2.G.A.2)

1. 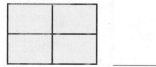 _____

2.  _____

▶ **Parts of a Whole** **Write a fraction that names the shaded part.** (3.NF.A.1)

3. _____

4. _____

5. _____

▶ **Read and Write Fractions** **Write a fraction for the shaded part. Write a fraction for the unshaded part.** (3.NF.A.1)

6.   shaded: _____

unshaded: _____

7.   shaded: _____

unshaded: _____

The electricity that powers our appliances is converted from many sources of energy. About $\frac{5}{10}$ is made from coal, about $\frac{2}{10}$ from natural gas, and about $\frac{2}{10}$ from nuclear power. About how much of our electricity comes from sources other than coal, natural gas, or nuclear power?

Vocabulary Builder

▶ **Visualize It** ••

Complete the bubble map using the words with a ✓.

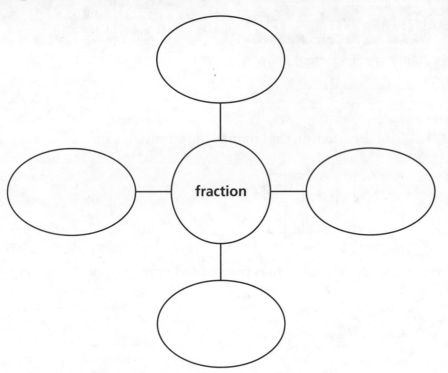

Review Words
Associative Property of Addition
Commutative Property of Addition
✓ denominator
fraction
✓ numerator
simplest form

Preview Words
✓ mixed number
✓ unit fraction

▶ **Understand Vocabulary** ••••••••••••••••••••••••••••••

Write the word or phrase that matches the description.

1. When the numerator and denominator have only 1 as a common factor

   _____

2. A number that names a part of a whole or part of a group

   _____

3. An amount given as a whole number and a fraction

   _____

4. The number in a fraction that tells how many equal parts are in the whole or in the group _____

5. A fraction that has a numerator of one _____

• **Interactive Student Edition**
• **Multimedia eGlossary**

Chapter 7 Vocabulary

**Associative Property
of Addition**

propiedad asociativa
de la suma

3

**Commutative Property
of Addition**

propiedad conmutativa
de la suma

12

denominator

denominador

22

fraction

fracción

36

mixed number

número mixto

54

numerator

numerador

56

simplest form

mínima expresión

84

unit fraction

fracción unitaria

94

The property that states that when the order of two addends is changed, the sum is the same

Example: 4 + 5 = 5 + 4

The property that states that you can group addends in different ways and still get the same sum

Example: 3 + (8 + 5) = (3 + 8) + 5

A number that names a part of a whole or part of a group

Example:

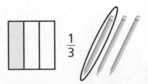

$\frac{1}{3}$

The number below the bar in a fraction that tells how many equal parts are in the whole or in the group

Example: $\frac{3}{4}$ ← denominator

The number above the bar in a fraction that tells how many parts of the whole or group are being considered

Example: $\frac{1}{5}$ ← numerator

An amount given as a whole number and a fraction

Example: $2\frac{3}{6}$ is a mixed number

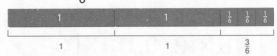

whole number part → $2\frac{3}{6}$ ← fraction part

A fraction that has a numerator of one

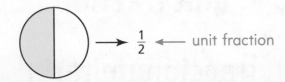

→ $\frac{1}{2}$ ← unit fraction

A fraction is in simplest form when the numerator and denominator have only 1 as a common factor

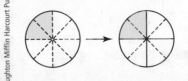

$\frac{2}{8} = \frac{1}{4}$

↑
simplest form

Bingo

For 3 to 6 players

Materials

- 1 set of word cards
- 1 bingo board for each player
- game markers

How to Play

1. The caller chooses a card and reads the definition. Then the caller puts the card in a second pile.

2. Players put a marker on the word that matches the definition each time they find it on their bingo boards.

3. Repeat Steps 1 and 2 until a player marks 5 boxes in a line going down, across, or on a slant and calls "Bingo."

4. Check the answers. Have the player who said "Bingo" read the words aloud while the caller checks the definitions on the cards in the second pile.

Word Box

Associative Property of Addition
Commutative Property of Addition
denominator
fraction
mixed number
numerator
simplest form
unit fraction

The Write Way

Reflect

Choose one idea. Write about it.

- Is $\frac{3}{4}$ a unit fraction? Explain why or why not.
- Explain what is most important to understand about mixed numbers.
- Write a creative story that includes addition and subtraction of fractions.

Name _____

Add and Subtract Parts of a Whole

Essential Question When can you add or subtract parts of a whole?

Common Core Number and Operations—Fractions—4.NF.B.3a
MATHEMATICAL PRACTICES
MP2, MP4

Investigate

Materials ■ fraction circles ■ color pencils

Ms. Clark has the following pie pieces left over from a bake sale.

She will combine the pieces so they are on the same dish.
How much pie will be on the dish?

A. Model the problem using fraction circles. Draw a picture of your model. Then write the sum.

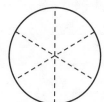 + 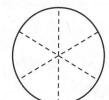 =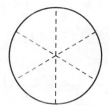

_____ + _____ = _____

So, _____ of a pie is on the dish.

B. Suppose Ms. Clark eats 2 pieces of the pie. How much pie will be left on the dish? Model the problem using fraction circles. Draw a picture of your model. Then write the difference.

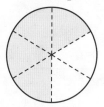

_____ − _____ = _____

So, _____ of the pie is left on the dish.

Draw Conclusions

1. Kevin says that when you combine 3 pieces of pie and 1 piece of pie, you have 4 pieces of pie. Explain how Kevin's statement is related to the equation $\frac{3}{6} + \frac{1}{6} = \frac{4}{6}$.

_____

_____

_____

2. Isabel wrote the equation $\frac{1}{2} + \frac{1}{6} = \frac{4}{6}$ and Jonah wrote $\frac{3}{6} + \frac{1}{6} = \frac{4}{6}$ to represent combining the pie pieces. Explain why both equations are correct.

_____

3. **THINK SMARTER** If there is $\frac{4}{6}$ of a pie on a plate, what part of the pie is missing from the plate? Write an equation to justify your answer.

_____

Make Connections

You can only join or separate parts that refer to the same whole.

Suppose Randy has $\frac{1}{4}$ of a round cake and $\frac{1}{4}$ of a square cake.

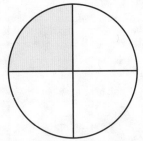 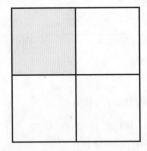

Math Talk

MATHEMATICAL PRACTICES ④

Interpret a Result Give an example of a situation where the equation $\frac{1}{4} + \frac{1}{4} = \frac{2}{4}$ makes sense. Explain your reasoning.

a. Are the wholes the same? Explain.

_____

b. Does the sum $\frac{1}{4} + \frac{1}{4} = \frac{2}{4}$ make sense in this situation? Explain.

_____

_____

Name _____

Use the model to write an equation.

1.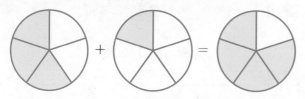

_____

2.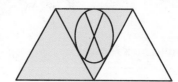

_____

3.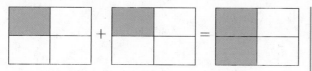

_____

4.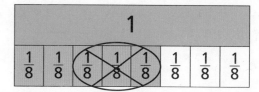

_____

Use the model to solve the equation.

5. $\dfrac{3}{4} - \dfrac{1}{4} =$ _____

6. $\dfrac{5}{6} + \dfrac{1}{6} =$ _____

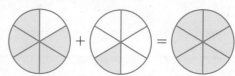

Problem Solving • Applications Real World

7. **MATHEMATICAL PRACTICE ② Reason Abstractly** Sean has $\dfrac{1}{5}$ of a cupcake and $\dfrac{1}{5}$ of a large cake.

a. Are the wholes the same? Explain.

_____

b. Does the sum $\dfrac{1}{5} + \dfrac{1}{5} = \dfrac{2}{5}$ make sense in this situation? Explain.

_____

8. **GO DEEPER** Carrie's dance class learned $\dfrac{1}{5}$ of a new dance on Monday, and $\dfrac{2}{5}$ of the dance on Tuesday. What fraction of the dance is left for the class to learn on Wednesday?

_____

Sense or Nonsense?

9. **THINK SMARTER** Samantha and Kim used different models to help find $\frac{1}{3} + \frac{1}{6}$. Whose model makes sense? Whose model is nonsense? Explain your reasoning below each model.

Samantha's Model

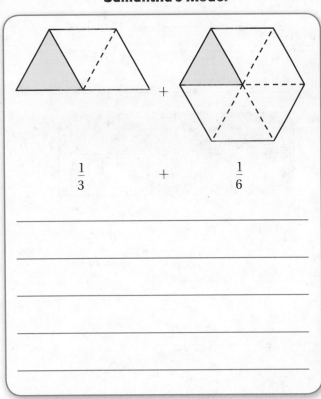

$$\frac{1}{3} \quad + \quad \frac{1}{6}$$

_____

_____

_____

_____

Kim's Model

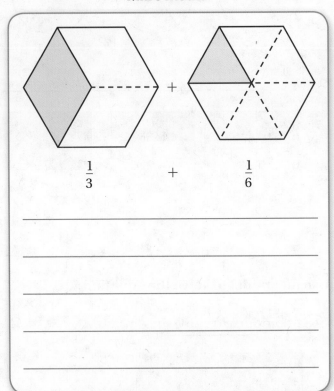

$$\frac{1}{3} \quad + \quad \frac{1}{6}$$

_____

_____

_____

_____

10. **GO DEEPER** Draw a model you could use to add $\frac{1}{4} + \frac{1}{2}$.

11. **THINK SMARTER +** Cindy has two jars of paint. One jar is $\frac{3}{8}$ full. The other jar is $\frac{2}{8}$ full.

Use the fractions to write an equation that shows the amount of paint Cindy has.

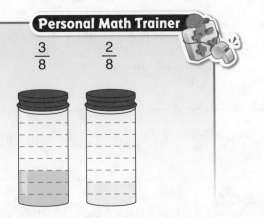

Personal Math Trainer

$$\frac{3}{8} \qquad \frac{2}{8}$$

$$\boxed{\frac{1}{8}} \quad \boxed{\frac{2}{8}} \quad \boxed{\frac{3}{8}} \quad \boxed{\frac{5}{8}} \quad \boxed{\frac{7}{8}}$$

_____ + _____ = _____

Name _____

Add and Subtract Parts of a Whole

COMMON CORE STANDARD—4.NF.B.3a
Build fractions from unit fractions by applying and extending previous understandings of operations on whole numbers.

Use the model to write an equation.

1.

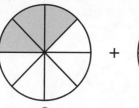

Think: $\dfrac{3}{8}$ + $\dfrac{2}{8}$ = $\dfrac{5}{8}$

$\dfrac{3}{8} + \dfrac{2}{8} = \dfrac{5}{8}$

2.

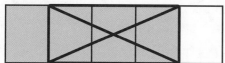

_____

3.

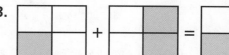

_____

Use the model to solve the equation.

4.

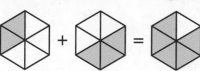

$\dfrac{2}{6} + \dfrac{3}{6} =$ _____

5.

$\dfrac{3}{5} - \dfrac{2}{5} =$ _____

Problem Solving Real World

6. Jake ate $\dfrac{4}{8}$ of a pizza. Millie ate $\dfrac{3}{8}$ of the same pizza. How much of the pizza was eaten by Jake and Millie?

_____

7. **WRITE** ▸ *Math* Draw a fraction circle to model $\dfrac{5}{6} - \dfrac{1}{6}$ and write the difference.

Lesson Check (4.NF.B.3a)

1. A whole pie is cut into 8 equal slices. Three of the slices are served. How much of the pie is left?

2. An orange is divided into 6 equal wedges. Jody eats 1 wedge. Then she eats 3 more wedges. How much of the orange did Jody eat?

Spiral Review (4.OA.C.5, 4.NBT.B.5, 4.NF.A.1, 4.NF.A.2)

3. Put these distances in order from least to greatest: $\frac{3}{16}$ mile, $\frac{1}{8}$ mile, $\frac{3}{4}$ mile

4. Jeremy walked $\frac{6}{8}$ of the way to school and ran the rest of the way. What fraction, in simplest form, shows the part of the way that Jeremy walked?

5. An elevator starts on the 100th floor of a building. It descends 4 floors every 10 seconds. At what floor will the elevator be 60 seconds after it starts?

6. For a school play, the teacher asked the class to set up chairs in 20 rows with 25 chairs in each row. After setting up all the chairs, they were 5 chairs short. How many chairs did the class set up?

FOR MORE PRACTICE GO TO THE Personal Math Trainer

Write Fractions as Sums

Essential Question How can you write a fraction as a sum of fractions with the same denominators?

 Common Core **Number and Operations— Fractions—4.NF.B.3b**
MATHEMATICAL PRACTICES
MP2, MP3, MP8

🔑 Unlock the Problem (Real World)

Emilio cut a sandwich into 8 equal pieces and ate 1 piece. He has $\frac{7}{8}$ of the sandwich left. Emilio put each remaining piece on a snack plate. How many snack plates did he use? What part of the sandwich did he put on each plate?

Each piece of the sandwich is $\frac{1}{8}$ of the whole. $\frac{1}{8}$ is called a **unit fraction** because it tells the part of the whole that 1 piece represents. A unit fraction always has a numerator of 1.

🔒 Example 1 Write $\frac{7}{8}$ as a sum of unit fractions.

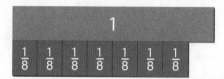

$$\frac{7}{8} = \text{\_\_\_\_} + \text{\_\_\_\_} + \text{\_\_\_\_} + \text{\_\_\_\_} + \text{\_\_\_\_} + \text{\_\_\_\_} + \text{\_\_\_\_}$$

The number of addends represents the number of plates used.

The unit fractions represent the part of the sandwich on each plate.

So, Emilio used _____ plates. He put _____ of a sandwich on each plate.

1. What if Emilio ate 3 pieces of the sandwich instead of 1 piece? How many snack plates would he need? What part of the sandwich would be on each plate? Explain.

_____

_____

_____

_____

🔒 Example 2 Write a fraction as a sum.

Kevin and Isabel are going to share a whole pizza. The pizza is cut into 6 equal slices. They will put the slices on two separate dishes. What part of the whole pizza could be on each dish?

Shade the models to show three different ways Kevin and Isabel could share the pizza. Write an equation for each model.

Think: $\frac{6}{6}$ = 1 whole pizza.

$=$ _____ $+$ _____

$=$ _____ $+$ _____

$=$ _____ $+$ _____

Math Talk

MATHEMATICAL PRACTICES ⑧

Use Repeated Reasoning
If there were 8 dishes, could $\frac{1}{6}$ of the whole pizza be on each dish? Explain.

2. What if 3 friends share the pizza and they put the pizza slices on three separate dishes? What part of the pizza could be on each dish? Write equations to support your answer.

_____

_____

Name _____

 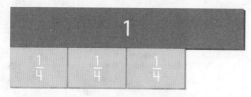
1. Write $\frac{3}{4}$ as a sum of unit fractions.

1		
$\frac{1}{4}$	$\frac{1}{4}$	$\frac{1}{4}$

$\frac{3}{4} =$ _____ + _____ + _____

Write the fraction as a sum of unit fractions.

2.

1					
$\frac{1}{6}$	$\frac{1}{6}$	$\frac{1}{6}$	$\frac{1}{6}$	$\frac{1}{6}$	$\frac{1}{6}$

$\frac{5}{6} =$ _____

3.

1		
$\frac{1}{3}$	$\frac{1}{3}$	$\frac{1}{3}$

$\frac{2}{3} =$ _____

Math Talk

MATHEMATICAL PRACTICES ②

Use Reasoning How is the numerator in $\frac{5}{6}$ related to the number of addends in the sum of its unit fractions?

On Your Own

Write the fraction as a sum of unit fractions.

4. $\frac{4}{12} =$ _____

5. $\frac{6}{8}$ _____

Write the fraction as a sum of fractions three different ways.

6. $\frac{8}{10}$

_____

_____

_____

7. $\frac{6}{6}$

_____

_____

_____

8. **MATHEMATICAL PRACTICE ③ Compare Representations** How many different ways can you write a fraction that has a numerator of 2 as a sum of fractions? Explain.

_____

_____

Unlock the Problem *Real World*

9. **THINK SMARTER** Holly's garden is divided into 5 equal sections. She will fence the garden into 3 areas by grouping some equal sections together. What part of the garden could each fenced area be?

a. What information do you need to use?

_____

_____

b. How can writing an equation help you solve the problem? _____

_____

_____

c. How can drawing a model help you write an equation?

_____

_____

d. Show how you can solve the problem.

e. Complete the sentence.

The garden can be fenced into _____,

_____, and _____ parts or _____,

_____, and _____ parts.

10. **GO DEEPER** Leena walked $\frac{2}{3}$ of a mile. What is $\frac{2}{3}$ written as a sum of unit fractions with a denominator of 9?

_____

11. **THINK SMARTER** Ellie's mom sells toys. She sold $\frac{7}{10}$ of the toys. Select a way $\frac{7}{10}$ can be written as a sum of fractions. Mark all that apply.

Ⓐ $\frac{4}{10} + \frac{1}{10} + \frac{1}{10} + \frac{1}{10}$

Ⓑ $\frac{4}{10} + \frac{3}{10} + \frac{1}{10} + \frac{1}{10} + \frac{1}{10}$

Ⓒ $\frac{1}{10} + \frac{2}{10} + \frac{3}{10} + \frac{1}{10}$

Write Fractions as Sums

COMMON CORE STANDARD—4.NF.B.3b
Build fractions from unit fractions by applying and extending previous understandings of operations on whole numbers.

Write the fraction as a sum of unit fractions.

1. $\dfrac{4}{5} =$ _____ $\dfrac{1}{5} + \dfrac{1}{5} + \dfrac{1}{5} + \dfrac{1}{5}$ _____

Think: Add $\frac{1}{5}$ four times.

2. $\dfrac{3}{8} =$ _____

3. $\dfrac{6}{12} =$ _____

4. $\dfrac{4}{4} =$ _____

Write the fraction as a sum of fractions three different ways.

5. $\dfrac{7}{10}$

_____

_____

_____

6. $\dfrac{6}{6}$

_____

_____

_____

Problem Solving · Real World

7. Petra is asked to color $\frac{6}{6}$ of her grid. She must use 3 colors: blue, red, and pink. There must be more blue sections than red sections or pink sections. What are the different ways Petra can color the sections of her grid and follow all the rules?

_____

_____

_____

8. **WRITE** *Math* Write $\frac{9}{12}$ as a sum of unit fractions.

_____

_____

_____

Lesson Check

1. Jorge wants to write $\frac{4}{5}$ as a sum of unit fractions. What should he write?

2. What fraction is equivalent to the expression $\frac{4}{8} + \frac{2}{8} + \frac{1}{8}$?

Spiral Review

3. An apple is cut into 6 equal slices. Nancy eats 2 of the slices. What fraction of the apple is left?

4. Which of these numbers is a prime number: 1, 11, 21, 51?

5. A teacher has a bag of 100 unit cubes. She gives an equal number of cubes to each of the 7 groups in her class. She gives each group as many cubes as she can. How many unit cubes are left over?

6. Jessie sorted the coins in her bank. She made 7 stacks of 6 dimes and 8 stacks of 5 nickels. She then found 1 dime and 1 nickel. How many dimes and nickels does Jessie have in all?

FOR MORE PRACTICE GO TO THE Personal Math Trainer

Add Fractions Using Models

Essential Question How can you add fractions with like denominators using models?

 Number and Operations—Fractions—4.NF.B.3d *Also 4.MD.A.2*
MATHEMATICAL PRACTICES
MP2, MP3, MP4

Unlock the Problem Real World

Ms. Clark made a loaf of bread. She used $\frac{1}{8}$ of the bread for a snack and $\frac{5}{8}$ of the bread for lunch. How much did she use for a snack and lunch?

One Way Use a picture.

$\frac{1}{8}$ is _____ eighth-size piece of bread.

$\frac{5}{8}$ is _____ eighth-size pieces of bread.

Shade 1 eighth-size piece. Then shade 5 eighth-size pieces.

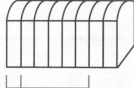

↑ snack   ↑ lunch

Think: The pieces you shaded represent the pieces Ms. Clark used.

So, Ms. Clark used _____ eighth-size

pieces, or $\frac{}{8}$ of the bread.

Another Way Use fraction strips.

The 1 strip represents the whole loaf.

Each $\frac{1}{8}$ part represents 1 eighth-size piece of bread.

Shade $\frac{1}{8}$. Then shade $\frac{5}{8}$.

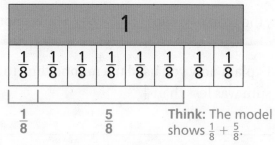

$\frac{1}{8}$ $\frac{5}{8}$

Think: The model shows $\frac{1}{8} + \frac{5}{8}$.

How many $\frac{1}{8}$-size parts are shaded? _____

Write the sum. $\frac{1}{8} + \frac{5}{8} = \frac{}{8}$

So, Ms. Clark used _____ of the bread.

---

1. Explain how the numerator of the sum is related to the fraction strip model.

_____

_____

 MATHEMATICAL PRACTICES ②

Reason Abstractly
Explain why $\frac{1}{8} + \frac{5}{8} \neq \frac{6}{16}$.

2. Explain how the denominator of the sum is related to the fraction strip model.

_____

_____

🔒 Example

Jacob needs two strips of wood to make masts for a miniature sailboat. One mast will be $\frac{3}{6}$ foot long. The other mast will be $\frac{2}{6}$ foot long. He has a strip of wood that is $\frac{4}{6}$ foot long. Is this strip of wood long enough to make both masts?

Shade the model to show $\frac{3}{6} + \frac{2}{6}$.

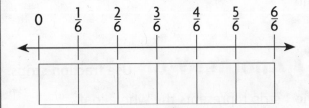

Write the sum. $\frac{3}{6} + \frac{2}{6} = \frac{}{6}$

Is the sum less than or greater than $\frac{4}{6}$? _____

So, the strip of wood _____ long enough to make both masts.

---

3. Explain how you used the number line to determine if the sum was less than $\frac{4}{6}$.

_____

_____

4. What if each mast was $\frac{2}{6}$ foot long? Could Jacob use the strip of wood to make both masts? Explain.

Share and Show MATH BOARD

1. Adrian's cat ate $\frac{3}{5}$ of a bag of cat treats in September and $\frac{1}{5}$ of the same bag of cat treats in October. What part of the bag of cat treats did Adrian's cat eat in both months?

Use the model to find the sum $\frac{3}{5} + \frac{1}{5}$.

How many fifth-size pieces are shown? _____

$\frac{3}{5} + \frac{1}{5} = \frac{}{5}$ of a bag

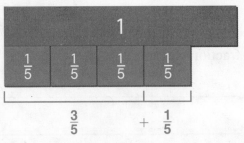

Name _____

Use the model to find the sum.

2.

1			
$\frac{1}{4}$	$\frac{1}{4}$	$\frac{1}{4}$	$\frac{1}{4}$

$\frac{1}{4}$ + $\frac{2}{4}$

$\frac{1}{4} + \frac{2}{4} =$ _____

3.

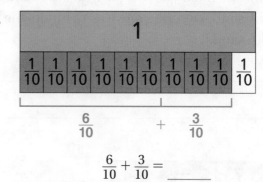

$\frac{6}{10}$ + $\frac{3}{10}$

$\frac{6}{10} + \frac{3}{10} =$ _____

Find the sum. Use models to help.

4. $\frac{3}{6} + \frac{3}{6} =$ _____

5. $\frac{5}{8} + \frac{2}{8} =$ _____

6. $\frac{1}{3} + \frac{1}{3} =$ _____

On Your Own

 Math Talk

MATHEMATICAL PRACTICES ③

Apply Explain how to add $\frac{2}{6} + \frac{3}{6}$.

Find the sum. Use models or *i*Tools to help.

7. $\frac{5}{8} + \frac{2}{8} =$ _____

8. $\frac{2}{5} + \frac{2}{5} =$ _____

9. $\frac{4}{6} + \frac{1}{6} =$ _____

10. **GO DEEPER** Jason is making a fruit drink. He mixes $\frac{2}{8}$ quart of grape juice with $\frac{3}{8}$ quart of apple juice. Then he adds $\frac{1}{8}$ quart of lemonade. How much fruit drink does Jason make?

_____

Problem Solving • Applications Real World

11. **THINK SMARTER** A sum has five addends. Each addend is a unit fraction. The sum is 1. What are the addends?

_____

12. **THINK SMARTER** In a survey, $\frac{4}{12}$ of the students chose Friday and $\frac{5}{12}$ chose Saturday as their favorite day of the week. What fraction shows the students who chose Friday or Saturday as their favorite day? Shade the model to show your answer.

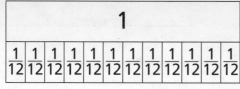

_____ of the students chose Friday or Saturday.

13. **MATHEMATICAL PRACTICE 4** **Model Mathematics** Jin is putting colored sand in a jar. She filled $\frac{2}{10}$ of the jar with blue sand and $\frac{4}{10}$ of the jar with pink sand. Describe one way to model the part of the jar filled with sand.

_____

_____

Connect to Art

Stained Glass Windows

Have you ever seen a stained glass window in a building or home? Artists have been designing stained glass windows for hundreds of years.

Help design the stained glass sail on the boat below.

Materials ■ color pencils

Look at the eight triangles in the sail. Use the guide below to color the triangles:

- $\frac{2}{8}$ blue
- $\frac{3}{8}$ red
- $\frac{2}{8}$ orange
- $\frac{1}{8}$ yellow

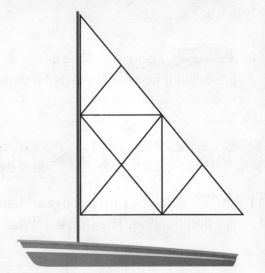

14. **MATHEMATICAL PRACTICE 4** **Write an Equation** Write an equation that shows the fraction of triangles that are red or blue.

15. **GO DEEPER** What color is the greatest part of the sail? Write a fraction for that color. How do you know that fraction is greater than the other fractions? Explain.

_____

_____

_____

Add Fractions Using Models

Common Core

COMMON CORE STANDARD—4.NF.B.3d
Build fractions from unit fractions by applying and extending previous understandings of operations on whole numbers.

Find the sum. Use fraction strips to help.

1. $\dfrac{2}{6} + \dfrac{1}{6} = $ _____ $\dfrac{3}{6}$ _____

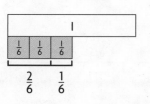

2. $\dfrac{4}{10} + \dfrac{5}{10} = $ _____

3. $\dfrac{1}{3} + \dfrac{2}{3} = $ _____

4. $\dfrac{2}{4} + \dfrac{1}{4} = $ _____

5. $\dfrac{2}{12} + \dfrac{4}{12} = $ _____

6. $\dfrac{1}{6} + \dfrac{2}{6} = $ _____

Problem Solving · Real World

7. Lola walks $\dfrac{4}{10}$ mile to her friend's house. Then she walks $\dfrac{5}{10}$ mile to the store. How far does she walk in all?

_____

8. Evan eats $\dfrac{1}{8}$ of a pan of lasagna and his brother eats $\dfrac{2}{8}$ of it. What fraction of the pan of lasagna do they eat?

_____

9. Jacqueline buys $\dfrac{2}{4}$ yard of green ribbon and $\dfrac{1}{4}$ yard of pink ribbon. How many yards of ribbon does she buy?

_____

10. Shu mixes $\dfrac{2}{3}$ pound of peanuts with $\dfrac{1}{3}$ pound of almonds. How many pounds of nuts does Shu mix?

_____

11. **WRITE** ▸*Math* Find a recipe in a book or online that includes the amount of salt as a fraction. Model how to find the amount of salt needed when the recipe is doubled.

Lesson Check (4.NF.B.3d)

1. Mary Jane has $\frac{3}{8}$ of a medium pizza left. Hector has $\frac{2}{8}$ of another medium pizza left. How much pizza do they have altogether? Use models to help.

2. Jeannie ate $\frac{1}{4}$ of an apple. Kelly ate $\frac{2}{4}$ of the apple. How much did they eat together? Use models to help.

Spiral Review (4.NBT.B.5, 4.NBT.B.6, 4.NF.A.1)

3. Karen is making 14 different kinds of greeting cards. She is making 12 of each kind. How many greeting cards is she making?

4. Jefferson works part time and earns $1,520 in four weeks. How much does he earn each week?

5. By installing efficient water fixtures, the average American can reduce water use to about 45 gallons of water per day. Using such water fixtures, about how many gallons of water would the average American use in December?

6. Collin is making a bulletin board and note center. He is using square cork tiles and square dry-erase tiles. One of every 3 squares will be a cork square. If he uses 12 squares for the center, how many will be cork squares?

FOR MORE PRACTICE
GO TO THE
Personal Math Trainer

Name _____

Subtract Fractions Using Models

Essential Question How can you subtract fractions with like denominators using models?

**Number and Operations—
Fractions—4.NF.B.3d** *Also 4.MD.A.2*
MATHEMATICAL PRACTICES
MP1, MP2, MP4, MP6

Unlock the Problem Real World

A rover needs to travel $\frac{5}{8}$ mile to reach its destination. It has already traveled $\frac{3}{8}$ mile. How much farther does the rover need to travel?

Compare fractions to find the difference.

STEP 1 Shade the model.

Shade the model to show the total distance.

Then shade the model to show how much distance the rover has already covered.

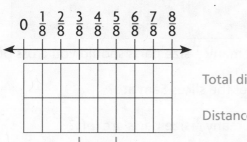

Total distance

Distance traveled

Think: The difference is _____.

STEP 2 Write the difference.

$$\frac{5}{8} - \frac{3}{8} = \frac{}{8}$$

So, the rover needs to travel _____ mile farther.

1. Explain how the model shows how much farther the rover needs to travel.

_____

_____

2. Explain how you can use the model to find $\frac{6}{8} - \frac{2}{8}$.

_____

_____

🔓 Example

Sam ordered a small pizza, which was cut into 6 equal slices. He ate $\frac{2}{6}$ of the pizza and put the rest away for later. How much of the pizza did he put away for later?

Find $1 - \frac{2}{6}$.

- How much pizza did Sam begin with?

  _____

- How many slices are in the whole? _____

- How many slices did Sam eat? _____

🔓 One Way Use a picture.

Shade 1 whole.

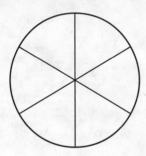

Cross out the parts Sam ate.

Think: He ate $\frac{2}{6}$ of the pizza, or 2 sixth-size parts.

How many sixth-size parts are left? _____

So, Sam put _____ of the pizza away for later.

🔓 Another Way Use fraction strips.

Use six $\frac{1}{6}$-size parts to model the whole pizza.

How many $\frac{1}{6}$-size parts should you cross out to model the slices Sam ate? _____

How many $\frac{1}{6}$-size parts are left? _____

Write the difference.

$1 - \dfrac{}{} = \dfrac{}{}$

 Math Talk

MATHEMATICAL PRACTICES ④

Use Models Explain why it makes sense to think of 1 whole as $\frac{6}{6}$ in this problem.

3. Explain how the equation $\frac{6}{6} - \frac{2}{6} = \frac{4}{6}$ is related to the problem situation.

_____

_____

4. Sam ate $\frac{2}{3}$ of the pizza and put the rest away for later. Explain how you can use the circle to find how much of the pizza Sam put away for later.

_____

_____

_____

Name _____

1. Lisa needs $\frac{4}{5}$ pound of shrimp to make shrimp salad. She has $\frac{1}{5}$ pound of shrimp. How much more shrimp does Lisa need to make the salad?

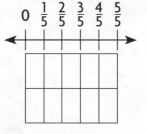

Subtract $\frac{4}{5} - \frac{1}{5}$. Use the model to help.

Shade the model to show how much shrimp Lisa needs.

Then shade the model to show how much shrimp Lisa has. Compare the difference between the two shaded rows.

$\frac{4}{5} - \frac{1}{5} = \frac{}{5}$ pound

Lisa needs _____ pound more shrimp.

Use the model to find the difference.

✓ 2. $\frac{3}{6} - \frac{2}{6} = \frac{}{6}$

3. $\frac{8}{10} - \frac{3}{10} = \frac{}{10}$

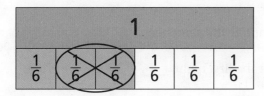

Subtract. Use models to help.

4. $\frac{5}{8} - \frac{2}{8} =$ _____

✓ 5. $\frac{7}{12} - \frac{2}{12} =$ _____

6. $\frac{3}{4} - \frac{2}{4} =$ _____

On Your Own

Subtract. Use models to help.

7. $\frac{2}{3} - \frac{1}{3} =$ _____

8. $\frac{7}{8} - \frac{5}{8} =$ _____

Math Talk MATHEMATICAL PRACTICES ②

Reason Abstractly Why does the numerator change when you subtract fractions with like denominators, but the denominator doesn't?

9. **THINK SMARTER** Explain how you could find the unknown addend in $\frac{2}{6} +$ _____ $= 1$ without using a model.

_____

_____

_____

Unlock the Problem

10. **GO DEEPER** Mrs. Ruiz served a pie for dessert two nights in a row. The drawings below show the pie after her family ate dessert on each night. What fraction of the pie did they eat on the second night?

First night   Second night

 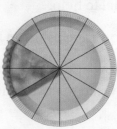

a. What do you need to know? _____

_____

b. How can you find the number of pieces eaten on the second night? _____

_____

c. Explain the steps you used to solve the problem.

_____

_____

_____

d. Complete the sentences.

After the first night, _____ pieces were left.

After the second night, _____ pieces were left.

So, _____ of the pie was eaten on the second night.

11. **MATHEMATICAL PRACTICE ⑥ Make Connections Between Models** Judi ate $\frac{7}{8}$ of a small pizza and Jack ate $\frac{2}{8}$ of a second small pizza. How much more of a pizza did Judi eat?

_____

12. **THINK SMARTER** Keiko sewed $\frac{3}{4}$ yard of lace on her backpack. Pam sewed $\frac{1}{4}$ yard of lace on her backpack. Shade the model to show how much more lace Keiko sewed on her backpack than Pam.

1			
$\frac{1}{4}$	$\frac{1}{4}$	$\frac{1}{4}$	$\frac{1}{4}$

Keiko sewed _____ yard more lace on her backpack than Pam.

Subtract Fractions Using Models

Common Core

COMMON CORE STANDARD—4.NF.B.3d
*Build fractions from unit fractions by applying
and extending previous understandings of
operations on whole numbers.*

Subtract. Use fraction strips to help.

1. $\frac{4}{5} - \frac{1}{5} =$ _____ $\frac{3}{5}$

1

| $\frac{1}{5}$ | $\frac{1}{5}$ | $\frac{1}{5}$ | $\frac{1}{5}$ |

2. $\frac{3}{4} - \frac{1}{4} =$ _____

1

| $\frac{1}{4}$ | $\frac{1}{4}$ | $\frac{1}{4}$ |

$\frac{1}{4}$

$\frac{2}{4}$

3. $\frac{5}{6} - \frac{1}{6} =$ _____

4. $\frac{7}{8} - \frac{1}{8} =$ _____

Problem Solving · Real World

Use the table for 5 and 6.

5. Ena is making trail mix. She buys the
   items shown in the table. How many
   more pounds of pretzels than raisins
   does she buy?

   _____

6. How many more pounds of granola than
   banana chips does she buy?

   _____

Item	Weight (in pounds)
Pretzels	$\frac{7}{8}$
Peanuts	$\frac{4}{8}$
Raisins	$\frac{2}{8}$
Banana Chips	$\frac{3}{8}$
Granola	$\frac{5}{8}$

7. **WRITE** ▸ *Math* List and describe the steps you would use to
   model $\frac{7}{10} - \frac{4}{10}$.

   _____

   _____

Lesson Check (4.NF.B.3d)

1. Lee reads for $\frac{3}{4}$ hour in the morning and $\frac{2}{4}$ hour in the afternoon. How much longer does Lee read in the morning than in the afternoon? Use models to help.

2. What equation does the model below represent?

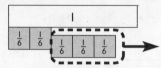

Spiral Review (4.NBT.B.5, 4.NF.A.2, 4.NF.B.3d)

3. A city received 2 inches of rain each day for 3 days. The meteorologist said that if the rain had been snow, each inch of rain would have been 10 inches of snow. How much snow would that city have received in the 3 days?

4. At a party there were four large submarine sandwiches, all the same size. During the party, $\frac{2}{3}$ of the chicken sandwich, $\frac{3}{4}$ of the tuna sandwich, $\frac{7}{12}$ of the roast beef sandwich, and $\frac{5}{6}$ of the veggie sandwich were eaten. Which sandwich had the least amount left?

5. Deena uses $\frac{3}{8}$ cup milk and $\frac{2}{8}$ cup oil in a recipe. How much liquid is this?

6. In the car lot, $\frac{4}{12}$ of the cars are white and $\frac{3}{12}$ of the cars are blue. What fraction of the cars in the lot are either white or blue?

FOR MORE PRACTICE
GO TO THE
Personal Math Trainer

Name _____

Add and Subtract Fractions

Essential Question How can you add and subtract fractions with like denominators?

Common Core

Number and Operations—Fractions—4.NF.B.3d
MATHEMATICAL PRACTICES
MP2, MP6, MP7

Unlock the Problem (Real World)

Julie is making a poster for a book report. The directions say to use $\frac{1}{5}$ of the poster to describe the setting, $\frac{2}{5}$ of the poster to describe the characters, and the rest of the poster to describe the plot. What part of the poster will she use to describe the plot?

🔑 **Example** Use a model.

Shade _____ to represent the part for the setting.

Shade _____ to represent the part for the characters.

1				
$\frac{1}{5}$	$\frac{1}{5}$	$\frac{1}{5}$	$\frac{1}{5}$	$\frac{1}{5}$

- Write an equation for the part of the poster used for

  the setting and characters. _____

- What does the part of the model that is not shaded represent?

  _____

- Write an equation for the part of the poster she will use for the plot.

  _____

So, Julie will use _____ of the poster to describe the plot.

 Math Talk

MATHEMATICAL PRACTICES ⑦

Look for Structure Why should Julie divide her poster into 5 equal parts instead of 3 equal parts?

1. What's the Error? Luke says $\frac{1}{5} + \frac{2}{5} = \frac{3}{10}$. Describe his error.

_____

_____

_____

Common Denominators Fractions with common denominators represent wholes divided into the same number of equal-size parts. To add or subtract fractions with the same denominator, you can add or subtract the number of parts given in the numerators.

🔑 Example Complete each equation.

Words	Fractions
1 fourth-size part + 2 fourth-size parts = _____ fourth-size parts	$\frac{1}{4} + \frac{2}{4} = \frac{}{4}$
3 sixth-size parts + 2 sixth-size parts = _____	$\frac{3}{6} + \frac{2}{6} = \underline{}$
7 tenth-size parts − 4 tenth-size parts = _____	$\underline{} - \underline{} = \underline{}$

Share and Show

Math Talk

MATHEMATICAL PRACTICES ②

Reason Abstractly
Explain why $\frac{11}{12} - \frac{5}{6} \neq \frac{6}{6}$.

1. 9 twelfth-size parts − 5 twelfth-size parts = _____

$\frac{9}{12} - \frac{5}{12} =$ _____

Find the sum or difference.

2. $\frac{3}{12} + \frac{8}{12} =$ _____

3. $\frac{1}{3} + \frac{1}{3} =$ _____

4. $\frac{3}{4} - \frac{1}{4} =$ _____

✓ **5.** $\frac{2}{6} + \frac{2}{6} =$ _____

6. $\frac{3}{8} + \frac{1}{8} =$ _____

✓ **7.** $\frac{6}{10} - \frac{2}{10} =$ _____

On Your Own

Find the sum or difference.

8. $\frac{1}{2} + \frac{1}{2} =$ _____

9. $\frac{5}{6} - \frac{4}{6} =$ _____

10. $\frac{4}{5} - \frac{2}{5} =$ _____

Practice: Copy and Solve **Find the sum or difference.**

11. $\frac{1}{4} + \frac{1}{4} =$ _____

12. $\frac{9}{10} - \frac{5}{10} =$ _____

13. $\frac{1}{12} + \frac{7}{12} =$ _____

14. **GO DEEPER** Christopher mixes $\frac{3}{8}$ gallon of red paint with $\frac{5}{8}$ gallon of blue paint to make purple paint. He uses $\frac{2}{8}$ gallon of the purple paint. How much purple paint is left?

Name _____

15. **MATHEMATICAL PRACTICE 6** A city worker is painting a stripe down the center of Main Street. Main Street is $\frac{8}{10}$ mile long. The worker painted $\frac{4}{10}$ mile of the street. **Explain** how to find what part of a mile is left to paint.

_____

_____

_____

16. **THINK SMARTER** **Sense or Nonsense?** Brian says that when you add or subtract fractions with the same denominator, you can add or subtract the numerators and keep the same denominator. Is Brian correct? Explain.

_____

_____

_____

_____

_____

17. **GO DEEPER** The length of a rope was $\frac{6}{8}$ yard. Jeff cut the rope into 3 pieces. Each piece is a different length measured in eighths of a yard. What is the length of each piece of rope?

_____

18. **THINK SMARTER** For 18a–18d, choose Yes or No to show if the sum or difference is correct.

18a. $\frac{3}{5} + \frac{1}{5} = \frac{4}{5}$ ○ Yes   ○ No

18b. $\frac{1}{4} + \frac{2}{4} = \frac{3}{8}$ ○ Yes   ○ No

18c. $\frac{5}{8} - \frac{4}{8} = \frac{1}{8}$ ○ Yes   ○ No

18d. $\frac{4}{9} - \frac{2}{9} = \frac{6}{9}$ ○ Yes   ○ No

Sense or Nonsense?

19. Harry says that $\frac{1}{4} + \frac{1}{8} = \frac{2}{8}$. Jane says $\frac{1}{4} + \frac{1}{8} = \frac{3}{8}$. Whose answer makes sense? Whose answer is nonsense? Explain your reasoning. Draw a model to help.

	Harry
	$\frac{1}{4} + \frac{1}{8} = \frac{2}{8}$

	Jane
	$\frac{1}{4} + \frac{1}{8} = \frac{3}{8}$

Model

Harry

Jane

Add and Subtract Fractions

COMMON CORE STANDARD—4.NF.B.3d
Build fractions from unit fractions by applying
and extending previous understandings of
operations on whole numbers.

Find the sum or difference.

1. $\frac{4}{12} + \frac{8}{12} =$ _____ $\frac{12}{12}$

1											
$\frac{1}{12}$	$\frac{1}{12}$	$\frac{1}{12}$	$\frac{1}{12}$	$\frac{1}{12}$	$\frac{1}{12}$	$\frac{1}{12}$	$\frac{1}{12}$	$\frac{1}{12}$	$\frac{1}{12}$	$\frac{1}{12}$	$\frac{1}{12}$

$\frac{4}{12}$ $\frac{8}{12}$

2. $\frac{3}{6} - \frac{1}{6} =$ _____

1					
$\frac{1}{6}$	$\frac{1}{6}$	$\frac{1}{6}$	$\frac{1}{6}$	$\frac{1}{6}$	$\frac{1}{6}$
$\frac{1}{6}$	$\frac{1}{6}$	$\frac{1}{6}$	$\frac{1}{6}$	$\frac{1}{6}$	$\frac{1}{6}$

$\frac{2}{6}$

3. $\frac{4}{5} - \frac{3}{5} =$ _____

4. $\frac{6}{10} + \frac{3}{10} =$ _____

5. $1 - \frac{3}{8} =$ _____

6. $\frac{1}{4} + \frac{2}{4} =$ _____

Problem Solving · Real World

Use the table for 7 and 8.

7. Guy finds how far his house is from several locations and makes the table shown. How much farther away from Guy's house is the library than the cafe?

_____

8. If Guy walks from his house to school and back, how far does he walk?

_____

Distance from Guy's House	
Location	Distance (in miles)
Library	$\frac{9}{10}$
School	$\frac{5}{10}$
Store	$\frac{7}{10}$
Cafe	$\frac{4}{10}$
Yogurt Shop	$\frac{6}{10}$

9. **WRITE** ▸Math Compare how you would model and record finding the sum and difference of two rocks weighing $\frac{2}{8}$ pound and $\frac{3}{8}$ pound.

_____

_____

Lesson Check (4.NF.B.3d)

1. Mr. Angulo buys $\frac{5}{8}$ pound of red grapes and $\frac{3}{8}$ pound of green grapes. How many pounds of grapes did Mr. Angulo buy?

2. What equation does the model below represent?

1							
$\frac{1}{8}$	$\frac{1}{8}$	$\frac{1}{8}$	$\frac{1}{8}$	$\frac{1}{8}$	$\frac{1}{8}$	$\frac{1}{8}$	$\frac{1}{8}$
$\frac{1}{8}$	$\frac{1}{8}$	$\frac{1}{8}$	$\frac{1}{8}$	$\frac{1}{8}$	$\frac{1}{8}$	$\frac{1}{8}$	$\frac{1}{8}$

Spiral Review (4.OA.A.3, 4.NBT.B.5, 4.NF.B.3d)

3. There are 6 muffins in a package. How many packages will be needed to feed 48 people if each person has 2 muffins?

4. Camp Oaks gets 32 boxes of orange juice and 56 boxes of apple juice. Each shelf in the cupboard can hold 8 boxes of juice. What is the least number of shelves needed for all the juice boxes?

5. A machine makes 18 parts each hour. If the machine operates 24 hours a day, how many parts can it make in one day?

6. What equation does the model below represent?

FOR MORE PRACTICE
GO TO THE
Personal Math Trainer

Name _____

✓ Mid-Chapter Checkpoint

Vocabulary

Choose the best term from the box.

Vocabulary
fraction
simplest form
unit fraction

1. A _____ always has a numerator of 1. (p. 391)

Concepts and Skills

Write the fraction as a sum of unit fractions. (4.NF.B.3b)

2. $\frac{3}{10} =$ _____

3. $\frac{6}{6} =$ _____

Use the model to write an equation. (4.NF.B.3a)

4.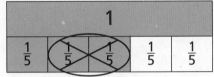

_____

5.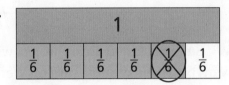

_____

Use the model to solve the equation. (4.NF.B.3a)

6. $\frac{3}{8} + \frac{2}{8} =$ _____

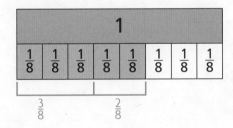

7. $\frac{4}{10} + \frac{5}{10} =$ _____

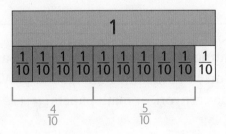

Find the sum or difference. (4.NF.B.3d)

8. $\frac{9}{12} - \frac{7}{12} =$ _____

9. $\frac{2}{3} + \frac{1}{3} =$ _____

10. $\frac{1}{5} + \frac{3}{5} =$ _____

11. $\frac{2}{6} + \frac{2}{6} =$ _____

12. $\frac{4}{4} - \frac{2}{4} =$ _____

13. $\frac{7}{8} - \frac{4}{8} =$ _____

14. Tyrone mixed $\frac{7}{12}$ quart of red paint with $\frac{1}{12}$ quart of yellow paint. How much paint does Tyrone have in the mixture? (4.NF.B.3d)

_____

15. Jorge lives $\frac{6}{8}$ mile from school and $\frac{2}{8}$ mile from a ballpark. How much farther does Jorge live from school than from the ballpark? (4.NF.B.3d)

_____

16. **GO DEEPER** Su Ling started an art project with 1 yard of felt. She used $\frac{2}{6}$ yard on Tuesday and $\frac{3}{6}$ yard on Wednesday. How much felt does Su Ling have left? (4.NF.B.3d)

_____

17. Eloise hung artwork on $\frac{2}{5}$ of a bulletin board. She hung math papers on $\frac{1}{5}$ of the same bulletin board. What part of the bulletin board has artwork or math papers? (4.NF.B.3d)

_____

Name _____

Rename Fractions and Mixed Numbers

Essential Question How can you rename mixed numbers as fractions greater than 1 and rename fractions greater than 1 as mixed numbers?

Common Core Number and Operations— Fractions—4.NF.B.3b *Also 4.MD.A.2*
MATHEMATICAL PRACTICES
MP2, MP6, MP7, MP8

Unlock the Problem

Mr. Fox has $2\frac{3}{6}$ loaves of corn bread. Each loaf was cut into $\frac{1}{6}$-size pieces. If he has 14 people over for dinner, is there enough bread for each person to have 1 piece?

A **mixed number** is a number represented by a whole number and a fraction. You can write a mixed number as a fraction.

To find how many $\frac{1}{6}$-size pieces are in $2\frac{3}{6}$, write $2\frac{3}{6}$ as a fraction.

- What is the size of 1 piece of bread relative to the whole?

_____

- How much bread does Mr. Fox need for 14 people?

_____

🔓 Example Write a mixed number as a fraction.

THINK	**MODEL AND RECORD**

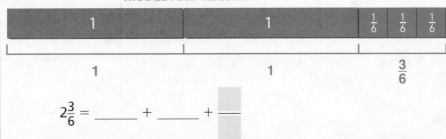

STEP 1 Model $2\frac{3}{6}$.

$$2\frac{3}{6} = \underline{\quad} + \underline{\quad} + \underline{\quad}$$

STEP 2 Find how many $\frac{1}{6}$-size pieces are in each whole. Model $2\frac{3}{6}$ using only $\frac{1}{6}$-size pieces.

$$2\frac{3}{6} = \underline{\quad} + \underline{\quad} + \underline{\quad}$$

STEP 3 Find the total number of $\frac{1}{6}$-size pieces in $2\frac{3}{6}$.

Think: Find $\frac{6}{6} + \frac{6}{6} + \frac{3}{6}$.

$$2\frac{3}{6} = \underline{\quad}$$

There are _____ sixth-size pieces in $2\frac{3}{6}$.

So, there is enough bread for 14 people to each have 1 piece.

Math Talk

MATHEMATICAL PRACTICES ⑦

Look for Structure Give an example of how to write a mixed number as a fraction without using a model.

🔑 Example   Write a fraction greater than 1 as a mixed number.

To weave a bracelet, Charlene needs 7 pieces of brown thread. Each piece of thread must be $\frac{1}{3}$ yard long. How much thread should she buy to weave the bracelet?

Write $\frac{7}{3}$ as a mixed number.

THINK	MODEL AND RECORD
STEP 1 Model $\frac{7}{3}$.	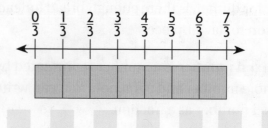 $\frac{7}{3} = \underline{\quad} + \underline{\quad} + \underline{\quad} + \underline{\quad} + \underline{\quad} + \underline{\quad} + \underline{\quad}$
STEP 2 Find how many wholes are in $\frac{7}{3}$, and how many thirds are left over.	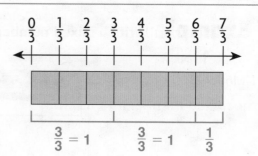 $\frac{3}{3} = 1 \qquad \frac{3}{3} = 1 \qquad \frac{1}{3}$ $\frac{7}{3} = \underline{\quad} + \underline{\quad} + \underline{\quad}$
STEP 3 Write $\frac{7}{3}$ as a mixed number.	$\frac{7}{3} = \boxed{}\,\dfrac{\boxed{}}{\boxed{}}$

So, Charlene should buy _____ yards of thread.

Share and Show

Write the unknown numbers. Write mixed numbers above the number line and fractions greater than one below the number line.

1.

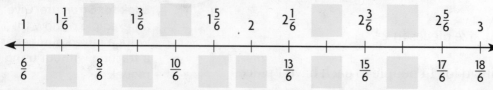

Name _____

Write the mixed number as a fraction.

2. $1\frac{1}{8}$

3. $1\frac{3}{5}$

4. $1\frac{2}{3}$

_____

Write the fraction as a mixed number.

5. $\frac{11}{4}$

6. $\frac{6}{5}$

7. $\frac{13}{10}$

_____

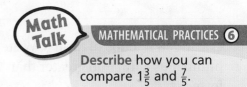

Math Talk

MATHEMATICAL PRACTICES 6

Describe how you can compare $1\frac{3}{5}$ and $\frac{7}{5}$.

On Your Own

Write the mixed number as a fraction.

8. $2\frac{7}{10}$

9. $3\frac{2}{3}$

10. $4\frac{2}{5}$

_____

MATHEMATICAL PRACTICE 8 Use Repeated Reasoning Algebra Find the unknown numbers.

11. $\frac{13}{7} = 1\frac{\blacksquare}{7}$

12. $\blacksquare\frac{5}{6} = \frac{23}{6}$

13. $\frac{57}{11} = \blacksquare\frac{\blacksquare}{11}$

_____

14. **GO DEEPER** Pen has $\frac{1}{2}$-cup and $\frac{1}{8}$-cup measuring cups. What are two ways he could measure out $1\frac{3}{4}$ cups of flour?

_____

15. **GO DEEPER** Juanita is making bread. She needs $3\frac{1}{2}$ cups of flour. Juanita only has a $\frac{1}{4}$-cup measuring cup. How many $\frac{1}{4}$ cups of flour will Juanita use to prepare the bread?

_____

Problem Solving • Applications

Use the recipe to solve 16–18.

16. **MATHEMATICAL PRACTICE ② Reason Quantitatively** Cal is making energy squares. How many $\frac{1}{2}$ cups of peanut butter are used in the recipe?

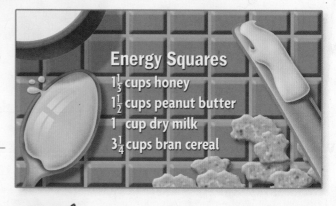

Energy Squares
$1\frac{1}{3}$ cups honey
$1\frac{1}{2}$ cups peanut butter
1 cup dry milk
$3\frac{1}{4}$ cups bran cereal

17. **THINK SMARTER** Suppose Cal wants to make 2 times as many energy squares as the recipe makes. How many cups of bran cereal should he use? Write your answer as a mixed number and as a fraction greater than 1 in simplest form.

WRITE ▸ *Math* • **Show Your Work**

18. Cal added $2\frac{3}{8}$ cups of raisins. Write this mixed number as a fraction greater than 1 in simplest form.

19. **GO DEEPER** Jenn is preparing brown rice. She needs $1\frac{1}{2}$ cups of brown rice and 2 cups of water. Jenn has only a $\frac{1}{8}$-cup measuring cup. How many $\frac{1}{8}$ cups each of rice and water will Jenn use to prepare the rice?

20. **THINK SMARTER** Draw a line to show the mixed number and fraction that have the same value.

$1\frac{2}{5}$ $2\frac{3}{8}$ $4\frac{1}{3}$ $1\frac{2}{3}$

•   •   •   •

•   •   •   •

$\frac{30}{3}$ $\frac{13}{3}$ $\frac{4}{3}$ $\frac{8}{5}$

Name _____

Rename Fractions and Mixed Numbers

 Common Core

COMMON CORE STANDARD—4.NF.B.3b
Build fractions from unit fractions by applying and extending previous understandings of operations on whole numbers.

Write the mixed number as a fraction.

1. $2\frac{3}{5}$

Think: Find $\frac{5}{5} + \frac{5}{5} + \frac{3}{5}$.

$\frac{13}{5}$ _____

2. $4\frac{1}{3}$

_____

3. $1\frac{2}{5}$

_____

4. $3\frac{2}{3}$

_____

5. $4\frac{1}{8}$

_____

6. $1\frac{7}{10}$

_____

7. $5\frac{1}{2}$

_____

8. $2\frac{3}{8}$

_____

Write the fraction as a mixed number.

9. $\frac{31}{6}$

_____

10. $\frac{20}{10}$

_____

11. $\frac{15}{8}$

_____

12. $\frac{13}{6}$

_____

Problem Solving • Real World

13. A recipe calls for $2\frac{2}{4}$ cups of raisins, but Julie only has a $\frac{1}{4}$ cup measuring cup. How many $\frac{1}{4}$ cups does Julie need to measure out $2\frac{2}{4}$ cups of raisins?

_____

14. If Julie needs $3\frac{1}{4}$ cups of oatmeal, how many $\frac{1}{4}$ cups of oatmeal will she use?

_____

15. **WRITE** ▸ *Math* Draw and explain how you can use a number line to rename a fraction greater than 1 as a mixed number.

_____

_____

_____

Lesson Check (4.NF.B.3c)

1. Write a mixed number that is equivalent to $\frac{16}{3}$.

2. Stacey filled her $\frac{1}{2}$ cup measuring cup seven times to have enough flour for a cake recipe. How much flour does the cake recipe call for?

Spiral Review (4.NBT.B.5, 4.NBT.B.6, 4.NF.A.1, 4.NF.B.3d)

3. Becki put some stamps into her stamp collection book. She put 14 stamps on each page. If she completely filled 16 pages, how many stamps did she put in the book?

4. Brian is driving 324 miles to visit some friends. He wants to get there in 6 hours. How many miles does he need to drive each hour?

5. During a bike challenge, riders have to collect various colored ribbons. Each $\frac{1}{2}$ mile they collect a red ribbon, each $\frac{1}{8}$ mile they collect a green ribbon, and each $\frac{1}{4}$ mile they collect a blue ribbon. Which colors of ribbons will be collected at the $\frac{3}{4}$ mile marker?

6. Stephanie had $\frac{7}{8}$ pound of bird seed. She used $\frac{3}{8}$ pound to fill a bird feeder. How much bird seed does Stephanie have left?

FOR MORE PRACTICE
GO TO THE
Personal Math Trainer

Name _____

Add and Subtract Mixed Numbers

Essential Question How can you add and subtract mixed numbers with like denominators?

Common Core Number and Operations—
Fractions—4.NF.B.3c *Also 4.MD.A.2*
MATHEMATICAL PRACTICES
MP1, MP2, MP4, MP8

Unlock the Problem

After a party, there were $1\frac{4}{6}$ quesadillas left on one tray and $2\frac{3}{6}$ quesadillas left on another tray. How many quesadillas were left?

- What operation will you use?

_____

- Is the sum of the fractional parts of the mixed numbers greater than 1?

_____

Example Add mixed numbers.

THINK	MODEL	RECORD
STEP 1 Add the fractional parts of the mixed numbers.	**Think:** Shade to model $\frac{4}{6} + \frac{3}{6}$. 	$1\frac{4}{6}$ $+ 2\frac{3}{6}$ ———
STEP 2 Add the whole-number parts of the mixed numbers.	**Think:** Shade to model $1 + 2$. 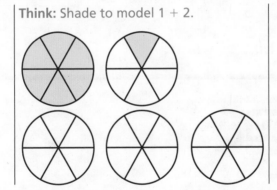	$1\frac{4}{6}$ $+ 2\frac{3}{6}$ ——— $\frac{7}{6}$

STEP 3 Rename the sum.

Think: $\frac{7}{6}$ is greater than 1. Group the wholes together to rename the sum.

The model shows a total of ▢ wholes and ── left over.

$$3\frac{7}{6} = 3 + \frac{6}{6} + \underline{\quad}$$

$$= 3 + 1 + \underline{\ \ } = \underline{\quad}\ \underline{\ \ }$$

So, _____ quesadillas were left.

Math Talk

MATHEMATICAL PRACTICES ②

Reason Abstractly When modeling sums such as $\frac{4}{6}$ and $\frac{3}{6}$, why is it helpful to combine parts into wholes when possible? Explain.

Example Subtract mixed numbers.

Alejandro had $3\frac{4}{6}$ quesadillas. His family ate $2\frac{3}{6}$ of the quesadillas. How many quesadillas are left?

Find $3\frac{4}{6} - 2\frac{3}{6}$.

MODEL	RECORD
Shade the model to show $3\frac{4}{6}$. Then cross out $2\frac{3}{6}$ to model the subtraction.	Subtract the fractional parts of the mixed numbers. Then subtract the whole-number parts of the mixed numbers.

$$3\frac{4}{6}$$
$$-\ 2\frac{3}{6}$$

The difference is _____.

So, there are _____ quesadillas left.

 **Share and Show** MATH BOARD

Write the sum as a mixed number with the fractional part less than 1.

1.  $1\frac{1}{6}$ Add whole numbers.   Add fractions.

$+3\frac{3}{6}$

$+$ _____ $+$ _____

$+$ _____ $=$ _____

2. $1\frac{4}{5}$

$+7\frac{2}{5}$

✓ **3.** $2\frac{1}{2}$

$+3\frac{1}{2}$

Name _____

Find the difference.

4. $3\dfrac{7}{12}$
　　$-2\dfrac{5}{12}$
　　—————

5. $4\dfrac{2}{3}$
　　$-3\dfrac{1}{3}$
　　—————

☑ **6.** $6\dfrac{9}{10}$
　　$-3\dfrac{7}{10}$
　　—————

Math Talk

MATHEMATICAL PRACTICES ⑧

Draw Conclusions
Explain how adding and subtracting mixed numbers is different from adding and subtracting fractions.

On Your Own

Write the sum as a mixed number with the fractional part less than 1.

7. $7\dfrac{4}{6}$
　　$+4\dfrac{3}{6}$
　　—————

8. $8\dfrac{1}{3}$
　　$+3\dfrac{2}{3}$
　　—————

9. $5\dfrac{4}{8}$
　　$+3\dfrac{5}{8}$
　　—————

10. $3\dfrac{5}{12}$
　　$+4\dfrac{2}{12}$
　　—————

Find the difference.

11. $5\dfrac{7}{8}$
　　$-2\dfrac{3}{8}$
　　—————

12. $5\dfrac{7}{12}$
　　$-4\dfrac{1}{12}$
　　—————

13. $3\dfrac{5}{10}$
　　$-1\dfrac{3}{10}$
　　—————

14. $7\dfrac{3}{4}$
　　$-2\dfrac{2}{4}$
　　—————

Practice: Copy and Solve **Find the sum or difference.**

15. $1\dfrac{3}{8} + 2\dfrac{7}{8}$

16. $6\dfrac{5}{8} - 4$

17. $9\dfrac{1}{2} + 8\dfrac{1}{2}$

18. $6\dfrac{3}{5} + 4\dfrac{3}{5}$

19. $8\dfrac{7}{10} - \dfrac{4}{10}$

20. $7\dfrac{3}{5} - 6\dfrac{3}{5}$

Problem Solving • Applications

Solve. Write your answer as a mixed number.

WRITE ▸ *Math*
Show Your Work

21. **MATHEMATICAL PRACTICE ①** **Make Sense of Problems** The driving distance from Alex's house to the museum is $6\frac{7}{10}$ miles. What is the round-trip distance?

22. **THINK SMARTER** The driving distance from the sports arena to Kristina's house is $10\frac{9}{10}$ miles. The distance from the sports arena to Luke's house is $2\frac{7}{10}$ miles. How much greater is the driving distance between the sports arena and Kristina's house than between the sports arena and Luke's house?

23. Pedro biked from his house to the nature preserve, a distance of $23\frac{4}{5}$ miles. Sandra biked from her house to the lake, a distance of $12\frac{2}{5}$ miles. How many miles less did Sandra bike than Pedro?

24. **GO DEEPER** During the Martinez family trip, they drove from home to a ski lodge, a distance of $55\frac{4}{5}$ miles, and then drove an additional $12\frac{4}{5}$ miles to visit friends. If the family drove the same route back home, what was the distance traveled during their trip?

25. **THINK SMARTER** For 25a–25d, select True or False for each statement.

25a. $2\frac{3}{8} + 1\frac{6}{8}$ is equal to $4\frac{1}{8}$.   ○ True   ○ False

25b. $3\frac{6}{12} + 1\frac{4}{12}$ is equal to $2\frac{2}{12}$.   ○ True   ○ False

25c. $5\frac{5}{6} - 2\frac{4}{6}$ is equal to $1\frac{3}{6}$.   ○ True   ○ False

25d. $5\frac{5}{8} - 3\frac{2}{8}$ is equal to $2\frac{3}{8}$.   ○ True   ○ False

Add and Subtract Mixed Numbers

Common Core

COMMON CORE STANDARD—4.NF.B.3c
Build fractions from unit fractions by applying and extending previous understandings of operations on whole numbers.

Find the sum. Write the sum as a mixed number, so the fractional part is less than 1.

1. $6\frac{4}{5}$
$+ 3\frac{3}{5}$
$\overline{9\frac{7}{5}} = 10\frac{2}{5}$

2. $4\frac{1}{2}$
$+ 2\frac{1}{2}$

3. $2\frac{2}{3}$
$+ 3\frac{2}{3}$

4. $6\frac{4}{5}$
$+ 7\frac{4}{5}$

5. $9\frac{3}{6}$
$+ 2\frac{2}{6}$

6. $8\frac{4}{12}$
$+ 3\frac{6}{12}$

7. $4\frac{3}{8}$
$+ 1\frac{5}{8}$

8. $9\frac{5}{10}$
$+ 6\frac{3}{10}$

Find the difference.

9. $6\frac{7}{8}$
$- 4\frac{3}{8}$

10. $4\frac{2}{3}$
$- 3\frac{1}{3}$

11. $6\frac{4}{5}$
$- 3\frac{3}{5}$

12. $7\frac{3}{4}$
$- 2\frac{1}{4}$

Problem Solving · Real World

13. James wants to send two gifts by mail. One package weighs $2\frac{3}{4}$ pounds. The other package weighs $1\frac{3}{4}$ pounds. What is the total weight of the packages?

14. **WRITE** ▸*Math* Describe how adding and subtracting mixed numbers can help you with recipes.

Lesson Check (4.NF.B.3c)

1. Brad has two lengths of copper pipe to fit together. One has a length of $2\frac{5}{12}$ feet and the other has a length of $3\frac{7}{12}$ feet. How many feet of pipe does he have?

2. A pattern calls for $2\frac{1}{4}$ yards of material and $1\frac{1}{4}$ yards of lining. How much total fabric is needed?

Spiral Review (4.OA.A.3, 4.NBT.B.4, 4.NBT.B.5, 4.NBT.B.6)

3. Shanice has 23 baseball trading cards of star players. She agrees to sell them for $16 each. How much money will she make from selling the cards?

4. Nanci is volunteering at the animal shelter. She wants to spend an equal amount of time playing with each dog. She has 145 minutes to play with all 7 dogs. About how much time can she spend with each dog?

5. Frieda has 12 red apples and 15 green apples. She is going to share the apples equally among 8 people and keep any extra apples for herself. How many apples will Frieda keep for herself?

6. The Lynch family bought a house for $75,300. A few years later, they sold the house for $80,250. How much greater was the selling price than the purchase price?

**FOR MORE PRACTICE
GO TO THE
Personal Math Trainer**

Name _____

Subtraction with Renaming

Essential Question How can you rename a mixed number to help you subtract?

Number and Operations—Fractions—4.NF.B.3c Also 4.MD.A.2
MATHEMATICAL PRACTICES
MP1, MP4, MP7

⚿ Unlock the Problem Real World

Ramon, Chandler, and Chase go bike riding on weekends. On one weekend, Chase rode his bike for 3 hours, Chandler rode her bike for $2\frac{1}{4}$ hours, and Ramon rode his bike for $1\frac{3}{4}$ hours. How much longer did Chandler ride her bike than Ramon did?

• Which operation will you use?

_____

• In the problem, circle the numbers that you need to use to find a solution.

🔑 **Use a model. Find $2\frac{1}{4} - 1\frac{3}{4}$.**

Shade the model to show how long Chandler rode her bike.
Then shade the model to show how long Ramon rode his bike.

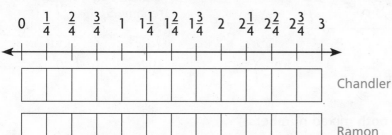

Think: The difference is _____.

So, Chandler rode her bike _____ hour longer than Ramon did.

---

1. If you have 1 fourth-size part, can you take away 3 fourth-size parts? Explain.

_____

_____

2. If you have 1 whole and 1 fourth-size part, can you take away 3 fourth-size parts? Explain.

_____

_____

Math Talk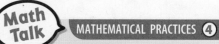

MATHEMATICAL PRACTICES ④

Use Models How can you use models to find how much longer Chase rode his bike than Chandler did?

🔓 One Way — Rename the first mixed number.

Find the difference. $5\frac{1}{8} - 3\frac{3}{8}$

STEP 1

Rename $5\frac{1}{8}$ as a mixed number with a fraction greater than 1.

Think:

$$5\frac{1}{8} = 4 + 1 + \frac{1}{8}$$

$$= 4 + \frac{\boxed{}}{8} + \frac{1}{8}$$

$$= \boxed{}$$

STEP 2

Subtract the mixed numbers.

$$5\frac{1}{8} = \boxed{}$$

$$-3\frac{3}{8} = -3\frac{3}{8}$$

$$\overline{\boxed{}}$$

Math Talk

MATHEMATICAL PRACTICES ⑦

Look for Structure
Explain why you need to rename $5\frac{1}{8}$.

🔓 Another Way — Rename both mixed numbers.

Find the difference. $3\frac{4}{12} - 1\frac{6}{12}$

STEP 1

Rename both mixed numbers as fractions greater than 1.

$$3\frac{4}{12} = \frac{\boxed{}}{12} \qquad 1\frac{6}{12} = \frac{\boxed{}}{12}$$

STEP 2

Subtract the fractions greater than 1.

$$\frac{\boxed{}}{12}$$

$$-\frac{\boxed{}}{12}$$

$$\overline{\boxed{}}$$

- Explain how you could rename 5 to subtract $3\frac{1}{4}$.

_____

_____

Name _____

1. Rename both mixed numbers as fractions. Find the difference.

$$3\frac{3}{6} = \frac{}{6}$$

$$-1\frac{4}{6} = -\frac{}{6}$$

Find the difference.

2. $1\frac{1}{3}$
$-\frac{2}{3}$

3. $4\frac{7}{10}$
$-1\frac{9}{10}$

4. $3\frac{5}{12}$
$-\frac{8}{12}$

Math Talk MATHEMATICAL PRACTICES ④

Model Mathematics
Describe how you would model $\frac{13}{6} - \frac{8}{6}$.

On Your Own

Find the difference.

5. $8\frac{1}{10}$
$-2\frac{9}{10}$

6. 2
$-1\frac{1}{4}$

7. $4\frac{1}{5}$
$-3\frac{2}{5}$

Practice: Copy and Solve **Find the difference.**

8. $4\frac{1}{6} - 2\frac{5}{6}$

9. $6\frac{9}{12} - 3\frac{10}{12}$

10. $3\frac{3}{10} - \frac{7}{10}$

11. $4 - 2\frac{3}{5}$

12. **GO DEEPER** Lisa mixed $4\frac{2}{6}$ cups of orange juice with $3\frac{1}{6}$ cups of pineapple juice to make fruit punch. She and her friends drank $3\frac{4}{6}$ cups of the punch. How much of the fruit punch is left?

© Houghton Mifflin Harcourt Publishing Company

Problem Solving • Applications

Rename the fractions to solve.

Many instruments are coiled or curved so that they are easier for the musician to play, but they would be quite long if straightened out completely.

13. **MATHEMATICAL PRACTICE ❶ Analyze Relationships** Trumpets and cornets are brass instruments. Fully stretched out, the length of a trumpet is $5\frac{1}{4}$ feet and the length of a cornet is $4\frac{2}{4}$ feet. The trumpet is how much longer than the cornet?

_____

14. **THINK SMARTER** Tubas, trombones, and French horns are brass instruments. Fully stretched out, the length of a tuba is 18 feet, the length of a trombone is $9\frac{11}{12}$ feet, and the length of a French horn is $17\frac{1}{12}$ feet. The tuba is how much longer than the French horn? The French horn is how much longer than the trombone?

WRITE *Math* • **Show Your Work**

_____

15. **GO DEEPER** The pitch of a musical instrument is related to its length. In general, the greater the length of a musical instrument, the lower its pitch. Order the brass instruments identified on this page from lowest pitch to the highest pitch.

_____

Personal Math Trainer

16. **THINK SMARTER +** Alicia had $3\frac{1}{6}$ yards of fabric. After making a tablecloth, she had $1\frac{4}{6}$ yards of fabric. Alicia said she used $2\frac{3}{6}$ yards of fabric for the tablecloth. Do you agree? Explain.

_____

_____

_____

Name _____

Subtraction with Renaming

Common Core

COMMON CORE STANDARD—4.NF.B.3c
Build fractions from unit fractions by applying and extending previous understandings of operations on whole numbers.

Find the difference.

1. $5\frac{1}{3} \longrightarrow 4\frac{4}{3}$
    $-3\frac{2}{3} \longrightarrow 3\frac{2}{3}$
    _____
    $1\frac{2}{3}$

2. 6
    $-3\frac{2}{5}$
    _____

3. $5\frac{1}{4}$
    $-2\frac{3}{4}$
    _____

4. $9\frac{3}{8}$
    $-8\frac{7}{8}$
    _____

5. $12\frac{3}{10}$
    $-7\frac{7}{10}$
    _____

6. $8\frac{1}{6}$
    $-3\frac{5}{6}$
    _____

7. $7\frac{3}{5}$
    $-4\frac{4}{5}$
    _____

8. $10\frac{1}{2}$
    $-8\frac{1}{2}$
    _____

9. $7\frac{1}{6}$
    $-2\frac{5}{6}$
    _____

10. $9\frac{3}{12}$
    $-4\frac{7}{12}$
    _____

11. $9\frac{1}{10}$
    $-8\frac{7}{10}$
    _____

12. $9\frac{1}{3}$
    $-\frac{2}{3}$
    _____

Problem Solving

13. Alicia buys a 5-pound bag of rocks for a fish tank. She uses $1\frac{1}{8}$ pounds for a small fish bowl. How much is left?

14. Xavier made 25 pounds of roasted almonds for a fair. He has $3\frac{1}{2}$ pounds left at the end of the fair. How many pounds of roasted almonds did he sell at the fair?

_____   _____

15. **WRITE** ▸ *Math* Explain when you know you need to rename a mixed number to subtract.

_____

_____

_____

Lesson Check

1. Reggie is making a double-layer cake. The recipe for the first layer calls for $2\frac{1}{4}$ cups of sugar. The recipe for the second layer calls for $1\frac{1}{4}$ cups of sugar. Reggie has 5 cups of sugar. How much will he have left after making both recipes?

2. Kate has $4\frac{3}{8}$ yards of fabric and needs $2\frac{7}{8}$ yards to make a skirt. How much extra fabric will she have left after making the skirt?

Spiral Review

3. Paulo has 128 glass beads to use to decorate picture frames. He wants to use the same number of beads on each frame. If he decorates 8 picture frames, how many beads will he put on each frame?

4. Madison is making party favors. She wants to make enough favors so each guest gets the same number of favors. She knows there will be 6 or 8 guests at the party. What is the least number of party favors Madison should make?

5. A shuttle bus makes 4 round-trips between two shopping centers each day. The bus holds 24 people. If the bus is full on each one-way trip, how many passengers are carried by the bus each day?

6. To make a fruit salad, Marvin mixes $1\frac{3}{4}$ cups of diced peaches with $2\frac{1}{4}$ cups of diced pears. How many cups of peaches and pears are in the fruit salad?

FOR MORE PRACTICE
GO TO THE
Personal Math Trainer

Fractions and Properties of Addition

Essential Question How can you add fractions with like denominators using the properties of addition?

Common Core Number and Operations—
Fractions—4.NF.B.3c

MATHEMATICAL PRACTICES
MP2, MP7, MP8

CONNECT The Associative and Commutative Properties of Addition can help you group and order addends to find sums mentally. You can use mental math to combine fractions that have a sum of 1.

- The Commutative Property of Addition states that when the order of two addends is changed, the sum is the same. For example, $4 + 5 = 5 + 4$.

- The Associative Property of Addition states that when the grouping of addends is changed, the sum is the same. For example, $(5 + 8) + 4 = 5 + (8 + 4)$.

Unlock the Problem (Real World)

The map shows four lighthouses in the Florida Keys and their distances apart in miles. The Dry Tortugas Lighthouse is the farthest west, and the Alligator Reef Lighthouse is the farthest east.

What is the distance from the Dry Tortugas Lighthouse to the Alligator Reef Lighthouse, traveling between the four lighthouses?

Gulf of Mexico

$70\frac{5}{10}$ $43\frac{6}{10}$ $34\frac{5}{10}$

Dry Tortugas Lighthouse   Key West Lighthouse   Sombrero Key Lighthouse   Alligator Reef Lighthouse

🔑 **Use the properties to order and group.**

Add. $70\frac{5}{10} + 43\frac{6}{10} + 34\frac{5}{10}$

$$70\frac{5}{10} + 43\frac{6}{10} + 34\frac{5}{10} = \text{\_\_\_\_\_} + \text{\_\_\_\_\_} + \text{\_\_\_\_\_}$$

$$= (\text{\_\_\_\_\_} + \text{\_\_\_\_\_}) + \text{\_\_\_\_\_}$$

$$= (\text{\_\_\_\_\_}) + \text{\_\_\_\_\_}$$

$$= \text{\_\_\_\_\_}$$

Use the Commutative Property to order the addends so that the fractions with a sum of 1 are together.

Use the Associative Property to group the addends that you can add mentally.

Add the grouped numbers, and then add the other mixed number.

Write the sum.

So, the distance from the Dry Tortugas Lighthouse to the Alligator Reef Lighthouse, traveling between the four lighthouses,

is _____ miles.

Try This! Use the properties and mental math to solve. Show each step, and name the property used.

$1\frac{1}{3} + (2 + 3\frac{2}{3})$

Share and Show MATH BOARD

1. Complete. Name the property used.

$\left(3\frac{4}{10} + 5\frac{2}{10}\right) + \frac{6}{10} = \left(5\frac{2}{10} + 3\frac{4}{10}\right) +$ _____ _____

$= 5\frac{2}{10} + \left(3\frac{4}{10} +$ _____ $\right)$ _____

$= 5\frac{2}{10} +$ _____

$=$ _____

Math Talk

MATHEMATICAL PRACTICES ②

Reason Abstractly
Describe how you could use the properties to find the sum $1\frac{1}{3} + 2\frac{5}{8} + 1\frac{2}{3}$.

Use the properties and mental math to find the sum.

2. $\left(2\frac{7}{8} + 3\frac{2}{8}\right) + 1\frac{1}{8}$

3. $1\frac{2}{5} + \left(1 + \frac{3}{5}\right)$

4. $5\frac{3}{6} + \left(5\frac{5}{6} + 4\frac{3}{6}\right)$

5. $\left(1\frac{1}{4} + 1\frac{1}{4}\right) + 2\frac{3}{4}$

6. $\left(12\frac{4}{9} + 1\frac{2}{9}\right) + 3\frac{5}{9}$

7. $\frac{3}{12} + \left(1\frac{8}{12} + \frac{9}{12}\right)$

Name _____

Use the properties and mental math to find the sum.

8. $\left(45\frac{1}{3} + 6\frac{1}{3}\right) + 38\frac{2}{3}$

9. $\frac{1}{2} + \left(103\frac{1}{2} + 12\right)$

10. $\left(3\frac{5}{10} + 10\right) + 11\frac{5}{10}$

11. GO DEEPER Pablo is training for a marathon. He ran $5\frac{4}{8}$ miles on Friday, $6\frac{5}{8}$ miles on Saturday, and $7\frac{4}{8}$ miles on Sunday. How many miles did he run on all three days?

12. GO DEEPER At lunchtime, Dale's Diner served a total of $2\frac{2}{6}$ pots of vegetable soup, $3\frac{5}{6}$ pots of chicken soup, and $4\frac{3}{6}$ pots of tomato soup. How many pots of soup were served in all?

Problem Solving • Applications Real World

Use the expressions in the box for 13–14.

13. Which property of addition would you use to regroup the addends in Expression A?

_____

14. THINK SMARTER Which two expressions have the same value?

_____

A	$\frac{1}{8} + \left(\frac{7}{8} + \frac{4}{8}\right)$
B	$\frac{1}{2} + 2$
C	$\frac{3}{7} + \left(\frac{1}{2} + \frac{4}{7}\right)$
D	$\frac{1}{3} + \frac{4}{3} + \frac{2}{3}$

15. THINK SMARTER Match the equation with the property used.

$\frac{6}{12} + \left(\frac{6}{12} + \frac{3}{12}\right) = \left(\frac{6}{12} + \frac{6}{12}\right) + \frac{3}{12}$ •

$3\frac{2}{5} + \left(5\frac{4}{5} + 2\frac{1}{5}\right) = 3\frac{2}{5} + \left(2\frac{1}{5} + 5\frac{4}{5}\right)$ •

$\left(4\frac{1}{6} + 3\frac{5}{6}\right) + 2\frac{2}{6} = \left(3\frac{5}{6} + 4\frac{1}{6}\right) + 2\frac{2}{6}$ •

$\left(1\frac{1}{8} + \frac{5}{8}\right) + 3\frac{3}{8} = 1\frac{1}{8} + \left(\frac{5}{8} + 3\frac{3}{8}\right)$ •

• Commutative Property

• Associative Property

Pose a Problem

16. **GO DEEPER**   Costumes are being made for the high school musical. The table at the right shows the amount of fabric needed for the costumes of the male and female leads. Alice uses the expression $7\frac{3}{8} + 1\frac{5}{8} + 2\frac{4}{8}$ to find the total amount of fabric needed for the costume of the female lead.

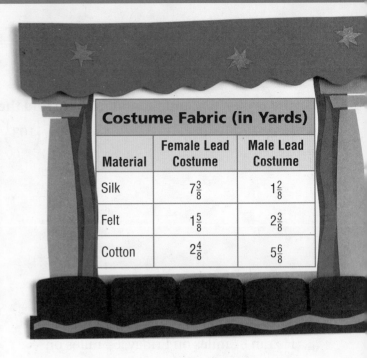

Costume Fabric (in Yards)		
Material	Female Lead Costume	Male Lead Costume
Silk	$7\frac{3}{8}$	$1\frac{2}{8}$
Felt	$1\frac{5}{8}$	$2\frac{3}{8}$
Cotton	$2\frac{4}{8}$	$5\frac{6}{8}$

To find the value of the expression using mental math, Alice used the properties of addition.

$$7\frac{3}{8} + 1\frac{5}{8} + 2\frac{4}{8} = \left(7\frac{3}{8} + 1\frac{5}{8}\right) + 2\frac{4}{8}$$

Alice added $7 + 1$ and was able to quickly add $\frac{3}{8}$ and $\frac{5}{8}$ to the sum of 8 to get 9. She added $2\frac{4}{8}$ to 9, so her answer was $11\frac{4}{8}$.

So, the amount of fabric needed for the costume of the female lead actor is $11\frac{4}{8}$ yards.

Write a new problem using the information for the costume for the male lead actor.

Pose a Problem	Solve your problem. Check your solution.

- **MATHEMATICAL PRACTICE ⑦ Identify Relationships** Explain how using the properties of addition makes both problems easier to solve.

Fractions and Properties of Addition

COMMON CORE STANDARD—4.NF.B.3c
Build fractions from unit fractions by applying
and extending previous understandings of
operations on whole numbers.

Use the properties and mental math to find the sum.

1. $5\frac{1}{3} + \left(2\frac{2}{3} + 1\frac{1}{3}\right)$

$5\frac{1}{3} + (4)$

$\underline{\quad 9\frac{1}{3} \quad}$

2. $10\frac{1}{8} + \left(3\frac{5}{8} + 2\frac{7}{8}\right)$

_____

3. $8\frac{1}{5} + \left(3\frac{2}{5} + 5\frac{4}{5}\right)$

_____

4. $6\frac{3}{4} + \left(4\frac{2}{4} + 5\frac{1}{4}\right)$

_____

5. $\left(6\frac{3}{6} + 10\frac{4}{6}\right) + 9\frac{2}{6}$

_____

6. $\left(6\frac{2}{5} + 1\frac{4}{5}\right) + 3\frac{1}{5}$

_____

Problem Solving

7. Nate's classroom has three tables of different lengths. One has a length of $4\frac{1}{2}$ feet, another has a length of 4 feet, and a third has a length of $2\frac{1}{2}$ feet. What is the length of all three tables when pushed end to end?

_____

8. Mr. Warren uses $2\frac{1}{4}$ bags of mulch for his garden and another $4\frac{1}{4}$ bags for his front yard. He also uses $\frac{3}{4}$ bag around a fountain. How many total bags of mulch does Mr. Warren use?

_____

9. **WRITE** *Math* Describe how the Commutative and Associative Properties of Addition can make adding mixed numbers easier.

_____

_____

_____

_____

Lesson Check (4.NF.B.3c)

1. A carpenter cut a board into three pieces. One piece was $2\frac{5}{6}$ feet long. The second piece was $3\frac{1}{6}$ feet long. The third piece was $1\frac{5}{6}$ feet long. How long was the board?

2. Harry works at an apple orchard. He picked $45\frac{7}{8}$ pounds of apples on Monday. He picked $42\frac{3}{8}$ pounds of apples on Wednesday. He picked $54\frac{1}{8}$ pounds of apples on Friday. How many pounds of apples did Harry pick those three days?

Spiral Review (4.OA.B.4, 4.NBT.B.5, 4.NBT.B.6, 4.NF.B.3c)

3. There were 6 oranges in the refrigerator. Joey and his friends ate $3\frac{2}{3}$ oranges. How many oranges were left?

4. Darlene was asked to identify which of the following numbers is prime:

   2, 12, 21, 39

   Which number should she choose?

5. A teacher has 100 chairs to arrange for an assembly into equal rows. Write one way the chairs could be arranged. Include the number of rows and the number of chairs in each row.

6. Nic bought 28 folding chairs for $16 each. How much money did Nic spend on chairs?

FOR MORE PRACTICE
GO TO THE
Personal Math Trainer

Name _____

Problem Solving • Multistep Fraction Problems

Essential Question How can you use the strategy *act it out* to solve multistep problems with fractions?

Number and Operations—
Fractions—4.NF.B.3d *Also 4.MD.A.2*
MATHEMATICAL PRACTICES
MP1, MP3, MP4

Unlock the Problem

A gift shop sells walnuts in $\frac{3}{4}$-pound bags. Ann will buy some bags of walnuts and repackage them into 1-pound bags. What is the least number of $\frac{3}{4}$-pound bags Ann could buy, if she wants to fill each 1-pound bag, without leftovers?

Read the Problem

What do I need to find?

I need to find how many

_____ bags of walnuts Ann needs to make 1-pound bags of walnuts, without leftovers.

What information do I need to use?

The bags she will buy contain

_____ pound of walnuts. She will repackage the walnuts into

_____ -pound bags.

How will I use the information?

I can use fraction circles to

_____ the problem.

Solve the Problem

Describe how to act it out. Use fraction circles.

One $\frac{3}{4}$-pound bag   Not enough for a 1-pound bag

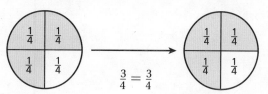

$\frac{3}{4} = \frac{3}{4}$

Two $\frac{3}{4}$-pound bags   One 1-pound bag with $\frac{2}{4}$ pound left over

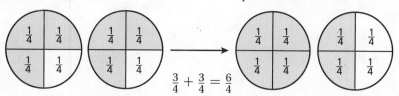

$\frac{3}{4} + \frac{3}{4} = \frac{6}{4}$

Three $\frac{3}{4}$-pound bags have $\frac{3}{4} + \frac{3}{4} + \frac{3}{4} = \frac{}{4}$ pounds of

walnuts. This makes _____ 1-pound bags with _____ pound left over.

Four $\frac{3}{4}$-pound bags have $\frac{3}{4} + \frac{3}{4} + \frac{3}{4} + \frac{3}{4} = \frac{}{4}$-pounds of walnuts.

This makes _____ 1-pound bags with _____ left over.

So, Ann could buy _____ $\frac{3}{4}$-pound bags of walnuts.

❶ Try Another Problem

At the end of dinner, a restaurant had several dishes of quiche, each with 2 sixth-size pieces of quiche. The chef was able to combine these pieces to make 2 whole quiches, with no leftovers. How many dishes did the chef combine?

Read the Problem	Solve the Problem
What do I need to find?	**Describe how to act it out.**
What information do I need to use?	
How will I use the information?	

So, the chef combined _____ dishes each with $\frac{2}{6}$ quiche.

Name _____

Unlock the Problem

✓ Underline the question.
✓ Circle the important facts.
✓ Cross out unneeded information.

Share and Show

1. Last week, Sia ran $1\frac{1}{4}$ miles each day for 5 days and then took 2 days off. Did she run at least 6 miles last week?

   First, model the problem. Describe your model.

   _____

   _____

   _____

   Then, regroup the parts in the model to find the number of whole miles Sia ran.

   Sia ran _____ whole miles and _____ mile.

   Finally, compare the total number of miles she ran to 6 miles.

   $6\frac{1}{4}$ miles ◯ 6 miles

   So, Sia _____ run at least 6 miles last week.

WRITE *Math*
Show Your Work

2. What if Sia ran only $\frac{3}{4}$ mile each day? Would she have run at least 6 miles last week? Explain.

   _____

   _____

3. A quarter is $\frac{1}{4}$ dollar. Noah has 20 quarters. How much money does he have? Explain.

   _____

   _____

   _____

4. **THINK SMARTER** How many $\frac{2}{5}$ parts are in 2 wholes?

   _____

On Your Own

5. A company shipped 15,325 boxes of apples and 12,980 boxes of oranges. How many more boxes of apples than oranges did the company ship?

_____

6. **MATHEMATICAL PRACTICE ①** **Analyze** A fair sold a total of 3,300 tickets on Friday and Saturday. It sold 100 more on Friday than on Saturday. How many tickets did the fair sell on Friday?

_____

7. **THINK SMARTER** Emma walked $\frac{1}{4}$ mile on Monday, $\frac{2}{4}$ mile on Tuesday, and $\frac{3}{4}$ mile on Wednesday. If the pattern continues, how many miles will she walk on Friday? Explain how you found the number of miles.

_____

_____

_____

_____

_____

8. **GO DEEPER** Jared painted a mug $\frac{5}{12}$ red and $\frac{4}{12}$ blue. What part of the mug is **not** red or blue?

_____

9. **THINK SMARTER** Choose the number that correctly completes the sentence.

Each day, Mrs. Hewes knits $\frac{1}{3}$ of a scarf in the morning and $\frac{1}{3}$ of a scarf in the afternoon.

It will take Mrs. Hewes

| 2 |
| 3 |
| 4 |

days to knit 2 scarves.

Name _____

Problem Solving • Multistep Fraction Problems

Common Core

COMMON CORE STANDARD—4.NF.B.3d
Build fractions from unit fractions by applying
and extending previous understandings of
operations on whole numbers.

Read each problem and solve.

1. Each child in the Smith family was given an orange cut
   into 8 equal sections. Each child ate $\frac{5}{8}$ of the orange. After
   combining the leftover sections, Mrs. Smith noted that there
   were exactly 3 full oranges left. How many children are in the
   Smith family?

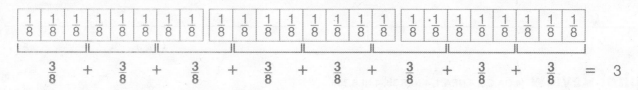

$$\frac{3}{8} + \frac{3}{8} + \frac{3}{8} + \frac{3}{8} + \frac{3}{8} + \frac{3}{8} + \frac{3}{8} + \frac{3}{8} = 3$$

There are 8 addends, so there are 8 children in the Smith family.

_____ **8 children** _____

2. Val walks $2\frac{3}{5}$ miles each day. Bill runs 10 miles once every
   4 days. In 4 days, who covers the greater distance?

   _____

3. Chad buys peanuts in 2-pound bags. He repackages them
   into bags that hold $\frac{5}{6}$ pound of peanuts. How many 2-pound
   bags of peanuts should Chad buy so that he can fill the
   $\frac{5}{6}$-pound bags without having any peanuts left over?

   _____

4. **WRITE** ▸*Math* Write a word problem that involves adding or
   subtracting two fractions. Draw a model and describe how you
   would act out the problem to solve it.

   _____

   _____

   _____

1. Karyn cuts a length of ribbon into 4 equal pieces, each $1\frac{1}{4}$ feet long. How long was the ribbon?

2. Several friends each had $\frac{2}{5}$ of a bag of peanuts left over from the baseball game. They realized that they could have bought 2 fewer bags of peanuts between them. How many friends went to the game?

Spiral Review (4.OA.C.5, 4.NF.A.1, 4.NF.B.3b, 4.NF.B.3d)

3. A frog made three jumps. The first was $12\frac{5}{6}$ inches. The second jump was $8\frac{3}{6}$ inches. The third jump was $15\frac{1}{6}$ inches. What was the total distance the frog jumped?

4. LaDanian wants to write the fraction $\frac{4}{6}$ as a sum of unit fractions. What expression should he write?

5. Greta made a design with squares. She colored 8 out of the 12 squares blue. What fraction of the squares did she color blue?

6. The teacher gave this pattern to the class: the first term is 5 and the rule is *add* 4, *subtract* 1. Each student says one number. The first student says 5. Victor is tenth in line. What number should Victor say?

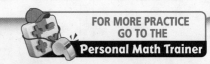

FOR MORE PRACTICE
GO TO THE
Personal Math Trainer

✓ Chapter 7 Review/Test

Personal Math Trainer
Online Assessment
and Intervention

1. A painter mixed $\frac{1}{4}$ quart of red paint with $\frac{3}{4}$ blue paint to make purple paint.

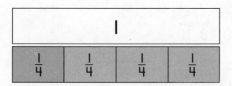

How much purple paint did the painter make?

☐ quart of purple paint

2. Ivan biked $1\frac{2}{3}$ hours on Monday, $2\frac{1}{3}$ hours on Tuesday, and $2\frac{2}{3}$ hours on Wednesday. What is the total number of hours Ivan spent biking?

Ivan spent ☐ hours biking.

Personal Math Trainer

3. THINK SMARTER + Tricia had $4\frac{1}{8}$ yards of fabric to make curtains. When she finished she had $2\frac{3}{8}$ yards of fabric left. She said she used $2\frac{2}{8}$ yards of fabric for the curtains. Do you agree? Explain.

GO DIGITAL Assessment Options
Chapter Test

4. Miguel's class went to the state fair. The fairground is divided into sections. Rides are in $\frac{6}{10}$ of the fairground. Games are in $\frac{2}{10}$ of the fairground. Farm exhibits are in $\frac{1}{10}$ of the fairground.

Part A

Use the model. What fraction of the fairground is rides and games?

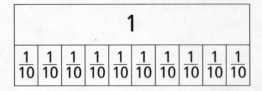

The fraction of the fairground with games and rides is ⬜.

Part B

How much greater is the part of the fairground with rides than with farm exhibits? Explain how the model could be used to find the answer.

⬜

5. Rita is making chili. The recipe calls for $2\frac{3}{4}$ cups of tomatoes. How many cups of tomatoes, written as a fraction greater than one, are used in the recipe?

⬜ cups

6. Lamar's mom sells sports equipment online. She sold $\frac{9}{10}$ of the sports equipment. Select a way $\frac{9}{10}$ can be written as a sum of fractions. Mark all that apply.

Ⓐ $\frac{1}{10} + \frac{1}{10} + \frac{1}{10} + \frac{1}{10} + \frac{2}{10}$ Ⓓ $\frac{4}{10} + \frac{1}{10} + \frac{1}{10} + \frac{3}{10}$

Ⓑ $\frac{3}{10} + \frac{2}{10} + \frac{3}{10} + \frac{1}{10}$ Ⓔ $\frac{4}{10} + \frac{3}{10} + \frac{1}{10} + \frac{1}{10} + \frac{1}{10}$

Ⓒ $\frac{2}{10} + \frac{2}{10} + \frac{2}{10} + \frac{2}{10}$ Ⓕ $\frac{2}{10} + \frac{2}{10} + \frac{2}{10} + \frac{3}{10}$

7. Bella brought $\frac{8}{10}$ gallon of water on a hiking trip. She drank $\frac{6}{10}$ gallon of water. How much water is left?

[____] gallon

8. In a survey, $\frac{6}{10}$ of the students chose Saturday and $\frac{1}{10}$ chose Monday as their favorite day of the week. What fraction shows the students who chose Saturday or Monday as their favorite day?

Part A

Shade the model to show your answer.

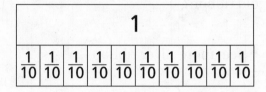

[____] of the students chose Monday or Saturday.

Part B

How are the numerator and denominator of your answer related to the model? Explain.

[   ]

9. Match the equation with the property used.

$\frac{6}{10} + \left(\frac{4}{10} + \frac{3}{10}\right) = \left(\frac{6}{10} + \frac{4}{10}\right) + \frac{3}{10}$ •

$1\frac{1}{4} + \left(3 + 2\frac{1}{4}\right) = 1\frac{1}{4} + \left(2\frac{1}{4} + 3\right)$ •   • Commutative Property

$\left(2\frac{6}{10} + \frac{1}{10}\right) + 3\frac{9}{10} = 2\frac{6}{10} + \left(\frac{1}{10} + 3\frac{9}{10}\right)$ •   • Associative Property

$\left(3\frac{4}{7} + 2\frac{1}{7}\right) + 6\frac{3}{7} = \left(2\frac{1}{7} + 3\frac{4}{7}\right) + 6\frac{3}{7}$ •

10. For numbers 10a–10e, select Yes or No to show if the sum or difference is correct.

10a. $\frac{2}{8} + \frac{1}{8} = \frac{3}{8}$ ○ Yes ○ No

10b. $\frac{4}{5} + \frac{1}{5} = \frac{5}{5}$ ○ Yes ○ No

10c. $\frac{4}{6} + \frac{1}{6} = \frac{5}{12}$ ○ Yes ○ No

10d. $\frac{6}{12} - \frac{4}{12} = \frac{2}{12}$ ○ Yes ○ No

10e. $\frac{7}{9} - \frac{2}{9} = \frac{9}{9}$ ○ Yes ○ No

11. Gina has $5\frac{2}{6}$ feet of silver ribbon and $2\frac{4}{6}$ of gold ribbon. How much more silver ribbon does Gina have than gold ribbon?

    [   ] feet more silver ribbon

12. Jill is making a long cape. She needs $4\frac{1}{3}$ yards of blue fabric for the outside of the cape. She needs $3\frac{2}{3}$ yards of purple fabric for the lining of the cape.

    Part A

    Jill incorrectly subtracted the two mixed numbers to find how much more blue fabric than purple fabric she should buy. Her work is shown below.

    $4\frac{1}{3} - 3\frac{2}{3} = \frac{12}{3} - \frac{9}{3} = \frac{3}{3}$

    Why is Jill's work incorrect?

    [   ]

    Part B

    How much more blue fabric than purple fabric should Jill buy? Show your work.

    [   ]

Name _____

13. Russ has two jars of glue. One jar is $\frac{1}{5}$ full. The other jar is $\frac{2}{5}$ full.

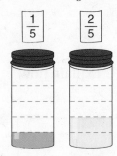

Use the fractions to write an equation to find the amount of glue Russ has.

$\boxed{\frac{1}{5}}$ $\boxed{\frac{2}{5}}$ $\boxed{\frac{3}{5}}$ $\boxed{\frac{4}{5}}$ $\boxed{} + \boxed{} = \boxed{}$

14. Gertie ran $\frac{3}{4}$ mile during physical education class. Sarah ran $\frac{2}{4}$ mile during the same class. How much farther did Gertie run than Sarah? Shade the model to show your answer.

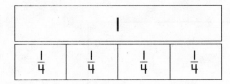

Gertie ran $\boxed{}$ mile farther than Sarah.

15. Teresa planted marigolds in $\frac{2}{8}$ of her garden and petunias in $\frac{3}{8}$ of her garden. What fraction of the garden has marigolds and petunias?

Teresa's garden has $\boxed{}$ marigolds and petunias.

16. Draw a line to show the mixed number and fraction that have the same value.

- $3\frac{2}{7}$ • $4\frac{5}{8}$ • $2\frac{3}{5}$ • $2\frac{3}{8}$

- $\frac{21}{8}$ • $\frac{37}{3}$ • $\frac{21}{7}$ • $\frac{37}{8}$

17. GO DEEPER Each day, Tally's baby sister eats $\frac{1}{4}$ cup of rice cereal in the morning and $\frac{1}{4}$ cup of rice cereal in the afternoon.

It will take Tally's sister $\boxed{\begin{array}{c} 2 \\ 3 \\ 4 \end{array}}$ days to eat 2 cups of rice cereal.

18. Three girls are selling cases of popcorn to earn money for a band trip. In week 1, Emily sold $2\frac{3}{4}$ cases, Brenda sold $4\frac{1}{4}$ cases, and Shannon sold $3\frac{1}{2}$ cases.

Part A

How many cases of popcorn have the girls sold in all? Explain how you found your answer.

Part B

The girls must sell a total of 35 cases in order to have enough money for the trip. Suppose they sell the same amount in week 2 and week 3 of the sale as in week 1. Will the girls have sold enough cases of popcorn to go on the trip? Explain.

19. Henry ate $\frac{3}{8}$ of a sandwich. Keith ate $\frac{4}{8}$ of the same sandwich. How much more of the sandwich did Keith eat than Henry?

of the sandwich

20. For numbers 20a–20d, choose True or False for each sentence.

20a. $1\frac{4}{9} + 2\frac{6}{9}$ is equal to $4\frac{1}{9}$.   ○ True   ○ False

20b. $3\frac{5}{6} + 2\frac{3}{6}$ is equal to $5\frac{2}{6}$.   ○ True   ○ False

20c. $4\frac{5}{8} - 2\frac{4}{8}$ is equal to $2\frac{3}{8}$.   ○ True   ○ False

20d. $5\frac{5}{8} - 3\frac{2}{8}$ is equal to $2\frac{3}{8}$.   ○ True   ○ False

21. Justin lives $4\frac{3}{5}$ miles from his grandfather's house. Write the mixed number as a fraction greater than one.

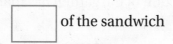

$$4\frac{3}{5} = $$

Multiply Fractions by Whole Numbers

✓ Show What You Know

Check your understanding of important skills.

Name _____

▶ **Relate Addition to Multiplication** **Complete.** (2.OA.C.4)

1.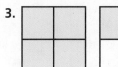

___ + ___ + ___ + ___ = ___

___ × ___ = ___

2.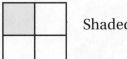

___ + ___ + ___ = ___

___ × ___ = ___

▶ **Read and Write Mixed Numbers** **Write a mixed number for the shaded part. Write a fraction for the unshaded part.** (4.NF.B.3c)

3.

Shaded: _____

Unshaded: _____

4.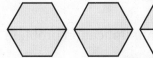

Shaded: _____

Unshaded: _____

▶ **Model Fractions and Mixed Numbers** **Write a fraction or mixed number for the model.** (4.NF.B.3c)

5. _____

6. _____

Math in the Real World

The budget for Carter Museum's annual party is $10,000. Food accounts for $\frac{1}{2}$ of the budget, beverages for $\frac{1}{4}$, and decorations for $\frac{1}{10}$ of the budget. The remainder is spent on staffing the party. How much money is spent on staffing the party?

Vocabulary Builder

▶ **Visualize It**

Complete the bubble map using the review words.

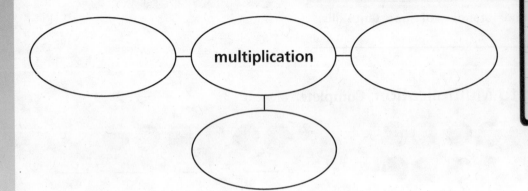

Review Words

fraction

Identity Property
 of Multiplication

multiple

product

unit fraction

▶ **Understand Vocabulary**

Write the word or phrase that matches the description.

1. A _____ can name a part of a group or a whole.

2. You can write _____ of 10 such as 10, 20, 30, and so on.

3. _____ have one as the numerator.

4. The answer to a multiplication problem is called the

   _____.

5. _____ states that the product of any number and 1 is that number.

GO DIGITAL
• **Interactive Student Edition**
• **Multimedia eGlossary**

Chapter 8 Vocabulary

equation

ecuación

27

fraction

fracción

36

Identity Property of Multiplication

propiedad de identidad de la multiplicación

41

mixed number

número mixto

54

multiple

múltiplo

55

pattern

patrón

63

product

producto

72

unit fraction

fracción unitaria

94

A number that names a part of a whole or part of a group

Example:

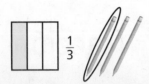

$\frac{1}{3}$

A number sentence which shows that two quantities are equal

Example: $3 + 1 = 4$

An amount given as a whole number and a fraction

Example: $2\frac{3}{6}$ is a mixed number

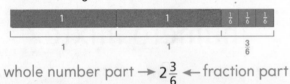

whole number part → $2\frac{3}{6}$ ← fraction part

The property that states that the product of any number and 1 is that number

Example: $9 \times 1 = 9$

An ordered set of numbers or objects; the order helps you predict what will come next

Examples: 2, 4, 6, 8, 10

The product of a number and a counting number is called a multiple of the number

Example:

$$\begin{array}{cccc} 3 & 3 & 3 & 3 \\ \times 1 & \times 2 & \times 3 & \times 4 \\ \hline 3 & 6 & 9 & 12 \end{array}$$

← counting numbers
← multiples of 3

A fraction that has a numerator of one

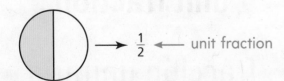

$\frac{1}{2}$ ← unit fraction

The answer to a multiplication problem

Example: $4 \times 5 = 20$

↑
product

Pick It

For 3 players

Materials

- 4 sets of word cards

How to Play

1. Each player is dealt 5 cards. The remaining cards are a draw pile.

2. To take a turn, ask any player if he or she has a word that matches one of your word cards.

3. If the player has the word, he or she gives you the word card, and you must give the definition of the word.

   - If you are correct, keep the card and put the matching pair in front of you. Take another turn.

   - If you are wrong, return the card. Your turn is over.

4. If the player does not have the word, he or she answers, "Pick it." Then you take a card from the draw pile.

5. If the card you draw matches one of your word cards, follow the directions for Step 3 above. If it does not, your turn is over.

6. The game is over when one player has no cards left. The player with the most matches wins.

Word Box
equation
fraction
Identity Property of Multiplication
mixed number
multiple
pattern
product
unit fraction

The Write Way

Reflect

Choose one idea. Write about it in the space below.

- Explain how to find multiples of a unit fraction.

- Pablo practiced piano $1\frac{1}{2}$ hours 3 times a week. Elsa practiced $\frac{3}{4}$ hour 5 times a week. Explain how you know who practiced for more time each week.

- Write two questions you have about multiplying fractions by whole numbers.

Name _____

Multiples of Unit Fractions

Essential Question How can you write a fraction as a product of a whole number and a unit fraction?

Common Core   **Number and Operations— Fractions—4.NF.B.4a**
MATHEMATICAL PRACTICES
MP4, MP6, MP7

Unlock the Problem

At a pizza party, each pizza was cut into 6 equal slices. At the end of the party, there was $\frac{5}{6}$ of a pizza left. Roberta put each of the leftover slices in its own freezer bag. How many bags did she use? What part of a pizza did she put in each bag?

- How many slices of pizza were eaten?

  _____

- What fraction of the pizza is 1 slice?

  _____

Example Write $\frac{5}{6}$ as the product of a whole number and a unit fraction.

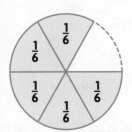

The picture shows $\frac{5}{6}$ or

_____ sixth-size parts.

Each sixth-size part of the pizza can be shown by the

unit fraction _____.

Remember

You can use multiplication to show repeated addition.

3×4 means $4 + 4 + 4$.

4×2 means $2 + 2 + 2 + 2$.

You can use unit fractions to show $\frac{5}{6}$ in two ways.

$\frac{5}{6} =$ _____ $+$ _____ $+$ _____ $+$ _____ $+$ _____

$\frac{5}{6} =$ _____ $\times \frac{1}{6}$

The number of addends, or the multiplier, represents the number of bags used.

The unit fractions represent the part of a pizza in each bag.

So, Roberta used _____ bags. She put _____ of a pizza in each bag.

Math Talk

MATHEMATICAL PRACTICES ⑦

Look for Structure Give an example of how you would write a fraction greater than 1 as a mixed number.

- Explain how you can write $\frac{3}{2}$ as the product of a whole number and a unit fraction.

  _____

  _____

  _____

Multiples The product of a number and a counting number is a multiple of the number. You have learned about multiples of whole numbers.

The products 1×4, 2×4, 3×4, and so on are multiples of 4. The numbers 4, 8, 12, and so on are multiples of 4.

You can also find multiples of unit fractions.

🔑 $1 \times \frac{1}{4}$ is $\frac{1}{4}$. Use models to write the next four multiples of $\frac{1}{4}$. Complete the last model.

$\frac{1}{4}$	$\frac{1}{4}$	$\frac{1}{4}$	$\frac{1}{4}$
$\frac{1}{4}$	$\frac{1}{4}$	$\frac{1}{4}$	$\frac{1}{4}$

$2 \times \frac{1}{4}$

$= \frac{2}{4}$

$\frac{1}{4}$	$\frac{1}{4}$	$\frac{1}{4}$	$\frac{1}{4}$
$\frac{1}{4}$	$\frac{1}{4}$	$\frac{1}{4}$	$\frac{1}{4}$
$\frac{1}{4}$	$\frac{1}{4}$	$\frac{1}{4}$	$\frac{1}{4}$

$3 \times \underline{}$

$= \frac{}{4}$

$\frac{1}{4}$	$\frac{1}{4}$	$\frac{1}{4}$	$\frac{1}{4}$
$\frac{1}{4}$	$\frac{1}{4}$	$\frac{1}{4}$	$\frac{1}{4}$
$\frac{1}{4}$	$\frac{1}{4}$	$\frac{1}{4}$	$\frac{1}{4}$
$\frac{1}{4}$	$\frac{1}{4}$	$\frac{1}{4}$	$\frac{1}{4}$

$4 \times \underline{}$

$= \frac{}{4}$

$\frac{1}{4}$	$\frac{1}{4}$	$\frac{1}{4}$	$\frac{1}{4}$
$\frac{1}{4}$	$\frac{1}{4}$	$\frac{1}{4}$	$\frac{1}{4}$
$\frac{1}{4}$	$\frac{1}{4}$	$\frac{1}{4}$	$\frac{1}{4}$
$\frac{1}{4}$	$\frac{1}{4}$	$\frac{1}{4}$	$\frac{1}{4}$
$\frac{1}{4}$	$\frac{1}{4}$	$\frac{1}{4}$	$\frac{1}{4}$

$\underline{} \times \underline{}$

$= \underline{}$

Multiples of $\frac{1}{4}$ are $\frac{1}{4}$, ⬜, ⬜, ⬜, and ⬜.

🔑 Use a number line to write multiples of $\frac{1}{5}$.

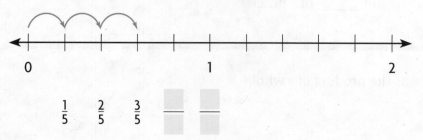

$\frac{1}{5}$ $\frac{2}{5}$ $\frac{3}{5}$ ⬜ ⬜

Multiples of $\frac{1}{5}$ are $\frac{1}{5}$, ⬜, ⬜, ⬜, and ⬜.

Name _____

1. Use the picture to complete the equations.

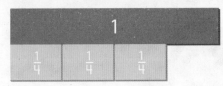

$\frac{3}{4} = $ _____ + _____ + _____

$\frac{3}{4} = $ _____ $\times \frac{1}{4}$

Write the fraction as a product of a whole number and a unit fraction.

2. $\frac{4}{5} = $ _____

3. $\frac{3}{10} = $ _____

4. $\frac{8}{3} = $ _____

List the next four multiples of the unit fraction.

5. $\frac{1}{6}$, ____, ____, ____,

6. $\frac{1}{3}$, ____, ____, ____,

Math Talk

MATHEMATICAL PRACTICES ⑥

Attend to Precision
Explain why $\frac{8}{5}$ is a multiple of $\frac{1}{5}$.

On Your Own

Write the fraction as a product of a whole number and a unit fraction.

7. $\frac{5}{6} = $ _____

8. $\frac{9}{4} = $ _____

9. $\frac{3}{100} = $ _____

List the next four multiples of the unit fraction.

10. $\frac{1}{10}$, ____, ____, ____,

11. $\frac{1}{8}$, ____, ____, ____,

Problem Solving • Applications

12. MATHEMATICAL PRACTICE ⑥ Robyn uses $\frac{1}{2}$ cup of blueberries to make each loaf of blueberry bread. **Explain** how many loaves of blueberry bread she can make with $2\frac{1}{2}$ cups of blueberries.

_____

13. GO DEEPER Nigel cut a loaf of bread into 12 equal slices. His family ate some of the bread and now $\frac{5}{12}$ of the loaf is left. Nigel wants to put each of the leftover slices in its own bag. How many bags does Nigel need?

_____

14. THINK SMARTER Which fraction is a multiple of $\frac{1}{5}$? Mark all that apply.

○ $\frac{4}{5}$ ○ $\frac{5}{9}$

○ $\frac{5}{7}$ ○ $\frac{3}{5}$

Sense or Nonsense?

15. THINK SMARTER Whose statement makes sense? Whose statement is nonsense? Explain your reasoning.

There is no multiple of $\frac{1}{6}$ between $\frac{3}{6}$ and $\frac{4}{6}$.

$\frac{4}{5}$ is a multiple of $\frac{1}{4}$.

Gavin

_____

_____

_____

_____

_____

_____

_____

Abigail

_____

_____

_____

_____

_____

_____

_____

- For the statement that is nonsense, write a new statement that makes sense.

_____

_____

Multiples of Unit Fractions

Common Core

COMMON CORE STANDARD—4.NF.B.4a
Build fractions from unit fractions by applying and extending previous understandings of operations on whole numbers.

Write the fraction as a product of a whole number and a unit fraction.

1. $\frac{5}{6}$ = ___ $5 \times \frac{1}{6}$ ___

2. $\frac{7}{8}$ = _____

3. $\frac{5}{3}$ = _____

4. $\frac{9}{10}$ = _____

5. $\frac{3}{4}$ = _____

6. $\frac{11}{12}$ = _____

List the next four multiples of the unit fraction.

7. $\frac{1}{5}$, ___, ___, ___, ___

8. $\frac{1}{8}$, ___, ___, ___, ___

Problem Solving · Real World

9. So far, Monica has read $\frac{5}{6}$ of a book. She has read the same number of pages each day for 5 days. What fraction of the book does Monica read each day?

_____

10. Nicholas buys $\frac{3}{8}$ pound of cheese. He puts the same amount of cheese on 3 sandwiches. How much cheese does Nicholas put on each sandwich?

_____

11. **WRITE** ▸*Math* Explain how to write $\frac{5}{3}$ as a product of a whole number and a unit fraction.

_____

_____

_____

Lesson Check (4.NF.B.4a)

1. Selena walks from home to school each morning and back home each afternoon. Altogether, she walks $\frac{2}{3}$ mile each day. How far does Selena live from school?

2. Will uses $\frac{3}{4}$ cup of olive oil to make 3 batches of salad dressing. How much oil does Will use for one batch of salad dressing?

Spiral Review (4.OA.B.4, 4.NF.A.1, 4.NF.B.3b, 4.NF.B.3d)

3. Liza bought $\frac{5}{8}$ pound of trail mix. She gives $\frac{2}{8}$ pound of trail mix to Michael. How much trail mix does Liza have left?

4. Leigh has a piece of rope that is $6\frac{2}{3}$ feet long. How do you write $6\frac{2}{3}$ as a fraction greater than 1?

5. A group of students have the following house numbers : 29, 39, 59, and 79. Randy's house number is a composite number. What is Randy's house number?

6. Mindy buys 12 cupcakes. Nine of the cupcakes have chocolate frosting and the rest have vanilla frosting. What fraction of the cupcakes have vanilla frosting?

**FOR MORE PRACTICE
GO TO THE
Personal Math Trainer**

Name _____

Multiples of Fractions

Essential Question How can you write a product of a whole number and a fraction as a product of a whole number and a unit fraction?

Common Core — Number and Operations—Fractions—**4.NF.B.4b** *Also 4.NF.B.4c*

MATHEMATICAL PRACTICES
MP2, MP7, MP8

Unlock the Problem (Real World)

Jen is making 4 pans of baked ziti. For each pan, she needs $\frac{2}{3}$ cup cheese. Her measuring cup can scoop $\frac{1}{3}$ cup of cheese. How many scoops of cheese does she need for the 4 pans?

Example 1 Use a model to write the product of $4 \times \frac{2}{3}$ as the product of a whole number and a unit fraction.

$\frac{1}{3}$	$\frac{1}{3}$	$\frac{1}{3}$

Think: $\frac{2}{3}$ is 2 third-size parts.

$\frac{2}{3} =$ _____ + _____ or $2 \times$ _____ .

There are 4 pans of baked ziti. Each pan needs $\frac{2}{3}$ cup cheese.

$\frac{1}{3}$	$\frac{1}{3}$	$\frac{1}{3}$

← 1 pan: $2 \times \frac{1}{3} = \frac{2}{3}$

$\frac{1}{3}$	$\frac{1}{3}$	$\frac{1}{3}$

← 2 pans: $2 \times 2 \times \frac{1}{3} = 4 \times \frac{1}{3} = \frac{4}{3}$

$\frac{1}{3}$	$\frac{1}{3}$	$\frac{1}{3}$

← 3 pans: $3 \times 2 \times \frac{1}{3} = 6 \times \frac{1}{3} = \frac{6}{3}$

$\frac{1}{3}$	$\frac{1}{3}$	$\frac{1}{3}$

← 4 pans: $4 \times 2 \times \frac{1}{3} = 8 \times \frac{1}{3} = \frac{8}{3}$

$4 \times \frac{2}{3} = 4 \times$ _____ $\times \frac{1}{3} =$ _____ $\times \frac{1}{3} = \frac{\square}{3}$

So, Jen needs _____ third-size scoops of cheese for 4 pans of ziti.

Math Talk

MATHEMATICAL PRACTICES ⑦

Identify Relationships
Explain how this model of $4 \times \frac{2}{3}$ is related to a model of 4×2.

1. What if Jen decides to make 10 pans of ziti? Describe a pattern you could use to find the number of scoops of cheese she would need.

_____

_____

Multiples You have learned to write multiples of unit fractions. You can also write multiples of non-unit fractions.

Example 2 Use a number line to write multiples of $\frac{2}{5}$.

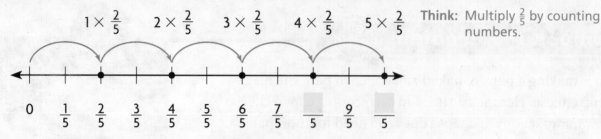

Think: Multiply $\frac{2}{5}$ by counting numbers.

Multiples of $\frac{2}{5}$ are $\frac{2}{5}$, ⬜ , ⬜ , ⬜ , and ⬜ .

$3 \times \frac{2}{5} = \frac{6}{5}$. Write $\frac{6}{5}$ as a product of a whole number and a unit fraction.

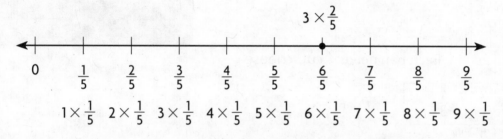

$$3 \times \frac{2}{5} = \frac{6}{5} = \underline{\qquad} \times \underline{\qquad}$$

2. Explain how to use repeated addition to write the multiple of a fraction as the product of a whole number and a unit fraction.

_____

_____

Share and Show

1. Write three multiples of $\frac{3}{8}$.

$1 \times \frac{3}{8} = \underline{\qquad}$

$2 \times \frac{3}{8} = \underline{\qquad}$

$3 \times \frac{3}{8} = \underline{\qquad}$

Multiples of $\frac{3}{8}$ are _____ , _____ , and _____ .

Name _____

List the next four multiples of the fraction.

 2. $\frac{3}{6}$, ___ , ___ , ___ ,

3. $\frac{2}{10}$, ___ , ___ , ___ ,

Write the product as the product of a whole number and a unit fraction.

 4.

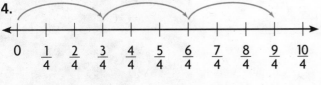

$3 \times \frac{3}{4} =$ _____

5.

$2 \times \frac{4}{6} =$ _____

Math Talk

MATHEMATICAL PRACTICES ②

Use Reasoning Explain how to write a product of a whole number and a fraction as a product of a whole number and a unit fraction.

On Your Own

List the next four multiples of the fraction.

6. $\frac{4}{5}$, ___ , ___ , ___ ,

7. $\frac{2}{4}$, ___ , ___ , ___ ,

Write the product as the product of a whole number and a unit fraction.

8.

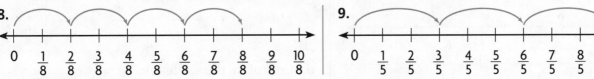

$4 \times \frac{2}{8} =$ _____

9.

$3 \times \frac{3}{5} =$ _____

10. **MATHEMATICAL PRACTICE ⑧** Use Repeated Reasoning Are $\frac{6}{10}$ and $\frac{6}{30}$ multiples of $\frac{3}{10}$? Explain.

_____

_____

11. **GO DEEPER** Which is greater, $4 \times \frac{2}{7}$ or $3 \times \frac{3}{7}$? Explain.

_____

© Houghton Mifflin Harcourt Publishing Company

12. **THINK SMARTER** Josh is watering his plants. He gives each of 2 plants $\frac{3}{5}$ pint of water. His watering can holds $\frac{1}{5}$ pint. How many times will he fill his watering can to water both plants?

a. What do you need to find?

_____

b. What information do you need to use?

_____

_____

c. How can drawing a model help you solve the problem?

_____

_____

_____

_____

_____

_____

d. Show the steps you use to solve the problem.

e. Complete the sentence.

Josh will fill his watering can _____ times.

13. **THINK SMARTER+** Alma is making 3 batches of tortillas. She adds $\frac{3}{4}$ cup of water to each batch. The measuring cup holds $\frac{1}{4}$ cup. How many times must Alma measure $\frac{1}{4}$ cup of water to have enough for the tortillas? Shade the model to show your answer.

Alma must measure $\frac{1}{4}$ cup [ ] times.

$\frac{1}{4}$	$\frac{1}{4}$	$\frac{1}{4}$	$\frac{1}{4}$
$\frac{1}{4}$	$\frac{1}{4}$	$\frac{1}{4}$	$\frac{1}{4}$
$\frac{1}{4}$	$\frac{1}{4}$	$\frac{1}{4}$	$\frac{1}{4}$

Multiples of Fractions

COMMON CORE STANDARD—4.NF.B.4a
Build fractions from unit fractions by applying and extending previous understandings of operations on whole numbers.

List the next four multiples of the fraction.

1. $\frac{3}{5}$, ____, ____, ____, ____

2. $\frac{2}{6}$, ____, ____, ____, ____

Write the product as the product of a whole number and a unit fraction.

3.

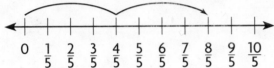

$2 \times \frac{4}{5} =$ _____

4.

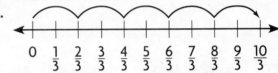

$5 \times \frac{2}{3} =$ _____

Problem Solving

5. Jessica is making 2 loaves of banana bread. She needs $\frac{3}{4}$ cup of sugar for each loaf. Her measuring cup can only hold $\frac{1}{4}$ cup of sugar. How many times will Jessica need to fill the measuring cup in order to get enough sugar for both loaves of bread?

_____

6. A group of four students is performing an experiment with salt. Each student must add $\frac{3}{8}$ teaspoon of salt to a solution. The group only has a $\frac{1}{8}$-teaspoon measuring spoon. How many times will the group need to fill the measuring spoon in order to perform the experiment?

_____

7. **WRITE** ▸*Math* Explain how to write $3 \times \frac{3}{8}$ as the product of a whole number and a unit fraction.

_____

_____

_____

Lesson Check (4.NF.B.4b)

1. Eloise made a list of some multiples of $\frac{8}{5}$. Write 5 fractions that could be in Eloise's list.

2. David is filling five $\frac{3}{4}$-quart bottles with a sports drink. His measuring cup only holds $\frac{1}{4}$ quart. How many times will David need to fill the measuring cup in order to fill the 5 bottles?

Spiral Review (4.NBT.B.6, 4.OA.A.3, 4.NF.B.3c, 4.NF.A.2)

3. Ira has 128 stamps in his stamp album. He has the same number of stamps on each of the 8 pages. How many stamps are on each page?

4. Ryan is saving up for a bike that costs $198. So far, he has saved $15 per week for the last 12 weeks. How much more money does Ryan need in order to be able to buy the bike?

5. Tina buys $3\frac{7}{8}$ yards of material at the fabric store. She uses it to make a skirt. Afterward, she has $1\frac{3}{8}$ yards of the fabric leftover. How many yards of material did Tina use?

6. Order these fractions from **least** to **greatest:** $\frac{2}{3}$, $\frac{7}{12}$, $\frac{3}{4}$

FOR MORE PRACTICE
GO TO THE
Personal Math Trainer

Name _____

 **Mid-Chapter Checkpoint**

Vocabulary

Choose the best term from the box.

Vocabulary
multiple
product
unit fraction

1. A _____ of a number is the product of the number and a counting number. (p. 456)

2. A _____ always has a numerator of 1. (p. 455)

Concepts and Skills

List the next four multiples of the unit fraction. (4.NF.B.4a)

3. $\frac{1}{2}$, ☐ , ☐ , ☐

4. $\frac{1}{5}$, ☐ , ☐ , ☐ , ☐

Write the fraction as a product of a whole number and a unit fraction. (4.NF.B.4a)

5. $\frac{4}{10} =$ _____

6. $\frac{8}{12} =$ _____

7. $\frac{3}{4} =$ _____

List the next four multiples of the fraction. (4.NF.B.4b)

8. $\frac{2}{5}$, ☐ , ☐ , ☐

9. $\frac{5}{6}$, ☐ , ☐ , ☐

Write the product as the product of a whole number and a unit fraction. (4.NF.B.4b)

10.
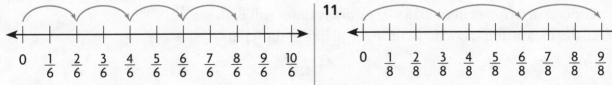

$$4 \times \frac{2}{6} =$$ _____

11.
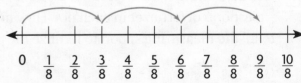

$$3 \times \frac{3}{8} =$$ _____

12. Pedro cut a sheet of poster board into 10 equal parts. His brother used some of the poster board and now $\frac{8}{10}$ is left. Pedro wants to make a sign from each remaining part of the poster board. How many signs can he make? (4.NF.B.4a)

_____

13. Ella is making 3 batches of banana milkshakes. She needs $\frac{3}{4}$ gallon of milk for each batch. Her measuring cup holds $\frac{1}{4}$ gallon. How many times will she need to fill the measuring cup to make all 3 batches of milkshakes? (4.NF.B.4b)

_____

14. Darren cut a lemon pie into 8 equal slices. His friends ate some of the pie and now $\frac{5}{8}$ is left. Darren wants to put each slice of the leftover pie on its own plate. What part of the pie will he put on each plate? (4.NF.B.4a)

_____

15. **GO DEEPER** Beth is putting liquid fertilizer on the plants in 4 flowerpots. Her measuring spoon holds $\frac{1}{8}$ teaspoon. The directions say to put $\frac{5}{8}$ teaspoon of fertilizer in each pot. How many times will Beth need to fill the measuring spoon to fertilize the plants in the 4 pots? (4.NF.B.4b)

_____

Name _____

Multiply a Fraction by a Whole Number Using Models

Common Core **Number and Operations—Fractions—4.NF.B.4b** *Also 4.NF.B.4c*
MATHEMATICAL PRACTICES
MP2, MP4, MP7

Essential Question How can you use a model to multiply a fraction by a whole number?

Unlock the Problem Real World

Rafael practices the violin for $\frac{3}{4}$ hour each day. He has a recital in 3 days. How much time will he practice in 3 days?

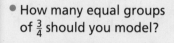

• How many equal groups of $\frac{3}{4}$ should you model?

_____

Example 1 Use a model to multiply $3 \times \frac{3}{4}$.

Think: $3 \times \frac{3}{4}$ is 3 groups of $\frac{3}{4}$ of a whole. Shade the model to show 3 groups of $\frac{3}{4}$.

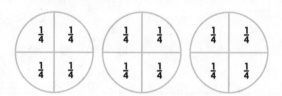

1 group of $\frac{3}{4}$ = _____

2 groups of $\frac{3}{4}$ = _____

3 groups of $\frac{3}{4}$ = _____

$3 \times \frac{3}{4}$ = _____

So, Rafael will practice for _____ hours in all.

Math Talk

MATHEMATICAL PRACTICES ②

Reason Abstractly If you multiply $4 \times \frac{2}{6}$, is the product greater than or less than 4? Explain.

1. Explain how you can use repeated addition with the model to find the product $3 \times \frac{3}{4}$.

_____

_____

2. Rafael's daily practice of $\frac{3}{4}$ hour is in sessions that last for $\frac{1}{4}$ hour each. Describe how the model shows the number of practice sessions Rafael has in 3 days.

_____

_____

🔓 Example 2 Use a pattern to multiply.

You know how to use a model and repeated addition to multiply a fraction by a whole number. Look for a pattern in the table to discover another way to multiply a fraction by a whole number.

Multiplication Problem		Whole Number (Number of Groups)	Fraction (Size of Groups)	Product
$\frac{1}{6}$ $\frac{1}{6}$ $\frac{1}{6}$ $\frac{1}{6}$ $\frac{1}{6}$ $\frac{1}{6}$ / $\frac{1}{6}$ $\frac{1}{6}$ $\frac{1}{6}$ $\frac{1}{6}$ $\frac{1}{6}$ $\frac{1}{6}$	$2 \times \frac{1}{6}$	2	$\frac{1}{6}$ of a whole	$\frac{2}{6}$
$\frac{1}{6}$ $\frac{1}{6}$ $\frac{1}{6}$ $\frac{1}{6}$ $\frac{1}{6}$ $\frac{1}{6}$ / $\frac{1}{6}$ $\frac{1}{6}$ $\frac{1}{6}$ $\frac{1}{6}$ $\frac{1}{6}$ $\frac{1}{6}$	$2 \times \frac{2}{6}$	2	$\frac{2}{6}$ of a whole	$\frac{4}{6}$
$\frac{1}{6}$ $\frac{1}{6}$ $\frac{1}{6}$ $\frac{1}{6}$ $\frac{1}{6}$ $\frac{1}{6}$ / $\frac{1}{6}$ $\frac{1}{6}$ $\frac{1}{6}$ $\frac{1}{6}$ $\frac{1}{6}$ $\frac{1}{6}$	$2 \times \frac{3}{6}$	2	$\frac{3}{6}$ of a whole	$\frac{6}{6}$

When you multiply a fraction by a whole number, the numerator

in the product is the product of the _____ and the

_____ of the fraction. The denominator in the product

is the same as the _____ of the fraction.

3. How do you multiply a fraction by a whole number without using a model or repeated addition?

_____

_____

4. Describe two different ways to find the product $4 \times \frac{2}{3}$.

_____

_____

_____

© Houghton Mifflin Harcourt Publishing Company

Name _____

1. Find the product of $3 \times \frac{5}{8}$.

1 group of $\frac{5}{8} = \dfrac{}{8}$

2 groups of $\frac{5}{8} = \dfrac{}{8}$

3 groups of $\frac{5}{8} = \dfrac{}{8}$

$3 \times \frac{5}{8} =$ _____

3 groups of $\frac{5}{8}$

Multiply.

 2.

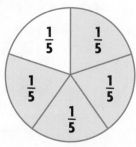

$2 \times \frac{4}{5} =$ _____

3.

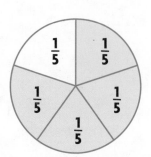

$4 \times \frac{2}{3} =$ _____

4. $5 \times \frac{3}{10} =$ _____

5. $4 \times \frac{5}{6} =$ _____

Math Talk MATHEMATICAL PRACTICES ④

Model Mathematics
Describe how to model
Exercise 5.

On Your Own

Multiply.

6. $2 \times \frac{7}{12} =$ _____

7. $6 \times \frac{3}{8} =$ _____

8. $5 \times \frac{2}{4} =$ _____

9. $3 \times \frac{4}{6} =$ _____

10. $2 \times \frac{5}{10} =$ _____

11. $4 \times \frac{2}{8} =$ _____

MATHEMATICAL PRACTICE ⑦ **Look for a Pattern** **Algebra** Write the unknown number.

12. $\boxed{} \times \frac{2}{3} = \frac{12}{3}$

13. $5 \times \dfrac{\boxed{}}{4} = \frac{10}{4}$

14. $2 \times \dfrac{7}{\boxed{}} = \frac{14}{8}$

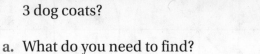 **Unlock the Problem**

15. **THINK SMARTER** Lisa makes clothes for pets. She needs $\frac{5}{6}$ yard of fabric to make 1 dog coat. How much fabric does she need to make 3 dog coats?

a. What do you need to find?

_____

b. What information do you need?

_____

c. Show the steps you use to solve the problem.

d. Complete the sentence.

   Lisa needs _____ yards of fabric to make 3 dog coats.

16. **GO DEEPER** Manuel's small dog eats $\frac{2}{4}$ bag of dog food in 1 month. His large dog eats $\frac{3}{4}$ bag of dog food in 1 month. How many bags do both dogs eat in 6 months?

_____

17. **THINK SMARTER** Select the correct product for the equation.

$\frac{24}{12}$ $\frac{18}{12}$ $\frac{24}{7}$ $\frac{18}{7}$

$9 \times \frac{2}{12} =$ [ ] $3 \times \frac{6}{7} =$ [ ]

$6 \times \frac{4}{7} =$ [ ] $8 \times \frac{3}{12} =$ [ ]

Name _____

Multiply a Fraction by a Whole Number Using Models

COMMON CORE STANDARD—4.NF.B.4
Build fractions from unit fractions by applying and extending previous understandings of operations on whole numbers..

Multiply.

1. $2 \times \dfrac{5}{6} = $ _____ $\dfrac{10}{6}$

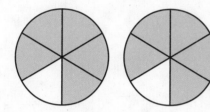

2. $3 \times \dfrac{2}{5} = $ _____

3. $7 \times \dfrac{3}{10} = $ _____

4. $3 \times \dfrac{5}{12} = $ _____

5. $6 \times \dfrac{3}{4} = $ _____

6. $4 \times \dfrac{2}{5} = $ _____

Problem Solving · Real World

7. Matthew walks $\dfrac{5}{8}$ mile to the bus stop each morning. How far will he walk in 5 days?

8. Emily uses $\dfrac{2}{3}$ cup of milk to make one batch of muffins. How many cups of milk will Emily use if she makes 3 batches of muffins?

_____   _____

9. **WRITE** ▸ *Math* Explain how you can use a model to find $4 \times \dfrac{3}{8}$. Include a drawing and a solution.

_____

_____

_____

_____

Lesson Check (4.NF.B.4b)

1. Aleta's puppy gained $\frac{3}{8}$ pound each week for 4 weeks. Altogether, how much weight did the puppy gain during the 4 weeks?

2. Pedro mixes $\frac{3}{4}$ teaspoon of plant food into each gallon of water. How many teaspoons of plant food should Pedro mix into 5 gallons of water?

Spiral Review (4.NF.A.2, 4.NF.B.3b, 4.NF.B.3c, 4.NF.B.4a)

3. Ivana has $\frac{3}{4}$ pound of hamburger meat. She makes 3 hamburger patties. Each patty weighs the same amount. How much does each hamburger patty weigh?

4. Write $\frac{7}{10}$ as a sum of fractions two different ways.

5. Lance wants to find the total length of 3 boards. He uses the expression $3\frac{1}{2} + (2 + 4\frac{1}{2})$. How can Lance rewrite the expression using both the Associative and Commutative Properties of Addition?

6. Fill in the blank with a symbol that makes this statement true:

$$\frac{5}{12} \bigcirc \frac{1}{3}$$

FOR MORE PRACTICE
GO TO THE
Personal Math Trainer

Name _____

Multiply a Fraction or Mixed Number by a Whole Number

 Common Core Number and Operations—Fractions—4.NF.B.4c

MATHEMATICAL PRACTICES
MP1, MP7, MP8

Essential Question How can you multiply a fraction by a whole number to solve a problem?

Unlock the Problem Real World

Christina is planning a dance routine. At the end of each measure of music, she will make a $1\frac{1}{4}$ turn. How many turns will she make after the first 3 measures of music?

You can multiply a mixed number by a whole number.

- Will Christina make more or less than $1\frac{1}{4}$ turns in 3 measures of music?

  _____

- What operation will you use to solve the problem?

  _____

Example

STEP 1 Write and solve an equation.

$3 \times 1\frac{1}{4} = 3 \times \rule{1cm}{0.15mm} = \rule{1cm}{0.15mm}$ Write $1\frac{1}{4}$ as a fraction. Multiply.

STEP 2 Write the product as a mixed number.

$$\frac{15}{4} = \underbrace{\frac{1}{4} + \frac{1}{4} + \frac{1}{4} + \frac{1}{4}}_{1} + \underbrace{\rule{0.4cm}{0.15mm} + \rule{0.4cm}{0.15mm} + \rule{0.4cm}{0.15mm} + \rule{0.4cm}{0.15mm}}_{1} + \underbrace{\rule{0.4cm}{0.15mm} + \rule{0.4cm}{0.15mm} + \rule{0.4cm}{0.15mm} + \rule{0.4cm}{0.15mm}}_{1} + \frac{1}{4} + \frac{1}{4} + \frac{1}{4}$$

$= \rule{0.8cm}{0.15mm} + \dfrac{}{}$ Combine the wholes. Then combine the remaining parts.

$= \dfrac{}{}$ Write the mixed number.

So, Christina will make _____ turns.

 Math Talk **MATHEMATICAL PRACTICES** ⑧

Generalize How is writing the mixed number as a fraction in Step 2 related to division?

1. If you multiply $3 \times \frac{1}{4}$, is the product greater than or less than 3? Explain.

   _____

2. Explain how you can tell that $3 \times 1\frac{1}{4}$ is greater than 3 without finding the exact product.

   _____

Rename Mixed Numbers and Fractions You can use multiplication and division to rename fractions and mixed numbers.

 Write $8\frac{1}{5}$ as a fraction.

$8\frac{1}{5} = 8 + \frac{1}{5}$

$= (8 \times \underline{\hspace{1cm}}) + \frac{1}{5}$ Use the Identity Property of Multiplication.

$= \left(8 \times \dfrac{}{}\right) + \frac{1}{5}$ Rename 1.

$= \dfrac{}{} + \dfrac{}{}$ Multiply.

$= \dfrac{}{}$ Add.

 Write $\frac{32}{5}$ as a mixed number.

Find how many groups of $\frac{5}{5}$ are in $\frac{32}{5}$.

- Divide 32 by 5.
- The whole-number quotient is the number of wholes in $\frac{32}{5}$.
- The remainder is the number of fifths left over.

There are 6 groups of $\frac{5}{5}$, or 6 wholes. There are 2 fifths, or $\frac{2}{5}$ left over.

$\dfrac{32}{5} = \boxed{}\dfrac{}{}$

Try This! Find $5 \times 2\frac{2}{3}$. Write the product as a mixed number.

$5 \times 2\frac{2}{3} = 5 \times \dfrac{}{}$ Write $2\frac{2}{3}$ as a fraction.

$= \dfrac{}{}$ Multiply.

$= \dfrac{}{}$ Divide the numerator by 3.

3. Explain why your solution to $5 \times 2\frac{2}{3} = 13\frac{1}{3}$ is reasonable.

_____

_____

4. Sense or Nonsense? To find $5 \times 2\frac{2}{3}$, Dylan says he can find $(5 \times 2) + \left(5 \times \frac{2}{3}\right)$. Does this make sense? Explain.

_____

_____

476

Name _____

1. $2 \times 3\frac{2}{3} = 2 \times$ _____

$=$ _____

$=$ _____

Multiply. Write the product as a mixed number.

☑ **2.** $6 \times \frac{2}{5} =$ _____

3. $3 \times 2\frac{3}{4}$ _____

☑ **4.** $2 \times 1\frac{5}{6} =$ _____

Math Talk MATHEMATICAL PRACTICES ①

Evaluate Reasonableness How do you know your answer to Exercise 3 is reasonable?

On Your Own

Multiply. Write the product as a mixed number.

5. $4 \times \frac{5}{8} =$ _____

6. $6 \times \frac{5}{12} =$ _____

7. $3 \times 2\frac{1}{2} =$ _____

8. $2 \times 2\frac{2}{3} =$ _____

9. $5 \times 1\frac{2}{4} =$ _____

10. $4 \times 2\frac{2}{5} =$ _____

MATHEMATICAL PRACTICE ⑦ **Look for a Pattern** **Algebra** Write the unknown number.

11. ▨ $\times 2\frac{1}{3} = 9\frac{1}{3}$

12. $3 \times 2\frac{2}{▨} = 7\frac{2}{4}$

13. $3 \times ▨\frac{3}{8} = 4\frac{1}{8}$

14. Describe two different ways to write $\frac{7}{3}$ as a mixed number.

_____

_____

_____

_____

Problem Solving • Applications

Use the recipe for 15–18.

15. Otis plans to make 3 batches of sidewalk chalk. How much plaster of Paris does he need?

_____

16. What's the Question? The answer is $\frac{32}{3}$.

_____

_____

17. THINK SMARTER Patty has 2 cups of warm water. Is that enough water to make 4 batches of sidewalk chalk? Explain how you know without finding the exact product.

> ### Sidewalk Chalk Recipe
> $\frac{3}{4}$ cup warm water
>
> $1\frac{1}{2}$ cups plaster of Paris
>
> $2\frac{2}{3}$ tablespoons powdered paint

_____

_____

18. GO DEEPER Rita makes sidewalk chalk 2 days a week. Each of those days, she spends $1\frac{1}{4}$ hours making the chalk. How much time does Rita spend making sidewalk chalk in 3 weeks?

_____

Personal Math Trainer

19. THINK SMARTER + Oliver has music lessons Monday, Wednesday, and Friday. Each lesson is $\frac{3}{4}$ of an hour. Oliver says he will have lessons for $3\frac{1}{2}$ hours this week. Without multiplying, explain how you know Oliver is incorrect.

Multiply a Fraction or Mixed Number by a Whole Number

COMMON CORE STANDARD—4.NF.B.4c
Build fractions from unit fractions by applying and extending previous understandings of operations on whole numbers.

Multiply. Write the product as a mixed number.

1. $5 \times \dfrac{3}{10} =$ ____ $1\dfrac{5}{10}$ ____

2. $3 \times \dfrac{3}{5} =$ ____

3. $5 \times \dfrac{3}{4} =$ ____

4. $4 \times 1\dfrac{1}{5} =$ ____

5. $2 \times 2\dfrac{1}{3} =$ ____

6. $5 \times 1\dfrac{1}{6} =$ ____

Problem Solving · Real World

7. Brielle exercises for $\dfrac{3}{4}$ hour each day for 6 days in a row. Altogether, how many hours does she exercise during the 6 days?

   _____

8. A recipe for quinoa calls for $2\dfrac{2}{3}$ cups of milk. Conner wants to make 4 batches of quinoa. How much milk does he need?

   _____

9. **WRITE** ▸ Math Write a word problem that you can solve by multiplying a mixed number by a whole number. Include a solution.

   _____

   _____

   _____

   _____

Lesson Check (4.NF.B.4c)

1. A mother is $1\frac{3}{4}$ times as tall as her son. Her son is 3 feet tall. How tall is the mother?

2. The cheerleaders are making a banner that is 8 feet wide. The length of the banner is $1\frac{1}{3}$ times the width of the banner. How long is the banner?

Spiral Review (4.NF.B.3c, 4.NF.B.4a, 4.NF.B.4b)

3. Karleigh walks $\frac{5}{8}$ mile to school every day. How far does she walk to school in 5 days?

4. Write a fraction that is a multiple of $\frac{4}{5}$.

5. Jo cut a key lime pie into 8 equal-size slices. The next day, $\frac{7}{8}$ of the pie is left. Jo puts each slice on its own plate. How many plates does she need?

6. Over the weekend, Ed spent $1\frac{1}{4}$ hours doing his math homework and $1\frac{3}{4}$ hours doing his science project. Altogether, how much time did Ed spend doing homework over the weekend?

FOR MORE PRACTICE
GO TO THE
Personal Math Trainer

Name _____

Problem Solving • Comparison Problems with Fractions

Essential Question How can you use the strategy *draw a diagram* to solve comparison problems with fractions?

Common Core   Number and Operations—
Fractions—4.NF.B.4c
MATHEMATICAL PRACTICES
MP1, MP6, MP7

🔑 Unlock the Problem (Real World)

The deepest part of the Grand Canyon is about $1\frac{1}{6}$ miles deep. The deepest part of the ocean is located in the Mariana Trench, in the Pacific Ocean. The deepest part of the ocean is almost 6 times as deep as the deepest part of the Grand Canyon. About how deep is the deepest part of the ocean?

Read the Problem	**Solve the Problem**
What do I need to find? I need to find _____ _____ _____	Draw a bar model. Compare the depth of the deepest part of the Grand Canyon and the deepest part of the ocean, in miles. _____ $\boxed{1\frac{1}{6}}$ _____ ⬚⬚⬚⬚⬚⬚ m
What information do I need to use? The deepest part of the Grand Canyon is about _____ miles deep. The deepest part of the ocean is about _____ times as deep.	Write an equation and solve. m is the deepest part of _____, in miles. $m =$ _____ ⬚ _____ Write an equation. $m =$ _____ ⬚ _____ Write the mixed number as a fraction.
How will I use the information? I can _____ to compare the depths.	$m =$ _____ Multiply. $m =$ _____ Write the fraction as a whole number.

So, the deepest part of the ocean is about _____ miles deep.

Try Another Problem

Mountains are often measured by the distance they rise above sea level. Mount Washington rises more than $1\frac{1}{10}$ miles above sea level. Mount Everest rises about 5 times as high. About how many miles above sea level does Mount Everest rise?

Read the Problem	Solve the Problem
What do I need to find?	
What information do I need to use?	
How will I use the information?	

So, Mount Everest rises about _____ miles above sea level.

- How did drawing a diagram help you solve the problem?

_____

_____

Math Talk

MATHEMATICAL PRACTICES ⑦

Look for Structure What strategy could you use to find the height of Mount Everest?

Name _____

Unlock the Problem

✓ Use the Problem Solving MathBoard.
✓ Underline important facts.

1. Komodo dragons are the heaviest lizards on Earth. A baby Komodo dragon is $1\frac{1}{4}$ feet long when it hatches. Its mother is 6 times as long. How long is the mother?

   First, draw a bar model to show the problem.

   WRITE ▶ Math
   Show Your Work

   Then, write the equation you need to solve.

   _____

   Finally, find the length of the mother Komodo dragon.

   The mother Komodo dragon is _____ feet long.

2. **THINK SMARTER** What if a male Komodo dragon is 7 times as long as the baby Komodo dragon? How long is the male? How much longer is the male than the mother?

   _____

✅ 3. The smallest hummingbird is the Bee hummingbird. It has a mass of about $1\frac{1}{2}$ grams. A Rufous hummingbird's mass is 3 times the mass of the Bee hummingbird. What is the mass of a Rufous hummingbird?

   _____

✅ 4. Sloane needs $\frac{3}{4}$ hour to drive to her grandmother's house. It takes her 5 times as long to drive to her cousin's house. How long does it take to drive to her cousin's house?

   _____

On Your Own

Use the table for 5 and 6.

Payton has a variety of flowers in her garden. The table shows the average heights of the flowers.

Flower	Height
tulip	$1\frac{1}{4}$ feet
daisy	$2\frac{1}{2}$ feet
tiger lily	$3\frac{1}{3}$ feet
sunflower	$7\frac{3}{4}$ feet

5. **MATHEMATICAL PRACTICE 1** **Make Sense of Problems** What is the difference between the height of the tallest flower and the height of the shortest flower in Payton's garden?

_____

WRITE ▶ Math
Show Your Work

6. **THINK SMARTER** Payton says her average sunflower is 7 times the height of her average tulip. Do you agree or disagree with her statement? Explain your reasoning.

_____

_____

_____

7. **GO DEEPER** Miguel ran $1\frac{3}{10}$ miles on Monday. On Friday, Miguel ran 3 times as far as he did on Monday. How much farther did Miguel run on Friday than he did on Monday?

_____

Personal Math Trainer

8. **THINK SMARTER +** The table shows the lengths of different types of turtles at a zoo.

Turtle Name	Type of Turtle	Length
Tuck	Common Snapping Turtle	$1\frac{1}{6}$ feet
Lolly	Leatherback Sea Turtle	$5\frac{5}{6}$ feet
Daisy	Loggerhead Sea Turtle	$3\frac{1}{2}$ feet

For numbers 8a–8d, select True or False for each statement.

8a. Daisy is 4 times as long as Tuck.　　○ True　　○ False

8b. Lolly is 5 times as long as Tuck.　　○ True　　○ False

8c. Daisy is 3 times as long as Tuck.　　○ True　　○ False

8d. Lolly is 2 times as long as Daisy.　　○ True　　○ False

Problem Solving • Comparison Problems with Fractions

COMMON CORE STANDARD—4.NF.B.4c
Build fractions from unit fractions by applying and extending previous understandings of operations on whole numbers.

Read each problem and solve.

1. A shrub is $1\frac{2}{3}$ feet tall. A small tree is 3 times as tall as the shrub. How tall is the tree?

   t is the height of the tree, in feet.

   $t = 3 \times 1\frac{2}{3}$

   $t = 3 \times \frac{5}{3}$

   $t = \frac{15}{3}$

   $t = 5$

   So, the tree is 5 feet tall.

   shrub $\boxed{1\frac{2}{3}}$

   tree $\boxed{1\frac{2}{3}}\ \boxed{1\frac{2}{3}}\ \boxed{1\frac{2}{3}}$

   _____5 feet_____

2. You run $1\frac{3}{4}$ miles each day. Your friend runs 4 times as far as you do. How far does your friend run each day?

   _____

3. At the grocery store, Ayla buys $1\frac{1}{3}$ pounds of ground turkey. Tasha buys 2 times as much ground turkey as Ayla. How much ground turkey does Tasha buy?

   _____

4. **WRITE** ▸*Math* Draw a bar model that shows a pen is 4 times as long as an eraser that is $1\frac{1}{3}$ inches long.

Lesson Check (4.NF.B.4c)

1. A Wilson's Storm Petrel is a small bird with a wingspan of $1\frac{1}{3}$ feet. A California Condor is a larger bird with a wingspan almost 7 times as wide as the wingspan of the petrel. About how wide is the wingspan of the California Condor? (It may be helpful to draw a model.)

2. The walking distance from the Empire State Building in New York City to Times Square is about $\frac{9}{10}$ mile. The walking distance from the Empire State Building to Sue's hotel is about 8 times as far. About how far is Sue's hotel from the Empire State Building? (It may be helpful to draw a model.)

Spiral Review (4.OA.B.4, 4.NF.A.2, 4.NF.B.3d, 4.NF.B.4c)

3. Write an expression that is equal to $3 \times 2\frac{1}{4}$.

4. At a bake sale, Ron sells $\frac{7}{8}$ of an apple pie and $\frac{5}{8}$ of a cherry pie. Altogether, how much pie does he sell at the bake sale?

5. Write one measurement that is between $\frac{3}{16}$ inch and $\frac{7}{8}$ inch on a ruler.

6. Write a composite number that is less than 5.

**FOR MORE PRACTICE
GO TO THE
Personal Math Trainer**

Name _____

1. What are the next four multiples of $\frac{1}{8}$?

```



```

2. THINK SMARTER ✛   Marta is making 3 servings of fruit salad. She adds $\frac{3}{8}$ cup blueberries for each serving. Her measuring cup holds $\frac{1}{8}$ cup. How many times must Marta measure $\frac{1}{8}$ cup of blueberries to have enough for the fruit salad? Shade the models to show your answer.

$\frac{1}{8}$	$\frac{1}{8}$	$\frac{1}{8}$	$\frac{1}{8}$	$\frac{1}{8}$	$\frac{1}{8}$	$\frac{1}{8}$	$\frac{1}{8}$
$\frac{1}{8}$	$\frac{1}{8}$	$\frac{1}{8}$	$\frac{1}{8}$	$\frac{1}{8}$	$\frac{1}{8}$	$\frac{1}{8}$	$\frac{1}{8}$
$\frac{1}{8}$	$\frac{1}{8}$	$\frac{1}{8}$	$\frac{1}{8}$	$\frac{1}{8}$	$\frac{1}{8}$	$\frac{1}{8}$	$\frac{1}{8}$

Marta must measure $\frac{1}{8}$ cup _____ times.

3. Mickey exercises $\frac{3}{4}$ hour every day. How many hours does he exercise in 8 days?

_____ hours

4. Molly is baking for the Moms and Muffins event at her school. She will bake 4 batches of banana muffins. She needs $1\frac{3}{4}$ cups of bananas for each batch of muffins.

Part A

Molly completed the multiplication below and said she needed 8 cups of bananas for 4 batches of muffins. What is Molly's error?

$$4 \times 1\frac{3}{4} = 4 \times \frac{8}{4} = \frac{32}{4} = 8$$

Part B

What is the correct number of cups Molly needs for 4 batches of muffins? Explain how you found your answer.

5. Which fraction is a multiple of $\frac{1}{9}$? Mark all that apply.

○ $\frac{3}{9}$ ○ $\frac{9}{12}$ ○ $\frac{2}{9}$

○ $\frac{4}{9}$ ○ $\frac{9}{10}$ ○ $\frac{9}{9}$

6. Mimi recorded a soccer game that lasted $1\frac{2}{3}$ hours. She watched it 3 times over the weekend to study the plays. How many hours did Mimi spend watching the soccer game? Show your work.

7. Theo is comparing shark lengths. He learned that a horn shark is $2\frac{3}{4}$ feet long. A blue shark is 4 times as long. Complete the model. Then find the length of a blue shark.

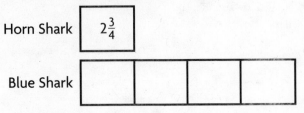

Horn Shark | $2\frac{3}{4}$

Blue Shark

A blue shark is ☐ feet long.

8. Joel made a number line showing the multiples of $\frac{3}{5}$.

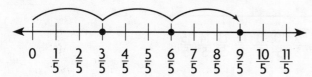

The product $2 \times \frac{3}{5}$ is shown by the fraction ⬚ on the number line.

9. Bobby has baseball practice Monday, Wednesday, and Friday. Each practice is $2\frac{1}{2}$ hours. Bobby says he will have practice for 4 hours this week.

Part A

Without multiplying, explain how you know Bobby is incorrect.

Part B

How long will Bobby have baseball practice this week? Write your answer as a mixed number. Show your work.

10. Look at the number line. Write the missing fractions.

11. Ana's dachshund weighed $5\frac{5}{8}$ pounds when it was born. By age 4, the dog weighed 6 times as much. Fill each box with a number or symbol from the list to show how to find the weight of Ana's dog at age 4. Not all numbers and symbols may be used.

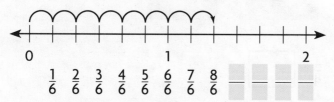

weight = ⬚ ⬚ ⬚

12. Asta made a fraction number line to help her find $3 \times \frac{4}{5}$.

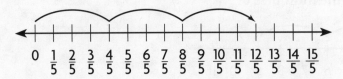

Select a way to write $3 \times \frac{4}{5}$ as the product of a whole number and a unit fraction.

$$3 \times \frac{4}{5} = \boxed{\begin{array}{c} 4 \times \frac{3}{5} \\[4pt] 12 \times \frac{1}{5} \\[4pt] 6 \times \frac{1}{5} \end{array}}$$

13. Yusif wants to give $\frac{1}{3}$ of his total toy car collection to each of 2 of his friends. How much of his total toy car collection will he give away?

14. Select the correct product for the equation.

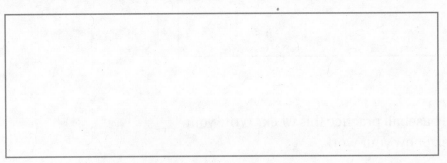

$4 \times \frac{5}{8} = \boxed{}$ $4 \times \frac{4}{8} = \boxed{}$

Name _____

15. The lengths of different types of snakes at a zoo
are shown in the table.

For numbers 15a–15d, select True or False for
the statement.

Snake's Name	Type of Snake	Length
Kenny	Kenyan Sand Boa	$1\frac{1}{2}$ feet
Bobby	Ball Python	$4\frac{1}{2}$ feet
Puck	Blood Python	$7\frac{1}{2}$ feet

15a. Bobby is 4 times
as long as Kenny. ○ True ○ False

15b. Bobby is 3 times
as long as Kenny. ○ True ○ False

15c. Puck is 5 times
as long as Kenny. ○ True ○ False

15d. Puck is 2 times
as long as Bobby. ○ True ○ False

16. Hank used $3\frac{1}{2}$ bags of seed to plant grass in his front yard. He used
3 times as much seed to plant grass in his back yard. How much
seed did Hank need for the backyard?

_____ bags

17. Jess made a big kettle of rice and beans. He used $1\frac{1}{2}$ cups of beans.
He used 4 times as much rice.

Part A

Draw a model to show the problem.

Part B

Use your model to write an equation. Then solve the equation to
find the amount of rice Jess needs.

18. Mrs. Burnham is making modeling clay for her class. She needs $\frac{2}{3}$ cup of warm water for each batch.

Part A

Mrs. Burnham has a 1-cup measure that has no other markings. Can she make 6 batches of modeling clay using only the 1-cup measure? Describe two ways you can find the answer.

Part B

The modeling clay recipe also calls for $\frac{1}{2}$ cup of cornstarch. Nikki says Mrs. Burnham will also need 4 cups of cornstarch. Do you agree or disagree? Explain.

19. Donna buys some fabric to make place mats. She needs $\frac{1}{5}$ yard of each type of fabric. She has 9 different types of fabrics to make her design. Use the following equation. Write the number in the box to make the statement true.

$$\frac{9}{5} = \underline{\hspace{2cm}} \times \frac{1}{5}$$

20. Mr. Tuyen uses $\frac{5}{8}$ of a tank of gas each week to drive to and from his job. How many tanks of gas does Mr. Tuyen use in 5 weeks? Write your answer two different ways.

Mr. Tuyen uses _____ or _____ tanks of gas.

21. **GO DEEPER** Rico is making 4 batches of salsa. Each batch needs $\frac{2}{3}$ cup of corn. He only has a $\frac{1}{3}$-cup measure. How many times must Rico measure $\frac{1}{3}$ cup of corn to have enough for all of the salsa?

_____ times

Chapter 9 — Relate Fractions and Decimals

✓ Show What You Know

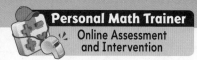

Personal Math Trainer
Online Assessment and Intervention

Check your understanding of important skills.

Name _____

▶ **Count Coins** **Find the total value.** (2.MD.C.8)

1.

Total value: _____

2.

Total value: _____

▶ **Equivalent Fractions**

Write two equivalent fractions for the picture. (3.NF.A.3b)

3.

_____

4.

_____

▶ **Fractions with Denominators of 10**

Write a fraction for the words. You may draw a picture. (3.NF.A.1)

5. three tenths _____

6. six tenths _____

7. eight tenths _____

8. nine tenths _____

Math in the Real World

The Hudson River Science Barge, docked near New York City, provides a demonstration of how renewable energy can be used to produce food for large cities. Vegetables grown on the barge require _____ of the water needed by field crops. Use these clues to find the fraction and decimal for the missing amount.

• The number is less than one and has two decimal places.
• The digit in the hundredths place has a value of $\frac{5}{100}$.
• The digit in the tenths place has a value of $\frac{2}{10}$.

Chapter 9   493

▶ **Visualize It** ································

Complete the Semantic Map by using words with a ✓.

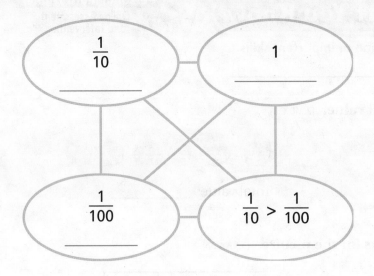

▶ **Understand Vocabulary** ·····················

Draw a line to match each word with its definition.

Word	Definition
1. decimal	• Two or more decimals that name the same amount
2. decimal point	• One part out of one hundred equal parts
3. tenth	• A number with one or more digits to the right of the decimal point
4. hundredth	• One part out of ten equal parts
5. equivalent decimals	• A symbol used to separate dollars from cents in money amounts and to separate the ones and the tenths places in decimals

• **Interactive Student Edition**
• **Multimedia eGlossary**

Chapter 9 Vocabulary

compare

comparar

14

decimal

decimal

19

decimal point

punto decimal

20

equivalent decimals

decimales equivalentes

28

equivalent fractions

fracciones equivalentes

29

hundredth

centésimo

40

tenth

décimo

89

whole

entero

96

A number with one or more digits to the right of the decimal point

Examples: 0.5, 0.06, and 12.679 are decimals.

To describe whether numbers are equal to, less than, or greater than each other

Ones	.	Tenths	Hundredths
1	.	1	5
1	.	3	

1.3 > 1.15

Two or more decimals that name the same amount

Ones	.	Tenths	Hundredths
0	.	8	
0	.	8	0

Example: 0.8 and 0.80 are equivalent decimals.

A symbol used to separate dollars from cents in money amounts, and to separate the ones and the tenths places in a decimal

Example: 6.4
↑ decimal point

One of one hundred equal parts

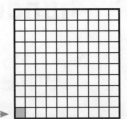

hundredth →

Two or more fractions that name the same amount

Example: $\frac{3}{4}$ and $\frac{6}{8}$ name the same amount.

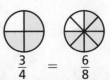

$\frac{3}{4}$ = $\frac{6}{8}$

All of the parts of a shape or group

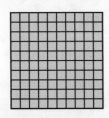

One of ten equal parts

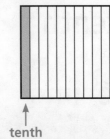

tenth

Matchup

For 2 to 3 players

Materials

- 1 set of word cards

How to Play

1. Put the cards face-down in rows. Take turns to play.

2. Choose two cards and turn them face-up.

   - If the cards show a word and its meaning, it's a match. Keep the pair and take another turn.

   - If the cards do not match, turn them back over.

3. The game is over when all cards have been matched. The players count their pairs. The player with the most pairs wins.

Word Box
compare
decimal
decimal point
equivalent decimals
equivalent fractions
hundredth
tenth
whole

The Write Way

Materials

Choose one idea. Write about it.

- Write a paragraph that uses at three of these words or phrases.

  decimal   decimal point   hundredth   tenth   whole

- Explain in your own words what equivalent decimals are.

- As the writer of a math advice column, you often hear from readers about their struggles to relate fraction and decimal forms. Write a letter explaining what those readers need to know to better understand this subject.

Name _____

Relate Tenths and Decimals

Essential Question How can you record tenths as fractions and decimals?

Common Core
Number and Operations—Fractions—4.NF.C.6
MATHEMATICAL PRACTICES
MP2, MP5, MP6

Unlock the Problem

Ty is reading a book about metamorphic rocks. He has read $\frac{7}{10}$ of the book. What decimal describes the part of the book Ty has read?

A **decimal** is a number with one or more digits to the right of the **decimal point**. You can write tenths and hundredths as fractions or decimals.

One Way Use a model and a place-value chart.

Fraction

Shade $\frac{7}{10}$ of the model.

Think: The model is divided into 10 equal parts. Each part represents one **tenth**.

Write: _____

Read: seven tenths

Decimal

$\frac{7}{10}$ is 7 tenths.

Ones	.	Tenths	Hundredths
	.		

↑ decimal point

Write: _____

Read: _____

Another Way Use a number line.

Label the number line with decimals that are equivalent to the fractions. Locate the point $\frac{7}{10}$.

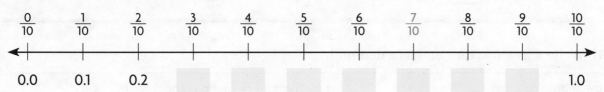

_____ names the same amount as $\frac{7}{10}$.

So, Ty read 0.7 of the book.

Math Talk

MATHEMATICAL PRACTICES ②

Use Reasoning How is the size of one whole related to the size of one tenth?

- How can you write 0.1 as a fraction? Explain.

_____

Tara rode her bicycle $1\frac{6}{10}$ miles. What decimal describes how far she rode her bicycle?

You have already written a fraction as a decimal. You can also write a mixed number as a decimal.

One Way Use a model and a place-value chart.

Fraction

Shade $1\frac{6}{10}$ of the model.

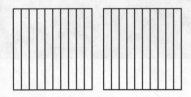

Write: _____

Read: one and six tenths

Decimal

$1\frac{6}{10}$ is 1 whole and 6 tenths.

Think: Use the ones place to record wholes.

Ones	.	Tenths	Hundredths
	.		

Write: _____

Read: _____

Another Way Use a number line.

Label the number line with equivalent mixed numbers and decimals. Locate the point $1\frac{6}{10}$.

$1\frac{0}{10}$ $1\frac{1}{10}$ $1\frac{2}{10}$ $1\frac{3}{10}$ .... W .... $2\frac{0}{10}$

1.0 .... 2.0

_____ names the same amount as $1\frac{6}{10}$.

So, Tara rode her bicycle _____ miles.

Try This! Write 1 as a fraction and as a decimal.

Shade the model to show 1.

Fraction: _____

Think: 1 is 1 whole and 0 tenths.

Ones	.	Tenths	Hundredths
	.		

Decimal: _____

Name _____

1. Write five tenths as a fraction and as a decimal.

Fraction: _____ Decimal: _____

Ones	.	Tenths	Hundredths
	.		

Write the fraction or mixed number and the decimal shown by the model.

2.

_____ _____

3.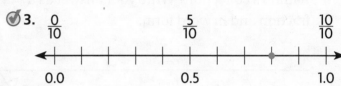

_____ _____

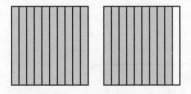

MATHEMATICAL PRACTICES 6

Attend to Precision How can you write $1\frac{3}{10}$ as a decimal? Explain.

On Your Own

Write the fraction or mixed number and the decimal shown by the model.

4.

_____ _____

5.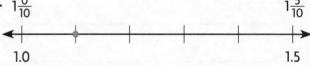

_____ _____

6.

_____ _____

7. $3\frac{0}{10}$ $3\frac{5}{10}$ $4\frac{0}{10}$

_____ _____

Practice: Copy and Solve Write the fraction or mixed number as a decimal.

8. $5\frac{9}{10}$

9. $\frac{1}{10}$

10. $\frac{7}{10}$

11. $8\frac{9}{10}$

12. $\frac{6}{10}$

13. $6\frac{3}{10}$

14. $\frac{5}{10}$

15. $9\frac{7}{10}$

Problem Solving • Applications

Use the table for 16–19.

Ramon's Rock Collection	
Name	**Type**
Basalt	Igneous
Rhyolite	Igneous
Granite	Igneous
Peridotite	Igneous
Scoria	Igneous
Shale	Sedimentary
Limestone	Sedimentary
Sandstone	Sedimentary
Mica	Metamorphic
Slate	Metamorphic

16. What part of the rocks listed in the table are igneous? Write your answer as a decimal.

_____

17. Sedimentary rocks make up what part of Ramon's collection? Write your answer as a fraction and in word form.

_____

18. **THINK SMARTER** What part of the rocks listed in the table are metamorphic? Write your answer as a fraction and as a decimal.

_____

▲ Granite– Igneous

▲ Mica–Metamorphic

▲ Sandstone– Sedimentary

19. **MATHEMATICAL PRACTICE ⑤ Communicate** Niki wrote the following sentence in her report: "Metamorphic rocks make up 2.0 of Ramon's rock collection." Describe her error.

_____

_____

20. **GO DEEPER** Josh paid for three books with two $20 bills. He received $1 in change. Each book was the same price. How much did each book cost?

_____

21. **THINK SMARTER** Select a number shown by the model. Mark all that apply.

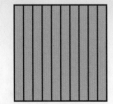 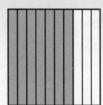

$1\frac{7}{10}$ $\frac{70}{10}$ 1.7

7   0.7 $\frac{17}{10}$

Relate Tenths and Decimals

COMMON CORE STANDARD—4.NF.C.6
Understand decimal notation for fractions, and compare decimal fractions.

Write the fraction or mixed number and the decimal shown by the model.

1. 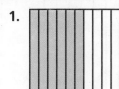 Think: The model is divided into 10 equal parts. Each part represents one tenth.

$\frac{6}{10}$; 0.6

2.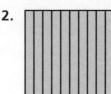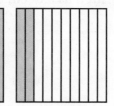

_____

3. $2\frac{0}{10}$ $2\frac{5}{10}$

2.0   2.5

_____

Write the fraction or mixed number as a decimal.

4. $\frac{4}{10}$ 5. $3\frac{1}{10}$ 6. $\frac{7}{10}$ 7. $6\frac{5}{10}$ 8. $\frac{9}{10}$

Problem Solving · Real World

9. There are 10 sports balls in the equipment closet. Three are kickballs. Write the portion of the balls that are kickballs as a fraction, as a decimal, and in word form.

10. Peyton has 2 pizzas. Each pizza is cut into 10 equal slices. She and her friends eat 14 slices. What part of the pizzas did they eat? Write your answer as a decimal.

11. **WRITE** ▸ Math Do 0.3 and 3.0 have the same value? Explain.

_____

_____

Lesson Check (4.NF.C.6)

1. Valerie has 10 CDs in her music case. Seven of the CDs are pop music CDs. What is this amount written as a decimal?

2. What decimal amount is modeled below?

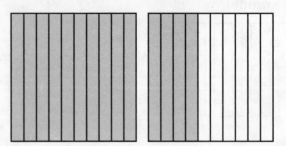

_____

Spiral Review (4.OA.B.4, 4.NF.A.1, 4.NF.B.3b)

3. Write one number that is a factor of 13.

4. An art gallery has 18 paintings and 4 photographs displayed in equal rows on a wall, with the same number of each type of art in each row. What could be the number of rows?

_____

5. How do you write the mixed number shown as a fraction greater than 1?

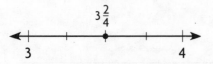

6. What fraction of this model, in simplest form, is shaded?

_____

FOR MORE PRACTICE
GO TO THE
Personal Math Trainer

Relate Hundredths and Decimals

Essential Question How can you record hundredths as fractions and decimals?

Common Core **Number and Operations—Fractions—4.NF.C.6**
MATHEMATICAL PRACTICES
MP1, MP2, MP7

Unlock the Problem

In the 2008 Summer Olympic Games, the winning time in the men's 100-meter butterfly race was only $\frac{1}{100}$ second faster than the second-place time. What decimal represents this fraction of a second?

You can write hundredths as fractions or decimals.

• Circle the numbers you need to use.

One Way Use a model and a place-value chart.

Fraction	Decimal
Shade $\frac{1}{100}$ of the model.	Complete the place-value chart. $\frac{1}{100}$ is 1 hundredth.

  Think: The model is divided into 100 equal parts. Each part represents one **hundredth**.

Ones	.	Tenths	Hundredths
0	.	0	1

Write: _____

Read: one hundredth

Write: _____

Read: one hundredth

Another Way Use a number line.

Label the number line with equivalent decimals. Locate the point $\frac{1}{100}$.

© Houghton Mifflin Harcourt Publishing Company • Image Credits: (tr) ©Corbis

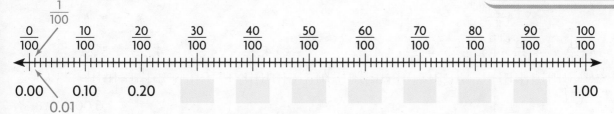

$\frac{1}{100}$

| $\frac{0}{100}$ | $\frac{10}{100}$ | $\frac{20}{100}$ | $\frac{30}{100}$ | $\frac{40}{100}$ | $\frac{50}{100}$ | $\frac{60}{100}$ | $\frac{70}{100}$ | $\frac{80}{100}$ | $\frac{90}{100}$ | $\frac{100}{100}$ |

0.00   0.10   0.20   1.00
  0.01

Math Talk

MATHEMATICAL PRACTICES ②

Use Reasoning How is the size of one tenth related to the size of one hundredth?

_____ names the same amount as $\frac{1}{100}$.

So, the winning time was _____ second faster.

Alicia won her 400-meter freestyle race by $4\frac{25}{100}$ seconds. How can you write this mixed number as a decimal?

🔑 One Way Use a model and a place-value chart.

Mixed Number

Shade the model to show $4\frac{25}{100}$.

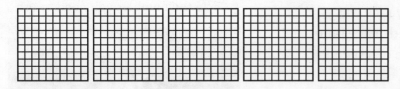

Write: _____

Read: four and twenty-five hundredths

Decimal

Complete the place-value chart.

Think: Look at the model above. $4\frac{25}{100}$ is 4 wholes and 2 tenths 5 hundredths.

Ones	.	Tenths	Hundredths
	.		

Write: _____

Read: _____

🔑 Another Way Use a number line.

Label the number line with equivalent mixed numbers and decimals. Locate the point $4\frac{25}{100}$.

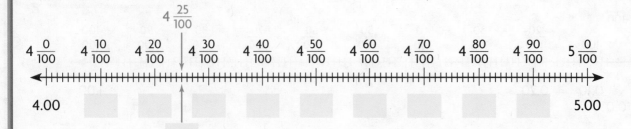

_____ names the same amount as $4\frac{25}{100}$.

So, Alicia won her race by _____ seconds.

Name _____

1. Shade the model to show $\frac{31}{100}$.

   Write the amount as a decimal. _____

Ones	.	Tenths	Hundredths
	.		

Write the fraction or mixed number and the decimal shown by the model.

✓2.   _____ _____

3.   _____ _____

✓4.

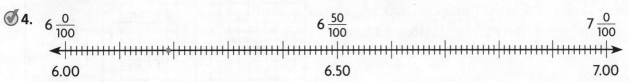

_____ _____

Math Talk

MATHEMATICAL PRACTICES ⑦

Look for Structure Are 0.5 and 0.50 equivalent? Explain.

On Your Own

Write the fraction or mixed number and the decimal shown by the model.

5.   _____ _____

6.   _____ _____

7.

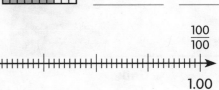

_____ _____

Practice: Copy and Solve Write the fraction or mixed number as a decimal.

8. $\frac{9}{100}$ 9. $4\frac{55}{100}$ 10. $\frac{10}{100}$ 11. $9\frac{33}{100}$ 12. $\frac{92}{100}$ 13. $14\frac{16}{100}$

Problem Solving • Applications

14. THINK SMARTER Shade the grids to show three different ways to represent $\frac{16}{100}$ using models.

15. MATHEMATICAL PRACTICE 1 **Describe Relationships**
Describe how one whole, one tenth, and one hundredth are related.

_____

_____

16. THINK SMARTER Shade the model to show $1\frac{24}{100}$. Then write the mixed number in decimal form.

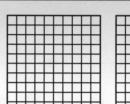 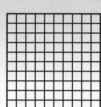

17. GO DEEPER The Memorial Library is 0.3 mile from school. Whose statement makes sense? Whose statement is nonsense? Explain your reasoning.

I am going to walk 3 tenths mile to the Memorial Library after school.

I am going to walk 3 miles to the Memorial Library after school.

Gabe	Tara

Name _____

Relate Hundredths and Decimals

Common Core

COMMON CORE STANDARD—4.NF.C.6
Understand decimal notation for fractions, and compare decimal fractions.

Write the fraction or mixed number and the decimal shown by the model.

1. 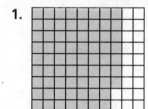 Think: The whole is divided into one hundred equal parts, so each part is one hundredth.

$\frac{77}{100}$; 0.77

2.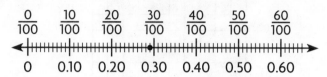

_____

3.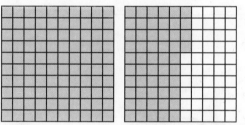

_____

4.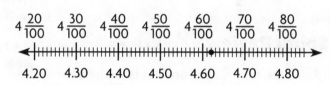

_____

Write the fraction or mixed number as a decimal.

5. $\frac{37}{100}$

6. $8\frac{11}{100}$

7. $\frac{98}{100}$

8. $25\frac{50}{100}$

9. $\frac{6}{100}$

_____

Problem Solving

10. There are 100 pennies in a dollar. What fraction of a dollar is 61 pennies? Write it as a fraction, as a decimal, and in word form.

11. **WRITE** ▸*Math* Describe a situation where it is easier to use decimals than fractions, and explain why.

_____

_____

Lesson Check (4.NF.C.6)

1. What decimal represents the shaded section of the model below?

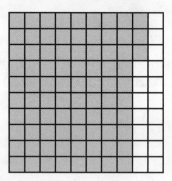

2. There were 100 questions on the unit test. Alondra answered 97 of the questions correctly. What decimal represents the fraction of questions Alondra answered correctly?

Spiral Review (4.OA.C.5, 4.NF.B.3b, 4.NF.B.3d, 4.NF.B.4c)

3. Write an expression that is equivalent to $\frac{7}{8}$.

4. What is $\frac{9}{10} - \frac{6}{10}$?

5. Misha used $\frac{1}{4}$ of a carton of 12 eggs to make an omelet. How many eggs did she use?

6. Kurt used the rule *add* 4, *subtract* 1 to generate a pattern. The first term in his pattern is 5. Write a number that could be in Kurt's pattern.

506

FOR MORE PRACTICE
GO TO THE
Personal Math Trainer

Equivalent Fractions and Decimals

Essential Question How can you record tenths and hundredths as fractions and decimals?

 Common Core Number and Operations—Fractions—4.NF.C.5 *Also 4.NF.C.6*
MATHEMATICAL PRACTICES
MP2, MP6, MP7

Unlock the Problem

Daniel spent a day hiking through a wildlife preserve. During the first hour of the hike, he drank $\frac{6}{10}$ liter of water. How many hundredths of a liter did he drink?

- Underline what you need to find.
- How can you represent hundredths?

_____

One Way Write $\frac{6}{10}$ as an equivalent fraction with a denominator of 100.

MODEL   RECORD

 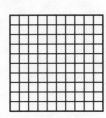

$$\frac{6}{10} = \frac{6 \times \boxed{}}{10 \times \boxed{}} = \frac{\boxed{}}{100}$$

$$\frac{6}{10} = \frac{\boxed{}}{100}$$

Another Way Write $\frac{6}{10}$ as a decimal.

Think: 6 tenths is the same as 6 tenths 0 hundredths.

Ones	.	Tenths	Hundredths

So, Daniel drank _____, or _____ liter of water.

- Explain why 6 tenths is equivalent to 60 hundredths.

 Math Talk

MATHEMATICAL PRACTICES 6
Explain how you can write 0.2 as hundredths.

_____

_____

Jasmine collected 0.30 liter of water in a jar during a rainstorm. How many tenths of a liter did she collect?

Equivalent decimals are decimals that name the same amount. You can write 0.30 as a decimal that names tenths.

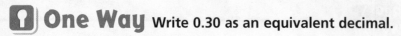 **One Way** Write 0.30 as an equivalent decimal.

Show 0.30 in the place-value chart.

Ones	.	Tenths	Hundredths

Think: There are no hundredths.

0.30 is equivalent to _____ tenths.

Write 0.30 as _____.

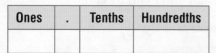 **Another Way** Write 0.30 as a fraction with a denominator of 10.

STEP 1 Write 0.30 as a fraction.

0.30 is _____ hundredths.

30 hundredths written as a fraction is _____.
_____

STEP 2 Write $\frac{30}{100}$ as an equivalent fraction with a denominator of 10.

Think: 10 is a common factor of the numerator and the denominator.

$$\frac{30}{100} = \frac{30 \div \boxed{}}{100 \div \boxed{}} = \frac{\boxed{}}{10}$$

So, Jasmine collected _____, or _____ liter of water.

 **Share and Show**

1. Write $\frac{4}{10}$ as hundredths.

Write $\frac{4}{10}$ as an equivalent fraction.

$$\frac{4}{10} = \frac{4 \times \boxed{}}{10 \times \boxed{}} = \frac{\boxed{}}{100}$$

Fraction: _____

Write $\frac{4}{10}$ as a decimal.

Ones	.	Tenths	Hundredths
	.		

Decimal: _____

Name _____

**Write the number as hundredths in fraction form
and decimal form.**

☑ 2. $\frac{7}{10}$

3. 0.5

4. $\frac{3}{10}$

**Write the number as tenths in fraction form
and decimal form.**

☑ 5. 0.40

6. $\frac{80}{100}$

7. $\frac{20}{100}$

On Your Own

Practice: Copy and Solve Write the number as
hundredths in fraction form and decimal form.

8. $\frac{8}{10}$

9. $\frac{2}{10}$

10. 0.1

Math Talk

MATHEMATICAL PRACTICES ②

Reason Abstractly Explain whether
you can write 0.25 as tenths.

Practice: Copy and Solve Write the number as tenths in fraction
form and decimal form.

11. $\frac{60}{100}$

12. $\frac{90}{100}$

13. 0.70

THINK SMARTER Write the number as an equivalent mixed number
with hundredths.

14. $1\frac{4}{10}$

15. $3\frac{5}{10}$

16. $2\frac{9}{10}$

© Houghton Mifflin Harcourt Publishing Company

Problem Solving • Applications

17. **THINK SMARTER** Carter says that 0.08 is equivalent to $\frac{8}{10}$. Describe and correct Carter's error.

_____

_____

_____

18. **THINK SMARTER** For numbers 18a–18e, choose True or False for the statement.

18a. 0.6 is equivalent to $\frac{6}{100}$. ○ True ○ False

18b. $\frac{3}{10}$ is equivalent to 0.30. ○ True ○ False

18c. $\frac{40}{100}$ is equivalent to $\frac{4}{10}$. ○ True ○ False

18d. 0.40 is equivalent to $\frac{4}{100}$. ○ True ○ False

18e. 0.5 is equivalent to 0.50. ○ True ○ False

Connect to Science

Inland Water

How many lakes and rivers does your state have? The U.S. Geological Survey defines inland water as water that is surrounded by land. The Atlantic Ocean, the Pacific Ocean, and the Great Lakes are not considered inland water.

19. **WRITE** ▸ Math Just over $\frac{2}{100}$ of the entire United States is inland water. Write $\frac{2}{100}$ as a decimal.

_____

20. **MATHEMATICAL PRACTICE 6** Can you write 0.02 as tenths? **Explain.**

_____

_____

21. About 0.17 of the area of Rhode Island is inland water. Write 0.17 as a fraction.

_____

22. **GO DEEPER** Louisiana's lakes and rivers cover about $\frac{1}{10}$ of the state. Write $\frac{1}{10}$ as hundredths in words, fraction form, and decimal form.

_____

Equivalent Fractions and Decimals

Common Core   **COMMON CORE STANDARD—4.NF.C.5**
Understand decimal notation for fractions, and compare decimal fractions.

Write the number as hundredths in fraction form and decimal form.

1. $\frac{5}{10}$

$\frac{5}{10} = \frac{5 \times 10}{10 \times 10} = \frac{50}{100}$

Think: 5 tenths is the same as 5 tenths and 0 hundredths. Write 0.50.

$\frac{50}{100}$; 0.50

2. $\frac{9}{10}$

3. 0.2

4. 0.8

Write the number as tenths in fraction form and decimal form.

5. $\frac{40}{100}$

6. $\frac{10}{100}$

7. 0.60

Problem Solving (Real World)

8. Billy walks $\frac{6}{10}$ mile to school each day. Write $\frac{6}{10}$ as hundredths in fraction form and in decimal form.

9. **WRITE** *Math* Write $\frac{5}{10}$ in three equivalent forms.

_____

_____

_____

_____

Lesson Check (4.NF.C.5)

1. The fourth-grade students at Harvest School make up 0.3 of all students at the school. What fraction is equivalent to 0.3?

2. Kyle and his brother have a marble set. Of the marbles, 12 are blue. This represents $\frac{50}{100}$ of all the marbles. What decimal is equivalent to $\frac{50}{100}$?

Spiral Review (4.OA.C.5, 4.NF.A.1, 4.NF.B.4c, 4.NF.C.6)

3. Jesse won his race by $3\frac{45}{100}$ seconds. What is this number written as a decimal?

4. Marge cut 16 pieces of tape for mounting pictures on poster board. Each piece of tape was $\frac{3}{8}$ inch long. How much tape did Marge use?

5. Of Katie's pattern blocks, $\frac{9}{12}$ are triangles. What is $\frac{9}{12}$ in simplest form?

6. A number pattern has 75 as its first term. The rule for the pattern is *subtract* 6. What is the sixth term?

FOR MORE PRACTICE GO TO THE
Personal Math Trainer

Name _____

Relate Fractions, Decimals, and Money

Essential Question How can you relate fractions, decimals, and money?

 Common Core Number and Operations—
Fractions—4.NF.C.6

MATHEMATICAL PRACTICES
MP2, MP4, MP6

Unlock the Problem

Together, Julie and Sarah have $1.00 in quarters. They want to share the quarters equally. How many quarters should each girl get? How much money is this?

> **Remember**
> 1 dollar = 100 cents
> 1 quarter = 25 cents
> 1 dime = 10 cents
> 1 penny = 1 cent

🔑 **Use the model to relate money, fractions, and decimals.**

4 quarters = 1 dollar = $1.00

$0.25 $0.25 $0.25 $0.25

1 quarter is $\frac{25}{100}$, or $\frac{1}{4}$ of a dollar.

2 quarters are $\frac{50}{100}$, $\frac{2}{4}$, or $\frac{1}{2}$ of a dollar.

$\frac{1}{2}$ of a dollar = $0.50, or 50 cents.

Circle the number of quarters each girl should get.

So, each girl should get 2 quarters, or $ _____.

🔑 Examples Use money to model decimals.

1 dollar	10 dimes = 1 dollar	100 pennies = 1 dollar

$1.00, or _____ cents	1 dime = $\frac{1}{10}$, or 0.10 of a dollar $ _____, or 10 cents	1 penny = $\frac{1}{100}$, or 0.01 of a dollar $ _____, or 1 cent

 Math Talk

MATHEMATICAL PRACTICES ④

Model Mathematics Model 68 pennies. What part of a dollar do you have? Explain.

Relate Money and Decimals Think of dollars as ones, dimes as tenths, and pennies as hundredths.

$1.56

Dollars	.	Dimes	Pennies
1	.	5	6

Think: $1.56 = 1 dollar and 56 pennies

There are 100 pennies in 1 dollar.
So, $1.56 = 156 pennies.

1.56 dollars

Ones	.	Tenths	Hundredths
1	.	5	6

Think: 1.56 = 1 one and 56 hundredths

There are 100 hundredths in 1 one.
So, 1.56 = 156 hundredths.

▣ More Examples Shade the decimal model to show the money amount. Then write the money amount and a fraction in terms of dollars.

Ⓐ

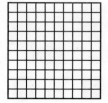

_____ , or $\frac{21}{100}$ of a dollar

Ⓑ

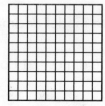 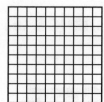

$1.46, or $1\frac{}{100}$ dollars

Try This! Complete the table to show how money, fractions, mixed numbers, and decimals are related.

$ Bills and Coins	Money Amount	Fraction or Mixed Number	Decimal
	$0.03		0.03
	$0.25	$\frac{25}{100}$, or $\frac{1}{4}$	
2 quarters 1 dime		$\frac{60}{100}$, or $\frac{6}{10}$	
2 $1 bills 5 nickels			

Math Talk

MATHEMATICAL PRACTICES ②

Reason Abstractly Would you rather have $0.25 or $\frac{3}{10}$ of a dollar? Explain.

Name _____

1. Write the amount of money as a decimal in terms of dollars.

   5 pennies = $\frac{5}{100}$ of a dollar = _____ of a dollar.

Write the total money amount. Then write the amount as a fraction or a mixed number and as a decimal in terms of dollars.

2.

   _____

✓3.

   _____

Write as a money amount and as a decimal in terms of dollars.

4. $\frac{92}{100}$ _____

5. $\frac{7}{100}$ _____

6. $\frac{16}{100}$ _____

✓7. $\frac{53}{100}$ _____

On Your Own

MATHEMATICAL PRACTICES ⑥

Make Connections How are $0.84 and $\frac{84}{100}$ of a dollar related?

Write the total money amount. Then write the amount as a fraction or a mixed number and as a decimal in terms of dollars.

8.

   _____

9.

   _____

Write as a money amount and as a decimal in terms of dollars.

10. $\frac{27}{100}$ _____

11. $\frac{4}{100}$ _____

12. $\frac{75}{100}$ _____

13. $\frac{100}{100}$ _____

Write the total money amount. Then write the amount as a fraction and as a decimal in terms of dollars.

14. 1 quarter 6 dimes 8 pennies

    _____

15. 3 dimes 5 nickels 20 pennies

    _____

MATHEMATICAL PRACTICE 6 Make Connections **Algebra** Complete to tell the value of each digit.

16. $1.05 = \underline{\hspace{1cm}}$ dollar $+ \underline{\hspace{1cm}}$ pennies, $1.05 = \underline{\hspace{1cm}}$ one $+ \underline{\hspace{1cm}}$ hundredths

17. $5.18 = \underline{\hspace{1cm}}$ dollars $+ \underline{\hspace{1cm}}$ dime $+ \underline{\hspace{1cm}}$ pennies

   $5.18 = \underline{\hspace{1cm}}$ ones $+ \underline{\hspace{1cm}}$ tenth $+ \underline{\hspace{1cm}}$ hundredths

Problem Solving • Applications

Use the table for 18–19.

18. The table shows the coins three students have. Write Nick's total amount as a fraction in terms of dollars.

   _____

Pocket Change				
Name	**Quarters**	**Dimes**	**Nickels**	**Pennies**
Kim	1	3	2	3
Tony	0	6	1	6
Nick	2	4	0	2

19. **THINK SMARTER** Kim spent $\frac{40}{100}$ of a dollar on a snack. Write as a money amount the amount she has left.

   _____

20. **GO DEEPER** Travis has $\frac{1}{2}$ of a dollar. He has at least two different types of coins in his pocket. Draw two possible sets of coins that Travis could have.

21. **THINK SMARTER** Complete the table.

$ Bills and Coins	Money Amount	Fraction or Mixed Number	Decimal
6 pennies		$\frac{6}{100}$	0.06
	$0.50		0.50
		$\frac{70}{100}$ or $\frac{7}{10}$	0.70
3 $1 bills 9 pennies			3.09

Name _____

Relate Fractions, Decimals, and Money

COMMON CORE STANDARD—4.NF.C.6
Understand decimal notation for fractions, and compare decimal fractions.

Write the total money amount. Then write the amount as a fraction or a mixed number and as a decimal in terms of dollars.

1.

$0.18; $\frac{18}{100}$; 0.18
_____

2.

_____

Write as a money amount and as a decimal in terms of dollars.

3. $\frac{25}{100}$ **4.** $\frac{79}{100}$ **5.** $\frac{31}{100}$ **6.** $\frac{8}{100}$ **7.** $\frac{42}{100}$

_____ _____ _____ _____ _____

Write the money amount as a fraction in terms of dollars.

8. $0.87 **9.** $0.03 **10.** $0.66 **11.** $0.95 **12.** $1.00

_____ _____ _____ _____ _____

Write the total money amount. Then write the amount as a fraction and as a decimal in terms of dollars.

13. 2 quarters 2 dimes **14.** 3 dimes 4 pennies **15.** 8 nickels 12 pennies

_____ _____ _____

Problem Solving

16. Kate has 1 dime, 4 nickels, and 8 pennies. Write Kate's total amount as a fraction in terms of a dollar.

17. **WRITE** ▸*Math* Jeffrey says he has 6.8 dollars. How do you write the decimal 6.8 when it refers to money? Explain.

_____

Lesson Check (4.NF.C.6)

1. Write the total amount of money shown as a fraction in terms of a dollar.

2. Crystal has $\frac{81}{100}$ of a dollar. What could be the coins Crystal has?

_____

_____

_____

Spiral Review (4.NF.A.1, 4.NF.C.6)

3. Joel gives $\frac{1}{3}$ of his baseball cards to his sister. Write a fraction that is equivalent to $\frac{1}{3}$.

4. Penelope bakes pretzels. She salts $\frac{3}{8}$ of the pretzels. Write a fraction that is equivalent to $\frac{3}{8}$.

_____

_____

5. What decimal is shown by the shaded area in the model?

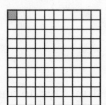

6. Mr. Guzman has 100 cows on his dairy farm. Of the cows, 57 are Holstein. What decimal represents the portion of cows that are Holstein?

_____

_____

© Houghton Mifflin Harcourt Publishing Company

FOR MORE PRACTICE GO TO THE
Personal Math Trainer

Problem Solving • Money

Essential Question How can you use the strategy *act it out* to solve problems that use money?

 Common Core **Measurement and Data—4.MD.A.2**
MATHEMATICAL PRACTICES
MP1, MP2, MP6

Unlock the Problem Real World

Together, Marnie and Serena have $1.20. They want to share the money equally. How much money will each girl get?

Use the graphic organizer to solve the problem.

Read the Problem	Solve the Problem
What do I need to find? I need to find the _____ _____	You can make $1.20 with 4 quarters and 2 _____. Circle the coins to show two sets with equal value.
What information do I need to use? I need to use the total amount, _____, and divide the amount into _____ equal parts.	
How will I use the information? I will use coins to model the _____ and act out the problem.	So, each girl gets _____ quarters and _____ dime. Each girl gets $_____.

- Describe another way you could act out the problem with coins.

_____

_____

🔑 Try Another Problem

Josh, Tom, and Chuck each have $0.40. How much money do they have together?

Read the Problem	Solve the Problem
What do I need to find?	
What information do I need to use?	
How will I use the information?	

• How can you solve the problem using dimes and nickels?

_____

_____

Math Talk

MATHEMATICAL PRACTICES ①

Describe What other strategy might you use to solve the problem? Explain.

Name _____

Unlock the Problem

√ Circle the question.
√ Underline the important facts.
√ Cross out unneeded information.

1. Juan has $3.43. He is buying a paint brush that costs $1.21 to paint a model race car. How much will Juan have after he pays for the paint brush?

   First, use bills and coins to model $3.43.

WRITE ▸ Math
Show Your Work

   Next, you need to subtract. Remove bills and coins that have a value of $1.21. Mark Xs to show what you remove.

   Last, count the value of the bills and coins that are left. How much will Juan have left?

   _____

2. What if Juan has $3.43, and he wants to buy a paint brush that costs $2.28? How much money will Juan have left then? Explain.

   _____

   _____

   _____

   _____

3. Sophia has $2.25. She wants to give an equal amount to each of her 3 young cousins. How much will each cousin receive?

   _____

On Your Own

4. Marcus saves $13 each week. In how many weeks will he have saved at least $100?

_____

5. **MATHEMATICAL PRACTICE 1** **Analyze Relationships** Hoshi has $50. Emily has $23 more than Hoshi. Karl has $16 less than Emily. How much money do they have all together?

_____

6. **THINK SMARTER** Four girls have $5.00 to share equally. How much money will each girl get? Explain.

_____

_____

_____

WRITE ▸ Math
Show Your Work

7. **Go DEEPER** What if four girls want to share $5.52 equally? How much money will each girl get? Explain.

_____

_____

_____

Personal Math Trainer

8. **THINK SMARTER +** Aimee and three of her friends have three quarters and one nickel. If Aimee and her friends share the money equally, how much will each person get? Explain how you found your answer.

Problem Solving • Money

 COMMON CORE STANDARD—4.MD.A.2
*Solve problems involving measurement and
conversion of measurements from a larger unit to
a smaller unit.*

Use the *act it out* strategy to solve.

1. Carl wants to buy a bicycle bell that costs $4.50.
   Carl has saved $2.75 so far. How much more
   money does he need to buy the bell?

   Use 4 $1 bills and 2 quarters to model $4.50.
   Remove bills and coins that have a value of $2.75.
   First, remove 2 $1 bills and 2 quarters.

   Next, exchange one $1 bill for 4 quarters and
   remove 1 quarter.

   Count the amount that is left.
   So, Carl needs to save $1.75 more.

   _____ $1.75

2. Together, Xavier, Yolanda, and Zachary have
   $4.44. If each person has the same amount, how
   much money does each person have?

   _____

3. Marcus, Nan, and Olive each have $1.65 in their
   pockets. They decide to combine the money. How
   much money do they have altogether?

   _____

4. Jessie saves $6 each week. In how many weeks
   will she have saved at least $50?

   _____

5. **WRITE** ▸ *Math* Write a money problem you can solve
   using sharing, joining, or separating.

   _____

   _____

Lesson Check (4.MD.A.2)

1. Four friends earned $5.20 for washing a car. They shared the money equally. How much did each friend get?

2. Write a decimal that represents the value of one $1 bill and 5 quarters.

Spiral Review (4.OA.B.4, 4.NF.A.1, 4.NF.A.2, 4.NF.C.6)

3. Bethany has 9 pennies. What fraction of a dollar is this?

4. Michael made $\frac{9}{12}$ of his free throws at practice. What is $\frac{9}{12}$ in simplest form?

5. I am a prime number between 30 and 40. What number could I be?

6. Fill in the blank with a symbol that makes this statement true:

$$\frac{2}{5} \bigcirc \frac{1}{2}$$

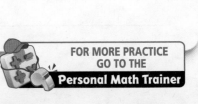

FOR MORE PRACTICE
GO TO THE
Personal Math Trainer

Name _____

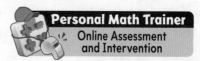

Vocabulary

Choose the best term from the box to complete the sentence.

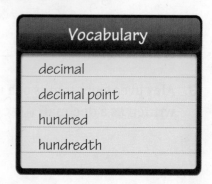

Vocabulary
decimal
decimal point
hundred
hundredth

1. A symbol used to separate the ones and the tenths place is

   called a _____. (p. 495)

2. The number 0.4 is written as a _____. (p. 495)

3. A _____ is one of one hundred equal parts of a
   whole. (p. 501)

Concepts and Skills

Write the fraction or mixed number and the decimal shown
by the model. (4.NF.C.6)

4.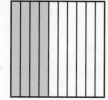

   _____   _____

5.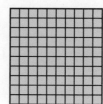

   _____   _____

Write the number as hundredths in fraction form
and decimal form. (4.NF.C.5)

6. $\frac{8}{10}$

7. 0.5

8. $\frac{6}{10}$

   _____   _____   _____

Write the fraction or mixed number as a money amount,
and as a decimal in terms of dollars. (4.NF.C.6)

9. $\frac{65}{100}$

10. $1\frac{48}{100}$

11. $\frac{4}{100}$

   _____   _____   _____

12. Ken's turtle competed in a 0.50-meter race. His turtle had traveled $\frac{49}{100}$ meter when the winning turtle crossed the finish line. What is $\frac{49}{100}$ written as a decimal? (4.NF.C.6)

_____

13. Alex lives eight tenths of a mile from Sarah. What is eight tenths written as a decimal? (4.NF.C.6)

_____

14. **GO DEEPER** What fraction and decimal, in hundredths, is equivalent to $\frac{7}{10}$? (4.NF.C.5)

_____

15. Elaine found the following in her pocket. How much money was in her pocket? (4.NF.C.6)

_____

16. Three girls share $0.60. Each girl gets the same amount. How much money does each girl get? (4.MD.A.2)

_____

17. The deli scale weighs meat and cheese in hundredths of a pound. Sam put $\frac{5}{10}$ pound of pepperoni on the deli scale. What weight does the deli scale show? (4.NF.C.5)

_____

Add Fractional Parts of 10 and 100

Essential Question How can you add fractions when the denominators are 10 or 100?

 Common Core Number and Operations— Fractions—4.NF.C.5 *Also* 4.MD.A.2
MATHEMATICAL PRACTICES
MP2, MP7, MP8

🔑 Unlock the Problem (Real World)

The fourth grade classes are painting designs on tile squares to make a mural. Mrs. Kirk's class painted $\frac{3}{10}$ of the mural. Mr. Becker's class painted $\frac{21}{100}$ of the mural. What part of the mural is painted?

You know how to add fractions with parts that are the same size. You can use equivalent fractions to add fractions with parts that are not the same size.

🔒 Example 1 Find $\frac{3}{10} + \frac{21}{100}$.

STEP 1 Write $\frac{3}{10}$ and $\frac{21}{100}$ as a pair of fractions with a common denominator.

Think: 100 is a multiple of 10. Use 100 as the common denominator.

$$\frac{3}{10} = \frac{3 \times \boxed{}}{10 \times \boxed{}} = \frac{\boxed{}}{100}$$

Think: $\frac{21}{100}$ already has 100 in the denominator.

So, $\frac{\boxed{}}{100}$ of the mural is painted.

STEP 2 Add.

Think: Write $\frac{3}{10} + \frac{21}{100}$ using fractions with a common denominator.

$$\frac{30}{100} + \frac{21}{100} = \frac{\boxed{}}{100}$$

 Math Talk

MATHEMATICAL PRACTICES ⑧

Draw Conclusions When adding tenths and hundredths, can you always use 100 as a common denominator? Explain.

Try This! Find $\frac{4}{100} + \frac{1}{10}$.

A Write $\frac{1}{10}$ as $\frac{10}{100}$.

$$\frac{1}{10} = \frac{1 \times \boxed{}}{10 \times \boxed{}} = \frac{\boxed{}}{100}$$

B Add.

$$\frac{\boxed{}}{100} + \frac{10}{100} = \frac{\boxed{}}{100}$$

So, $\frac{4}{100} + \frac{10}{100} = \frac{14}{100}$

🔑 Example 2 Add decimals.

Sean lives 0.5 mile from the store. The store is 0.25 mile from his grandmother's house. Sean is going to walk to the store and then to his grandmother's house. How far will he walk?

Find 0.5 + 0.25.

STEP 1 Write 0.5 + 0.25 as a sum of fractions.

Think: 0.5 is 5 tenths.   Think: 0.25 is 25 hundredths.

$$0.5 = \underline{} \qquad\qquad 0.25 = \underline{}$$

Write 0.5 + 0.25 as $\underline{}$ + $\underline{}$

STEP 2 Write $\frac{5}{10} + \frac{25}{100}$ as a sum of fractions with a common denominator.

Think: Use 100 as a common denominator. Rename $\frac{5}{10}$.

$$\frac{5}{10} = \frac{5 \times }{10 \times } = \frac{}{100}$$

Write $\frac{5}{10} + \frac{25}{100}$ as $\underline{}$ + $\underline{}$.

STEP 3 Add.

$$\frac{50}{100} + \frac{25}{100} = \underline{}$$

STEP 4 Write the sum as a decimal.

$$\frac{75}{100} = \underline{}$$

So, Sean will walk _____ mile.

Math Talk

MATHEMATICAL PRACTICES ⑦

Identify Relationships
Explain why you can think of $0.25 as either $\frac{1}{4}$ dollar or $\frac{25}{100}$ dollar.

Try This! Find $0.25 + $0.40.

$0.25 + $0.40 = _____

Remember
A money amount less than a dollar can be written as a fraction of a dollar.

© Houghton Mifflin Harcourt Publishing Company

Name _____

1. Find $\frac{7}{10} + \frac{5}{100}$.

Think: Write the addends as fractions with a common denominator.

$$\frac{}{100} + \frac{}{100} = \frac{}{}$$

Find the sum.

2. $\frac{1}{10} + \frac{11}{100} =$ _____

3. $\frac{36}{100} + \frac{5}{10} =$ _____

4. $\$0.16 + \$0.45 = \$$ _____

5. $\$0.08 + \$0.88 = \$$ _____

On Your Own

6. $\frac{6}{10} + \frac{25}{100} =$ _____

7. $\frac{7}{10} + \frac{7}{100} =$ _____

8. $\$0.55 + \$0.23 = \$$ _____

9. $\$0.19 + \$0.13 = \$$ _____

MATHEMATICAL PRACTICE ② **Reason Quantitatively** **Algebra** Write the number that makes the equation true.

10. $\frac{20}{100} + \frac{}{10} = \frac{60}{100}$

11. $\frac{2}{10} + \frac{}{100} = \frac{90}{100}$

12. GO DEEPER Jerry had 1 gallon of ice cream. He used $\frac{3}{10}$ gallon to make chocolate milkshakes and 0.40 gallon to make vanilla milkshakes. How much ice cream does Jerry have left after making the milkshakes?

_____

Problem Solving • Applications Real World

Use the table for 13–16.

Paving Stone Center	
Style	**Length (in meters)**
Rustic	$\frac{15}{100}$
Teakwood	$\frac{3}{10}$
Buckskin	$\frac{41}{100}$
Rainbow	$\frac{6}{10}$
Rose	$\frac{8}{100}$

13. **THINK SMARTER** Dean selects Teakwood stones and Buckskin stones to pave a path in front of his house. How many meters long will each set of one Teakwood stone and one Buckskin stone be?

_____

14. The backyard patio at Nona's house is made from a repeating pattern of one Rose stone and one Rainbow stone. How many meters long is each pair of stones?

_____

15. **GO DEEPER** For a stone path, Emily likes the look of a Rustic stone, then a Rainbow stone, and then another Rustic stone. How long will the three stones in a row be? Explain.

_____

_____

16. **WRITE ▸ Math** Which two stones can you place end-to-end to get a length of 0.38 meter? Explain how you found your answer.

_____

_____

17. **THINK SMARTER** Christelle is making a dollhouse. The dollhouse is $\frac{6}{10}$ meter tall without the roof. The roof is $\frac{15}{100}$ meter high. What is the height of the dollhouse with the roof? Choose a number from each column to complete an equation to solve.

$$\frac{6}{10} + \frac{15}{100} = \boxed{\begin{array}{c} \frac{6}{100} \\ \frac{60}{100} \\ \frac{61}{100} \end{array}} + \boxed{\begin{array}{c} \frac{15}{10} \\ \frac{5}{100} \\ \frac{15}{100} \end{array}} = \boxed{\begin{array}{c} \frac{65}{100} \\ \frac{7}{10} \\ \frac{75}{100} \end{array}} \text{ meter.}$$

Add Fractional Parts of 10 and 100

Common Core

COMMON CORE STANDARD—4.NF.C.5
Understand decimal notation for fractions, and compare decimal fractions.

Find the sum.

1. $\frac{2}{10} + \frac{43}{100}$

   $\frac{20}{100} + \frac{43}{100} = \frac{63}{100}$

   $\frac{63}{100}$

Think: Write $\frac{2}{10}$ as a fraction with a denominator of 100:

$\frac{2 \times 10}{10 \times 10} = \frac{20}{100}$

2. $\frac{17}{100} + \frac{6}{10}$

3. $\frac{9}{100} + \frac{9}{10}$

4. $\$0.25 + \$0.34$

 Problem Solving Real World

5. Ned's frog jumped $\frac{38}{100}$ meter. Then his frog jumped $\frac{4}{10}$ meter. How far did Ned's frog jump?

6. Keiko walks $\frac{5}{10}$ kilometer from school to the park. Then she walks $\frac{19}{100}$ kilometer from the park to her home. How far does Keiko walk?

7. **WRITE** ▸ *Math* Explain how you would use equivalent fractions to solve $0.5 + 0.10$.

_____

_____

_____

Lesson Check (4.NF.C.5)

1. In a fish tank, $\frac{2}{10}$ of the fish were orange and $\frac{5}{100}$ of the fish were striped. What fraction of the fish were orange or striped?

2. Greg spends $0.45 on an eraser and $0.30 on a pen. How much money does Greg spend?

Spiral Review (4.NF.A.1, 4.NF.B.3d, 4.MD.A.2)

3. Phillip saves $8 each month. How many months will it take him to save at least $60?

4. Ursula and Yi share a submarine sandwich. Ursula eats $\frac{2}{8}$ of the sandwich. Yi eats $\frac{3}{8}$ of the sandwich. How much of the sandwich do the two friends eat?

5. A carpenter has a board that is 8 feet long. He cuts off two pieces. One piece is $3\frac{1}{2}$ feet long and the other is $2\frac{1}{3}$ feet long. How much of the board is left?

6. Jeff drinks $\frac{2}{3}$ of a glass of juice. Write a fraction that is equivalent to $\frac{2}{3}$.

FOR MORE PRACTICE
GO TO THE
Personal Math Trainer

Compare Decimals

Essential Question How can you compare decimals?

 Common Core Number and Operations—
Fractions—4.NF.C.7
MATHEMATICAL PRACTICES
MP2, MP6, MP7

🔑 Unlock the Problem (Real World)

The city park covers 0.64 square mile.
About 0.18 of the park is covered by water,
and about 0.2 of the park is covered by
paved walkways. Is more of the park covered by
water or paved walkways?

- Cross out unnecessary information.
- Circle numbers you will use.
- What do you need to find?

_____

_____

🔒 One Way Use a model.

Shade 0.18.   Shade 0.2.

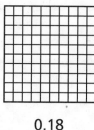   

0.18 ◯ 0.2

🔒 Other Ways

A Use a number line.

Locate 0.18 and 0.2 on a number line.

Think: 2 tenths is equivalent to 20 hundredths.

0.0   0.10   0.20   0.30   0.40   0.50

_____ is closer to 0, so 0.18 ◯ 0.2.

B Compare equal-size parts.

- 0.18 is _____ hundredths.

- 0.2 is 2 tenths, which is equivalent to _____ hundredths.

18 hundredths ◯ 20 hundredths, so 0.18 ◯ 0.2.

So, more of the park is covered by _____.

Math Talk

MATHEMATICAL PRACTICES ⑥

Compare How does the number
of tenths in 0.18 compare to the
number of tenths in 0.2? Explain.

Place Value You can compare numbers written as decimals by using place value. Comparing decimals is like comparing whole numbers. Always compare the digits in the greatest place-value position first.

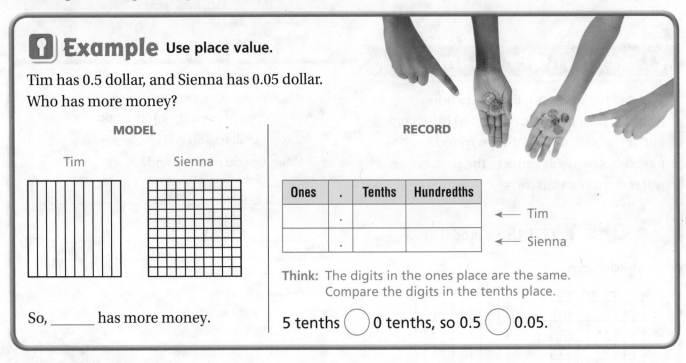

Example Use place value.

Tim has 0.5 dollar, and Sienna has 0.05 dollar. Who has more money?

MODEL

Tim   Sienna

So, _____ has more money.

RECORD

Ones	.	Tenths	Hundredths
	.			← Tim
	.			← Sienna

Think: The digits in the ones place are the same. Compare the digits in the tenths place.

5 tenths ◯ 0 tenths, so 0.5 ◯ 0.05.

- Compare the size of 1 tenth to the size of 1 hundredth. How could this help you compare 0.5 and 0.05? Explain.

_____

_____

_____

Try This! Compare 1.3 and 0.6. Write <, >, or =.

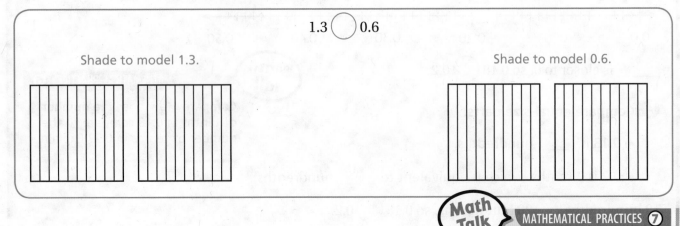

1.3 ◯ 0.6

Shade to model 1.3.

Shade to model 0.6.

Math Talk

MATHEMATICAL PRACTICES ⑦

Look for Structure How could you use place value to compare 1.3 and 0.6?

Name _____

1. Compare 0.39 and 0.42. Write <, >, or =.
   Shade the model to help.

   0.39 ◯ 0.42

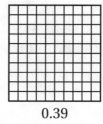

0.39

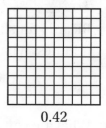

0.42

Compare. Write <, >, or =.

2. 0.26 ◯ 0.23

Ones	.	Tenths	Hundredths
	.		
	.		

3. 0.7 ◯ 0.54

Ones	.	Tenths	Hundredths
	.		
	.		

4. 1.15 ◯ 1.3

Ones	.	Tenths	Hundredths
	.		
	.		

5. 4.5 ◯ 2.89

Ones	.	Tenths	Hundredths
	.		
	.		

Math Talk

MATHEMATICAL PRACTICES ②

Reason Abstractly Can you compare 0.39 and 0.42 by comparing only the tenths? Explain.

On Your Own

Compare. Write <, >, or =.

6. 0.9 ◯ 0.81

7. 1.06 ◯ 0.6

8. 0.25 ◯ 0.3

9. 2.61 ◯ 3.29

MATHEMATICAL PRACTICE ② **Reason Quantitatively** **Compare. Write <, >, or =.**

10. 0.30 ◯ $\frac{3}{10}$

11. $\frac{4}{100}$ ◯ 0.2

12. 0.15 ◯ $\frac{1}{10}$

13. $\frac{1}{8}$ ◯ 0.8

14. **GO DEEPER** Robert had $14.53 in his pocket. Ivan had $14.25 in his pocket. Matt had $14.40 in his pocket. Who had more money, Robert or Matt? Did Ivan have more money than either Robert or Matt?

Unlock the Problem

15. **THINK SMARTER** Ricardo and Brandon ran a 1500-meter race. Ricardo finished in 4.89 minutes. Brandon finished in 4.83 minutes. What was the time of the runner who finished first?

a. What are you asked to find? _____

b. What do you need to do to find the answer? _____

_____

c. Solve the problem.

d. What was the time of the runner who finished first?

_____

e. Look back. Does your answer make sense? Explain.

_____

_____

_____

_____

16. **GO DEEPER** The Venus flytrap closes in 0.3 second and the waterwheel plant closes in 0.2 second. What decimal is halfway between 0.2 and 0.3? Explain.

_____

_____

_____

_____

17. **THINK SMARTER +** For numbers 17a–17c, compare then select True or False.

17a. 0.5 > 0.53   ○ True   ○ False

17b. 0.35 < 0.37   ○ True   ○ False

17c. $1.35 > $0.35   ○ True   ○ False

Compare Decimals

Common Core

COMMON CORE STANDARDS—4.NF.C.7
Understand decimal notation for fractions, and compare decimal fractions.

Compare. Write <, >, or =.

1. 0.35 $\left(<\right)$ 0.53

Think: 3 tenths is less
than 5 tenths.
So, 0.35 < 0.53

2. 0.6 $\bigcirc$ 0.60

3. 0.24 $\bigcirc$ 0.31

4. 0.94 $\bigcirc$ 0.9

5. 0.3 $\bigcirc$ 0.32

6. 0.45 $\bigcirc$ 0.28

7. 0.39 $\bigcirc$ 0.93

Use the number line to compare. Write *true* or *false*.

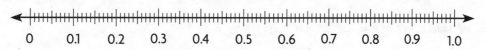

```
←|++++++|++++++|++++++|++++++|++++++|++++++|++++++|++++++|++++++|++++++|→
  0    0.1   0.2   0.3   0.4   0.5   0.6   0.7   0.8   0.9   1.0
```

8. 0.8 > 0.78

_____

9. 0.4 > 0.84

_____

10. 0.7 < 0.70

_____

11. 0.4 > 0.04

_____

Compare. Write *true* or *false*.

12. 0.09 > 0.1

_____

13. 0.24 = 0.42

_____

14. 0.17 < 0.32

_____

15. 0.85 > 0.82

_____

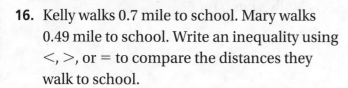

16. Kelly walks 0.7 mile to school. Mary walks 0.49 mile to school. Write an inequality using <, >, or = to compare the distances they walk to school.

_____

17. **WRITE** ▸*Math* Show or describe two different ways to complete the comparison using <, >, or =: 0.26 $\bigcirc$ 0.4.

_____

_____

_____

Lesson Check (4.NF.C.7)

1. Bob, Cal, and Pete each made a stack of baseball cards. Bob's stack was 0.2 meter high. Cal's stack was 0.24 meter high. Pete's stack was 0.18 meter high. Write a number sentence that compares Cal's stack of cards to Pete's stack of cards.

2. Three classmates spent money at the school supplies store. Mark spent 0.5 dollar, Andre spent 0.45 dollar, and Raquel spent 0.52 dollar. Write a number sentence that compares the money Andre spent to the money that Mark spent.

Spiral Review (4.NF.B.3c, 4.NF.B.4c, 4.NF.C.5, 4.NF.C.6)

3. Pedro has $0.35 in his pocket. Alice has $0.40 in her pocket. How much money do Pedro and Alice have altogether?

4. The measure 62 centimeters is equivalent to $\frac{62}{100}$ meter. What is this measure written as a decimal?

5. Joel has 24 sports trophies. Of the trophies, $\frac{1}{8}$ are soccer trophies. How many soccer trophies does Joel have?

6. Molly's jump rope is $6\frac{1}{3}$ feet long. Gail's jump rope is $4\frac{2}{3}$ feet long. How much longer is Molly's jump rope?

FOR MORE PRACTICE
GO TO THE
Personal Math Trainer

✓ Chapter 9 Review/Test

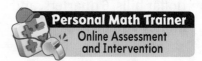

Personal Math Trainer
Online Assessment
and Intervention

1. Select a number shown by the model. Mark all that apply.

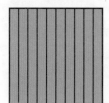 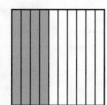 $\frac{14}{10}$ $\frac{40}{10}$ 1.4

   $1\frac{4}{10}$ 14   4.1

2. Rick has one dollar and twenty-seven cents to buy a notebook. Which names this money amount in terms of dollars? Mark all that apply.

   Ⓐ 12.7   Ⓓ 1.27

   Ⓑ 1.027   Ⓔ $1\frac{27}{100}$

   Ⓒ $1.27   Ⓕ $\frac{127}{10}$

3. For numbers 3a–3e, select True or False for the statement.

   3a. 0.9 is equivalent to 0.90.   ○ True   ○ False

   3b. 0.20 is equivalent to $\frac{2}{100}$.   ○ True   ○ False

   3c. $\frac{80}{100}$ is equivalent to $\frac{8}{10}$.   ○ True   ○ False

   3d. $\frac{6}{10}$ is equivalent to 0.60.   ○ True   ○ False

   3e. 0.3 is equivalent to $\frac{3}{100}$.   ○ True   ○ False

GO DIGITAL **Assessment Options**
Chapter Test

4. After selling some old books and toys, Gwen and her brother Max had 5 one-dollar bills, 6 quarters, and 8 dimes. They agreed to divide the money equally.

Part A

What is the total amount of money that Gwen and Max earned? Explain.

Part B

Max said that he and Gwen cannot get equal amounts of money because 5 one-dollar bills cannot be divided evenly. Do you agree with Max? Explain.

5. Harrison rode his bike $\frac{6}{10}$ of a mile to the park. Shade the model. Then write the decimal to show how far Harrison rode his bike.

Harrison rode his bike _____ mile to the park.

6. Amaldo spent $\frac{88}{100}$ of a dollar on a souvenir pencil from Zion National Park in Utah. What is $\frac{88}{100}$ written as a decimal in terms of dollars?

7. Tran has $5.82. He is saving for a video game that costs $8.95.

Tran needs _____ more to have enough money for the game.

Name _____

8. Cheyenne lives $\frac{7}{10}$ mile from school. A fraction in hundredths equal to $\frac{7}{10}$ is _____.

9. Write a decimal in tenths that is **less** than 2.42 but **greater** than 2.0.

_____

10. GO DEEPER Kylee and two of her friends are at a museum. They find two quarters and one dime on the ground.

Part A

If Kylee and her friends share the money equally, how much will each person get? Explain how you found your answer.

Part B

Kylee says that each person will receive $\frac{2}{10}$ of the money that was found. Do you agree? Explain.

11. Shade the model to show $1\frac{52}{100}$. Then write the mixed number in decimal form.

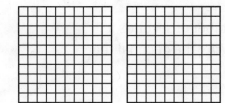

12. Henry is making a recipe for biscuits. A recipe calls for $\frac{5}{10}$ kilogram flour and $\frac{9}{100}$ kilogram sugar.

   Part A

   If Henry measures correctly and combines the two amounts, how much flour and sugar will he have? Show your work.

   Part B

   How can you write your answer as a decimal?

13. An orchestra has 100 musicians. $\frac{40}{100}$ of them play string instruments—violin, viola, cello, double bass, guitar, lute, and harp. What decimal is equivalent to $\frac{40}{100}$?

14. Complete the table.

$ Bills and Coins	Money Amount	Fraction or Mixed Number	Decimal
8 pennies		$\frac{8}{100}$	0.08
	$0.50		0.50
		$\frac{90}{100}$ or $\frac{9}{10}$	0.90
4 $1 bills 5 pennies			4.05

15. The point on the number line shows the number of seconds it took an athlete to run the forty-yard dash. Write the decimal that correctly names the point.

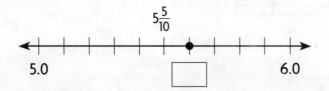

$5\frac{5}{10}$

5.0   6.0

16. Ingrid is making a toy car. The toy car is $\frac{5}{10}$ meter high without the roof. The roof is $\frac{18}{100}$ meter high. What is the height of the toy car with the roof? Choose a number from each column to complete an equation to solve.

$$\frac{5}{10} + \frac{18}{100} = \boxed{\begin{array}{c}\frac{5}{100}\\[4pt]\frac{15}{100}\\[4pt]\frac{50}{100}\end{array}} + \boxed{\begin{array}{c}\frac{18}{100}\\[4pt]\frac{81}{100}\\[4pt]\frac{18}{10}\end{array}} = \boxed{\begin{array}{c}\frac{68}{10}\\[4pt]\frac{32}{100}\\[4pt]\frac{68}{100}\end{array}} \text{ meter high.}$$

17. Callie shaded the model to represent the questions she answered correctly on a test. What decimal represents the part of the model that is shaded?

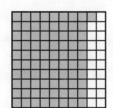

represents ☐

Personal Math Trainer

18. *THINK SMARTER +* For numbers 18a–18f, compare then select True or False.

18a. $0.21 < 0.27$ ○ True ○ False

18b. $0.4 > 0.45$ ○ True ○ False

18c. $\$3.21 > \$0.2$ ○ True ○ False

18d. $1.9 < 1.90$ ○ True ○ False

18e. $0.41 = 0.14$ ○ True ○ False

18f. $6.2 > 6.02$ ○ True ○ False

19. Fill in the numbers to find the sum.

$$\frac{4}{10} + \frac{\boxed{}}{100} = \frac{8}{\boxed{}}$$

20. Steve is measuring the growth of a tree. He drew this model to show the tree's growth in meters. Which fraction, mixed number, or decimal does the model show? Mark all that apply.

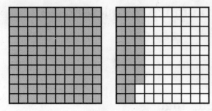

(A) 1.28

(B) 12.8

(C) 0.28

(D) $2\frac{8}{100}$

(E) $1\frac{28}{100}$

(F) $1\frac{28}{10}$

21. Luke lives 0.4 kilometer from a skating rink. Mark lives 0.25 kilometer from the skating rink.

Part A

Who lives closer to the skating rink? Explain.

Part B

How can you write each distance as a fraction? Explain.

Part C

Luke is walking to the skating rink to pick up a practice schedule. Then he is walking to Mark's house. Will he walk more than a kilometer or less than a kilometer? Explain.

Geometry, Measurement, and Data

 Common Core

CRITICAL AREA Understanding that geometric figures can be analyzed and classified based on their properties, such as having parallel sides, perpendicular sides, particular angle measures, and symmetry

Landscape architects can help design and plan outdoor spaces such as botanical gardens.

Landscape Architects

When people who live and work in big cities take breaks, they leave their tall buildings to relax in patches of green. A city garden may be small, but it gives people a chance to enjoy the beauty of nature.

Get Started

Design a garden that covers a whole city block. Decide on features to have in your garden and where they will be located. Mark off parts of your garden for each feature. Then find the number of square units the feature covers and record it on the design. Use the Important Facts to help you.

Important Facts
Features of a City Garden

 Benches   Snack bar

 Flower garden   Spring bulb garden

 Paths   Tree garden

 Shrub garden   Waterfall and fountain

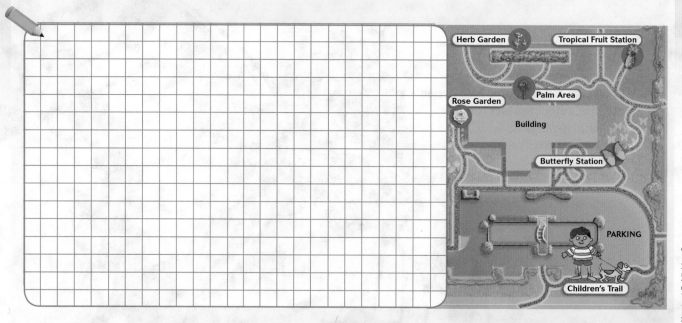

▲ This map is an example of how a city garden could be laid out.

Completed by _____

Two-Dimensional Figures

✓ Show What You Know

Check your understanding of important skills.

Name _____

▶ **Sides and Vertices** **Write the number of vertices.** (2.G.A.1)

1.
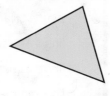

_____ vertices

2.

_____ vertices

3.

_____ vertices

▶ **Number of Sides** **Write the number of sides.** (2.G.A.1)

4.

_____ sides

5.

_____ sides

6.

_____ sides

▶ **Geometric Patterns** **Draw the next two shapes in the pattern.** (4.OA.C.5)

7.

The Isle of Wight Natural History Centre, off the coast of England, has shells of every size, shape, and color. Many shells have symmetry. Investigate this shell. Describe its shape in geometric terms. Then determine whether this shell has line symmetry.

Vocabulary Builder

▶ **Visualize It** ••

Complete the flow map by using the words with a ✓.

Geometry

What is it?   **What are some examples?**

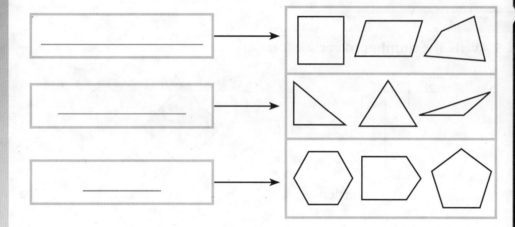

▶ **Understand Vocabulary** •••••••••••••••••••••••••

Complete the sentences by using preview words.

1. A shape has _____ if it can be folded about a line so that its two parts match exactly.

2. A figure that has no endpoints is called a _____.

3. A figure that has two endpoints is called a _____.

4. _____ are lines that never cross.

5. When two lines cross to form a square corner, the lines are _____.

• **Interactive Student Edition**
• **Multimedia eGlossary**

Chapter 10 Vocabulary

acute angle

ángulo agudo

1

intersecting lines

líneas secantes

42

line

línea

45

line of symmetry

eje de simetría

46

line segment

segmento

48

obtuse angle

ángulo obtuso

57

parallel lines

líneas paralelas

59

parallelogram

paralelogramo

60

Lines that cross each other at exactly one point

Example:

An angle that measures greater than 0° and less than 90°

Example:

An imaginary line on a shape about which the shape can be folded so that its two parts match exactly

Example:

line of symmetry →

A straight path of points in a plane that continues without end in both directions with no endpoints

Example:

S   T

An angle that measures greater than 90° and less than 180°

Example:

A part of a line that includes two points called endpoints and all the points between them

Example:

A   B

A quadrilateral whose opposite sides are parallel and of equal length

Example:

Lines in the same plane that never intersect and are always the same distance apart

Example:

perpendicular lines

líneas perpendiculares

66

point

punto

69

rectangle

rectángulo

77

rhombus

rombo

80

right angle

ángulo recto

81

square

cuadrado

85

straight angle

ángulo llano

88

trapezoid

trapecio

93

An exact location in space

Example: A •

Two lines that intersect to form four right angles

Example:

A quadrilateral with two pairs of parallel sides and four sides of equal length

Example:

A quadrilateral with two pairs of parallel sides, two pairs of sides of equal length, and four right angles

Example:

A quadrilateral with two pairs of parallel sides, four sides of equal length, and four right angles

Example:

An angle that forms a square corner

Example:

A quadrilateral with at least one pair of parallel sides

Examples:

An angle whose measure is 180°

Example:

X Y Z

Going to a Botanical Garden

Word Box

acute angle
intersecting lines
line
line of symmetry
line segment
obtuse angle
parallel lines
parallelogram
perpendicular
  lines
point
rectangle
rhombus
right angle
square
straight angle
trapezoid

For 2 players

Materials

- 1 red playing piece
- 1 blue playing piece
- 1 number cube

How to Play

1. Each player chooses a playing piece and puts it on START.

2. Toss the number cube to take a turn. Move your playing piece that many spaces.

3. If you land on these spaces:

   White Space Tell the meaning of the math term or use it in a sentence. If your answer is correct, jump to the next space with the same term.

   Green Space Follow the directions printed in the space. If there are no directions, stay where you are.

4. The first player to reach FINISH by exact count wins.

Game

HOW TO PLAY

1. Put your playing piece on START.
2. Toss the number cube and move your playing piece that many spaces.
3. If you land on one of these spaces:

White Space—Explain the math word or use it in a sentence. If your answer is correct, jump ahead to the next space with that word.

Green Space—Follow the directions in the space. If there are no directions, don't move.

4. The first player to reach FINISH by exact count wins.

MATERIALS

- 1 red playing piece
- 1 blue playing piece
- 1 number cube

548B

line segment | line of symmetry | square | rectangle | rhombus

parallel lines | perpendicular lines |  | trapezoid | parallelogram

square | rectangle | rhombus | parallelogram | trapezoid

acute angle | obtuse angle | intersecting lines | parallel lines | perpendicular lines

parallelogram | trapezoid | | perpendicular lines | parallel lines

straight angle | acute angle | obtuse angle | intersecting lines

548C

The Write Way

Reflect

Choose one idea. Write about it.

- Summarize how you can tell if two lines are intersecting, parallel, or perpendicular.

- Write the names of as many quadrilaterals that you can think of in three minutes.

- Explain what a *line of symmetry* is so that a child will understand the idea.

Name _____

Lines, Rays, and Angles

Essential Question How can you identify and draw points, lines, line segments, rays, and angles?

 **Common Core** Geometry—
4.G.A.1
MATHEMATICAL PRACTICES
MP4, MP6

🔑 Unlock the Problem

Everyday things can model geometric figures. For example, the period at the end of this sentence models a point. A solid painted stripe in the middle of a straight road models a line.

Term and Definition	Draw It	Read It	Write It	Example
A **point** is an exact location in space.	A •	point A	point A	
A **line** is a straight path of points that continues without end in both directions.	B ◄————————► C	line BC line CB	$\overleftrightarrow{BC}$ $\overleftrightarrow{CB}$	
A **line segment** is part of a line between two endpoints.	D •————————• E	line segment DE line segment ED	$\overline{DE}$ $\overline{ED}$	YIELD
A **ray** is a part of a line that has one endpoint and continues without end in one direction.	F •————————► G	ray FG	$\overrightarrow{FG}$	ONE WAY →

🔑 Activity 1 Draw and label $\overline{JK}$.

_____

 Math Talk

MATHEMATICAL PRACTICES ❻

Compare Explain how lines, line segments, and rays are related.

• Is there another way to name $\overline{JK}$? Explain.

_____

_____

Angles

Term and Definition	Draw It	Read It	Write It	Example
An **angle** is formed by two rays or line segments that have the same endpoint. The shared endpoint is called the vertex.	P, Q, R	angle PQR angle RQP angle Q	∠PQR ∠RQP ∠Q	

You can name an angle by the vertex. When you name an angle using 3 points, the vertex is always the point in the middle.

Angles are classified by the size of the opening between the rays.

A **right angle** forms a square corner.	A **straight angle** forms a line.	An **acute angle** is less than a right angle.	An **obtuse angle** is greater than a right angle and less than a straight angle.

🔓 Activity 2 Classify an angle.

Materials ■ paper

To classify an angle, you can compare it to a right angle.

Make a right angle by using a sheet of paper. Fold the paper twice evenly to model a right angle. Use the right angle to classify the angles below.
Write *acute*, *obtuse*, *right*, or *straight*.

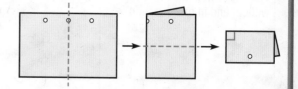

a.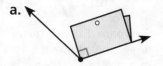
b.
c.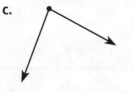
d.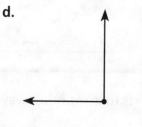

_____ _____ _____ _____

Share and Show

1. Draw and label $\overline{AB}$ in the space at the right.

   $\overline{AB}$ is a _____ .

Draw and label an example of the figure.

2. $\overleftrightarrow{XY}$

✓ 3. obtuse $\angle K$

4. right $\angle CDE$

Use Figure *M* for 5 and 6.

5. Name a line segment.

✓ 6. Name a right angle.

Figure M

On Your Own

Draw and label an example of the figure.

7. $\overrightarrow{PQ}$

8. acute $\angle RST$

9. straight $\angle WXZ$

Use Figure *F* for 10–15.

10. Name a ray.

11. Name an obtuse angle.

12. Name a line.

13. Name a line segment.

14. Name a right angle.

15. Name an acute angle.

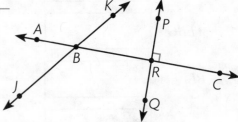

Figure F

Problem Solving · Applications

Use the picture of the bridge for 16 and 17.

16. Classify ∠A.

_____

17. 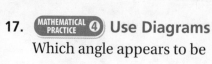 **Use Diagrams**

Which angle appears to be

obtuse? _____

18. **THINK SMARTER** How many different angles are in Figure X?
List them.

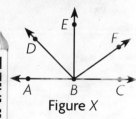

_____

_____

Figure X

19. **GO DEEPER** Vanessa drew the angle at the right and named it
∠TRS. Explain why Vanessa's name for the angle is incorrect.
Write a correct name for the angle.

_____

_____

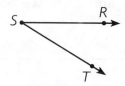

20. **THINK SMARTER** Write the word that describes
the part of Figure A.

| ray | line | line segment |

| acute angle | right angle |

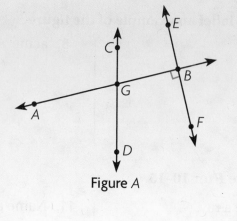

Figure A

$\overline{BG}$ [   ]

$\overleftrightarrow{CD}$ [   ]

∠FBG [   ]

$\overrightarrow{BE}$ [   ]

∠AGD [   ]

Lines, Rays, and Angles

Common
Core

COMMON CORE STANDARD—4.G.A.1
*Draw and identify lines and angles, and classify
shapes by properties of their lines and angles.*

Draw and label an example of the figure.

1. obtuse ∠ABC

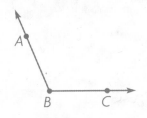

Think: An obtuse angle is greater than
a right angle. The middle letter, B, names
the vertex of the angle.

2. $\overrightarrow{GH}$

3. acute ∠JKL

4. $\overline{BC}$

Use the figure for 5–6.

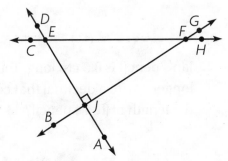

5. Name a line segment.

6. Name a right angle.

_____   _____

Use the figure at the right for 7–9.

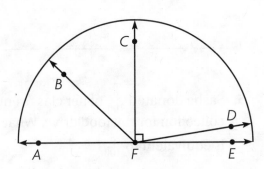

7. Classify ∠AFD. _____

8. Classify ∠CFE. _____

9. Name two acute angles.

_____

10. **WRITE** ►*Math* Draw and label a figure that has
4 points, 2 rays, and 1 right angle.

Lesson Check (4.G.A.1)

1. The hands of a clock show the time 12:25.

What kind of angle exists between the hands of the clock?

2. Use letters and symbols to name the figure shown below.

_____

Spiral Review (4.NF.B.3c, 4.NF.C.6, 4.NF.C.7, 4.MD.A.2)

3. Jan's pencil is 8.5 cm long. Ted's pencil is longer. Write a decimal that could represent the length of Ted's pencil?

4. Kayla buys a shirt for $8.19. She pays with a $10 bill. How much change should she receive?

_____

5. Sasha donated $\frac{9}{100}$ of her class's entire can collection for the food drive. What decimal is equivalent to $\frac{9}{100}$?

6. Jose jumped $8\frac{1}{3}$ feet. This was $2\frac{2}{3}$ feet farther than Lila jumped. How far did Lila jump?

FOR MORE PRACTICE
GO TO THE
Personal Math Trainer

Name _____

Classify Triangles by Angles

Essential Question How can you classify triangles by the size of their angles?

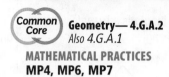

Common Core Geometry— 4.G.A.2
Also 4.G.A.1
MATHEMATICAL PRACTICES
MP4, MP6, MP7

🔑 Unlock the Problem

A triangle is a polygon with three sides and three angles. You can name a triangle by the vertices of its angles.

Triangle	Possible Names	
A B ⟍____⟍ C	△ABC	△ACB
	△BCA	△BAC
	△CAB	△CBA

Read Math

When you see "△ABC," say "triangle ABC."

An angle of a triangle can be right, acute, or obtuse.

🔓 Activity 1 Identify right, acute, and obtuse angles in triangles.

Materials ■ color pencils

Use the Triangle Color Guide to color the triangles below.

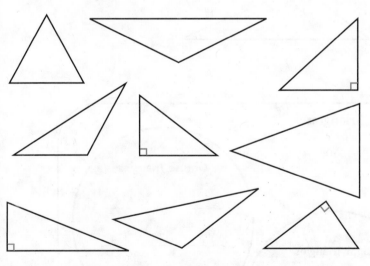

Triangle Color Guide	
RED	one right angle
BLUE	one obtuse angle
ORANGE	three acute angles

Math Talk

MATHEMATICAL PRACTICES ❼

Look for Structure Can a triangle have more than one obtuse angle? Explain.

Try This!

a. Name the triangle with one right angle. _____

b. Name the triangle with one obtuse angle. _____

c. Name the triangle with three acute angles. _____

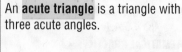

An **acute triangle** is a triangle with three acute angles.

An **obtuse triangle** is a triangle with one obtuse angle.

A **right triangle** is a triangle with one right angle.

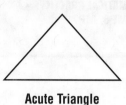

Acute Triangle

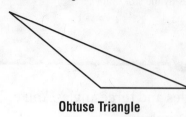

Obtuse Triangle

Right Triangle

Activity 2 Use a Venn diagram to classify triangles.

Write the names of the triangles in the Venn diagram.

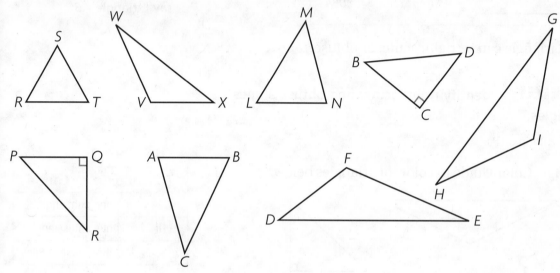

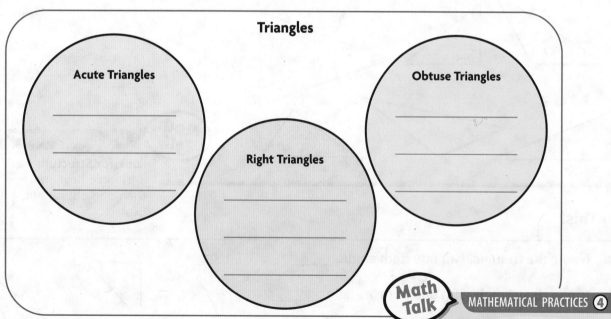

Triangles

Acute Triangles

_____

_____

_____

Right Triangles

_____

_____

_____

Obtuse Triangles

_____

_____

_____

Math Talk

MATHEMATICAL PRACTICES ④

Interpret a Result Explain why the three circles in this Venn diagram do not overlap.

Name _____

Share and Show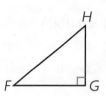

1. Name the triangle. Tell whether each angle is *acute*, *right*, or *obtuse*.

   A name for the triangle is _____.

   ∠F is _____.

   ∠G is _____.

   ∠H is _____.

Classify each triangle. Write *acute*, *right*, or *obtuse*.

2.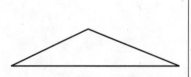

   _____

3.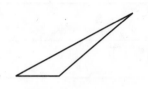

   _____

4.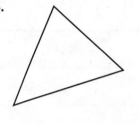

   _____

On Your Own

Classify each triangle. Write *acute*, *right*, or *obtuse*.

5.

   _____

6.

   _____

7.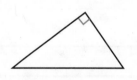

   _____

8. **THINK SMARTER** Cross out the figure that does not belong. Explain.

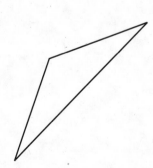 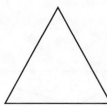 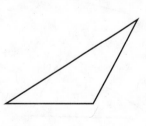 

_____

Problem Solving • Applications (Real World)

Use the Venn diagram for 9–10.

9. THINK SMARTER Which triangles do NOT have an obtuse angle? Explain.

_____

_____

10. MATHEMATICAL PRACTICE 6 How many triangles have *at least* two acute angles? **Explain.**

_____

_____

_____

_____

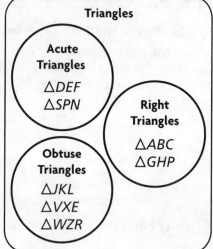

11. GO DEEPER Use the square shown at the right. Draw a line segment from point *M* to point *P*. Name and classify the triangles formed by the line segment.

_____

_____

_____

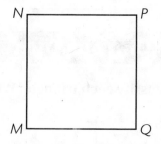

12. THINK SMARTER Write the letter of the triangle under its correct classification.

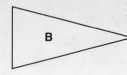

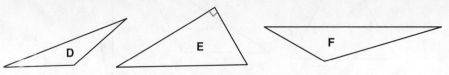

Acute Triangle	Obtuse Triangle	Right Triangle

Classify Triangles by Angles

COMMON CORE STANDARD—4.G.A.2
Draw and identify lines and angles and classify shapes by properties of their lines and angles.

Classify each triangle. Write *acute*, *right*, or *obtuse*.

1.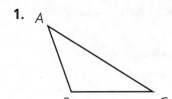

Think: Angles *A* and *C* are both acute.
Angle *B* is obtuse.

_____obtuse_____

2.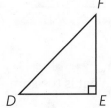

3.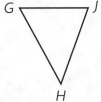

4.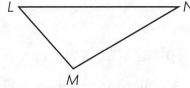

_____   _____   _____

Problem Solving

5. Use figure *ABCD* below. Draw a line segment from point *B* to point *D*. Name and classify the triangles formed.

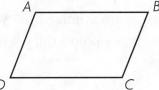

6. **WRITE** *Math* Draw and label an example of a right triangle, an acute triangle, and an obtuse triangle.

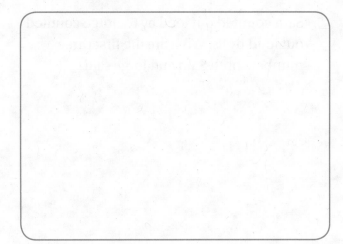

_____

_____

_____

Lesson Check (4.G.A.2)

1. Stephen drew this triangle. How many obtuse angles does the triangle have?

2. Joan was asked to draw a right triangle. How many right angles are in a right triangle?

Spiral Review (4.OA.B.4, 4.NBT.B.5, 4.NF.C.5, 4.G.A.1)

3. Oliver drew the figure below to show light traveling from the Sun to Earth. Name the figure he drew.

4. Armon added $\frac{1}{10}$ and $\frac{8}{100}$. What is the sum of these fractions?

5. Sam counted out loud by 6s. Jorge counted out loud by 8s. What are the first three numbers both Sam and Jorge said?

6. A basketball team averaged 105 points per game. How many points did the team score in 6 games?

FOR MORE PRACTICE
GO TO THE
Personal Math Trainer

Name _____

Parallel Lines and Perpendicular Lines

Essential Question How can you identify and draw parallel lines and perpendicular lines?

Common Core — Geometry—4.G.A.1
MATHEMATICAL PRACTICES
MP4, MP6, MP7

▲ Maglev trains use magnets to lift them above the tracks while moving.

Unlock the Problem

You can find models of lines in the world around you. For example, two streets that cross each other model intersecting lines. Metal rails on a train track that never cross model parallel lines.

Term and Definition	Draw It	Read It	Write It
Intersecting lines are lines in a plane that cross at exactly one point. Intersecting lines form four angles.	H, K, J, I, X	Line *HI* intersects line *JK* at point *X*.	$\overleftrightarrow{HI}$ and $\overleftrightarrow{JK}$ intersect at point *X*
Parallel lines are lines in a plane that are always the same distance apart. Parallel lines never intersect.	D, E, F, G	Line *DE* is parallel to line *FG*.	$\overleftrightarrow{DE} \parallel \overleftrightarrow{FG}$ The symbol ∥ means "is parallel to."
Perpendicular lines are lines in a plane that intersect to form four right angles.	N, L, M, O	Line *LM* is perpendicular to line *NO*.	$\overleftrightarrow{LM} \perp \overleftrightarrow{NO}$ The symbol ⊥ means "is perpendicular to."

Try This! Tell how the streets appear to be related. Write *perpendicular*, *parallel*, or *intersecting*.

- W 36th St and Broadway _____

- W 35th St and 7th Ave _____

- W 37th St and W 36th St _____

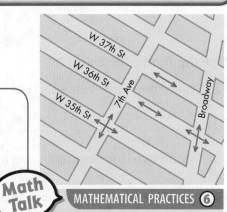

Math Talk

MATHEMATICAL PRACTICES ⑥

Use Math Vocabulary
Can two rays be parallel? Explain.

🔓 Activity Draw and label $\overrightarrow{YX} \perp \overrightarrow{YZ}$ intersecting at point Y.

Materials ■ straightedge

STEP 1: Draw and label $\overrightarrow{YX}$.

STEP 2: Then draw and label $\overrightarrow{YZ}$.

● How can you check if two rays are perpendicular?

STEP 3: Make sure $\overrightarrow{YX}$ and $\overrightarrow{YZ}$ intersect at point Y.

STEP 4: Make sure the rays are perpendicular.

1. Name the figure you drew.

_____

2. Can you classify the figure? Explain.

_____

_____

Share and Show MATH BOARD

1. Draw and label $\overline{QR} \parallel \overline{ST}$.

Think: Parallel lines never intersect. Parallel line segments are parts of parallel lines.

Use the figure for 2 and 3.

✔ **2.** Name two line segments that appear to be parallel.

_____

✔ **3.** Name two line segments that appear to be perpendicular.

_____

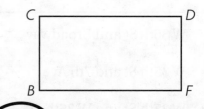

Math Talk

MATHEMATICAL PRACTICES ④

Use Symbols How could the symbols ⊥ and ∥ help you remember which relationships they describe?

Name _____

Use the figure for 4–5.

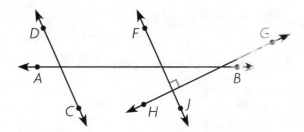

4. Name a pair of lines that are perpendicular.

    _____

5. Name a pair of lines that appear to be parallel.

    _____

Draw and label the figure described.

6. $\overline{RS} \parallel \overline{TU}$

7. $\overrightarrow{KL}$ and $\overrightarrow{KM}$

8. $\overline{CD} \perp \overline{DE}$

9. $\overleftrightarrow{JK} \perp \overleftrightarrow{LM}$

10. $\overleftrightarrow{ST}$ intersecting $\overleftrightarrow{UV}$ at point X

11. $\overleftrightarrow{AB} \parallel \overrightarrow{FG}$

Problem Solving • Applications (Real World)

Use the figure for 12–13.

12. **THINK SMARTER** Dan says that $\overleftrightarrow{HL}$ is parallel to $\overleftrightarrow{IM}$. Is Dan correct? Explain.

    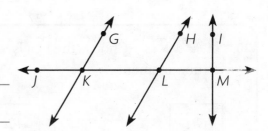

    _____

    _____

13. **GO DEEPER** Name two intersecting line segments that are not perpendicular.

    _____

Use the house plan at the right for 14–16.

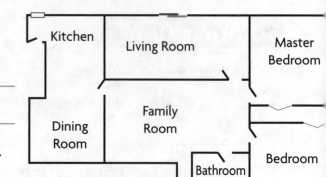

Kitchen · Living Room · Master Bedroom · Family Room · Dining Room · Bathroom · Bedroom

14. What geometric term describes a corner of the living room?

_____

_____

15. Name three parts of the plan that show line segments.

_____

_____

16. **THINK SMARTER** Name a pair of line segments that appear to be parallel.

_____

_____

Use the map at the right for 17–19.

17. Name a street that appears to be parallel to S 17th Street.

_____

_____

18. **MATHEMATICAL PRACTICE ④ Use Diagrams** Name a street that appears to be parallel to Vernon Street.

_____

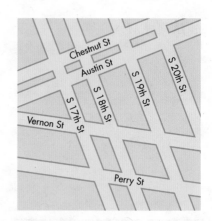

Chestnut St · Austin St · S 20th St · S 19th St · S 18th St · S 17th St · Vernon St · Perry St

19. Name a street that appears to be perpendicular to S 19th Street.

_____

20. **THINK SMARTER** Choose the labels to make a true statement.

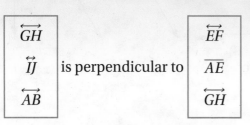

$$\overleftrightarrow{GH}$$
$$\overleftrightarrow{IJ}$$ is perpendicular to $$\overline{EF}$$
$$\overleftrightarrow{AB}$$ · $$\overline{AE}$$ · $$\overleftrightarrow{GH}$$

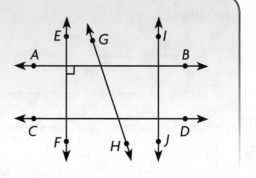

Name _____

Parallel Lines and Perpendicular Lines

COMMON CORE STANDARD—4.G.A.1
Draw and identify lines and angles, and classify shapes by properties of their lines and angles.

Use the figure for 1–2.

1. Name a pair of lines that appear to be perpendicular.

   Think: Perpendicular lines form right angles.
   $\overleftrightarrow{AB}$ and $\overleftrightarrow{EF}$ appear to form right angles.

   _____$\overleftrightarrow{AB}$ and $\overleftrightarrow{EF}$_____

2. Name a pair of lines that appear to be parallel.

   _____

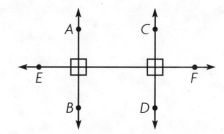

Draw and label the figure described.

3. $\overleftrightarrow{MN}$ and $\overleftrightarrow{PQ}$ intersecting at point R

4. $\overleftrightarrow{WX} \parallel \overleftrightarrow{YZ}$

5. $\overleftrightarrow{FH} \perp \overleftrightarrow{JK}$

Use the street map for 6–7.

6. Name two streets that intersect but do not appear to be perpendicular.

   _____

   _____

7. Name two streets that appear to be parallel to each other.

   _____

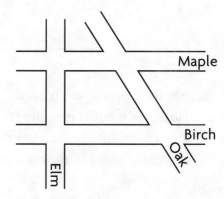

8. **WRITE** ▸*Math* Draw and label an example of two parallel lines that are perpendicular to a third line.

Lesson Check (4.G.A.1)

1. Write a capital letter that appears to have perpendicular line segments?

2. In the figure, which pair of line segments appear to be parallel?

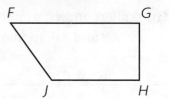

Spiral Review (4.NBT.B.5, 4.NBT.B.6 , 4.NF.A.2, 4.G.A.2)

3. Nolan drew a right triangle. How many acute angles did he draw?

4. Mike drank more than half the juice in his glass. What fraction of the juice could Mike have drunk?

5. A school principal ordered 1,000 pencils. He gave an equal number to each of 7 teachers until he had given out as many as possible. How many pencils were left?

6. A carton of juice contains 64 ounces. Ms. Wilson bought 6 cartons of juice. How many ounces of juice did she buy?

FOR MORE PRACTICE GO TO THE
Personal Math Trainer

Classify Quadrilaterals

Essential Question How can you sort and classify quadrilaterals?

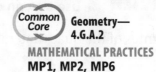

Geometry—
4.G.A.2

MATHEMATICAL PRACTICES
MP1, MP2, MP6

 Unlock the Problem Real World

A quadrilateral is a polygon with four sides and four angles. You can name a quadrilateral by the vertices of its angles.

Quadrilateral *ABCD* is a possible name for the figure shown at the right. Quadrilateral *ACBD* is not a possible name, since points *A* and *C* are not endpoints of the same side.

Assume that line segments that appear to be parallel are parallel.

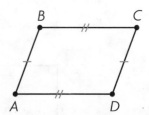

The tick marks on the line segments show that they have the same length. Sides *AD* and *BC* have the same length. Sides *AB* and *CD* have the same length.

Common Quadrilaterals

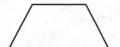

Trapezoid
- at least 1 pair of parallel sides

Parallelogram
- 2 pairs of parallel sides
- 2 pairs of sides of equal length

Rhombus
- 2 pairs of parallel sides
- 4 sides of equal length

Rectangle
- 2 pairs of parallel sides
- 2 pairs of sides of equal length
- 4 right angles

Square
- 2 pairs of parallel sides
- 4 sides of equal length
- 4 right angles

Activity 1 Identify right angles in quadrilaterals.

Materials ■ color pencils

Use the Quadrilateral Color Guide to color the quadrilaterals.

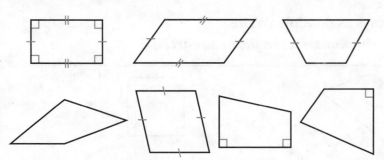

Quadrilateral Color Guide

RED:	exactly 4 right angles
BLUE:	exactly 2 right angles
ORANGE:	exactly 1 right angle

Math Talk · MATHEMATICAL PRACTICES ⑥

Can a quadrilateral have exactly 3 right angles? **Explain.**

🔑 Activity 2 Use a Venn diagram to sort quadrilaterals.

Write the names of the quadrilaterals in the Venn diagram.

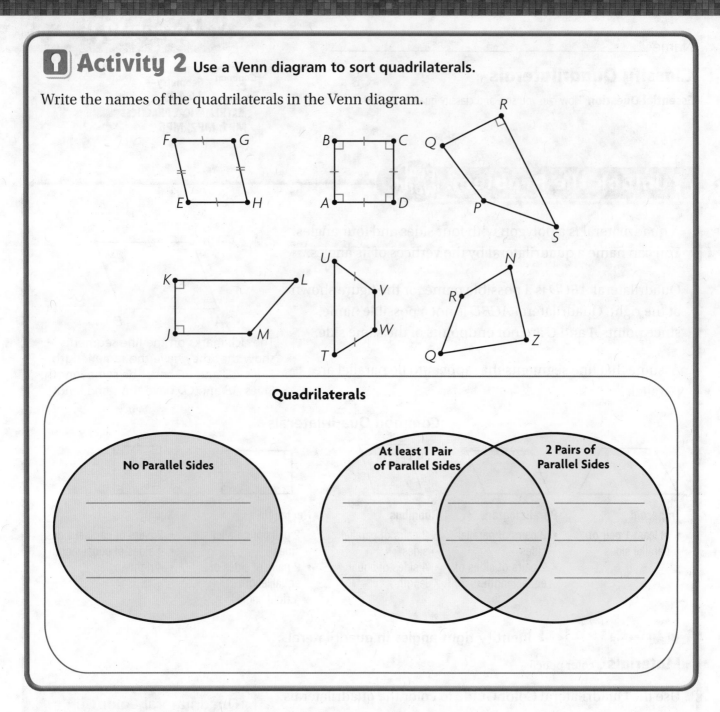

Quadrilaterals

No Parallel Sides

_____

_____

_____

At least 1 Pair of Parallel Sides

_____

_____

_____

2 Pairs of Parallel Sides

_____

_____

_____

Try This! Classify each figure as many ways as possible. Write *quadrilateral, trapezoid, parallelogram, rhombus, rectangle,* or *square.*

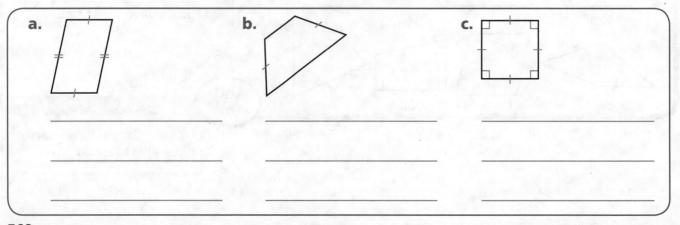

a.

_____

_____

b.

_____

_____

c.

_____

_____

Name _____

1. Tell whether the quadrilateral is also a trapezoid, parallelogram, rhombus, rectangle, or square.

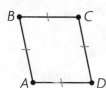

Think: _____ pairs of parallel sides

_____ sides of equal length

_____ right angles

Quadrilateral *ABCD* is also a _____

_____.

Classify each figure as many ways as possible. Write
quadrilateral, trapezoid, parallelogram, rhombus, rectangle, or *square.*

2.
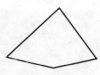

_____

_____

_____

3.

_____

_____

_____

4.

_____

_____

_____

Math Talk   MATHEMATICAL PRACTICES ②

Use Reasoning How would you classify a figure with 4 sides, none of which are parallel? Explain.

On Your Own

Classify each figure as many ways as possible.
Write *quadrilateral, trapezoid, parallelogram, rhombus, rectangle,* or *square.*

5.

_____

_____

6.

_____

_____

7.

_____

_____

Problem Solving • Applications Real World

8. **THINK SMARTER** Explain how a rhombus and square are alike, and how they are different.

_____

_____

_____

_____

_____

9. **THINK SMARTER** Classify the figure. Select all that apply.

- ○ quadrilateral
- ○ rectangle
- ○ trapezoid
- ○ rhombus
- ○ parallelogram
- ○ square

Connect to Art

The Louvre Museum is located in Paris, France. Architect I. M. Pei designed the glass and metal structure at the main entrance of the museum. This structure is called the Louvre Pyramid.

Below is a diagram of part of the entrance to the Louvre Pyramid.

10. **MATHEMATICAL PRACTICE ①** Describe the quadrilaterals you see in the diagram.

_____

_____

_____

_____

11. **GO DEEPER** How many triangles do you see in the diagram? Explain.

_____

_____

_____

_____

Name _____

Classify Quadrilaterals

Common Core

COMMON CORE STANDARD—4.G.A.2
Draw and identify lines and angles, and classify shapes by properties of their lines and angles.

Classify each figure as many ways as possible. Write
quadrilateral, trapezoid, parallelogram, rhombus, rectangle,
or square.

1.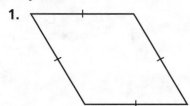

Think: 2 pairs of parallel sides
4 sides of equal length
0 right angles

quadrilateral, trapezoid, parallelogram, rhombus

2.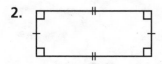

_____

_____

3.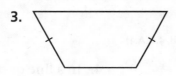

_____

_____

4.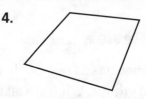

_____

_____

Problem Solving Real World

5. Alan drew a polygon with four sides and four angles. All four sides are equal. None of the angles are right angles. What figure did Alan draw?

_____

_____

6. Teresa drew a quadrilateral with 2 pairs of parallel sides and 4 right angles. What quadrilateral could she have drawn?

_____

_____

7. **WRITE** ▸*Math* Draw and label an example of each type of quadrilateral: trapezoid, parallelogram, rhombus, rectangle, and square.

Lesson Check (4.G.A.2)

1. Joey is asked to name a quadrilateral that is also a rhombus and has 2 pairs of parallel sides. What should be his answer?

2. What quadrilateral has at least one pair of parallel sides, but cannot be called a parallelogram?

Spiral Review (4.OA.B.4, 4.OA.C.5, 4.NF.B.3d, 4.G.A.1)

3. Terrence has 24 eggs to divide into equal groups. What are all the possible numbers of eggs that Terence could put in each group?

4. In a line of students, Jenna is number 8. The teacher says that a rule for a number pattern is *add 4*. The first student in line says the first term, 7. What number should Jenna say?

5. Lou eats $\frac{6}{8}$ of a pizza. What fraction of the pizza , in simplest form, is left over?

6. Name a capital letter that appears to have parallel lines.

FOR MORE PRACTICE
GO TO THE
Personal Math Trainer

 **Mid-Chapter Checkpoint**

Vocabulary

Choose the best term from the box to complete the sentence.

1. A _____ is part of a line between two endpoints. (p. 549)

2. A _____ forms a square corner. (p. 550)

3. An _____ is greater than a right angle and less than a straight angle. (p. 550)

4. The two-dimensional figure that has one endpoint is a

   _____. (p. 549)

5. An angle that forms a line is called a _____. (p. 550)

Concepts and Skills

6. On the grid to the right, draw a polygon that has 2 pairs of parallel sides, 2 pairs of sides equal in length, and 2 acute and 2 obtuse angles. Tell all the possible names for the figure. (4.G.A.2)

   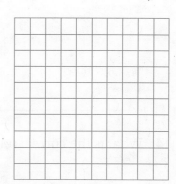

   _____

Draw the figure. (4.G.A.1)

7. parallel lines	8. obtuse $\angle ABC$	9. intersecting lines that are not perpendicular	10. acute $\angle RST$

11. Which triangle has one right angle? (4.G.A.2)

_____

12. A figure has 2 pairs of parallel sides, 2 pairs of sides of equal length, and 4 right angles. What quadrilateral best describes this figure? (4.G.A.2)

_____

13. Which quadrilateral can have 2 pairs of parallel sides, all sides with equal length, and no right angles? (4.G.A.2)

_____

14. What is the correct name of the figure shown? (4.G.A.1)

_____

15.  Describe the angles of an obtuse triangle. (4.G.A.2)

_____

_____

_____

_____

Line Symmetry

Essential Question How can you check if a shape has line symmetry?

Common Core Geometry—
4.G.A.3
MATHEMATICAL PRACTICES
MP2, MP3, MP6

Unlock the Problem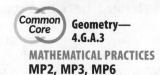

One type of symmetry found in geometric shapes is line symmetry. This sign is in the hills above Hollywood, California. Do any of the letters in the Hollywood sign show line symmetry?

A shape has **line symmetry** if it can be folded about a line so that its two parts match exactly.
A fold line, or a **line of symmetry**, divides a shape into two parts that are the same size and shape.

Activity Explore line symmetry.
Materials ■ pattern blocks ■ scissors

A Does the letter W have line symmetry?

STEP 1 Use pattern blocks to make the letter W.	**STEP 2** Trace the letter.

> **Math Idea**
>
> A vertical line goes up and down. ↕
>
> A horizontal line goes left and right. ↔
>
> A diagonal line goes through vertices of a polygon that are not next to each other. It can go up and down and left and right. ↗ ↙

STEP 3 Cut out the tracing.

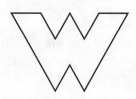

STEP 4 Fold the tracing over a vertical line.

Think: The two parts of the folded W match exactly. The fold line is a line of symmetry.

Math Talk

MATHEMATICAL PRACTICES ③

Apply How can you check to see if a shape has line symmetry?

So, the letter W _____ line symmetry.

B **Does the letter L have line symmetry?**

STEP 1

Use pattern blocks or grid paper to make the letter L.

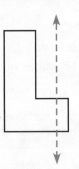

STEP 2

Trace the letter.

STEP 3

Cut out the tracing.

STEP 4

Fold the tracing over a vertical line.

Do the two parts match exactly?

_____

STEP 5

Then open it and fold it horizontally.

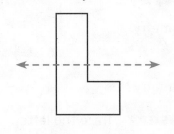

Do the two parts match exactly?

_____

STEP 6

Then open it and fold it diagonally.

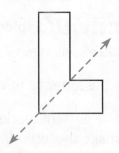

Do the two parts match exactly?

_____

So, the letter L _____ line symmetry.

1. Repeat Steps 1–6 for the remaining letters in HOLLYWOOD. Which letters have line symmetry?

_____

2. Do any of the letters have more than one line of symmetry? Explain.

_____

_____

Remember

You can fold horizontally, vertically, or diagonally to determine if the parts match exactly.

Name _____

Tell whether the parts on each side of the line match.
Is the line a line of symmetry? Write *yes* or *no*.

1.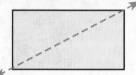

_____

2.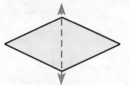

_____

3.

_____

✓4.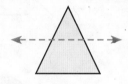

_____

Tell if the blue line appears to be a line of symmetry.
Write *yes* or *no*.

5.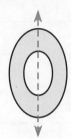

_____

6.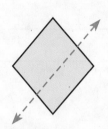

_____

7.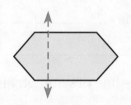

_____

✓8.

_____

Math Talk

MATHEMATICAL PRACTICES ②

Use Reasoning How can you use paper folding to check if a shape has line symmetry?

On Your Own

Tell if the blue line appears to be a line of symmetry.
Write *yes* or *no*.

9.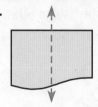

_____

10.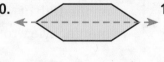

_____

11.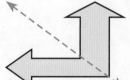

_____

12.

_____

13. **GO DEEPER** Which best describes the symmetry in the letter I?

I

_____

🔑 Unlock the Problem

14. Which shape has a correctly drawn line of symmetry?

   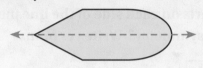   

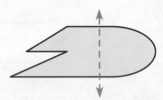   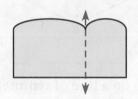

a. What do you need to find? _____

_____

b. How can you tell if the line of symmetry is correct?

_____

c. Tell how you solved the problem.

_____

_____

d. Circle the correct shape above.

15. **MATHEMATICAL PRACTICE ② Reason Abstractly** Draw a line of symmetry in the figure shown.

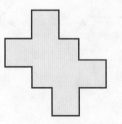

Personal Math Trainer

16. THINKSMARTER ✚ Evie's birthday is on the 18th of May. Since May is the 5th month, Evie wrote the date as shown.

Evie says all the numbers she wrote have line symmetry. Is she correct? Explain.

_____

_____

_____

Line Symmetry

Common Core **COMMON CORE STANDARD—4.G.A.3**
Draw and identify lines and angles, and classify shapes by properties of their lines and angles.

Tell if the dashed line appears to be a line of symmetry.
Write *yes* or *no*.

1.

____yes____

2.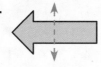

_____

3.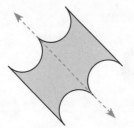

_____

4.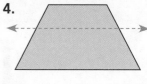

_____

Complete the design by reflecting over the line of symmetry.

5.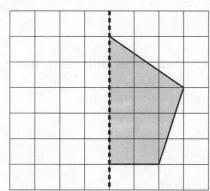

6.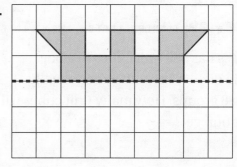

Problem Solving *Real World*

7. Kara uses the pattern at the right to make paper dolls. The dashed line represents a line of symmetry. A complete doll includes the reflection of the pattern over the line of symmetry. Complete the design to show what one of Kara's paper dolls looks like.

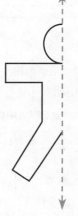

8. **WRITE** ▸*Math* Write a word that has line symmetry, like the word OHIO. Draw the line(s) of symmetry for each letter.

Lesson Check (4.G.A.3)

1. What word best describes the line of symmetry in the letter D?

_____

_____

2. Does the shape below show a correct line of symmetry? Explain.

_____

_____

Spiral Review (4.NBT.B.5, 4.NBT.B.6, 4.NF.A.2, 4.NF.B.4c)

3. The class has 360 unit cubes in a bag. Johnnie divides the unit cubes equally among 8 groups. How many unit cubes will each group get?

_____

4. There are 5,280 feet in one mile. How many feet are there in 6 miles?

_____

5. Sue has 4 pieces of wood. The lengths of her pieces of wood are $\frac{1}{3}$ foot, $\frac{2}{5}$ foot, $\frac{3}{10}$ foot, and $\frac{1}{4}$ foot. Which piece of wood is the shortest?

_____

6. Alice has $\frac{1}{5}$ as many miniature cars as Sylvester has. Sylvester has 35 miniature cars. How many miniature cars does Alice have?

_____

FOR MORE PRACTICE
GO TO THE
Personal Math Trainer

Name _____

Find and Draw Lines of Symmetry

Essential Question How do you find lines of symmetry?

Common Core Geometry—
4.G.A.3

MATHEMATICAL PRACTICES
MP1, MP3, MP8

🔑 Unlock the Problem

How many lines of symmetry does each polygon have?

🔒 Activity 1 Find lines of symmetry.

Materials ■ isometric and square dot paper ■ straightedge

STEP 1

Draw a triangle like the one shown, so all sides have equal length.

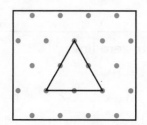

STEP 2

Fold the triangle in different ways to test for line symmetry. Draw along the fold lines that are lines of symmetry.

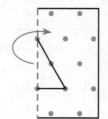

• Is there a line of symmetry if you fold the paper horizontally?

_____

STEP 3

Repeat the steps for each polygon shown. Complete the table.

Polygon	Triangle	Square	Parallelogram	Rhombus	Trapezoid	Hexagon
Number of Sides	3					
Number of Lines of Symmetry	3					

• In a regular polygon, all sides are of equal length and all angles are equal. What do you notice about the number of lines of symmetry in regular polygons?

_____

_____

MATHEMATICAL PRACTICES ⑧

Use Repeated Reasoning How many lines of symmetry does a circle have? Explain.

Activity 2 Make designs that have line symmetry.

Materials ■ pattern blocks

Make a design by using more than one pattern block.
Record your design. Draw the line or lines of symmetry.

Make a design with 2 lines of symmetry.

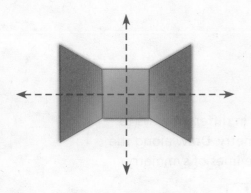

Make a design with 1 line of symmetry.

Make a design with more than 2 lines of symmetry.

Make a design with zero lines of symmetry.

Share and Show

1. The shape at the right has line symmetry.
   Draw the 2 lines of symmetry.

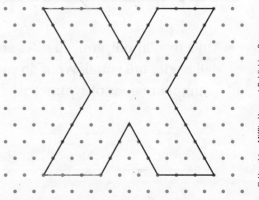

582

Name _____

Tell whether the shape appears to have zero lines, 1 line, or more than 1 line of symmetry. Write *zero*, *1*, or *more than 1*.

2.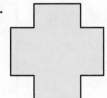

☑ 3.

4.

☑ 5.

_____   _____   _____   _____

On Your Own

Tell whether the shape appears to have zero lines, 1 line, or more than 1 line of symmetry. Write *zero*, *1*, or *more than 1*.

6.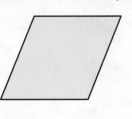

7.

8.

9.

Math Talk

MATHEMATICAL PRACTICES ①

Analyze Explain how you can find lines of symmetry for a shape.

Practice: Copy and Solve Does the design have line symmetry? Write *yes* or *no*. If your answer is *yes*, draw all lines of symmetry.

10.

11.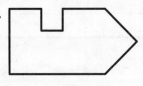

12.

13.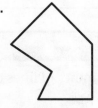

14. **GO DEEPER** Draw a figure that has 5 sides and exactly 1 line of symmetry.

Problem Solving • Applications

Use the chart for 15–17.

A	H	S
B	I	T
C	J	U
D	L	V
E	N	W

15. **GO DEEPER** Which letters appear to have only 1 line of symmetry?

_____

16. Which letters appear to have zero lines of symmetry?

_____

17. **THINK SMARTER** The letter C has horizontal symmetry. The letter A has vertical symmetry. Which letters appear to have both horizontal and vertical symmetry?

_____

18. **MATHEMATICAL PRACTICE ③** **Verify the Reasoning of Others** Jeff says that the shape has only 2 lines of symmetry.

Does his statement make sense? Explain.

_____

_____

_____

Personal Math Trainer

19. **THINK SMARTER +** Match each figure with the correct number of lines of symmetry it has.

G

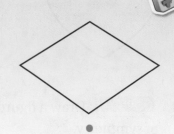

0 lines of symmetry	1 line of symmetry	2 lines of symmetry	More than 2 lines of symmetry

Name _____

Find and Draw Lines of Symmetry

Tell whether the shape appears to have zero
lines, 1 line, or more than 1 line of symmetry.
Write *zero*, *1*, or *more than 1*.

COMMON CORE STANDARD—4.G.A.3
*Draw and identify lines and angles, and classify
shapes by properties of their lines and angles.*

1.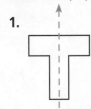

2.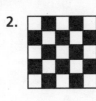

3.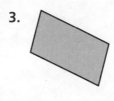

4.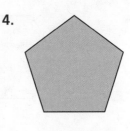

_____1_____   _____   _____   _____

Does the design have line symmetry? Write *yes* or *no*.
If your answer is yes, draw all lines of symmetry.

5.

6.

7.

8.

_____   _____   _____   _____

Draw a shape for the statement. Draw the line or lines of symmetry.

9. zero lines of symmetry

10. 1 line of symmetry

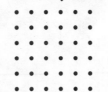

11. 2 lines of symmetry

Use the chart for 12.

0 2 3 4
5 6 8 9

12. Which number or numbers appear to have 2
lines of symmetry?

_____

13. **WRITE** ▸*Math* Draw a picture of a figure
that has more than 3 lines of symmetry.
Draw the lines of symmetry.

Lesson Check (4.G.A.3)

1. How many lines of symmetry does this shape appear to have?

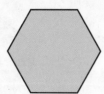

2. Draw a shape that has exactly 1 line of symmetry.

Spiral Review (4.NF.A.1, 4.NF.B.4b, 4.NF.C.6, 4.G.A.2)

3. Richard practiced each of 3 piano solos for $\frac{5}{12}$ hour. Expressed in simplest form, how long did he practice in all?

4. Write a decimal that is equivalent to three and ten hundredths.

5. Lynne used $\frac{3}{8}$ cup of flour and $\frac{1}{3}$ cup of sugar in a recipe. What number is a common denominator for $\frac{3}{8}$ and $\frac{1}{3}$?

6. Kevin draws a figure that has four sides. All sides have the same length. His figure has no right angles. What figure does Kevin draw?

FOR MORE PRACTICE
GO TO THE
Personal Math Trainer

Name _____

Problem Solving • Shape Patterns

Essential Question How can you use the strategy *act it out* to solve pattern problems?

Common Core Operations and Algebraic Thinking—
4.OA.C.5
MATHEMATICAL PRACTICES
MP5, MP6, MP7

🔑 Unlock the Problem *Real World*

You can find patterns in fabric, pottery, rugs, and wall coverings. You can see patterns in shape, size, position, color, or number of figures.

Sofia will use the pattern below to make a wallpaper border. What might be the next three figures in the pattern?

Use the graphic organizer below to solve the problem.

Read the Problem

What do I need to find?	What information do I need to use?	How will I use the information?
I need to find the next three _____ in the pattern.	I need to use the _____ of each figure in Sofia's pattern.	I will use pattern blocks to model the _____ and act out the problem.

Solve the Problem

 Math Talk

MATHEMATICAL PRACTICES ❼
Look for a Pattern How can you describe the shape pattern using numbers?

Describe how you acted out the problem to solve it.

I used a trapezoid and triangle to model the first

figure in the pattern. I used a _____ and

_____ to model the second figure in the pattern. I continued to model the pattern by repeating the models of the first two figures.

These are the next three figures in the pattern.

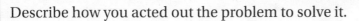

🔓 Try Another Problem

Draw what might be the next figure in the pattern.

Figure: 1   2   3   4 _____ 5

How can you describe this pattern?

Read the Problem

What do I need to find?	What information do I need to use?	How will I use the information?

Solve the Problem

1. Use the figures to write a number pattern. Then describe the pattern in the numbers.

_____

_____

_____

2. What might the tenth number in your pattern be? Explain.

_____

_____

Name _____

Unlock the Problem

√ Use the Problem Solving MathBoard.
√ Underline the important facts.
√ Choose a strategy you know.

Share and Show MATH BOARD

1. Marisol is making a pattern with blocks. What might the missing shape be?

   First, look at the blocks.

   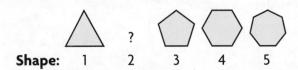

   Shape: 1   2   3   4   5

   Next, describe Marisol's pattern.

   _____

   _____

   Finally, draw the missing shape.

   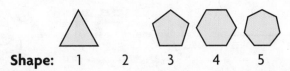

   Shape: 1   2   3   4   5

2. Use the shapes to write a number pattern. Then describe the pattern in the numbers.

   _____

   _____

3. **THINK SMARTER**   What if the pattern continued? Write an expression to describe the number of sides the sixth shape has in Marisol's pattern.

   _____

4. Sahil made a pattern using circles. The first nine circles are shown. Describe Sahil's pattern. If Sahil continues the pattern, what might the next three circles be?

   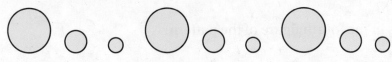

   _____

On Your Own

Use the toy quilt designs for 5–6.

5. THINK SMARTER Lu is making a quilt that is 20 squares wide and has 24 rows. The border of the quilt is made by using each toy design equally as often. Each square can hold one design. How many of each design does she use for the border?

_____

6. MATHEMATICAL PRACTICE ⑤ **Communicate** Starting in the first square of her quilt, Lu lined up her toy designs in this order: plane, car, fire truck, helicopter, crane, and wagon. Using this pattern unit, which design will Lu place in the fifteenth square? Explain how you found your answer.

_____

_____

_____

7. GO DEEPER Missy uses 1 hexagonal, 2 rectangular, and 4 triangular pieces of fabric to make 1 bug design for a quilt. If she uses 70 pieces in all to make bug designs, how many of each shape does she use?

_____

8. THINK SMARTER Norris drew the pattern shown.

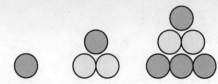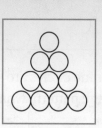

Label the circles to show the colors in the fourth figure of the pattern.

Problem Solving • Shape Patterns

Common Core

COMMON CORE STANDARD—4.OA.C.5
Generate and analyze patterns.

Solve each problem.

1. Marta is using this pattern to decorate a picture frame.
   Describe Marta's pattern. Draw what might be the next
   three figures in her pattern.

   ◺ □ □ ◺ ◺ □ □ ◺ □ □ ◺ □ □ ◺

   Possible answer: the pattern repeats: one triangle followed by

   two squares.

2. Describe a pattern. Draw what might be the next
   three figures in your pattern. How many circles are
   in the sixth figure in your pattern?

   ○
   ○   ○ ○
   ○   ○ ○   ○ ○ ○

   _____

   _____

3. **WRITE** ▸*Math* Find a pattern in your classroom. Describe and
   extend the pattern.

   _____

   _____

   _____

Lesson Check (4.OA.C.5)

1. Draw what might be the next three figures in this pattern?

⇑⇓⇓⇑⇑⇑⇓⇓⇓⇓⇑⇑⇑⇑⇑⇓⇓⇓⇓

2. Draw what might be the missing figure in the pattern below.

Spiral Review (4.OA.B.4, 4.NF.B.3d, 4.NF.B.4a, 4.NF.C.7)

3. Chad has two pieces of wood. One piece is $\frac{7}{12}$ foot long. The second piece is $\frac{5}{12}$ foot longer than the first piece. How long is the second piece?

4. Olivia finished a race in 40.64 seconds. Patty finished the race in 40.39 seconds. Miguel finished the race in 41.44 seconds. Chad finished the race in 40.46 seconds. Who finished the race in the least time?

5. Justin bought 6 ribbons for an art project. Each ribbon is $\frac{1}{4}$ yard long. How many yards of ribbon did Justin buy?

6. Kyle and Andrea were asked to make a list of prime numbers.

    Kyle: 1, 3, 7, 19, 23

    Andrea: 2, 3, 5, 7, 11

Whose list is correct?

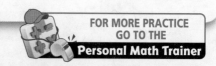

FOR MORE PRACTICE
GO TO THE
Personal Math Trainer

Name _____

✓ Chapter 10 Review/Test

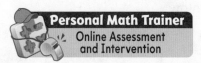

Personal Math Trainer
Online Assessment
and Intervention

1. Gavin is designing a kite. He sketched a picture of the kite.
   How many right angles does the kite appear to have?

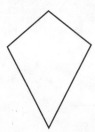

_____ right angles

2. Write the letter of the triangle under its correct classification.

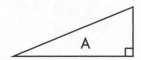 

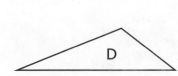

Acute Triangle	Obtuse Triangle	Right Triangle

3. Select the angles that identify an obtuse triangle. Mark all
   that apply.

   (A) acute, acute, acute

   (B) acute, acute, obtuse

   (C) right, acute, acute

   (D) obtuse, right, acute

© Houghton Mifflin Harcourt Publishing Company

GO DIGITAL Assessment Options
Chapter Test

4. Write the word that describes the part of Figure A written below.

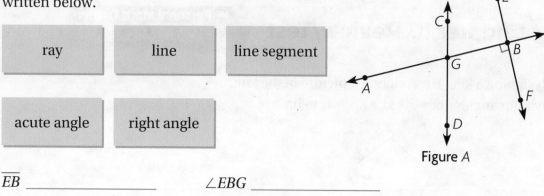

Figure A

ray	line	line segment

acute angle	right angle

$\overline{EB}$ _____ $\angle EBG$ _____

$\overleftrightarrow{AB}$ _____ $\angle CGB$ _____

$\overrightarrow{GA}$ _____

5. What term best describes the figure shown below?

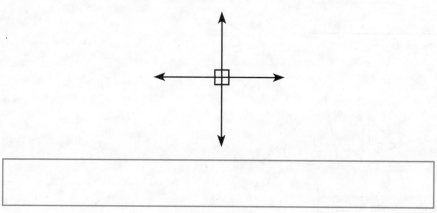

---

6. **THINK SMARTER +**   Naomi leaves for her trip to Los Angeles on the 12th day of August. Since August is the 8th month, Naomi wrote the date as shown.

Naomi says all the numbers she wrote have line symmetry. Is she correct? Explain your thinking.

Name _____

7. Max made a pennant that looks like a triangle. How can you classify the triangle based upon its angles?

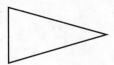

The triangle is a(n) _____ triangle.

8. Choose the labels to make a true statement.

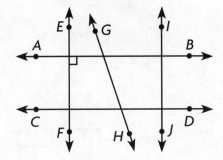

$$\begin{array}{|c|}\hline \overleftrightarrow{GH} \\ \overleftrightarrow{CD} \\ \overleftrightarrow{AB} \\ \hline \end{array}$$ is parallel to $$\begin{array}{|c|}\hline \overleftrightarrow{EF} \\ \overleftrightarrow{CD} \\ \overleftrightarrow{GH} \\ \hline \end{array}$$.

9. Classify the figure. Select all that apply.

○ quadrilateral   ○ rectangle

○ trapezoid   ○ rhombus

○ parallelogram   ○ square

10. Lily designed a deck in her backyard that looks like a quadrilateral that has only 1 pair of parallel sides. How can you classify the figure?

The quadrilateral is a _____.

11. Match each figure with the correct number of lines of symmetry it has.

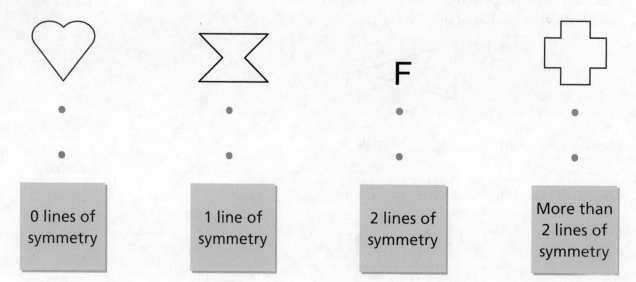

| 0 lines of symmetry | 1 line of symmetry | 2 lines of symmetry | More than 2 lines of symmetry |

12. Barb drew the pattern shown.

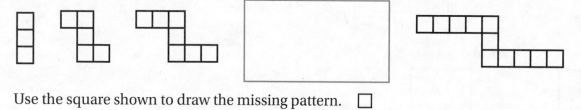

Use the square shown to draw the missing pattern. ☐

13. Claudia drew the figure below. Draw a line of symmetry on Claudia's figure.

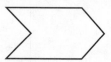

14. Write the word or words that best describe this figure.

15. How many acute angles does a right triangle have?

A right triangle has _____ acute angles.

Name _____

16. Mike drew a figure with opposite sides parallel. Write the pairs of parallel sides. What figure is it?

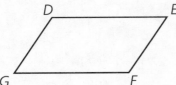

17. Circle the letter that does not have line symmetry.

DOTS

18. Joseph made a pattern using ovals and rectangles. The first four figures of his pattern are shown. Draw the next figure in the pattern.

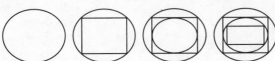

Figure 1   Figure 2   Figure 3   Figure 4   Figure 5

19. Jeremy drew Figure 1 and Louisa drew Figure 2.

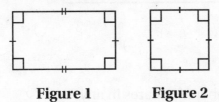

Figure 1   Figure 2

Part A

Jeremy says both figures are rectangles. Do you agree with Jeremy? Support your answer.

Part B

Louisa says both figures are rhombuses. Do you agree with Louisa? Support your answer.

20. Veronica found the number of lines of symmetry for the figure below. How many lines of symmetry does it have?

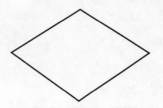

_____ lines of symmetry

21. GO DEEPER Jordan drew the pattern below.

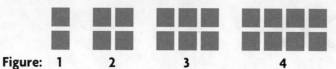

Figure: 1   2   3   4

Part A

Describe the pattern.

Part B

Write a rule using numbers to find the number of squares in any figure in the pattern.

Part C

Draw Figure 5.

Angles

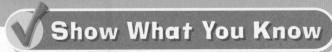 **Show What You Know**

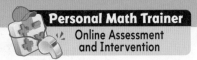

Personal Math Trainer
Online Assessment and Intervention

Check your understanding of important skills.

Name _____

▶ **Use a Metric Ruler** **Use a centimeter ruler to measure.**
Find the length in centimeters. (2.MD.A.1)

1.

_____ centimeters

2.

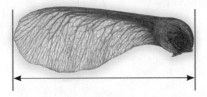

_____ centimeters

▶ **Classify Angles** **Classify the angle. Write** *acute, right,* **or** *obtuse*. (4.G.A.1)

3.

4.

_____

5.

_____

▶ **Parts of a Whole** **Write a fraction for each shaded part.** (3.NF.A.1)

6.

 _____

7.

 _____

8.

 _____

9.

 _____

Math in the Real World

The Sunshine Skyway Bridge crosses over Tampa Bay, Florida. Bridges and other building structures can model geometric figures. Look at the bridge in the photo at the left. Describe the geometric figures you see. Then classify the labeled angles and triangle.

Vocabulary Builder

▶ **Visualize It** •••••••••••••••••••••••••••••••

Complete the Bubble Map using review words.

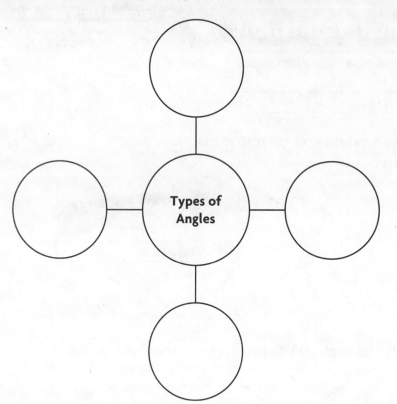

Review Words

acute

circle

obtuse

ray

right

straight

vertex

Preview Words

clockwise

counterclockwise

degree (°)

protractor

▶ **Understand Vocabulary** •••••••••••••••••••••••••

Draw a line to match each word with its definition.

1. protractor

2. degree(°)

3. clockwise

4. counterclockwise

• In the same direction in which the hands of a clock move

• In the opposite direction in which the hands of a clock move

• A tool for measuring the size of an angle

• The unit used for measuring angles

• **Interactive Student Edition**
• **Multimedia eGlossary**

Chapter 11 Vocabulary

acute angle

ángulo agudo

1

clockwise

en el sentido de las manecillas del reloj

8

counterclockwise

en sentido contrario a las manecillas del reloj

17

degree (°)

grado (°)

21

protractor

transportador

73

ray

semirrecta

76

right angle

ángulo recto

81

vertex

vértice

95

In the same direction in which the hands of a clock move

An angle that measures greater than 0° and less than 90°

Example:

The unit used for measuring angles and temperatures

In the opposite direction in which the hands of a clock move

A part of a line; it has one endpoint and continues without end in one direction

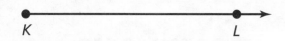

K   L

A tool for measuring the size of an angle

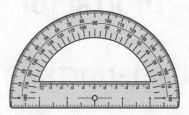

The point at which two rays of an angle meet or two (or more) line segments meet in a two-dimensional shape

vertex

An angle that forms a square corner

Example:

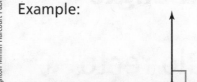

Picture It

Word Box
acute angle
clockwise
counterclockwise
degree(°)
protractor
ray
right angle
vertex

For 3 to 4 players

Materials
- timer
- sketch pad

How to Play

1. Take turns to play.

2. To take a turn, choose a word from the Word Box, but do not tell the word to the other players.

3. Set the timer for 1 minute.

4. Draw pictures and numbers on the sketch pad to give clues about the word. Do not use words.

5. The first player to guess the word before time runs out gets 1 point. If that player can use the word in a sentence, he or she gets 1 more point. Then that player gets a turn choosing a word.

6. The first player to score 10 points wins.

The Write Way

Reflect

Choose one idea. Write about it.

- Explain how to use a protractor to measure an angle or draw an angle.
- Illustrate and explain the difference between *clockwise* and *counterclockwise*. Use a separate piece of paper for your drawing.
- Write a creative story that includes a variety of angles.

Name _____

Angles and Fractional Parts of a Circle

Essential Question How can you relate angles and fractional parts of a circle?

Common Core   Measurement and Data—4.MD.C.5a

MATHEMATICAL PRACTICES
MP1, MP2, MP3

Investigate

Hands On

Materials ■ fraction circles

A. Place a $\frac{1}{12}$ piece on the circle. Place the tip of the fraction piece on the center of the circle. Trace the fraction piece to create an angle.

What parts of the fraction piece represent the rays

of the angle? _____

Where is the vertex of the angle?

_____

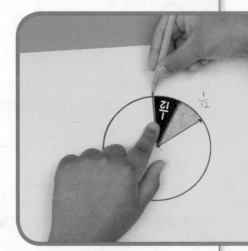

B. Shade the angle formed by the $\frac{1}{12}$ piece. Label it $\frac{1}{12}$.

C. Place the $\frac{1}{12}$ piece back on the shaded angle. Turn it counterclockwise. **Counterclockwise** is the direction opposite from the way the hands move on a clock.

Trace the fraction piece in its new position. How many twelfths have

you traced in all? _____ Label $\frac{2}{12}$.

D. Turn the fraction piece counterclockwise again and trace it. Label the total number of twelfths.

Continue until you reach the shaded angle.

How many times did you need to turn the $\frac{1}{12}$ piece to make a circle? _____

How many angles come together in the center of the circle? _____

Draw Conclusions

1. Compare the size of the angle formed by a $\frac{1}{4}$ piece and the size of the angle formed by a $\frac{1}{12}$ piece. Use a $\frac{1}{4}$ piece and your model on page 601 to help.

_____

_____

_____

2. Describe the relationship between the size of the fraction piece and the number of turns it takes to make a circle.

_____

_____

Make Connections

You can relate fractions and angles to the hands of a clock.

Let the hands of the clock represent the rays of an angle. Each 5-minute mark represents a $\frac{1}{12}$ turn **clockwise**.

15 minutes elapse.

The minute hand makes a

_____ turn clockwise.

30 minutes elapse.

The minute hand makes a

_____ turn clockwise.

45 minutes elapse.

The minute hand makes a

_____ turn clockwise.

60 minutes elapse.

The minute hand makes a

_____ turn clockwise.

MATHEMATICAL PRACTICES ③

Compare Representations
How is an angle formed in a circle using a $\frac{1}{4}$ fraction piece like a $\frac{1}{4}$ turn and 15 minutes elapsing on a clock?

© Houghton Mifflin Harcourt Publishing Company

602

Name _____

Tell what fraction of the circle the shaded angle represents.

1.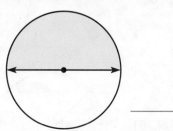
_____

2.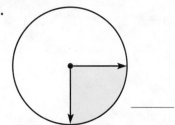
_____

3.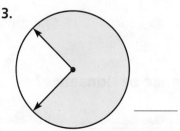
_____

4.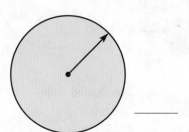
_____

5.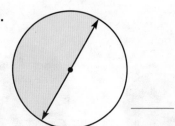
_____

6.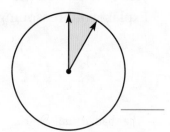
_____

Tell whether the angle on the circle shows a $\frac{1}{4}$, $\frac{1}{2}$, $\frac{3}{4}$, or 1 full turn clockwise or counterclockwise.

7.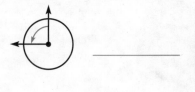
_____
_____

8.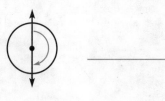
_____
_____

9.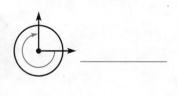
_____
_____

Problem Solving • Applications Real World

10. **MATHEMATICAL PRACTICE** Susan watched the game from 1 P.M. to 1:30 P.M. **Describe** the turn the minute hand made.

_____

11. **Go DEEPER** Compare the angles in Exercises 1 and 5. Does the position of the angle affect the size of the angle? Explain.

_____

_____

Personal Math Trainer

12. **THINK SMARTER +** Malcolm drew this angle on the circle. Which of the following describes the angle? Mark all that apply.

○ $\frac{3}{4}$ turn   ○ clockwise

○ $\frac{1}{4}$ turn   ○ counterclockwise

Sense or Nonsense?

13. **THINK SMARTER** Whose statement makes sense? Whose statement is nonsense? Explain your reasoning.

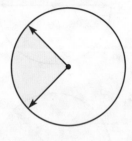

The shaded angle represents $\frac{3}{8}$ of the circle.

The shaded angle represents $\frac{1}{4}$ of the circle.

Carla's Statement	Adam's Statement
_____	_____
_____	_____
_____	_____
_____	_____

- For the statement that is nonsense, write a statement that makes sense.

  _____

- What is another way to describe the size of the angle? Explain.

  _____

Name _____

Angles and Fractional Parts of a Circle

Common Core

COMMON CORE STANDARD—4.MD.C.5a
Geometric measurement: understand concepts of angle and measure angles.

Tell what fraction of the circle the shaded angle represents.

1.

2.

3.

$\dfrac{1}{4}$
_____

_____

_____

Tell whether the angle on the circle shows a $\dfrac{1}{4}$, $\dfrac{1}{2}$, $\dfrac{3}{4}$, or 1 full turn clockwise or counterclockwise.

4.

5.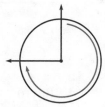

6.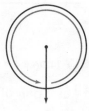

_____

_____

_____

_____

_____

_____

Problem Solving *Real World*

7. Shelley exercised for 15 minutes. Describe the turn the minute hand made.

Start

End

_____

_____

8. **WRITE** ▸*Math* Give a description of a $\dfrac{3}{4}$-turn of the minute hand on a clock face.

_____

_____

_____

_____

_____

_____

Lesson Check (4.MD.C.5a)

1. What fraction of the circle does the shaded angle represent?

_____

_____

2. Describe the turn shown below.

_____

_____

Spiral Review (4.OA.B.4, 4.NF.A.1, 4.NF.B.4c, 4.NF.C.7)

3. Write $\frac{2}{3}$ and $\frac{3}{4}$ as a pair of fractions with a common denominator.

_____

_____

4. Raymond bought $\frac{3}{4}$ of a dozen rolls. How many rolls did he buy?

_____

_____

5. List all the factors of 18.

6. Jonathan rode 1.05 miles on Friday, 1.5 miles on Saturday, 1.25 miles on Monday, and 1.1 miles on Tuesday. On which day did he ride the shortest distance?

_____

© Houghton Mifflin Harcourt Publishing Company

FOR MORE PRACTICE GO TO THE
Personal Math Trainer

Degrees

Essential Question How are degrees related to fractional parts of a circle?

Common Core **Measurement and Data—4.MD.C.5a, 4.MD.C.5b**
MATHEMATICAL PRACTICES
MP2, MP6, MP7

CONNECT You can use what you know about angles and fractional parts of a circle to understand angle measurement. Angles are measured in units called **degrees**. Think of a circle divided into 360 equal parts. An angle that turns through $\frac{1}{360}$ of the circle measures 1 degree.

> **Math Idea**
> The symbol for degrees is °.

🔑 Unlock the Problem Real World

The angle between two spokes on the bicycle wheel turns through $\frac{10}{360}$ of a circle. What is the measure of the angle formed between the spokes?

• What part of an angle does a spoke represent?

_____

_____

🔓 Example 1 Use fractional parts to find the angle measure.

Each $\frac{1}{360}$ turn measures _____ degree.

Ten $\frac{1}{360}$ turns measure _____ degrees.

So, the measure of the angle between the spokes is _____.

 Math Talk

MATHEMATICAL PRACTICES ②

Reason Abstractly How many degrees is the measure of an angle that turns through 1 whole circle? Explain.

▲ The Penny Farthing bicycle was built in the 1800s.

🔓 Example 2 Find the measure of a right angle.

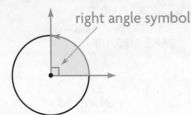

right angle symbol

Think: Through what fraction of a circle

does a right angle turn? _____

STEP 1 Write $\frac{1}{4}$ as an equivalent fraction with 360 in the denominator.

$$\frac{1}{4} = \frac{\boxed{}}{360}$$ Think: 4 × 9 = 36, so 4 × _____ = 360.

STEP 2 Write $\frac{90}{360}$ in degrees.

An angle that turns through $\frac{1}{360}$ of a circle measures _____.

An angle that turns through $\frac{90}{360}$ of a circle measures _____.

So, a right angle measures _____.

Try This! Find the measure of a straight angle.

Through what fraction of a circle does a straight angle turn? _____

Write $\frac{1}{2}$ as an equivalent fraction with 360 in the denominator.

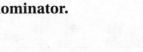

$$\frac{1}{2} = \frac{\boxed{}}{360}$$ Think: 2 × 18 = 36, so 2 × _____ = 360.

So, a straight angle measures _____.

1. How can you describe the measure of an acute angle in degrees?

_____

_____

2. How can you describe the measure of an obtuse angle in degrees?

_____

Share and Show MATH BOARD

1. Find the measure of the angle.

   Through what fraction of a circle does the angle turn? _____

   $\dfrac{1}{3} = \dfrac{\boxed{}}{360}$ Think: 3 × 12 = 36, so 3 × _____ = 360.

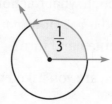

   So, the measure of the angle is _____.

Tell the measure of the angle in degrees.

2.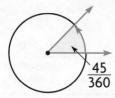

   _____

3.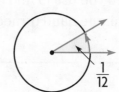

   _____

Math Talk   MATHEMATICAL PRACTICES ⑥

If an angle measures 60°, through what fraction of a circle does it turn? **Explain.**

On Your Own

Tell the measure of the angle in degrees.

4.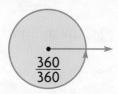

   _____

5.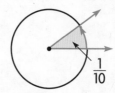

   _____

Classify the angle. Write *acute*, *obtuse*, *right*, or *straight*.

6.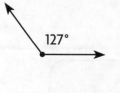
127°

_____

7.

_____

8.
37°

_____

9.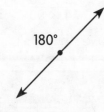
180°

_____

10. MATHEMATICAL PRACTICE ⑥ Is this an obtuse angle? **Explain.**

   _____

   _____

   _____

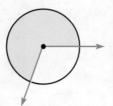

11. GO DEEPER Alex cut a circular pizza into 8 equal slices. He removed 2 of the slices of pizza. What is the measure of the angle made by the missing slices of pizza?

   _____

🔑 Unlock the Problem

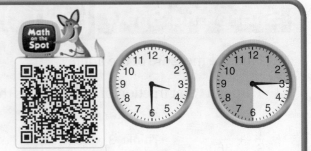

12. THINK SMARTER Ava started reading at 3:30 P.M. She stopped for a snack at 4:15 P.M. During this time, through what fraction of a circle did the minute hand turn? How many degrees did the minute hand turn?

a. What are you asked to find? _____

_____

b. What information can you use to find the fraction of a circle through which the minute hand turned?

_____

_____

c. How can you use the fraction of a circle through which the minute hand turned to find how many degrees it turned?

_____

_____

d. Show the steps to solve the problem.

STEP 1 $\dfrac{3 \times \boxed{}}{4 \times \boxed{}} = \dfrac{?}{360}$

STEP 2 $\dfrac{3 \times 90}{4 \times 90} = \dfrac{\boxed{}}{360}$

e. Complete the sentences.

From 3:30 P.M. to 4:15 P.M., the minute hand

made a _____ turn clockwise.

The minute hand turned _____ degrees.

---

13. THINK SMARTER An angle represents $\frac{1}{15}$ of a circle. Select the number to show how to find the measure of the angle in degrees.

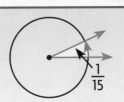

$\dfrac{1}{15} = \dfrac{1 \times \boxed{}}{15 \times \boxed{}} = \dfrac{\boxed{}}{360}$

The angle measures _____.

| 20 |
| 24 |
| 30 |

Degrees

Common Core

COMMON CORE STANDARDS—4.MD.C.5a, 4.MD.C.5b *Geometric measurement: understand concepts of angle and measure angles.*

Tell the measure of the angle in degrees.

1.
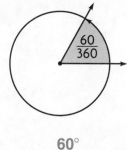

$\dfrac{60}{360}$

___60°___

2.
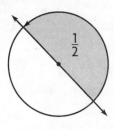

$\dfrac{1}{2}$

_____

3.
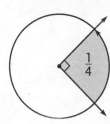

$\dfrac{1}{4}$

_____

Classify the angle. Write *acute, obtuse, right,* or *straight.*

4.
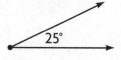

25°

_____

5.
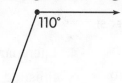

110°

_____

6.

60°

_____

7.
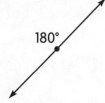

180°

_____

8.
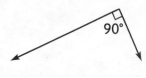

90°

_____

9.

50°

_____

Problem Solving *Real World*

Ann started reading at 4:00 P.M. and finished at 4:20 P.M.

10. Through what fraction of a circle did the minute hand turn?

_____

Start

End

11. **WRITE** ▸*Math* Give an example from everyday life of an angle that measures 90 degrees.

_____

_____

Lesson Check (4.MD.C.5a, 4.MD.C.5b)

1. What kind of angle is shown?

180°

2. How many degrees are in an angle that turns through $\frac{1}{4}$ of a circle?

Spiral Review (4.OA.A.3, 4.NF.B.3b, 4.NF.B.4a, 4.NF.C.5)

3. Mae bought 15 football cards and 18 baseball cards. She separated them into 3 equal groups. How many sports cards are in each group?

4. Each part of a race is $\frac{1}{10}$ mile long. Marsha finished 5 parts of the race. How far did Marsha race?

5. Jeff said his city got $\frac{11}{3}$ inches of snow. Write this fraction as a mixed number.

6. Amy ran $\frac{3}{4}$ mile. Write the distance Amy ran as a decimal.

FOR MORE PRACTICE
GO TO THE
Personal Math Trainer

Name _____

Measure and Draw Angles

Essential Question How can you use a protractor to measure and draw angles?

Measurement and Data—4.MD.C.6
MATHEMATICAL PRACTICES
MP1, MP5, MP6

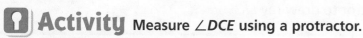

Unlock the Problem

Emma wants to make a clay sculpture of her daughter as she appears in the photo from her dance recital. How can she measure ∠DCE, or the angle formed by her daughter's arms?

A **protractor** is a tool for measuring the size of an angle.

Activity Measure ∠DCE using a protractor.

Materials ■ protractor

STEP 1 Place the center point of the protractor on vertex *C* of the angle.

STEP 2 Align the 0° mark on the scale of the protractor with ray *CE*.

STEP 3 Find where ray *CD* intersects the same scale. Read the angle measure on that scale. Extend the ray if you need to.

m∠*DCE* = _____

Read m∠*DCE* as "the measure of angle *DCE*".

So, the angle formed by Emma's daughter's

arms is _____.

Align center point and vertex.

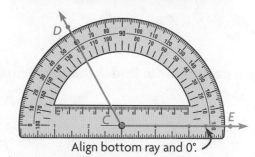

Align bottom ray and 0°.

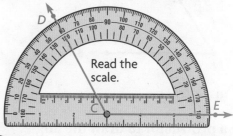

Read the scale.

Math Talk

MATHEMATICAL PRACTICES ⑤

Use Appropriate Tools Can you line up either ray of the angle with the protractor when measuring? Explain.

Draw Angles You can also use a protractor to draw an angle of a given measure.

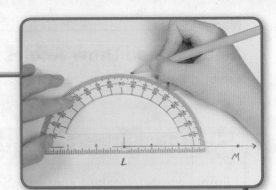

🔓 Activity Draw ∠*KLM* with a measure of 82°.

Materials ■ protractor

STEP 1 Use the straight edge of the protractor to draw and label ray *LM*.

STEP 2 Place the center point of the protractor on point *L*. Align ray *LM* with the 0° mark on the protractor.

STEP 3 Using the same scale, mark a point at 82°. Label the point *K*.

STEP 4 Use the straight edge of the protractor to draw ray *LK*.

Share and Show

1. Measure ∠*ABC*.

   Place the center of the protractor on point _____.

   Align ray *BC* with _____.

   Read where _____ intersects the same scale.

   So, m∠*ABC* is _____.

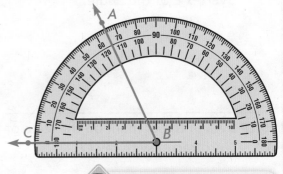

Use a protractor to find the angle measure.

2.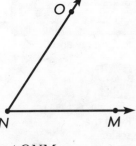

   m∠*ONM* = _____

☑ 3.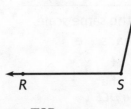

   m∠*TSR* = _____

! ERROR Alert

Be sure to use the correct scale on the protractor. Ask yourself: Is the measure reasonable?

Use a protractor to draw the angle.

4. 170°

☑ 5. 78°

Math Talk

MATHEMATICAL PRACTICES ⑥

Describe how drawing and measuring angles are similar.

Name _____

Use a protractor to find the angle measure.

6.
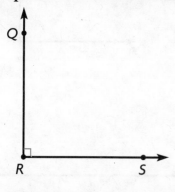

m∠QRS = _____

7.
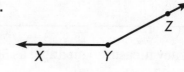

m∠XYZ = _____

Use a protractor to draw the angle.

8. 115°

9. 67°

Draw an example of each. Label the angle with its measure.

10. an acute angle

11. an obtuse angle

12. **GO DEEPER** Elizabeth is making a quilt with scraps of fabric. What is the difference between m∠ABC and m∠DEF?

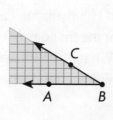
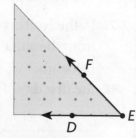

_____

13. **THINK SMARTER** Draw an angle with a measure of 0°. Describe your drawing.

_____

_____

Problem Solving • Applications (Real World)

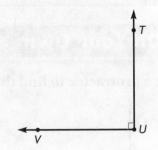

14. GO DEEPER Hadley wants to divide this angle into three angles with equal measure. What will the measure of each angle be?

_____

15. MATHEMATICAL PRACTICE ⑥ Tracy measured an angle as 50° that was actually 130°. **Explain** her error.

_____

_____

16. THINK SMARTER Choose the word and angle measure to complete a true statement about ∠QRS.

∠QRS is a(n)
| acute |
| obtuse |
| right |
angle that has a measure of
| 45°. |
| 115°. |
| 135°. |

Connect to Science

Earth's Axis

Earth revolves around the sun yearly. The Northern Hemisphere is the half of Earth that is north of the equator. The seasons of the year are due to the tilt of Earth's axis.

Use the diagrams and a protractor for 17–18.

17. In the Northern Hemisphere, Earth's axis is tilted away from the sun on the first day of winter, which is often on December 21. What is the measure of the marked angle on the first day of winter, the shortest day of the year?

_____

18. Earth's axis is not tilted away from or toward the sun on the first days of spring and fall, which are often on March 20 and September 22. What is the measure of the marked angle on the first day of spring or fall?

_____

Northern Hemisphere

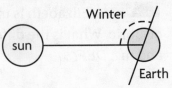

Winter
sun
Earth

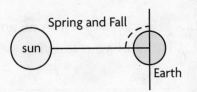

Spring and Fall
sun
Earth

Name _____

Measure and Draw Angles

Common Core **COMMON CORE STANDARD—4.MD.C.6**
Geometric measurement: understand concepts of angle and measure angles.

Use a protractor to find the angle measure.

1.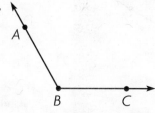

m∠ABC = ___120°___

2.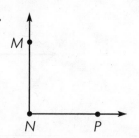

m∠MNP = _____

3.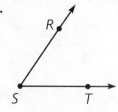

m∠RST = _____

Use a protractor to draw the angle.

4. 40°

5. 170°

 Problem Solving Real World

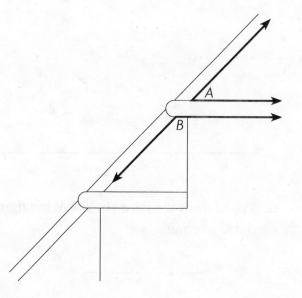

The drawing shows the angles a stair tread makes with a support board along a wall. Use your protractor to measure the angles.

6. What is the measure of ∠A? _____

7. What is the measure of ∠B? _____

8. **WRITE** ▸*Math* Find an angle at home. Measure the angle. Record the measure. Classify the angle.

_____

_____

_____

_____

Lesson Check (4.MD.C.6)

1. What is the measure of ∠ABC?

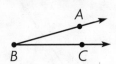

_____

2. What is the measure of ∠XYZ?

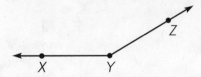

_____

Spiral Review (4.NBT.B.6, 4.NF.B.3c, 4.MD.C.5a, 4.G.A.1)

3. Derrick earned $1,472 during the 4 weeks he had his summer job. If he earned the same amount each week, how much did he earn each week?

4. Arthur baked $1\frac{7}{12}$ dozen muffins. Nina baked $1\frac{1}{12}$ dozen muffins. How many dozen muffins did they bake?

_____

_____

5. Trisha drew the figure below. What figure did she draw?

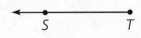

6. Measure and describe the turn shown by the angle. Be sure to tell about the size and direction of the turn.

_____

_____

FOR MORE PRACTICE GO TO THE Personal Math Trainer

Name _____

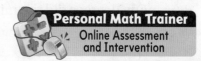

Personal Math Trainer
Online Assessment
and Intervention

Vocabulary

Choose the best term from the box.

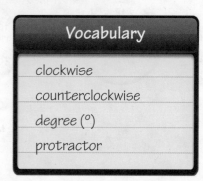

Vocabulary
clockwise
counterclockwise
degree (º)
protractor

1. The unit used to measure an angle is called

   a _____. (p. 607)

2. _____ is the opposite of the
   direction in which the hands of a clock move. (p. 601)

3. A _____ is a tool for measuring the size
   of an angle. (p. 613)

Concepts and Skills

**Tell whether the angle on the circle shows a $\frac{1}{4}$, $\frac{1}{2}$, $\frac{3}{4}$, or 1 full turn
clockwise or counterclockwise.** (4.MD.C.5a)

4.   5.   6.   7.

_____ _____ _____ _____

_____ _____ _____ _____

Tell the measure of the angle in degrees. (4.MD.C.5a, 4.MD.C.5b)

8.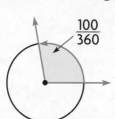

$\frac{100}{360}$

9.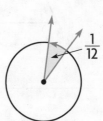

$\frac{1}{12}$

_____ _____

Use a protractor to draw the angle. (4.MD.C.6)

10. 75°   11. 127°

12. Phillip watched a beach volleyball game from 1:45 P.M. to 2:00 P.M. How many degrees did the minute hand turn? (4.MD.C.5a, 4.MD.C.5b)

_____

13. What angle does this piece of pie form? (4.MD.C.5a, 4.MD.C.5b)

_____

14. What is m∠*CBT*? Use a protractor to help you. (4.MD.C.6)

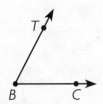

_____

_____

15. **GO DEEPER** Matt cut a circle into 8 equal sections. He drew an angle that measures the same as the total measure of 3 of the sections in the circle. What is the measure of the angle Matt drew? (4.MD.C.5a)

_____

Join and Separate Angles

Essential Question How can you determine the measure of an angle separated into parts?

Common Core **Measurement and Data—**
4.MD.C.7
MATHEMATICAL PRACTICES
MP1, MP4, MP6

Investigate

Hands On

Materials ■ construction paper ■ scissors ■ protractor

A. Use construction paper. Draw an angle that measures exactly 70°. Label it ∠ABC.

B. Cut out ∠ABC.

C. Separate ∠ABC by cutting it into two parts. Begin cutting at the vertex and cut between the rays.

What figures did you form? _____

D. Use a protractor to measure the two angles you formed.

Record the measures. _____

E. Find the sum of the angles you formed.

_____ + _____ = _____
   part + part = whole

> **Math Idea**
> You can think of ∠ABC as the whole and the two angles you formed as the parts of the whole.

F. Join the two angles. Compare m∠ABC to the sum of the measures of its parts. Explain how they compare.

_____

_____

_____

1. What if you cut ∠ABC into two different angles? What can you conclude about the sum of the measures of these two angles? Explain.

_____

_____

_____

2. **THINK SMARTER** Seth cut ∠ABC into 3 parts. Draw a model that shows two different ways he could have separated his angle.

3. Write a sentence that compares the measure of an angle to the sum of its parts.

_____

_____

Make Connections

Materials ■ protractor

You can write the measure of the angles shown in a circle as a sum.

STEP 1 Use a protractor to find the measure of each angle.

STEP 2 Label each angle with its measure.

STEP 3 Write the sum of the angle measures as an equation.

_____ + _____ + _____ = _____
part + part + part = whole

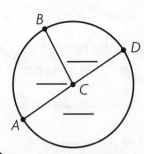

Math Talk

MATHEMATICAL PRACTICES ⑥

Use Math Vocabulary
Describe the angles shown in the circle above using the words *whole* and *part*.

Name _____

Add to find the measure of the angle. Write an equation to record your work.

1.

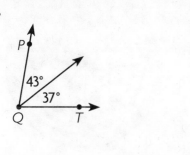

m∠PQT = _____

2.

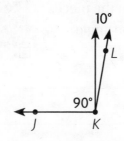

m∠JKL = _____

3.

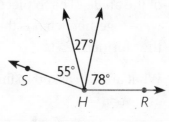

m∠RHS = _____

Use a protractor to find the measure of each angle. Label each angle with its measure. Write the sum of the angle measures as an equation.

4.

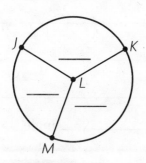

_____

5.

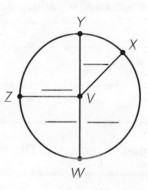

_____

6. MATHEMATICAL PRACTICE ④ **Use Diagrams** What is m∠QRT?

_____

7. GO DEEPER Look back at Exercise 1. Suppose you joined an angle measuring 10° to ∠PQT. Draw the new angle, showing all three parts. What type of angle is formed?

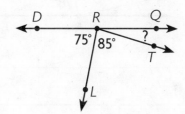

⚷ Unlock the Problem (Real World)

8. **THINK SMARTER** Stephanie, Kay, and Shane each ate an equal-sized piece of a pizza. The measure of the angle of each piece was 45°. When the pieces were together, what is the measure of the angle they formed?

a. What are you asked to find? _____

_____

b. What information do you need to use? _____

_____

_____

c. Tell how you can use addition to solve the problem. _____

_____

_____

_____

d. Complete the sentence. The three pieces of pizza formed a _____ angle.

---

9. What is the measure of ∠XZW? Write an equation to record your work.

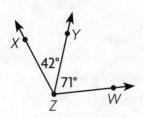

10. **THINK SMARTER +** What is m∠PRS? Use equations to explain and check your answer.

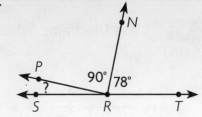

_____

_____

_____

_____

_____

Join and Separate Angles

Common Core   **COMMON CORE STANDARD—4.MD.C.7**
Geometric measurement: understand concepts of angle and measure angles.

Add to find the measure of the angle. Write an equation to record your work.

1.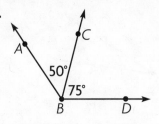

   _____ 50° + 75° = 125° _____

   m∠ABD = _____ 125° _____

2.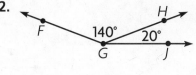

   _____

   m∠FGJ = _____

3.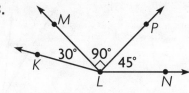

   _____

   m∠KLN = _____

Use a protractor to find the measure of each angle in the circle.

4. m∠ABC = _____

5. m∠DBE = _____

6. m∠CBD = _____

7. m∠EBA = _____

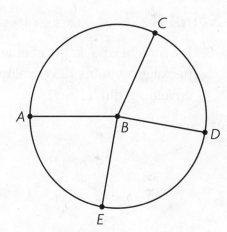

Problem Solving

8. Ned made the design at the right. Use a protractor. Find and write the measure of each of the 3 angles.

   _____

9. Write an equation to find the measure of the total angle.

   _____

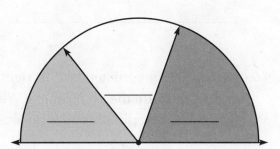

10. **WRITE** ▸*Math* How can you use addition and subtraction to put together and separate measures of an angle and its parts?

    _____

    _____

Lesson Check (4.MD.C.7)

1. What is the measure of ∠WXZ?

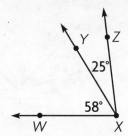

2. Write an equation that you can use to find the m∠MNQ.

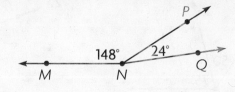

_____

_____

Spiral Review (4.NBT.B.5, 4.NF.B.3d, 4.MD.C.5a, 4.MD.C.5b, 4.G.A.2)

3. Joe bought 6 packages of envelopes. Each package contains 125 envelopes. How many envelopes did he buy?

4. Bill hiked $\frac{3}{10}$ mile on the Lake Trail. Then he hiked $\frac{5}{10}$ mile on the Rock Trail to get back to where he started. How many miles did he hike?

_____

_____

5. Ron drew a quadrilateral with 4 right angles and 4 sides with the same length. What figure best describes his quadrilateral?

6. How many degrees are in an angle that turns through $\frac{3}{4}$ of a circle?

_____

_____

FOR MORE PRACTICE GO TO THE
Personal Math Trainer

Problem Solving • Unknown Angle Measures

Essential Question How can you use the strategy *draw a diagram* to solve angle measurement problems?

 Common Core — Measurement and Data—
4.MD.C.7
MATHEMATICAL PRACTICES
MP1, MP2, MP4

Unlock the Problem

Mr. Tran is cutting a piece of kitchen tile as shown at the right. He needs tiles with 45° angles to make a design. After the cut, what is the angle measure of the part left over? Can Mr. Tran use both pieces in the design?

Use the graphic organizer below to solve the problem.

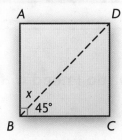

Read the Problem

What do I need to find?	**What information do I need to use?**	**How will I use the information?**
I need to find _____ _____	I can use the measures of the angles I know. _____ _____	I can draw a bar model and use the information to _____ _____

Solve the Problem

I can draw a bar model to represent the problem.
Then I can write an equation to solve the problem.

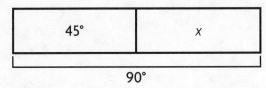

$$m\angle ABD + m\angle CBD = m\angle ABC$$

$$x + \text{\_\_\_\_\_} = \text{\_\_\_\_\_}$$

$$x = \text{\_\_\_\_\_}$$

The m∠ABD = _____.

Since both tiles measure _____, Mr. Tran can use both pieces in the design.

 Math Talk

MATHEMATICAL PRACTICES ④

Write an Equation What other equation can you write to solve the problem? Explain.

© Houghton Mifflin Harcourt Publishing Company

Try Another Problem

Marisol is building a frame for a sandbox, but the boards she has are too short. She must join two boards together to build a side as shown. At what angle did she cut the first board?

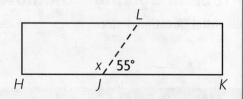

Read the Problem

What do I need to find?	What information do I need to use?	How will I use the information?

Solve the Problem

* Explain how you can check the answer to the problem.

_____

_____

Share and Show MATH BOARD

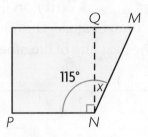

1. Laura cuts a square out of scrap paper as shown.
What is the angle measure of the piece left over?

First, draw a bar model to represent the problem.

Next, write the equation you need to solve.

_____

_____

Last, find the angle measure of the piece left over.

m∠*MNQ* = _____
So, the angle measure of the piece left over is _____.

2. Jackie trimmed a piece of scrap metal to make a
straight edge as shown. What is the measure of the
piece she trimmed off?

_____

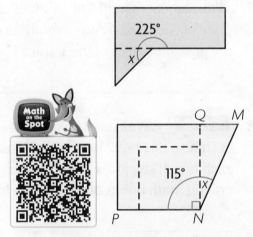

On Your Own

3. **THINK SMARTER** What if Laura cut a smaller square as
shown? Would m∠*MNQ* be different? Explain.

_____

_____

_____

4. **GO DEEPER** The map shows Marco's paper route. When
Marco turns right onto Center Street from Main Street,
what degree turn does he make? **Hint:** Draw a dashed
line to extend Oak Street to form a 180° angle.

_____

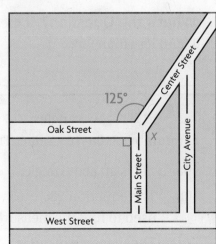

Problem Solving • Applications

5. **MATHEMATICAL PRACTICE 4** **Write an Equation** Two angles form a straight angle. One angle measures 89°. What is the measure of the other angle? Explain.

_____

_____

_____

6. **Pose a Problem** Look back at Problem 5. Write a similar problem about two angles that form a right angle.

_____

_____

_____

WRITE ▸ Math • **Show Your Work**

7. **GO DEEPER** Sam paid $20 for two T-shirts. The price of each T-shirt was a multiple of 5. What are the possible prices of the T-shirts?

_____

8. **GO DEEPER** Zayna has 3 boxes with 15 art books in each box. She has 2 bags with 11 math books in each bag. If she gives 30 books away, how many art and math books does she have left?

_____

9. **What's the Question?** It measures greater than 0° and less than 90°.

10. **THINK SMARTER** Two angles, ∠A and ∠B, form a straight angle. ∠A measures 65°. For numbers 10a–10c, select True or False for the statement.

10a.	∠B is an acute angle.	○ True	○ False
10b.	The equation 180° − 65° = x° can be used to find the measure of ∠B.	○ True	○ False
10c.	The measure of ∠B is 125°.	○ True	○ False

Problem Solving • Unknown
Angle Measures

Common Core

COMMON CORE STANDARD—4.MD.C.7
Geometric measurement: understand concepts of angle and measure angles.

Solve each problem. Draw a diagram to help.

1. Wayne is building a birdhouse. He is cutting a board as shown. What is the angle measure of the piece left over?

   Draw a bar model to represent the problem.

   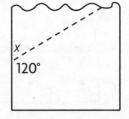

   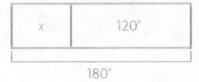

   $x + 120° = 180°$

   $x = 180° - 120°$

   $x = 60°$

   _____ 60°

2. An artist is cutting a piece of metal as shown. What is the angle measure of the piece left over?

   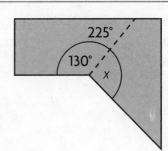

   _____

3. **WRITE** ▸ *Math* Give one example of when you would draw a diagram to solve an angle measurement problem.

   _____

   _____

   _____

   _____

Lesson Check (4.MD.C.7)

1. Angelo cuts a triangle from a sheet of paper as shown. What is the measure of $\angle x$ in the triangle?

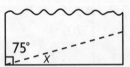

2. Cindy cuts a piece of wood as shown. What is the angle measure of the piece left over?

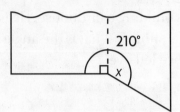

Spiral Review (4.OA.A.3, 4.NF.A.2, 4.NF.C.6, 4.MD.C.7)

3. Tyronne worked 21 days last month. He earned $79 each day. How much did Tyronne earn last month?

4. Meg inline skated for $\frac{7}{10}$ mile. Write this distance as a decimal.

5. Kerry ran $\frac{3}{4}$ mile. Sherrie ran $\frac{1}{2}$ mile. Marcie ran $\frac{2}{3}$ mile. List the friends in order from who ran the least distance to who ran the greatest distance.

6. What is the measure of $\angle ABC$?

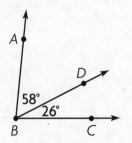

FOR MORE PRACTICE
GO TO THE
Personal Math Trainer

✓ Chapter 11 Review/Test

1. An angle represents $\frac{1}{12}$ of a circle. Use the numbers to show how to find the measure of the angle in degrees.

$$\frac{1}{12} = \frac{1 \times \boxed{}}{12 \times \boxed{}} = \frac{\boxed{}}{360}$$

The angle measure is _____.

24

30

36

2. Match the measure of each $\angle C$ with the measure of $\angle D$ that forms a straight angle.

$\angle C$	$\angle D$
	•145°
122° •	• 75°
35° •	•148°
62° •	• 58°
105° •	• 55°
	•118°

3. Katie drew an obtuse angle. Which could be the measure of the angle she drew? Mark all that apply.

(A) 35°   (C) 180°

(B) 157°   (D) 92°

4. Draw an angle that represents a $\frac{1}{4}$ turn counterclockwise on the circle.

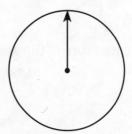

5. Renee drew the figure shown. For 5a–5c, select Yes or No to tell whether the statement is true.

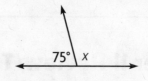

75° x

5a. The measure of a straight angle is 180°.   ○ Yes   ○ No

5b. To find the measure of x, Renee can subtract 75° from 180°.   ○ Yes   ○ No

5c. The measure of x is 115°.   ○ Yes   ○ No

6. [THINK SMARTER +] Trey drew this figure with a protractor.

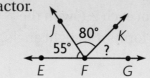

Part A

Write an equation that can be used to find m∠KFG.

Part B

What is the measure of ∠KFG? Describe how you solved the equation and how you can check your answer.

7. Use a protractor to find the measure of the angle.

The angle measures _____.

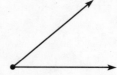

Name _____

8. Alex drew this angle on the circle.
   Which describes the angle?
   Mark all that apply.

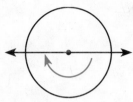

   (A) $\frac{1}{4}$ turn   (C) clockwise

   (B) $\frac{1}{2}$ turn   (D) counterclockwise

9. Miles has a piece of paper that is $\frac{1}{4}$ of a large circle.
   He cuts the paper into three equal parts from the
   center point of the circle. What is the angle
   measure of each part?

   The angle measures _____.

10. Use a protractor to find the measure of each
    angle. Write each angle and its measure in
    a box ordered by the measure of the angles
    from least to greatest.

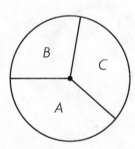

Angle:	Angle:	Angle:
Measure:	Measure:	Measure:

11. Use the numbers and symbols to write an equation that can be
    used to find the measure of the unknown angle.

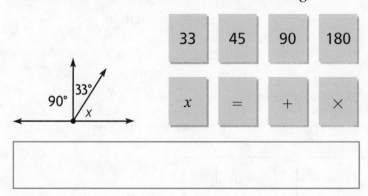

    What is the measure of the unknown angle? _____

12. Choose the word and angle measure to complete a true statement about ∠JKL.

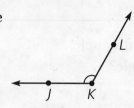

∠JKL is a(n)

acute
obtuse
right

angle that has a measure of

60°.
120°.
135°.

13. Vince began practicing piano at 5:15 P.M. He stopped at 5:35 P.M. How many degrees did the minute hand turn during Vince's practice time? Explain how you found your answer.

Start

Stop

14. An angle measures 125°. Through what fraction of a circle does the angle turn?

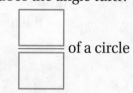 of a circle

15. Write the letter for each angle measure in the correct box.

A 125°   **B** 90°   **C** 180°   **D** 30°   **E** 45°   **F** 95°

acute	obtuse	right	straight

Name _____

16. For numbers 16a–16b, select the fraction that makes a true statement about the figure.

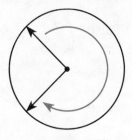

Figure 1   Figure 2

16a.   The angle in Figure 1 represents a $\begin{array}{c} \frac{1}{4} \\ \frac{1}{2} \\ \frac{3}{4} \end{array}$ turn.

16b.   The angle in Figure 2 represents a $\begin{array}{c} \frac{1}{4} \\ \frac{1}{2} \\ \frac{3}{4} \end{array}$ turn.

17. **GO DEEPER** Melanie cuts a rectangle out of a piece of scrap paper as shown. She wants to calculate the angle measure of the piece that is left over.

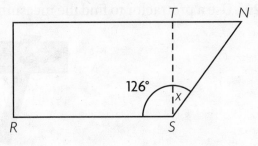

Part A

Draw a bar model to represent the problem.

Part B

Write and solve an equation to find x.

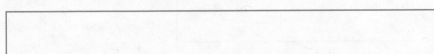

The angle measures _____.

18. Two angles, ∠A and ∠B, form a right angle. ∠A measures 32°. For numbers 18a–18c, select True or False for the statement.

18a.   ∠B is an acute angle.   ○ True   ○ False

18b.   The equation $180° - 32° = x°$ ○ True   ○ False
       can be used to find the
       measure of ∠B.

18c.   The measure of ∠B is 58°.   ○ True   ○ False

19. A circle is divided into parts. Which sum could represent the angle measures that make up the circle? Mark all that apply.

(A)   120° + 120° + 120° + 120°

(B)   25° + 40° + 80° + 105° + 110°

(C)   33° + 82° + 111° + 50° + 84°

(D)   40° + 53° + 72° + 81° + 90° + 34°

20. Use a protractor to find the measures of the unknown angles.

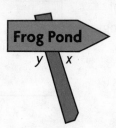

m∠x = _____   m∠y = _____

What do you notice about the measures of the unknown angles? Is this what you would have expected? Explain your reasoning.

Relative Sizes of Measurement Units

 Show What You Know

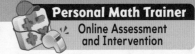
Check your understanding of important skills.

Name _____

▶ **Time to the Half Hour** **Read the clock. Write the time.** (2.MD.C.7)

1.

2.

3.

▶ **Multiply by 1-Digit Numbers** **Find the product.** (4.NBT.B.5)

4. 84
× 7

5. 536
× 8

6. 748
× 5

7. 2,524
× 2

8. 360
× 9

9. 296
× 3

10. $1,428
× 4

11. 64
× 5

Math in the Real World

A team was given a bucket of water and a sponge. The team had 1 minute to fill an empty half-gallon bucket with water using only the sponge. The line plot shows the amount of water squeezed into the bucket. Did the team squeeze enough water to fill the half-gallon bucket?

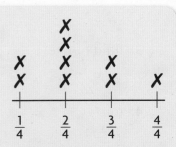

Amount of Water Squeezed into the Bucket (in cups)

Vocabulary Builder

▶ **Visualize It** ·····················

Complete the Brain Storming diagram by using words with a ✓.

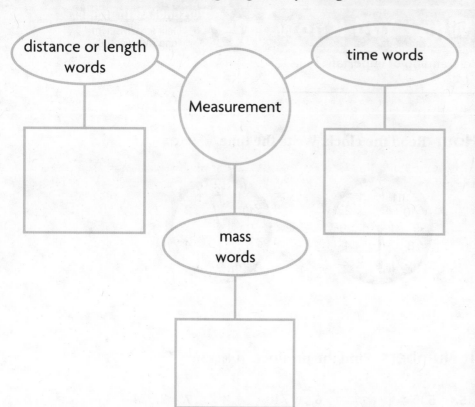

distance or length words

Measurement

time words

mass words

▶ **Understand Vocabulary** ·····················

Draw a line to match each word with its definition.

1. decimeter

2. second

3. fluid ounce

4. ton

5. line plot

• A customary unit for measuring liquid volume

• A graph that shows the frequency of data along a number line

• A customary unit used to measure weight

• A small unit of time

• A metric unit for measuring length or distance

• Interactive Student Edition
• Multimedia eGlossary

Chapter 12 Vocabulary

cup (c)

taza (tz)

18

fluid ounce (fl oz)

onza fluida (fl oz)

34

gallon (gal)

galón (gal)

37

half gallon

medio galón

38

kilometer (km)

kilómetro (km)

44

line plot

diagrama de puntos

47

liquid volume

volumen de un líquido

49

mile (mi)

milla (mi)

51

A customary unit used to measure liquid capacity and liquid volume

1 cup = 8 fluid ounces

A customary unit used to measure capacity and liquid volume
1 cup = 8 ounces

A customary unit for measuring capacity and liquid volume
1 half gallon = 2 quarts

 1 half gallon

A customary unit for measuring capacity and liquid volume
1 gallon = 4 quarts

 1 gallon

A graph that records each piece of data on a number line

Example:

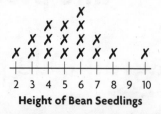

Height of Bean Seedlings

A metric unit for measuring length or distance
1 kilometer = 1,000 meters

A customary unit for measuring length or distance
1 mile = 5,280 feet

The measure of the space a liquid occupies

1 cup = 8 fluid ounces

1 pint = 2 cups

1 quart = 4 cups

Metric Units of Liquid Volume
1 liter (L) = 1,000 milliliters (mL)

milliliter (mL)

mililitro (mL)

52

millimeter (mm)

milímetro (mm)

53

ounce (oz)

onza (oz)

58

pint (pt)

pinta (pt)

67

pound (lb)

libra (lb)

70

quart (qt)

cuarto (ct)

74

second (sec)

segundo (seg)

83

ton (T)

tonelada (t)

92

A metric unit for measuring length or distance
1 centimeter = 10 millimeters

centimeters

A metric unit for measuring capacity and liquid volume
1 liter = 1,000 milliliters

1 milliliter

A customary unit for measuring capacity and liquid volume
1 pint = 2 cups

1 pint

A customary unit for measuring weight
1 pound = 16 ounces

about 1 ounce

A customary unit for measuring capacity and liquid volume
1 quart = 2 pints

A customary unit for measuring weight
1 pound = 16 ounces

about 1 pound

A customary unit used to measure weight
1 ton = 2,000 pounds

about 1 ton

A small unit of time
1 minute = 60 seconds

1 second

Bingo

For 3 to 6 players

Materials

- 1 set of word cards
- 1 Bingo board for each player
- game markers

How to Play

1. The caller chooses a card and reads the definition. Then the caller puts the card in a second pile.

2. Players put a marker on the word that matches the definition each time they find it on their Bingo boards.

3. Repeat Steps 1 and 2 until a player marks 5 boxes in a line going down, across, or on a slant and calls "Bingo."

4. Check the answers. Have the player who said "Bingo" read the words aloud while the caller checks the definitions on the cards in the second pile.

Word Box

cup
fluid ounce
gallon
half gallon
kilometer
line plot
liquid volume
mile
milliliter
millimeter
ounce
pint
pound
quart
second
ton

The Write Way

Reflect

Choose one idea. Write about it.

- Do 50 milliliters and 50 millimeters represent the same amount? Explain why or why not.
- Write a paragraph that uses at least three of these words.

  cup   mile   pound   second   ton

- Explain what is most important to understand about line plots.

Name _____

Measurement Benchmarks

Essential Question How can you use benchmarks to understand the relative sizes of measurement units?

Common Core Measurement and Data—
4.MD.A.1
MATHEMATICAL PRACTICES
MP1, MP2, MP3, MP7

Unlock the Problem Real World

Jake says the length of his bike is about four yards. Use the benchmark units below to determine if Jake's statement is reasonable.

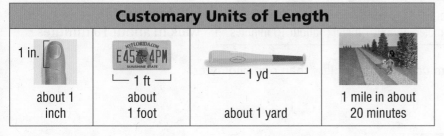

Customary Units of Length			
1 in. about 1 inch	⊢ 1 ft ⊣ about 1 foot	⊢ 1 yd ⊣ about 1 yard	1 mile in about 20 minutes

A **mile** is a customary unit for measuring length or distance. The benchmark shows the distance you can walk in about 20 minutes.

A baseball bat is about one yard long. Since Jake's bike is shorter than four times the length of a baseball bat, his bike is shorter than four yards long.

So, Jake's statement _____ reasonable.

Jake's bike is about _____ baseball bats long.

Example 1   Use the benchmark customary units.

Customary Units of Liquid Volume				
1 cup = 8 fluid ounces	1 pint	1 quart	1 half gallon	1 gallon

- About how much liquid is in a mug of hot chocolate? _____

Customary Units of Weight		
about 1 ounce	about 1 pound	about 1 ton

Math Talk

MATHEMATICAL PRACTICES ②

Use Reasoning Use benchmarks to explain how you would order the units of weight from heaviest to lightest.

- About how much does a grapefruit weigh? _____

© Houghton Mifflin Harcourt Publishing Company • Image Credits: (tr) ©hamurishi/Shutterstock

Benchmarks for Metric Units Like place value, the metric system is based on multiples of ten. Each unit is 10 times as large as the next smaller unit. Below are some common metric benchmarks.

🔒 Example 2 Use the benchmark metric units.

Metric Units of Length				
about 1 millimeter	about 1 centimeter	about 1 decimeter	about 1 meter	1 kilometer in about 10 minutes

A **kilometer** is a metric unit for measuring length or distance. The benchmark shows the distance you can walk in about 10 minutes.

- Is the length of your classroom greater than or less than one kilometer?

_____

Metric Units of Liquid Volume	
1 milliliter	1 liter

- About how much medicine is usually in a medicine bottle?

about 120 _____

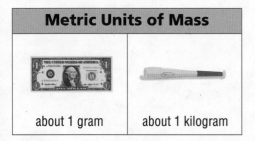

Metric Units of Mass	
about 1 gram	about 1 kilogram

- About how much is the mass of a paper clip?

_____

Math Talk

© Houghton Mifflin Harcourt Publishing Company

MATHEMATICAL PRACTICES ⑦

Look for Structure
Explain how benchmark measurements can help you decide which unit to use when measuring.

Name _____

Use benchmarks to choose the metric unit you would use to measure each.

1. mass of a strawberry

✓ 2. length of a cell phone

_____

_____

Metric Units
centimeter
meter
kilometer
gram
kilogram
milliliter
liter

Circle the better estimate.

3. width of a teacher's desk

   10 meters or 1 meter

4. the amount of liquid a punch bowl holds

   2 liters or 20 liters

✓ 5. distance between Seattle and San Francisco

   6 miles or 680 miles

MATHEMATICAL PRACTICES ③

Apply Which metric unit would you use to measure the distance across the United States? Explain.

On Your Own

Use benchmarks to choose the customary unit you would use to measure each.

6. length of a football field

7. weight of a pumpkin

_____

_____

Customary Units
inch
foot
yard
ounce
pound
cup
gallon

Circle the better estimate.

8. weight of a watermelon

   4 pounds or 4 ounces

9. the amount of liquid a fish tank holds

   10 cups or 10 gallons

Complete the sentence. Write *more* or *less*.

10. Matthew's large dog weighs _____ than one ton.

11. The amount of liquid a sink can hold is _____ than one cup of water.

12. A paper clip has a mass of _____ than one kilogram.

Problem Solving • Applications (Real World)

For 13–15, use benchmarks to explain your answer.

13. **THINK SMARTER** Cristina is making macaroni and cheese for her family. Would Cristina use 1 pound of macaroni or 1 ounce of macaroni?

_____

_____

14. Which is the better estimate for the length of a kitchen table, 200 centimeters or 200 meters?

_____

_____

15. **GO DEEPER** Jodi wants to weigh her cat and measure its standing height. Which two units should she use?

_____

16. **MATHEMATICAL PRACTICE ①** Evaluate Reasonableness Dalton used benchmarks to estimate that there are more cups than quarts in one gallon. Is Dalton's estimate reasonable? Explain.

_____

_____

17. **THINK SMARTER** Select the correct word to complete the sentence.

Justine is thirsty after running two miles.

She should drink | 1 pint
            1 meter | of water.
            10 pounds

Name _____

Measurement Benchmarks

COMMON CORE STANDARD—4.MD.A.1
Solve problems involving measurement and conversion of measurements from a larger unit to a smaller unit.

Use benchmarks to choose the customary unit you would use to measure each.

1. height of a computer

   foot
   _____

2. weight of a table

   _____

3. length of a semi-truck

   _____

4. the amount of liquid a bathtub holds

   _____

Customary Units	
ounce	yard
pound	mile
inch	gallon
foot	cup

Use benchmarks to choose the metric unit you would use to measure each.

5. mass of a grasshopper

   _____

6. the amount of liquid a water bottle holds

   _____

7. length of a soccer field

   _____

8. length of a pencil

   _____

Metric Units	
milliliter	centimeter
liter	meter
gram	kilometer
kilogram	

Circle the better estimate.

9. mass of a chicken egg

   50 grams   50 kilograms

10. length of a car

    12 miles   12 feet

11. amount of liquid a drinking glass holds

    8 ounces   8 quarts

Problem Solving Real World

12. What is the better estimate for the mass of a textbook, 1 gram or 1 kilogram?

    _____

13. What is the better estimate for the height of a desk, 1 meter or 1 kilometer?

    _____

14. **WRITE** ▸*Math* Use benchmarks to determine the customary and metric units you would use to measure the height of your house. Explain your answer.

    _____

    _____

© Houghton Mifflin Harcourt Publishing Company

1. What unit would be best to use for measuring the weight of a stapler?

_____

_____

2. Which is the best estimate for the length of a car?

_____

_____

Spiral Review (4.NF.B.4c, 4.NF.C.6, 4.MD.C.5a, 4.MD.C.5b, 4.G.A.2)

3. Bart practices his trumpet $1\frac{1}{4}$ hours each day. How many hours will he practice in 6 days?

_____

_____

4. Millie collected 100 stamps from different countries. Thirty-two of the stamps are from countries in Africa. What is $\frac{32}{100}$ written as a decimal?

_____

_____

5. Diedre drew a quadrilateral with 4 right angles and opposite sides of the same length. Name all the kinds of polygons that could be Diedre's quadrilateral.

_____

_____

6. How many degrees are in an angle that turns through $\frac{1}{2}$ of a circle?

FOR MORE PRACTICE
GO TO THE
Personal Math Trainer

Name _____

Customary Units of Length

Essential Question How can you use models to compare customary units of length?

 Common Core

Measurement and Data—4.MD.A.1
Also 4.MD.A.2
MATHEMATICAL PRACTICES
MP2, MP3, MP4

Unlock the Problem *Real World*

You can use a ruler to measure length. A ruler that is 1 foot long shows 12 inches in 1 foot. A ruler that is 3 feet long is called a yardstick. There are 3 feet in 1 yard.

How does the size of a foot compare to the size of an inch?

Activity

Materials ■ 1-inch grid paper ■ scissors ■ tape

STEP 1 Cut out the paper inch tiles. Label each tile 1 inch.

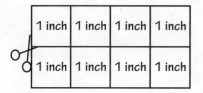

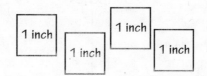

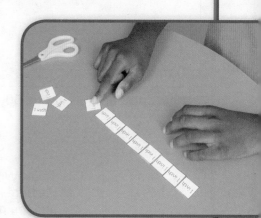

STEP 2 Place 12 tiles end-to-end to build 1 foot. Tape the tiles together.

1 foot											
1 inch	1 inch	1 inch	1 inch	1 inch	1 inch	1 inch	1 inch	1 inch	1 inch	1 inch	1 inch

STEP 3 Compare the size of 1 foot to the size of 1 inch.

1 foot											
1 inch	1 inch	1 inch	1 inch	1 inch	1 inch	1 inch	1 inch	1 inch	1 inch	1 inch	1 inch

1 inch

1 inch

Think: You need 12 inches to make 1 foot.

So, 1 foot is _____ times as long as 1 inch.

Math Talk

MATHEMATICAL PRACTICES ②

Use Reasoning Explain how you know the number of inches you need to make a yard.

Chapter 12 647

🔑 Example Compare measures.

Emma has 4 feet of thread. She needs 50 inches of thread to make some bracelets. How can she determine if she has enough thread to make the bracelets?

Since 1 foot is 12 times as long as 1 inch, you can write feet as inches by multiplying the number of feet by 12.

STEP 1 Make a table that relates feet and inches.

Feet	Inches
1	12
2	
3	
4	
5	

Think:

1 foot × 12 = 12 inches

2 feet × 12 = _____

3 feet × _____ = _____

4 feet × _____ = _____

5 feet × _____ = _____

STEP 2 Compare 4 feet and 50 inches.

4 feet   50 inches

Think: Write each measure in inches and compare using <, >, or =.

_____ ⟶ ◯ ⟵ _____

Emma has 4 feet of thread. She needs 50 inches of thread.

4 feet is _____ than 50 inches.

So, Emma _____ enough thread to make the bracelets.

MATHEMATICAL PRACTICES ②

Represent a Problem Explain how making a table helped you solve the problem.

- What if Emma had 5 feet of thread? Would she have enough thread to make the bracelets? Explain.

_____

_____

_____

648

Name _____

1. Compare the size of a yard to the size of a foot.
   Use a model to help.

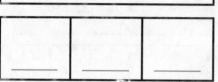

1 yard

Customary Units of Length
1 foot (ft) = 12 inches (in.)
1 yard (yd) = 3 feet
1 yard (yd) = 36 inches

_____   _____   _____

1 yard is _____ times as long as _____ foot.

Complete.

✓ 2. 2 feet = _____ inches   3. 3 yards = _____ feet   ✓ 4. 7 yards = _____ feet

MATHEMATICAL PRACTICES ④

Interpret a Result If you measured the length of your classroom in yards and then in feet, which unit would have a greater number of units? Explain.

On Your Own

Complete.

5. 4 yards = _____ feet   6. 10 yards = _____ feet   7. 7 feet = _____ inches

MATHEMATICAL PRACTICE ④ **Use Symbols Algebra** Compare using <, >, or =.

8. 1 foot ◯ 13 inches   9. 2 yards ◯ 6 feet   10. 6 feet ◯ 60 inches

Problem Solving • Applications

11. **THINK SMARTER** Joanna has 3 yards of fabric. She needs 100 inches of fabric to make curtains. Does she have enough fabric to make curtains? Explain. Make a table to help.

    _____

    _____

    _____

Yards	Inches
1	
2	
3	

12. **THINK SMARTER** Select the measures that are equal. Mark all that apply.

    (A) 4 feet   (C) 36 feet   (E) 15 feet

    (B) 12 yards   (D) 480 inches   (F) 432 inches

13. **GO DEEPER** Jasmine and Luke used fraction strips to compare the size of a foot to the size of an inch using fractions. They drew models to show their answers. Whose answer makes sense? Whose answer is nonsense? Explain your reasoning.

Jasmine's Work

1

$\frac{1}{12}$	$\frac{1}{12}$	$\frac{1}{12}$	$\frac{1}{12}$	$\frac{1}{12}$	$\frac{1}{12}$	$\frac{1}{12}$	$\frac{1}{12}$	$\frac{1}{12}$	$\frac{1}{12}$	$\frac{1}{12}$	$\frac{1}{12}$

1 inch is $\frac{1}{12}$ of a foot.

Luke's Work

1

$\frac{1}{3}$	$\frac{1}{3}$	$\frac{1}{3}$

1 inch is $\frac{1}{3}$ of a foot.

a. **MATHEMATICAL PRACTICE ③** **Apply** For the answer that is nonsense, write an answer that makes sense.

_____

_____

b. Look back at Luke's model. Which two units could you compare using his model? Explain.

_____

_____

_____

Customary Units of Length

Common Core Standard—4.MD.A.1
Solve problems involving measurement and conversion of measurements from a larger unit to a smaller unit.

Complete.

1. 3 feet = __36__ inches   Think: 1 foot = 12 inches,
so 3 feet = 3 × 12 inches, or 36 inches

2. 2 yards = _____ feet

3. 8 feet = _____ inches

4. 7 yards = _____ feet

5. 4 feet = _____ inches

6. 15 yards = _____ feet

7. 10 feet = _____ inches

Compare using <, >, or =.

8. 3 yards ◯ 10 feet

9. 5 feet ◯ 60 inches

10. 8 yards ◯ 20 feet

Problem Solving Real World

11. Carla has two lengths of ribbon. One ribbon is 2 feet long. The other ribbon is 30 inches long. Which length of ribbon is longer? **Explain.**

_____

_____

_____

_____

12. A football player gained 2 yards on one play. On the next play, he gained 5 feet. Was his gain greater on the first play or the second play? **Explain.**

_____

_____

_____

_____

13. **WRITE** ▶*Math* Write a problem that can be solved by comparing feet and inches using a model. Include a solution. Explain why you are changing from a larger unit to a smaller unit.

_____

_____

Lesson Check (4.MD.A.1)

1. Marta has 14 feet of wire to use to make necklaces. She needs to know the length in inches so she can determine how many necklaces to make. How many inches of wire does Marta have?

2. Jarod bought 8 yards of ribbon. He needs 200 inches to use to make curtains. How many inches of ribbon does he have?

Spiral Review (4.NF.C.6, 4.MD.A.1, 4.MD.A.2, 4.MD.C.5a)

3. Describe the turn shown below. (Be sure to include both the size and direction of the turn in your answer.)

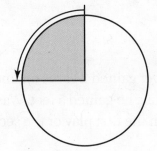

4. What decimal represents the shaded part of the model below?

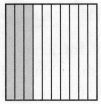

5. Three sisters shared $3.60 equally. How much did each sister get?

6. Which is the best estimate for the width of your index finger?

FOR MORE PRACTICE
GO TO THE
Personal Math Trainer

Name _____

Customary Units of Weight

Essential Question How can you use models to compare customary units of weight?

 Measurement and Data—4.MD.A.1
Also 4.MD.A.2
MATHEMATICAL PRACTICES
MP2, MP4, MP6

Unlock the Problem 〔Real World〕

Ounces and **pounds** are customary units of weight. How does the size of a pound compare to the size of an ounce?

🔑 Activity

Materials ■ color pencils

The number line below shows the relationship between pounds and ounces.

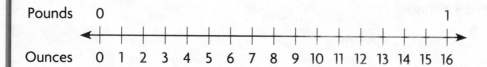

Pounds   0   1

Ounces 0 1 2 3 4 5 6 7 8 9 10 11 12 13 14 15 16

▲ You can use a spring scale to measure weight.

STEP 1 Use a color pencil to shade 1 pound on the number line.

STEP 2 Use a different color pencil to shade 1 ounce on the number line.

STEP 3 Compare the size of 1 pound to the size of 1 ounce.

You need _____ ounces to make _____ pound.

So, 1 pound is _____ times as heavy as 1 ounce.

 Math Talk

MATHEMATICAL PRACTICES ⑥

Attend to Precision How can you compare the size of 9 pounds to the size of 9 ounces?

- **MATHEMATICAL PRACTICE ⑥** **Explain** how the number line helped you to compare the sizes of the units.

_____

_____

_____

_____

🔒 Example · Compare measures.

Nancy needs 5 pounds of flour to bake pies for a festival. She has 90 ounces of flour. How can she determine if she has enough flour to bake the pies?

STEP 1 Make a table that relates pounds and ounces.

Pounds	Ounces
1	16
2	
3	
4	
5	

Think:

1 pound × 16 = 16 ounces

2 pounds × 16 = _____

3 pounds × _____ = _____

4 pounds × _____ = _____

5 pounds × _____ = _____

STEP 2 Compare 90 ounces and 5 pounds.

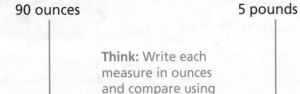

90 ounces   5 pounds

Think: Write each measure in ounces and compare using <, >, or =.

_____ ◯ _____

Nancy has 90 ounces of flour. She needs 5 pounds of flour.

90 ounces is _____ than 5 pounds.

So, Nancy _____ enough flour to make the pies.

Try This! There are 2,000 pounds in 1 **ton**.
Make a table that relates tons and pounds.

Tons	Pounds
1	2,000
2	
3	

1 ton is _____ times as heavy as 1 pound.

654

Name _____

Share and Show

1. 4 tons = _____ pounds

   Think: 4 tons × _____ = _____

Complete.

☑ 2. 5 tons = _____ pounds

3. 6 pounds = _____ ounces

Customary Units of Weight
1 pound (lb) = 16 ounces (oz)
1 ton (T) = 2,000 pounds

Math Talk MATHEMATICAL PRACTICES ④

Write an Equation What equation can you use to solve Exercise 4? Explain.

On Your Own

Complete.

☑ 4. 7 pounds = _____ ounces

5. 6 tons = _____ pounds

MATHEMATICAL PRACTICE ④ **Use Symbols Algebra** Compare using >, <, or =.

6. 1 pound ⬭ 15 ounces

7. 2 tons ⬭ 2 pounds

Problem Solving • Applications

8. A landscaping company ordered 8 tons of gravel. It sells the gravel in 50-pound bags. How many pounds of gravel did the company order?

   _____

9. **THINK SMARTER** If you could draw a number line that shows the relationship between tons and pounds, what would it look like? Explain.

   _____

   _____

   _____

10. **THINK SMARTER** Write the symbol that compares the weights correctly.

    [<]   [=]   [>]

    160 ounces _____ 10 pounds   600 pounds _____ 3 tons

11. 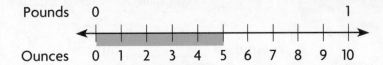 Alexis bought $\frac{1}{2}$ pound of grapes. How many ounces of grapes did she buy?

Dan drew the number line below to solve the problem. He says his model shows that there are 5 ounces in $\frac{1}{2}$ pound. What is his error?

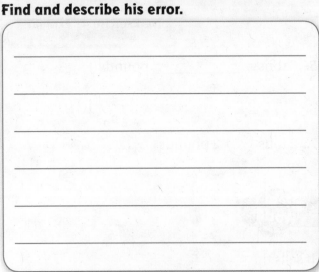

Look at the way Dan solved the problem. Find and describe his error.

Draw a correct number line and solve the problem.

So, Alexis bought _____ ounces of grapes.

- MATHEMATICAL PRACTICE **6** Look back at the number line you drew. How many ounces are in $\frac{1}{4}$ pound? **Explain.**

Customary Units of Weight

Common Core **Common Core Standard—4.MD.A.1**
Solve problems involving measurement and conversion of measurements from a larger unit to a smaller unit.

Complete.

1. 5 pounds = _____80_____ ounces

   Think: 1 pound = 16 ounces, so
   5 pounds = 5 × 16 ounces, or 80 ounces

2. 7 tons = _____ pounds

3. 2 pounds = _____ ounces

4. 3 tons = _____ pounds

5. 10 pounds = _____ ounces

Compare using <, >, or =.

6. 8 pounds ◯ 80 ounces

7. 1 ton ◯ 100 pounds

8. 3 pounds ◯ 50 ounces

9. 5 tons ◯ 1,000 pounds

Problem Solving ·Real World·

10. A company that makes steel girders can produce 6 tons of girders in one day. How many pounds is this?

    _____

11. Larry's baby sister weighed 6 pounds at birth. How many ounces did the baby weigh?

    _____

12. **WRITE** ▸*Math* Write a problem that can be solved by comparing pounds and ounces using a model. Include a solution. Explain why you are changing from a larger unit to a smaller unit.

    _____

    _____

    _____

Lesson Check (4.MD.A.1)

1. Ann bought 2 pounds of cheese to make lasagna. The recipe gives the amount of cheese needed in ounces. How many ounces of cheese did she buy?

2. A school bus weighs 7 tons. The weight limit for a bridge is given in pounds. What is this weight of the bus in pounds?

Spiral Review (4.NF.B.4c, 4.MD.A.1, 4.MD.C.7, 4.G.A.3)

3. What is the measure of ∠EHG?

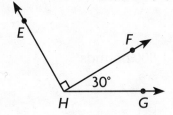

4. How many lines of symmetry does the square below have?

5. To make dough, Reba needs $2\frac{1}{2}$ cups of flour. How much flour does she need to make 5 batches of dough?

6. Judi's father is 6 feet tall. The minimum height to ride a rollercoaster is given in inches. How many inches tall is Judi's father?

FOR MORE PRACTICE GO TO THE
Personal Math Trainer

Name _____

Customary Units of Liquid Volume

Essential Question How can you use models to compare customary units of liquid volume?

Common Core Measurement and Data—4.MD.A.1
Also 4.MD.A.2
MATHEMATICAL PRACTICES
MP3, MP4, MP6, MP7

🔑 Unlock the Problem (Real World)

Liquid volume is the measure of the space a liquid occupies. Some basic units for measuring liquid volume are **gallons**, **half gallons**, **quarts**, **pints**, and **cups**.

The bars below model the relationships among some units of liquid volume. The largest units are gallons. The smallest units are **fluid ounces**.

1 cup = 8 fluid ounces

1 pint = 2 cups

1 quart = 4 cups

1 gallon

1 gallon															
1 half gallon								1 half gallon							
1 quart				1 quart				1 quart				1 quart			
1 pint		1 pint		1 pint		1 pint		1 pint		1 pint		1 pint		1 pint	
1 cup	1 cup	1 cup	1 cup	1 cup	1 cup	1 cup	1 cup	1 cup	1 cup	1 cup	1 cup	1 cup	1 cup	1 cup	1 cup
8 fluid ounces	8 fluid ounces	8 fluid ounces	8 fluid ounces	8 fluid ounces	8 fluid ounces	8 fluid ounces	8 fluid ounces	8 fluid ounces	8 fluid ounces	8 fluid ounces	8 fluid ounces	8 fluid ounces	8 fluid ounces	8 fluid ounces	8 fluid ounces

🔒 Example How does the size of a gallon compare to the size of a quart?

Math Talk

MATHEMATICAL PRACTICES ⑦

Look for a Pattern
Describe the pattern in the units of liquid volume.

STEP 1 Draw two bars that represent this relationship. One bar should show gallons and the other bar should show quarts.

STEP 2 Shade 1 gallon on one bar and shade 1 quart on the other bar.

STEP 3 Compare the size of 1 gallon to the size of 1 quart.

So, 1 gallon is _____ times as much as 1 quart.

1 Example Compare measures.

Serena needs to make 3 gallons of lemonade for the
lemonade sale. She has a powder mix that makes
350 fluid ounces of lemonade. How can she decide if
she has enough powder mix?

STEP 1 Use the model on page 659. Find the relationship
between gallons and fluid ounces.

1 gallon = _____ cups

1 cup = _____ fluid ounces

1 gallon = _____ cups × _____ fluid ounces

1 gallon = _____ fluid ounces

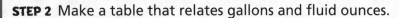

STEP 2 Make a table that relates gallons and fluid ounces.

Gallons	Fluid Ounces
1	128
2	
3	

Think:

1 gallon = 128 fluid ounces

2 gallons × 128 = _____ fluid ounces

3 gallons × 128 = _____ fluid ounces

STEP 3 Compare 350 fluid ounces and 3 gallons.

350 fluid ounces   3 gallons

Think: Write each
measure in fluid
ounces and compare
using <, >, or =.

_____ ◯ _____

Serena has enough mix to make 350 fluid ounces.
She needs to make 3 gallons of lemonade.

350 fluid ounces is _____ than 3 gallons.

So, Serena _____ enough mix to make 3 gallons
of lemonade.

Name _____

1. Compare the size of a quart to the size of a pint.
   Use a model to help.

1 quart

_____	_____

Customary Units of Liquid Volume
1 cup (c) = 8 fluid ounces (fl oz)
1 pint (pt) = 2 cups
1 quart (qt) = 2 pints
1 quart (qt) = 4 cups
1 gallon (gal) = 4 quarts
1 gallon (gal) = 8 pints
1 gallon (gal) = 16 cups

   1 quart is _____ times as much as _____ pint.

Complete.

✓ **2.** 2 pints = _____ cups

3. 3 gallons = _____ quarts

✓ **4.** 6 quarts = _____ cups

On Your Own

MATHEMATICAL PRACTICES ⑥

Make Connections Explain how the conversion chart above relates to the bar model in Exercise 1.

Use a model or _i_Tools to complete.

5. 4 gallons = _____ pints

6. 5 cups = _____ fluid ounces

MATHEMATICAL PRACTICE ④ **Use Symbols Algebra** Compare using >, <, or =.

7. 2 gallons ◯ 32 cups

8. 4 pints ◯ 6 cups

9. 5 quarts ◯ 11 pints

Problem Solving • Applications

10. THINK SMARTER A soccer team has 25 players. The team's thermos holds 4 gallons of water. If the thermos is full, is there enough water for each player to have 2 cups? Explain. Make a table to help.

_____

_____

_____

Gallons	Cups
1	
2	
3	
4	

11. **MATHEMATICAL PRACTICE 3** **Verify the Reasoning of Others** Whose statement makes sense? Whose statement is nonsense? Explain your reasoning.

1 pint is $\frac{1}{4}$ of a gallon.

1 pint is $\frac{1}{8}$ of a gallon.

Zach's Statement

_____

_____

_____

Angela's Statement

_____

_____

_____

12. **GO DEEPER** Peter's glasses each hold 8 fluid ounces. How many glasses of juice can Peter pour from a bottle that holds 2 quarts?

_____

13. **THINK SMARTER** A pitcher contains 5 quarts of water. Josy says the pitcher contains 10 cups of water. Explain Josy's error. Then find the correct number of cups the pitcher contains.

_____

_____

_____

Customary Units of Liquid Volume

Common Core **Common Core Standard—4.MD.A.1**
Solve problems involving measurement and conversion of measurements from a larger unit to a smaller unit.

Complete.

1. 6 gallons = ___24___ quarts

Think: 1 gallon = 4 quarts,
so 6 gallons = 6 × 4 quarts, or 24 quarts

2. 12 quarts = _____ pints

3. 6 cups = _____ fluid ounces

4. 9 pints = _____ cups

5. 10 quarts = _____ cups

6. 5 gallons = _____ pints

7. 3 gallons = _____ cups

Compare using <, >, or =.

8. 6 pints ◯ 60 fluid ounces

9. 3 gallons ◯ 30 quarts

10. 5 quarts ◯ 20 cups

11. 12 pints ◯ 6 cups

Problem Solving Real World

12. A chef makes $1\frac{1}{2}$ gallons of soup in a large pot. How many 1-cup servings can the chef get from this large pot of soup?

13. Kendra's water bottle contains 2 quarts of water. She wants to add drink mix to it, but the directions for the drink mix give the amount of water in fluid ounces. How many fluid ounces are in her bottle?

_____

_____

14. **WRITE** ▸*Math* Write a problem that can be solved by comparing quarts and cups using a model. Include a solution. Explain why you are changing from a larger unit to a smaller unit.

_____

_____

Lesson Check (4.MD.A.1)

1. Joshua drinks 8 cups of water a day. The recommended daily amount is given in fluid ounces. How many fluid ounces of water does he drink each day?

2. A cafeteria used 5 gallons of milk in preparing lunch. How many 1-quart containers of milk did the cafeteria use?

_____

_____

Spiral Review (4.NF.B.4a, 4.NF.C.6, 4.MD.A.1, 4.G.A.1)

3. Roy uses $\frac{1}{4}$ cup of batter for each muffin. Make a list to show the amounts of batter he will use depending on the number of muffins he makes.

4. Beth has $\frac{7}{100}$ of a dollar. What is the amount of money Beth has?

_____

_____

_____

_____

5. Name the figure that Enrico drew below.

6. A hippopotamus weighs 4 tons. Feeding instructions are given for weights in pounds. How many pounds does the hippopotamus weigh?

_____

_____

FOR MORE PRACTICE
GO TO THE
Personal Math Trainer

Name _____

Line Plots

Essential Question How can you make and interpret line plots with fractional data?

Common Core **Measurement and Data—4.MD.B.4**
Also 4.MD.A.2
MATHEMATICAL PRACTICES
MP2, MP3, MP4

🔑 Unlock the Problem

The data show the lengths of the buttons in Jen's collection. For an art project, she wants to know how many buttons are longer than $\frac{1}{4}$ inch.

You can use a line plot to solve the problem. A **line plot** is a graph that shows the frequency of data along a number line.

Length of Buttons in Jen's Collection (in inches)
$\frac{1}{4}, \frac{3}{4}, \frac{1}{4}, \frac{4}{4}, \frac{1}{4}, \frac{4}{4}$

Make a line plot to show the data.

🔑 Example 1

STEP 1 Order the data from least to greatest length and complete the tally table.

_____

_____

STEP 2 Label the fraction lengths on the number line below from the least value of the data to the greatest.

_____

STEP 3 Plot an *X* above the number line for each data point. Write a title for the line plot.

Buttons in Jen's Collection	
Length (in inches)	Tally
$\frac{1}{4}$	
$\frac{3}{4}$	
$\frac{4}{4}$	

_____

So, _____ buttons are longer than $\frac{1}{4}$ inch.

MATHEMATICAL PRACTICES ④

Use Models Explain how you labeled the numbers on the number line in Step 2.

1. How many buttons are in Jen's collection? _____

2. What is the difference in length between the longest button and the shortest button in Jen's collection? _____

Think: To find the difference, subtract the numerators. The denominators stay the same.

Chapter 12   665

🔓 Example 2

Some of the students in Ms. Lee's class walk to school. The data show the distances these students walk. What distance do most students walk?

Distance Students Walk to School (in miles)
$\frac{1}{2}$, $\frac{1}{2}$, $\frac{1}{4}$, $\frac{3}{4}$, $\frac{1}{4}$, $\frac{1}{2}$, $\frac{1}{2}$

Make a line plot to show the data.

STEP 1 Order the data from least to greatest distance and complete the tally table.

_____

STEP 2 Label the fraction lengths on the number line below from the least value of the data to the greatest.

STEP 3 Plot an *X* above the number line for each data point. Write a title for the line plot.

Distance Students Walk to School	
Distance (in miles)	Tally

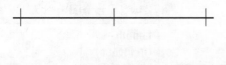

So, most students walk _____.

3. How many more students walk $\frac{1}{2}$ mile than $\frac{1}{4}$ mile to school?

_____

4. What is the difference between the longest distance and the shortest distance that students walk?

_____

5. What if a new student joins Ms. Lee's class who walks $\frac{3}{4}$ mile to school? How would the line plot change? Explain.

_____

Name _____

 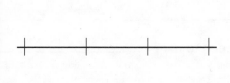
1. A food critic collected data on the lengths of time customers waited for their food. Order the data from least to greatest time. Make a tally table and a line plot to show the data.

Time Customers Waited for Food (in hours)
$\frac{1}{2}, \frac{1}{4}, \frac{3}{4}, \frac{1}{4}, \frac{1}{4}, \frac{1}{2}, 1$

Time Customers Waited for Food	
Time (in hours)	Tally

Math Talk

MATHEMATICAL PRACTICES ④

Use Graphs Explain how the line plot helped you answer the question for Exercise 2.

Use your line plot for 2 and 3.

2. On how many customers did the food critic collect data? _____

3. What is the difference between the longest time and the shortest time that customers waited? _____

On Your Own

4. **MATHEMATICAL PRACTICE** ④ **Use Models** The data show the lengths of the ribbons Mia used to wrap packages. Make a tally table and a line plot to show the data.

Ribbon Used to Wrap Packages	
Length (in yards)	Tally

Ribbon Length Used to Wrap Packages (in yards)
$\frac{1}{6}, \frac{2}{6}, \frac{5}{6}, \frac{3}{6}, \frac{2}{6}, \frac{6}{6}, \frac{3}{6}, \frac{2}{6}$

5. What is the difference in length between the longest ribbon and the shortest ribbon Mia used? _____

© Houghton Mifflin Harcourt Publishing Company

Unlock the Problem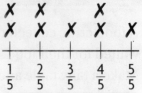

6. **GO DEEPER** The line plot shows the distances the students in Mr. Boren's class ran at the track in miles. Altogether, did the students run more or less than 5 miles?

a. What are you asked to find? _____

_____

b. What information do you need to use? _____

_____

c. How will the line plot help you solve the problem? _____

_____

d. What operation will you use to solve the problem? _____

e. Show the steps to solve the problem.

_____

_____

f. Complete the sentences.

The students ran a total of _____ miles.

The distance is _____ than 5 miles. Altogether the students ran _____ than 5 miles.

Distance Students Ran at the Track (in miles)

7. **THINK SMARTER** Lena collects antique spoons. The line plot shows the lengths of the spoons in her collection. If she lines up all of her spoons in order of size, what is the size of the middle spoon? Explain.

_____

_____

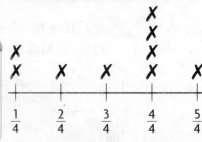

Length of Spoons (in feet)

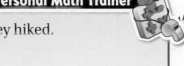

8. **THINK SMARTER +** A hiking group recorded the distances they hiked. Complete the line plot to show the data.

Distance Hiked (in miles)
$\frac{4}{8}, \frac{5}{8}, \frac{7}{8}, \frac{7}{8}, \frac{5}{8}, \frac{6}{8}, \frac{7}{8}, \frac{7}{8}, \frac{6}{8}$

Distance Hiked

Line Plots

Common Core   COMMON CORE STANDARD—4.MD.B.4
Represent and interpret data.

1. Some students compared the time they spend riding the school bus. Complete the tally table and line plot to show the data.

Time Spent on School Bus	
Time (in hours)	Tally
$\frac{1}{6}$	‖
$\frac{2}{6}$	
$\frac{3}{6}$	
$\frac{4}{6}$	

Time Spent on School Bus (in hours)
$\frac{1}{6}$, $\frac{3}{6}$, $\frac{4}{6}$, $\frac{2}{6}$, $\frac{3}{6}$, $\frac{1}{6}$, $\frac{3}{6}$, $\frac{3}{6}$

**Time Spent on
School Bus (in hours)**

Use your line plot for 2 and 3.

2. How many students compared times? _____

3. What is the difference between the longest time and shortest

   time students spent riding the bus? _____

Problem Solving · Real World

**For 4, make a tally table on a separate sheet of paper.
Make a line plot in the space below the problem.**

4.

Milk Drunk at Lunch (in quarts)
$\frac{1}{8}$, $\frac{2}{8}$, $\frac{2}{8}$, $\frac{4}{8}$, $\frac{1}{8}$, $\frac{3}{8}$, $\frac{4}{8}$, $\frac{2}{8}$, $\frac{3}{8}$, $\frac{2}{8}$

**Milk Drunk at Lunch
(in quarts)**

5. **WRITE** *Math* Write a problem that can be solved using a line plot. Draw and label the line plot and solve the problem.

_____

_____

_____

Lesson Check (4.MD.B.4)

Use the line plot for 1 and 2.

1. How many students were reading during study time?

_____

2. What is the difference between the longest time and shortest time spent reading?

_____

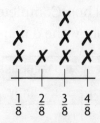

Time Spent Reading During Study Time (in hours)

Spiral Review (4.NF.C.5, 4.NF.C.6, 4.MD.A.1)

3. Bridget is allowed to play on-line games for $\frac{75}{100}$ of an hour each day. Write this fraction as a decimal.

_____

4. Bobby's collection of sports cards has $\frac{3}{10}$ baseball cards and $\frac{39}{100}$ football cards. The rest are soccer cards. What fraction of Bobby's sports cards are baseball or football cards?

_____

5. Jeremy gives his horse 12 gallons of water each day. How many 1-quart pails of water is that?

_____

6. An iguana at a pet store is 5 feet long. Measurements for iguana cages are given in inches. How many inches long is the iguana?

_____

FOR MORE PRACTICE GO TO THE Personal Math Trainer

Name _____

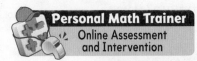
Vocabulary

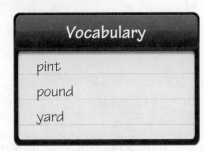

Vocabulary
pint
pound
yard

Choose the best term from the box to complete the sentence.

1. A _____ is a customary unit used to measure weight. (p. 653)

2. The cup and the _____ are both customary units for measuring liquid volume. (p. 659)

Concepts and Skills

Complete the sentence. Write *more* or *less*. (4.MD.A.1)

3. A cat weighs _____ than one ounce.

4. Serena's shoe is _____ than one yard long.

Complete. (4.MD.A.1)

5. 5 feet = _____ inches

6. 4 tons = _____ pounds

7. 4 cups = _____ pints

8. Mrs. Byrne's class went raspberry picking. The data show the weights of the cartons of raspberries the students picked. Make a tally table and a line plot to show the data. (4.MD.B.4)

Weight of Cartons of Raspberries Picked (in pounds)
$\frac{3}{4}, \frac{1}{4}, \frac{2}{4}, \frac{4}{4}, \frac{1}{4}, \frac{1}{4}, \frac{2}{4}, \frac{3}{4}, \frac{3}{4}$

Cartons of Raspberries Picked	
Weight (in pounds)	**Tally**

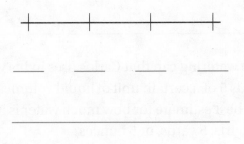

Use your line plot for 9 and 10. (4.MD.B.4)

9. What is the difference in weight between the heaviest carton

and lightest carton of raspberries? _____

10. How many pounds of raspberries did Mrs. Byrne's class pick in all? _____

11. A jug contains 2 gallons of water. How many quarts of water does the jug contain? (4.MD.A.1)

_____

12. Serena bought 4 pounds of dough to make pizzas. The recipe gives the amount of dough needed for a pizza in ounces. How many ounces of dough did she buy? (4.MD.A.1)

_____

13. GO DEEPER   Vicki has a 50 inch roll of ribbon. She used 3 feet of the ribbon to wrap a gift. How many inches of ribbon does she have left? (4.MD.A.1)

_____

14. The watering can that Carlos uses in his vegetable garden holds 5 of a certain unit of liquid volume. When full, what is the best estimate for how much water is in the watering can, 5 quarts, 5 yards, or 5 ounces? (4.MD.A.1)

_____

672

© Houghton Mifflin Harcourt Publishing Company • Image Credits: (br) ©Artville/Getty Images

Name _____

Metric Units of Length

Essential Question How can you use models to compare metric units of length?

Common Core **Measurement and Data—4.MD.A.1**
Also 4.MD.A.2
MATHEMATICAL PRACTICES
MP1, MP4, MP7, MP8

Investigate

Materials ■ ruler (meter) ■ scissors ■ tape

Meters (m), **decimeters** (dm), centimeters (cm), and **millimeters** (mm) are all metric units of length.

Build a meterstick to show how these units are related.

A. Cut out the meterstick strips.

B. Place the strips end-to-end to build 1 meter. Tape the strips together.

C. Look at your meter strip. What patterns do you notice about the sizes of the units?

1 meter is _____ times as long as 1 decimeter.

1 decimeter is _____ times as long as 1 centimeter.

1 centimeter is _____ times as long as 1 millimeter.

Describe the pattern you see.

_____

_____

> **Math Idea**
> If you lined up 1,000 metersticks end-to-end, the length of the metersticks would be 1 kilometer.

Draw Conclusions

1. Compare the size of 1 meter to the size of 1 centimeter. Use your meterstick to help.

_____

2. Compare the size of 1 meter to the size of 1 millimeter. Use your meterstick to help.

_____

_____

3. **THINK SMARTER** What operation could you use to find how many centimeters are in 3 meters? Explain.

_____

_____

_____

_____

Make Connections

You can use different metric units to describe the same length. For example, you can measure the length of a book as 3 decimeters or as 30 centimeters. Since the metric system is based on the number 10, decimals or fractions can be used to describe metric lengths as equivalent units.

Think of 1 meter as one whole. Use your meter strip to write equivalent units as fractions and decimals.

1 meter = 10 decimeters

Each decimeter is

_____ or _____ of a meter.

1 meter = 100 centimeters

Each centimeter is

_____ or _____ of a meter.

Complete the sentence.

• A length of 51 centimeters is _____ or _____ of a meter.

• A length of 8 decimeters is _____ or _____ of a meter.

• A length of 82 centimeters is _____ or _____ of a meter.

Math Talk MATHEMATICAL PRACTICES ⑦

Look for Structure Explain how you are able to locate and write decimeters and centimeters as parts of a meter on the meterstick.

674

Name _____

Metric Units of Length
1 centimeter (cm) = 10 millimeters (mm)
1 decimeter (dm) = 10 centimeters
1 meter (m) = 10 decimeters
1 meter (m) = 100 centimeters
1 meter (m) = 1,000 millimeters

Complete.

✓ **1.** 2 meters = _____ centimeters

2. 3 centimeters = _____ millimeters

3. 5 decimeters = _____ centimeters

MATHEMATICAL PRACTICE ④ Use Symbols Algebra Compare using <, >, or =.

4. 4 meters ◯ 40 decimeters

5. 5 centimeters ◯ 5 millimeters

6. 6 decimeters ◯ 65 centimeters

7. 7 meters ◯ 700 millimeters

Describe the length in meters. Write your answer as a fraction and as a decimal.

✓ **8.** 65 centimeters = _____ or _____ meter

9. 47 centimeters = _____ or _____ meter

10. 9 decimeters = _____ or _____ meter

11. 2 decimeters = _____ or _____ meter

Problem Solving • Applications

12. A new building is 25 meters tall. How many decimeters tall is the building?

_____

13. **GO DEEPER** Alexis is knitting a blanket 2 meters long. Every 2 decimeters, she changes the color of the yarn to make stripes. How many stripes will the blanket have? Explain.

_____

_____

_____

14. **THINK SMARTER** Julianne's desk is 75 centimeters long. She says her desk is 7.5 meters long. Describe her error.

_____

_____

15. **THINK SMARTER** Write the equivalent measurements in each column.

5,000 millimeters	500 centimeters	50 centimeters
$\frac{55}{100}$ meter	0.500 meter	0.55 meter
$\frac{500}{1,000}$ meter	550 millimeters	50 decimeters

5 meters	55 centimeters	500 millimeters

16. **THINK SMARTER** Aruna was writing a report on pecan trees. She made the table of information to the right.

Write a problem that can be solved by using the data.

Pecan Tree	
Average Measurements	
Length of nuts	3 cm to 5 cm
Height	21 m to 30 m
Width of trunk	18 dm
Width of leaf	10 cm to 20 cm

Pose a problem.

_____

_____

_____

_____

_____

Solve your problem.

- **MATHEMATICAL PRACTICE ①** **Describe** how you could change the problem by changing a unit in the problem. Then solve the problem.

_____

Metric Units of Length

Common Core

COMMON CORE STANDARD—4.MD.A.1
Solve problems involving measurement and
conversion of measurements from a larger unit
to a smaller unit.

Complete.

1. 4 meters = _____ 400 centimeters

Think: 1 meter = 100 centimeters,
so 4 meters = 4 × 100 centimeters,
or 400 centimeters

2. 8 centimeters = _____ millimeters

3. 5 meters = _____ decimeters

4. 9 meters = _____ millimeters

5. 7 meters = _____ centimeters

Compare using <, >, or =.

6. 8 meters ◯ 80 centimeters

7. 3 decimeters ◯ 30 centimeters

8. 4 meters ◯ 450 centimeters

9. 90 centimeters ◯ 9 millimeters

Describe the length in meters. Write your answer as a fraction and as a decimal.

10. 43 centimeters = _____ or

_____ meter

11. 6 decimeters = _____ or

_____ meter

Problem Solving · Real World

12. A flagpole is 4 meters tall. How many centimeters tall is the flagpole?

_____

13. Lucille runs the 50-meter dash in her track meet. How many decimeters long is the race?

_____

14. **WRITE** ▸ Math Find a measurement, in centimeters, of an object. Look through books, magazines, or the Internet. Then write the measurement as parts of a meter.

_____

_____

Lesson Check (4.MD.A.1)

1. A pencil is 15 centimeters long. How many millimeters long is that pencil?

2. John's father is 2 meters tall. How many centimeters tall is John's father?

Spiral Review (4.NF.B.4b, 4.NF.C.7, 4.MD.B.4)

3. Bruce reads for $\frac{3}{4}$ hour each night. How long will he read in 4 nights?

4. Mark jogged 0.6 mile. Caroline jogged 0.49 mile. Write an inequality to compare the distances they jogged.

Use the line plot for 5 and 6.

5. How many lawns were mowed?

6. What is the difference between the greatest amount and least amount of gasoline used to mow lawns?

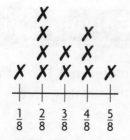

Gasoline Used to Mow Lawns in May (in Gallons)

FOR MORE PRACTICE GO TO THE Personal Math Trainer

Metric Units of Mass and Liquid Volume

Essential Question How can you compare metric units of mass and liquid volume?

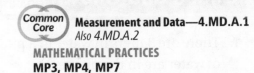

Common Core **Measurement and Data—4.MD.A.1**
Also 4.MD.A.2
MATHEMATICAL PRACTICES
MP3, MP4, MP7

🔑 Unlock the Problem Real World

Mass is the amount of matter in an object. Metric units of mass include kilograms (kg) and grams (g). Liters (L) and **milliliters** (mL) are metric units of liquid volume.

The charts show the relationship between these units.

Metric Units of Mass
1 kilogram (kg) = 1,000 grams (g)

Metric Units of Liquid Volume
1 liter (L) = 1,000 milliliters (mL)

🔑 Example 1 Compare kilograms and grams.

Becky planted a flower garden full of bluebonnets. She used 9 kilograms of soil. How many grams of soil is that?

number of kilograms		grams in 1 kilogram		total grams
9	×	1,000	=	_____

So, Becky used _____ grams of soil to plant her bluebonnets.

- Are kilograms heavier or lighter than grams?

  _____

- Will the number of grams be greater than or less than the number of kilograms?

  _____

- What operation will you use to solve the problem?

  _____

🔑 Example 2 Compare liters and milliliters.

Becky used 5 liters of water to water her bluebonnet garden. How many milliliters of water is that?

number of liters		milliliters in 1 liter		total milliliters
5	×	1,000	=	_____

So, Becky used _____ milliliters of water.

Math Talk MATHEMATICAL PRACTICES ❼

Identify Relationships Compare the size of a kilogram to the size of a gram. Then compare the size of a liter to the size of a milliliter.

1. There are 3 liters of water in a pitcher. How many milliliters of water are in the pitcher?

There are _____ milliliters in 1 liter. Since I am changing

from a larger unit to a smaller unit, I can _____ 3 by 1,000 to find the number of milliliters in 3 liters.

So, there are _____ milliliters of water in the pitcher.

Complete.

 **2.** 4 liters = _____ milliliters

 3. 6 kilograms = _____ grams

Math Talk

MATHEMATICAL PRACTICES ⑦

Look for Structure Explain how you can find the number of grams in 8 kilograms.

On Your Own

Complete.

4. 8 kilograms = _____ grams

5. 7 liters = _____ milliliters

MATHEMATICAL PRACTICE ④ Use Symbols Algebra Compare using <, >, or =.

6. 1 kilogram ◯ 900 grams

7. 2 liters ◯ 2,000 milliliters

MATHEMATICAL PRACTICE ⑦ Look for a Pattern Algebra Complete.

8.

Liters	Milliliters
1	1,000
2	
3	
	4,000
5	
6	
	7,000
8	
9	
10	

9.

Kilograms	Grams
1	1,000
2	
	3,000
4	
5	
6	
7	
	8,000
9	
10	

Name _____

Problem Solving • Applications

10. Frank wants to fill a fish tank with 8 liters of water. How many milliliters is that?

_____

11. **GO DEEPER** Kim has 3 water bottles. She fills each bottle with 1 liter of water. How many milliliters of water does she have?

_____

12. **GO DEEPER** Jared's empty backpack has a mass of 3 kilograms. He doesn't want to carry more than 7 kilograms on a trip. How many grams of equipment can Jared pack?

_____

13. **GO DEEPER** A large cooler contains 20 liters of iced tea and a small cooler contains 5 liters of iced tea. How many more milliliters of iced tea does the large cooler contain than the small cooler?

_____

14. **THINK SMARTER** A 500-gram bag of granola costs $4, and a 2-kilogram bag of granola costs $15. What is the least expensive way to buy 2,000 grams of granola? Explain.

_____

_____

_____

_____

15. **MATHEMATICAL PRACTICE ③** **Verify the Reasoning of Others** The world's largest apple had a mass of 1,849 grams. Sue said the mass was greater than 2 kilograms. Does Sue's statement make sense? Explain.

_____

_____

_____

_____

> **WRITE ▸** *Math*
> **Show Your Work**

Unlock the Problem Real World

16. **THINK SMARTER** Lori bought 600 grams of cayenne pepper and 2 kilograms of black pepper. How many grams of pepper did she buy in all?

black pepper   cayenne pepper

a. What are you asked to find?

_____

b. What information will you use?

_____

c. Tell how you might solve the problem.

_____

_____

_____

d. Show how you solved the problem.

_____

_____

_____

_____

e. Complete the sentences.

Lori bought _____ grams of cayenne pepper.

She bought _____ grams of black pepper.

_____ + _____ = _____ grams

So, Lori bought _____ grams of pepper in all.

17. **WRITE** ▸Math Jill has two rocks. One has a mass of 20 grams and the other has a mass of 20 kilograms. Which rock has the greater mass? Explain.

_____

_____

_____

18. **THINK SMARTER** For numbers 18a–18c, choose Yes or No to tell whether the measurements are equivalent.

18a. 5,000 grams and   ○ Yes   ○ No
      5 kilograms

18b. 300 milliliters   ○ Yes   ○ No
      and 3 liters

18c. 8 grams and   ○ Yes   ○ No
      8,000 kilograms

© Houghton Mifflin Harcourt Publishing Company

Name _____

Metric Units of Mass and Liquid Volume

 COMMON CORE STANDARDS—4.MD.A.1
4.MD.A.2 *Solve problems involving measurement and conversion of measurements from a larger unit to a smaller unit.*

Complete.

1. 5 liters = ___**5,000**___ milliliters

Think: 1 liter = 1,000 milliliters,
so 5 liters = 5 × 1,000 milliliters, or 5,000 milliliters

2. 3 kilograms = _____ grams

3. 8 liters = _____ milliliters

4. 7 kilograms = _____ grams

5. 9 liters = _____ milliliters

Compare using <, >, or =.

6. 8 kilograms $\bigcirc$ 850 grams

7. 3 liters $\bigcirc$ 3,500 milliliters

Problem Solving Real World

8. Kenny buys four 1-liter bottles of water. How many milliliters of water does Kenny buy?

_____

9. Mrs. Jones bought three 2-kilogram packages of flour. How many grams of flour did she buy?

_____

10. Colleen bought 8 kilograms of apples and 2.5 kilograms of pears. How many more grams of apples than pears did she buy?

_____

11. Dave uses 500 milliliters of juice for a punch recipe. He mixes it with 2 liters of ginger ale. How many milliliters of punch does he make?

_____

12. **WRITE** ▸ *Math* Write a problem that involves changing kilograms to grams. Explain how to find the solution.

_____

_____

_____

Lesson Check (4.MD.A.1, 4.MD.A.2)

1. During his hike, Milt drank 1 liter of water and 1 liter of sports drink. How many milliliters of liquid did he drink?

2. Larinda cooked a 4-kilogram roast. The roast left over after the meal weighed 3 kilograms. How many grams of roast were eaten during that meal?

Spiral Review (4.MD.A.1, 4.MD.C.6, 4.G.A.1)

3. Use a protractor to find the angle measure.

4. Draw a pair of parallel lines.

5. Carly bought 3 pounds of birdseed. How many ounces of birdseed did she buy?

6. A door is 8 decimeters wide. How wide is the door in centimeters?

FOR MORE PRACTICE
GO TO THE
Personal Math Trainer

Name _____

Units of Time

Essential Question How can you use models to compare units of time?

 Common Core **Measurement and Data—4.MD.A.1**
Also 4.MD.A.2
MATHEMATICAL PRACTICES
MP1, MP4, MP5, MP7

🔑 Unlock the Problem (Real World)

The analog clock below has an hour hand, a minute hand, and a **second** hand to measure time. The time is 4:30:12.

Read Math

Read 4:30:12 as 4:30 and 12 seconds, or 30 minutes and 12 seconds after 4.

• Are there more minutes or seconds in one hour?

_____

There are 60 seconds in a minute and 60 minutes in an hour. The clocks show how far the hands move for each length of time.

Start Time: 3:00:00

1 second elapses.

The time is now 3:00:01.

1 minute, or 60 seconds, elapses. The second hand has made a full turn clockwise.

The time is now 3:01:00.

1 hour, or 60 minutes, elapses. The minute hand has made a full turn clockwise.

The time is now 4:00:00.

🔑 Example 1 How does the size of an hour compare to the size of a second?

There are _____ minutes in an hour.

There are _____ seconds in a minute.

60 minutes × _____ = _____ seconds

There are _____ seconds in a hour.

So, 1 hour is _____ times as long as 1 second.

Think: Multiply the number of minutes in an hour by the number of seconds in a minute.

Math Talk

MATHEMATICAL PRACTICES ①

Analyze How many full turns clockwise does a minute hand make in 3 hours? Explain.

Chapter 12 **685**

🔑 Example 2 Compare measures.

Larissa spent 2 hours on her science project.
Cliff spent 200 minutes on his science project.
Who spent more time?

STEP 1 Make a table that relates hours and minutes.

Hours	Minutes
1	60
2	
3	

STEP 2 Compare 2 hours and 200 minutes.

2 hours   200 minutes

Think: Write each measure in minutes and compare using <, >, or =.

_____ ◯ _____

2 hours is _____ than 200 minutes.

So, _____ spent more time than _____ on the science project.

🔑 Activity Compare the length of a week to the length of a day.

Materials ■ color pencils

The number line below shows the relationship between days and weeks.

STEP 1 Use a color pencil to shade 1 week on the number line.

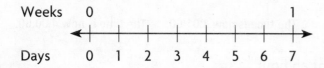

Weeks   0   1

Days   0   1   2   3   4   5   6   7

_____

STEP 2 Use a different color pencil to shade 1 day on the number line.

_____

STEP 3 Compare the size of 1 week to the size of 1 day.

There are _____ days in _____ week.

So, 1 week is _____ times as long as 1 day.

Name _____

Units of Time
1 minute (min) = 60 seconds (s)
1 hour (hr) = 60 minutes
1 day (d) = 24 hours
1 week (wk) = 7 days
1 year (yr) = 12 months (mo)
1 year (yr) = 52 weeks

1. Compare the length of a year to the length of a month. Use a model to help.

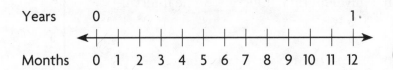

1 year is _____ times as long as _____ month.

Math Talk MATHEMATICAL PRACTICES ④

Use Models Explain how the number line helped you compare the length of a year and the length of a month.

Complete.

✓ 2. 2 minutes = _____ seconds   ✓ 3. 4 years = _____ months

On Your Own

Complete.

4. 3 minutes = _____ seconds   5. 4 hours = _____ minutes

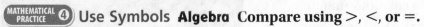 Use Symbols **Algebra** Compare using >, <, or =.

6. 3 years ◯ 35 months   7. 2 days ◯ 40 hours

Problem Solving • Applications

8. GO DEEPER Damien has lived in the apartment building for 5 years. Ken has lived there for 250 weeks. Who has lived in the building longer? Explain. Make a table to help.

_____

_____

Years	Weeks
1	
2	
3	
4	
5	

9. THINK SMARTER How many hours are in a week? Explain.

_____

_____

10. **MATHEMATICAL PRACTICE ⑤** **Communicate** Explain how you know that 9 minutes is less than 600 seconds.

_____

_____

11. **THINK SMARTER** Draw lines to match equivalent time intervals. Some intervals might not have a match.

1 hour	2 hours	5 hours	12 hours	48 hours
•	•	•	•	•

•	•	•	•	•
2 days	120 minutes	4 days	3,600 seconds	300 minutes

Connect ⎡to⎤ Science

One day is the length of time it takes Earth to make one complete rotation. One year is the time it takes Earth to revolve around the sun. To make the calendar match Earth's orbit time, there are leap years. Leap years add one extra day to the year. A leap day, February 29, is added to the calendar every four years.

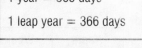

| 1 year = 365 days |
| 1 leap year = 366 days |

12. How many days are there in 4 years, if the fourth year is a leap year? Explain. Make a table to help.

_____

_____

Years	Days
1	
2	
3	
4	

13. Parker was born on February 29, 2008. The second time he is able to celebrate on his actual birthday is in 2016. How many days old will Parker be on February 29, 2016?

_____

Units of Time

COMMON CORE STANDARD—4.MD.A.1
Solve problems involving measurement and conversion of measurements from a larger unit to a smaller unit.

Complete.

1. 6 minutes = _____360_____ seconds   Think: 1 minute = 60 seconds,
   so 6 minutes = 6 × 60 seconds, or 360 seconds

2. 5 weeks = _____ days

3. 3 years = _____ weeks

4. 9 hours = _____ minutes

5. 9 minutes = _____ seconds

Compare using <, >, or =.

6. 2 years ◯ 14 months

7. 3 hours ◯ 300 minutes

8. 2 days ◯ 48 hours

9. 6 years ◯ 300 weeks

Problem Solving · Real World

10. Jody practiced a piano piece for 500 seconds. Bill practiced a piano piece for 8 minutes. Who practiced longer? **Explain.**

    _____

    _____

    _____

    _____

11. Yvette's younger brother just turned 3 years old. Fred's brother is now 30 months old. Whose brother is older? **Explain.**

    _____

    _____

    _____

    _____

12. **WRITE** ▸*Math* Explain how you can prove that 3 weeks is less than 24 days.

    _____

    _____

    _____

Lesson Check (4.MD.A.1)

1. Glen rode his bike for 2 hours. For how many minutes did Glen ride his bike?

2. Tina says that vacation starts in exactly 4 weeks. In how many days does vacation start?

Spiral Review (4.NF.B.3b, 4.NF.C.5, 4.MD.A.1, 4.MD.A.2)

3. Kayla bought $\frac{9}{4}$ pounds of apples. What is that weight as a mixed number?

4. Judy, Jeff, and Jim each earned $5.40 raking leaves. How much did they earn together?

5. Melinda rode her bike $\frac{54}{100}$ mile to the library. Then she rode $\frac{4}{10}$ mile to the store. How far did Melinda ride her bike in all? Write your answer as a decimal.

6. One day, the students drank 60 quarts of milk at lunch. How many pints of milk did the students drink?

**FOR MORE PRACTICE
GO TO THE
Personal Math Trainer**

Name _____

Problem Solving • Elapsed Time

Essential Question How can you use the strategy *draw a diagram* to solve elapsed time problems?

Common Core Measurement and Data—4.MD.A.2
Also 4.MD.A.1
MATHEMATICAL PRACTICES
MP1, MP4, MP5

🔑 Unlock the Problem Real World

Dora and her brother Kyle spent 1 hour and 35 minutes doing yard work. Then they stopped for lunch at 1:20 P.M. At what time did they start doing yard work?

Use the graphic organizer to help you solve the problem.

Read the Problem

What do I need to find?	What information do I need to use?	How will I use the information?
I need to find the time that Dora and Kyle _____.	I need to use the _____ and the time that they _____.	I can draw a time line to help me count backward and find the _____.

Solve the Problem

I draw a time line that shows the end time 1:20 P.M. Next, I count backward 1 hour and then 5 minutes at a time until I have 35 minutes.

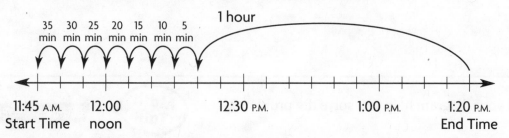

So, Dora and her brother Kyle started doing yard work at _____.

---

1. What if Dora and Kyle spent 50 minutes doing yard work and they stopped for lunch at 12:30 P.M.? What time would they have started doing yard work?

_____

🔍 Try Another Problem

Ben started riding his bike at 10:05 A.M. He stopped 23 minutes later when his friend Robbie asked him to play kickball. At what time did Ben stop riding his bike?

Read the Problem

What do I need to find?	What information do I need to use?	How will I use the information?

Solve the Problem

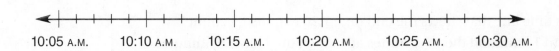

10:05 A.M. 10:10 A.M. 10:15 A.M. 10:20 A.M. 10:25 A.M. 10:30 A.M.

2. How did your diagram help you solve the problem?

_____

_____

_____

 Math Talk

MATHEMATICAL PRACTICES ①

Describe another way you could find the time an activity started or ended given the elapsed time and either the start or end time.

Name _____

Unlock the Problem

√ Use the Problem Solving MathBoard.
√ Choose a strategy you know.
√ Underline important facts.

Share and Show

1. Evelyn has dance class every Saturday. It lasts 1 hour and 15 minutes and is over at 12:45 P.M. At what time does Evelyn's dance class begin?

   First, write the problem you need to solve.

   _____

   Next, draw a time line to show the end time and the elapsed time.

11:00 A.M.   12:00   1:00 P.M.
                    noon

   Finally, find the start time.

   Evelyn's dance class begins at _____ .

2. **THINK SMARTER** What if Evelyn's dance class started at 11:00 A.M. and lasted 1 hour and 25 minutes? At what time would her class end? Describe how this problem is different from Problem 1.

   _____

   _____

3. Beth got on the bus at 8:06 A.M. Thirty-five minutes later, she arrived at school. At what time did Beth arrive at school?

   _____

4. Lyle went fishing for 1 hour and 30 minutes until he ran out of bait at 6:40 P.M. At what time did Lyle start fishing?

   _____

On Your Own

5. Mike and Jed went skiing at 10:30 A.M. They skied for 1 hour and 55 minutes before stopping for lunch. At what time did Mike and Jed stop for lunch?

_____

6. GO DEEPER Mike can run a mile in 12 minutes. He starts his run at 11:30 AM. and runs 4 miles. What time does Mike finish his run?

_____

WRITE ▸ _Math_
Show Your Work

7. MATHEMATICAL PRACTICE ⑤ **Communicate** Explain how you can use a diagram to determine the start time when the end time is 9:00 A.M. and the elapsed time is 26 minutes. What is the start time?

_____

_____

_____

_____

8. THINK SMARTER Bethany finished her math homework at 4:20 P.M. She did 25 multiplication problems in all. If each problem took her 3 minutes to do, at what time did Bethany start her math homework?

_____

9. THINK SMARTER Vincent began his weekly chores on Saturday morning at 11:20 A.M. He finished 1 hour and 10 minutes later. Draw a time line to show the end time.

11:00 A.M.   12:00   1:00 P.M.
                              noon

Vincent finished his chores at _____ P.M.

Problem Solving • Elapsed Time

COMMON CORE STANDARD—4.MD.A.2
*Solve problems involving measurement and
conversion of measurements from a larger unit
to a smaller unit.*

Read each problem and solve.

1. Molly started her piano lesson at 3:45 P.M.
   The lesson lasted 20 minutes. What time did the
   piano lesson end?

   Think: What do I need to find?
   How can I draw a diagram
   to help?

   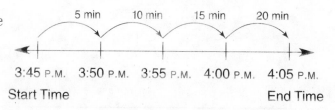

   _____ 4:05 P.M.

2. Brendan spent 24 minutes playing a computer
   game. He stopped playing at 3:55 P.M and went
   outside to ride his bike. What time did he start
   playing the computer game?

   _____

3. Aimee's karate class lasts 1 hour and
   15 minutes and is over at 5:00 P.M. What
   time does Aimee's karate class start?

   _____

4. Mr. Giarmo left for work at 7:15 A.M. Twenty-five
   minutes later, he arrived at his work. What time
   did Mr. Giarmo arrive at his work?

   _____

5. **WRITE** ▶*Math* Explain why it is important to know if a time
   is in the A.M. or in the P.M. when figuring out how much time
   has elapsed.

   _____

   _____

Lesson Check (4.MD.A.2)

1. Bobbie went snowboarding with friends at 10:10 A.M. They snowboarded for 1 hour and 43 minutes, and then stopped to eat lunch. What time did they stop for lunch?

2. The Cain family drove for 1 hour and 15 minutes and arrived at their camping spot at 3:44 P.M. What time did the Cain family start driving?

Spiral Review (4.NF.B.4b, 4.NF.C.5, 4.MD.A.1, 4.MD.A.2)

3. A praying mantis can grow up to 15 centimeters long. How long is this in millimeters?

4. Thom's minestrone soup recipe makes 3 liters of soup. How many milliliters of soup is this?

5. Stewart walks $\frac{2}{3}$ mile each day. List three multiples of $\frac{2}{3}$.

6. Angelica colored in 0.60 of the squares on her grid. Write 0.60 as tenths in fraction form.

FOR MORE PRACTICE
GO TO THE
Personal Math Trainer

Name _____

Mixed Measures

Essential Question How can you solve problems involving mixed measures?

 Measurement and Data—4.MD.A.2
Also 4.MD.A.1
MATHEMATICAL PRACTICES
MP2, MP3, MP8

 Unlock the Problem Real World

Herman is building a picnic table for a new campground. The picnic table is 5 feet 10 inches long. How long is the picnic table in inches?

- Is the mixed measure greater than or less than 6 feet?

_____

- How many inches are in 1 foot?

_____

 Change a mixed measure.

Think of 5 feet 10 inches as 5 feet + 10 inches.

Write feet as inches.

5 feet   **Think:** 5 feet × 12 = ⟶ [ ] inches
+ 10 inches   60 inches

                        + [ ] inches
                           [ ] inches

So, the picnic table is _____ inches long.

Example 1 Add mixed measures.

Herman built the picnic table in 2 days. The first day he worked for 3 hours 45 minutes. The second day he worked for 2 hours 10 minutes. How long did it take him to build the table?

STEP 1 Add the minutes.

   3 hr 45 min
+ 2 hr 10 min
         [ ] min

STEP 2 Add the hours.

   3 hr 45 min
+ 2 hr 10 min
   [ ] hr 55 min

So, it took Herman _____ to build the table.

Math Talk

MATHEMATICAL PRACTICES ⑧

Use Repeated Reasoning How is adding mixed measures similar to adding tens and ones? How is it different? Explain.

- What if Herman worked an extra 5 minutes on the picnic table? How long would he have worked on the table then? Explain.

_____

_____

🔒 Example 2 Subtract mixed measures.

Alicia is building a fence around the picnic area. She has a pole that is 6 feet 6 inches long. She cuts off 1 foot 7 inches from one end. How long is the pole now?

STEP 1 Subtract the inches.

Think: 7 inches is greater than 6 inches. You need to regroup to subtract.

6 ft 6 in. = 5 ft 6 in. + 12 in.

           = 5 ft _____ in.

$$
\begin{array}{r}
\overset{5}{\cancel{6}}\text{ft} \ \overset{18}{\cancel{6}}\text{in.} \\
- \ 1 \text{ ft } 7 \text{ in.} \\
\hline
 \text{in.}
\end{array}
$$

> **⚠ ERROR Alert**
> Be sure to check that you are regrouping correctly. There are 12 inches in 1 foot.

STEP 2 Subtract the feet.

$$
\begin{array}{r}
\overset{5}{\cancel{6}}\text{ft} \ \overset{18}{\cancel{6}}\text{in.} \\
- \ 1 \text{ ft } 7 \text{ in.} \\
\hline
\text{ft } 11 \text{ in.}
\end{array}
$$

So, the pole is now _____ long.

Try This! Subtract.

> 3 pounds 5 ounces − 1 pound 2 ounces

Share and Show

1. A truck is carrying 2 tons 500 pounds of steel. How many pounds of steel is the truck carrying?

Think of 2 tons 500 pounds as 2 tons + 500 pounds.
Write tons as pounds.

   2 tons   Think: 2 tons × 2,000 = ⟶   pounds

+ 500 pounds   _____ pounds   + _____ pounds

                                                    pounds

So, the truck is carrying _____ pounds of steel.

Name _____

Rewrite each measure in the given unit.

2. 1 yard 2 feet

_____ feet

3. 3 pints 1 cup

_____ cups

 4. 3 weeks 1 day

_____ days

Add or subtract.

5. 2 lb 4 oz
   + 1 lb 6 oz

 6. 3 gal 2 qt
   − 1 gal 3 qt

7. 5 hr 20 min
   − 3 hr 15 min

On Your Own

Rewrite each measure in the given unit.

8. 1 hour 15 minutes

_____ minutes

9. 4 quarts 2 pints

_____ pints

10. 10 feet 10 inches

_____ inches

Add or subtract.

11.   2 tons 300 lb
   − 1 ton 300 lb

12.   10 gal 8 c
   + 8 gal 9 c

13.   7 lb 6 oz
   − 2 lb 12 oz

Problem Solving • Applications Real World

14. **MATHEMATICAL PRACTICE 3 Apply** Ahmed fills 6 pitchers with juice. Each pitcher contains 2 quarts 1 pint. How many pints of juice does he have in all?

_____

15. Sense or Nonsense? Sam and Dave each solve the problem at the right. Sam says the sum is 4 feet 18 inches. Dave says the sum is 5 feet 6 inches. Whose answer makes sense? Whose answer is nonsense? Explain.

  2 ft 10 in.
+ 2 ft 8 in.

_____

_____

16. **THINK SMARTER** Jackson has a rope 1 foot 8 inches long. He cuts it into 4 equal pieces. How many inches long is each piece?

🔑 Unlock the Problem

17. Theo is practicing for a 5-kilometer race. He runs
5 kilometers every day and records his time. His normal
time is 25 minutes 15 seconds. Yesterday it took him only
23 minutes 49 seconds. How much faster was his time
yesterday than his normal time?

a. What are you asked to find?

_____

_____

b. What information do you know?

_____

_____

c. How will you solve the problem?

_____

d. Solve the problem.

    _____

e. Fill in the sentence.

Yesterday, Theo ran 5 kilometers in a time

that was _____ faster than his
normal time.

---

18. **GO DEEPER** Don has 5 pieces of pipe. Each
piece is 3 feet 6 inches long. If Don joins the
pieces end to end to make one long pipe,
how long will the new pipe be?

19. **THINK SMARTER +** Ana mixes
2 quarts 1 pint of apple juice and 1 quart
3 cups of cranberry juice. Will her mixture
be able to fit in a 1 gallon pitcher? Explain.

_____

_____

_____

_____

Mixed Measures

COMMON CORE STANDARD—4.MD.A.2
Solve problems involving measurement and
conversion of measurements from a larger unit to
a smaller unit.

Complete.

1. 8 pounds 4 ounces = _____132_____ ounces

Think: 8 pounds = 8 × 16 ounces, or 128 ounces.

128 ounces + 4 ounces = 132 ounces

2. 5 weeks 3 days = _____ days

3. 4 minutes 45 seconds = _____ seconds

4. 4 hours 30 minutes = _____ minutes

5. 3 tons 600 pounds = _____ pounds

Add or subtract.

6.   9 gal 1 qt
   + 6 gal 1 qt

7.   12 lb 5 oz
   − 7 lb 10 oz

8.   8 hr 3 min
   + 4 hr 12 min

Problem Solving

9. Michael's basketball team practiced for
2 hours 40 minutes yesterday and 3 hours
15 minutes today. How much longer did the
team practice today than yesterday?

10. Rhonda had a piece of ribbon that was
5 feet 3 inches long. She removed a 5-inch
piece to use in her art project. What is the
length of the piece of ribbon now?

_____

_____

11. **WRITE** ▸Math Write a subtraction problem involving
pounds and ounces. Solve the problem and show your work.

_____

_____

Lesson Check (4.MD.A.2)

1. Marsha bought 1 pound 11 ounces of roast beef and 2 pounds 5 ounces of corned beef. How much more corned beef did she buy than roast beef?

2. Theodore says there are 2 weeks 5 days left in the year. How many days are left in the year?

Spiral Review (4.NF.C.7, 4.MD.A.1, 4.MD.A.2, 4.G.A.2)

3. On one grid, 0.5 of the squares are shaded. On another grid, 0.05 of the squares are shaded. Compare the shaded parts of the grids using <, =, or >.

4. Classify the triangle by the size of its angles.

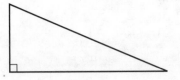

5. Sahil's brother is 3 years old. How many weeks old is his brother?

6. Sierra's swimming lessons last 1 hour 20 minutes. She finished her lesson at 10:50 A.M. At what time did her lesson start?

FOR MORE PRACTICE
GO TO THE
Personal Math Trainer

Name _____

Patterns in Measurement Units

Essential Question How can you use patterns to write number pairs for measurement units?

Common Core **Measurement and Data—
4.MD.A.1**
MATHEMATICAL PRACTICES
MP3, MP6, MP7

CONNECT The table at the right relates yards and feet. You can think of the numbers in the table as number pairs. 1 and 3, 2 and 6, 3 and 9, 4 and 12, and 5 and 15 are number pairs.

The number pairs show the relationship between yards and feet. 1 yard is equal to 3 feet, 2 yards is equal to 6 feet, 3 yards is equal to 9 feet, and so on.

Yards	Feet
1	3
2	6
3	9
4	12
5	15

Unlock the Problem (Real World)

Lillian made the table below to relate two units of time. What units of time does the pattern in the table show?

 Activity Use the relationship between the number pairs to label the columns of the table.

_____	_____
1	7
2	14
3	21
4	28
5	35

- List the number pairs.

  _____

- Describe the relationship between the numbers in each pair.

  _____

  _____

- Label the columns of the table.

  Think: What unit of time is 7 times as great as another unit?

Math Talk

MATHEMATICAL PRACTICES ⑦

Identify Relationships
Look at each number pair in the table. Could you change the order of the numbers in the number pairs? Explain why or why not.

© Houghton Mifflin Harcourt Publishing Company

Try This! Jasper made the table below to relate two customary units of liquid volume. What customary units of liquid volume does the pattern in the table show?

- List the number pairs.

  _____

___	___
1	4
2	8
3	12
4	16
5	20

- Describe the relationship between the numbers in each pair.

  _____

  _____

- Label the columns of the table.

  Think: What customary unit of liquid volume is 4 times as great as another unit?

- What other units could you have used to label the columns of the table above? Explain.

  _____

  _____

  _____

1. The table shows a pattern for two units of time. Label the columns of the table with the units of time.

Think: What unit of time is 24 times as great as another unit?

___	___
1	24
2	48
3	72
4	96
5	120

Math Talk

MATHEMATICAL PRACTICES ⑥

Explain how you labeled the columns of the table.

Name _____

Each table shows a pattern for two customary units. Label the columns of the table.

2.

___	___
1	2
2	4
3	6
4	8
5	10

3.

___	___
1	16
2	32
3	48
4	64
5	80

On Your Own

Each table shows a pattern for two customary units. Label the columns of the table.

4.

___	___
1	36
2	72
3	108
4	144
5	180

5.

___	___
1	12
2	24
3	36
4	48
5	60

Each table shows a pattern for two metric units of length. Label the columns of the table.

6.

___	___
1	10
2	20
3	30
4	40
5	50

7.

___	___
1	100
2	200
3	300
4	400
5	500

8. **GO DEEPER** List the number pairs for the table in Exercise 6. Describe the relationship between the numbers in each pair.

_____

_____

_____

Problem Solving • Applications

9. What's the Error? Maria wrote *Weeks* as the label for the first column of the table and *Years* as the label for the second column. Describe her error.

_____

_____

?	?
1	52
2	104
3	156
4	208
5	260

10. **MATHEMATICAL PRACTICE 3** **Verify the Reasoning of Others** The table shows a pattern for two metric units. Lou labels the columns *Meters* and *Millimeters*. Zayna labels them *Liters* and *Milliliters*. Whose answer makes sense? Whose answer is nonsense? Explain.

_____

_____

_____

?	?
1	1,000
2	2,000
3	3,000
4	4,000
5	5,000

11. **THINK SMARTER** Look at the following number pairs: 1 and 365, 2 and 730, 3 and 1,095. The number pairs describe the relationship between which two units of time? Explain.

_____

12. **THINK SMARTER** The tables show patterns for some units of measurement. Write the correct labels in each table.

Ounces	Days	Feet	Gallons	Hours	Inches	Pounds	Quarts

____	____
1	12
2	24
3	36
4	48

____	____
1	24
2	48
3	72
4	96

____	____
1	4
2	8
3	12
4	16

Patterns in Measurement Units

Common Core

COMMON CORE STANDARD—4.MD.A.1
Solve problems involving measurement and conversion of measurements from a larger unit to a smaller unit.

Each table shows a pattern for two customary units of time, liquid volume, or weight. Label the columns of the table.

1.

Gallons	Quarts
1	4
2	8
3	12
4	16
5	20

2.

1	2,000
2	4,000
3	6,000
4	8,000
5	10,000

3.

1	2
2	4
3	6
4	8
5	10

4.

1	60
2	120
3	180
4	240
5	300

Problem Solving (Real World)

Use the table for 5.

5. Marguerite made the table to compare two metric measures of length. Name a pair of units Marguerite could be comparing.

?	?
1	10
2	20
3	30
4	40
5	50

_____

6. **WRITE** ▸*Math* Draw a table to represent months and years. Explain how you labeled each column.

_____

_____

Lesson Check (4.MD.A.1)

1. Joanne made a table to relate two units of measure. The number pairs in her table are 1 and 16, 2 and 32, 3 and 48, 4 and 64. What are the best labels for Joanne's table?

2. Cade made a table to relate two units of time. The number pairs in his table are 1 and 24, 2 and 48, 3 and 72, 4 and 96. What are the best labels for Cade's table?

Spiral Review (4.NF.C.6, 4.MD.A.1, 4.MD.A.2, 4.MD.C.5a)

3. Anita has 2 quarters, 1 nickel, and 4 pennies. Write Anita's total amount as a fraction of a dollar.

4. The minute hand of a clock moves from 12 to 6. What describes the turn the minute hand makes?

5. Roderick has a dog that has a mass of 9 kilograms. What is the mass of the dog in grams?

6. Kari mixed 3 gallons 2 quarts of lemon-lime drink with 2 gallons 3 quarts of pink lemonade to make punch. How much more lemon-lime drink did Kari use than pink lemonade?

FOR MORE PRACTICE
GO TO THE
Personal Math Trainer

✓ Chapter 12 Review/Test

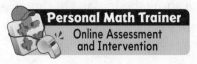

Personal Math Trainer
Online Assessment
and Intervention

1. Mrs. Miller wants to estimate the width of the steps in front of her house. Select the best benchmark for her to use.

Ⓐ her fingertip

Ⓑ the thickness of a dime

Ⓒ the width of a license plate

Ⓓ how far she can walk in 20 minutes

2. **GO DEEPER** Franco played computer chess for 3 hours. Lian played computer chess for 150 minutes. Compare the times spent playing computer chess. Complete the sentence.

_____ played for _____ longer than _____.

3. Select the measures that are equal. Mark all that apply.

Ⓐ 6 feet

Ⓑ 15 yards

Ⓒ 45 feet

Ⓓ 600 inches

Ⓔ 12 feet

Ⓕ 540 inches

4. Jackie made 6 quarts of lemonade. Jackie says she made 3 pints of lemonade. Explain Jackie's error. Then find the correct number of pints of lemonade.

GO DIGITAL Assessment Options
Chapter Test

5. Josh practices gymnastics each day after school. The data show the lengths of time Josh practiced gymnastics for 2 weeks.

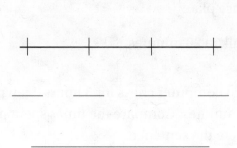

Time Practicing Gymnastics (in hours)
$\frac{1}{4}$, $\frac{1}{4}$, $\frac{3}{4}$, $\frac{3}{4}$, $\frac{1}{2}$, 1, 1, 1, $\frac{3}{4}$, 1

Part A

Make a tally table and line plot to show the data.

Time Practicing Gymnastics	
Time (in hours)	Tally

Part B

Explain how you used the tally table to label the numbers and plot the *X*s.

Part C

What is the difference between the longest time and shortest time Josh spent practicing gymnastics?

_____ hour

6. Select the correct word to complete the sentence.

Juan brings a water bottle with him to soccer practice.

A full water bottle holds

1 liter
10 milliliters
1 meter

of water.

7. Write the symbol that compares the weights correctly.

<	=	>

128 ounces _____ 8 pounds

8,000 pounds _____ 3 tons

8. Dwayne bought 5 yards of wrapping paper. How many inches of wrapping paper did he buy?

_____ inches

9. A sack of potatoes weighs 14 pounds 9 ounces. After Wendy makes potato salad for a picnic, the sack weighs 9 pounds 14 ounces. What is the weight of the potatoes Wendy used for the potato salad? Write the numbers to show the correct subtraction.

4	5	11	13	19	25	39

	14 pounds	9 ounces
	− 9 pounds	14 ounces
	⬚ pounds	⬚ ounces

10. Sabita made this table to relate two customary units of liquid volume.

Part A

List the number pairs for the table. Then describe the relationship between the numbers in each pair.

_____	_____
1	2
2	4
3	6
4	8
5	10

Part B

Label the columns of the table. Explain your answer.

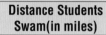
11. **THINK SMARTER +** The table shows the distances some students swam in miles. Complete the line plot to show the data.

Distance Students Swam(in miles)
$\frac{1}{8}, \frac{2}{8}, \frac{3}{8}, \frac{3}{8}, \frac{5}{8}, \frac{3}{8}, \frac{2}{8}, \frac{4}{8}, \frac{3}{8}, \frac{1}{8}, \frac{4}{8}, \frac{4}{8}$

Distance Students Swam (in miles)

What is the difference between the longest distance and the shortest distance the students swam?

 mile

12. An elephant living in a wildlife park weighs 4 tons. How many pounds does the elephant weigh?

_____ pounds

13. Katia bought two melons. She says the difference in mass between the melons is 5,000 grams. Which two melons did Katia buy?

(A) watermelon: 8 kilograms

(B) cantaloupe: 5 kilograms

(C) honeydew: 3 kilograms

(D) casaba melon: 2 kilograms

(E) crenshaw melon: 1 kilogram

14. Write the equivalent measurements in each column.

3,000 millimeters	300 centimeters	30 centimeters
$\frac{35}{100}$ meter	0.300 meter	0.35 meter
$\frac{300}{1,000}$ meter	350 millimeters	30 decimeters

3 meters	35 centimeters	300 millimeters

15. Cheryl is making a mixed fruit drink for a party. She mixes 7 pints each of apple juice and cranberry juice. How many fluid ounces of mixed fruit drink does Cheryl make?

_____ fluid ounces

16. Hamid's soccer game will start at 11:00 A.M., but the players must arrive at the field three-quarters of an hour early to warm up. The game must end by 1:15 P.M.

Part A

Hamid says he has to be at the field at 9:45 A.M. is Hamid correct? Explain your answer.

Part B

The park closes at 6:30 P.M. There is a 15-minute break between each game played at the park, and each game takes the same amount of time as Hamid's soccer game. How many more games can be played before the park closes? Explain your answer.

17. For numbers 17a–17e, select Yes or No to tell whether the measurements are equivalent.

17a. 7,000 grams and 7 kilograms ○ Yes ○ No

17b. 200 milliliters and 2 liters ○ Yes ○ No

17c. 6 grams and 6,000 kilograms ○ Yes ○ No

17d. 5 liters and 5,000 milliliters ○ Yes ○ No

17e. 2 milliliters and 2,000 liters ○ Yes ○ No

18. Draw lines to match equivalent time intervals.

$\frac{1}{2}$ hour   2 hours   3 hours   8 hours   72 hours

•   •   •   •   •

•   •   •   •   •

3 days   180 minutes   1,800 seconds   480 minutes   7,200 seconds

19. Anya arrived at the library on Saturday morning at 11:10 A.M. She left the library 1 hour 20 minutes later. Draw a time line to show the end time.

11:00 A.M.   12:00   1:00 P.M.
                               noon

Anya left the library at _____ P.M.

20. The tables show patterns for some units of measurement. Write the correct labels in each table.

| Pints | Days | Feet | Cups | Week | Yards | Inches | Quarts |

1	3
2	6
3	9
4	12

1	7
2	14
3	21
4	28

1	4
2	8
3	12
4	16

21. An Olympic swimming pool is 25 meters wide. How many decimeters wide is an Olympic swimming pool?

_____ decimeters wide

22. Frankie is practicing for a 5-kilometer race. His normal time is 31 minutes 21 seconds. Yesterday it took him only 29 minutes 38 seconds.

How much faster was Frankie yesterday than his normal time?

_____

Algebra: Perimeter and Area

Show What You Know

Personal Math Trainer
Online Assessment
and Intervention

Check your understanding of important skills.

Name _____

▶ **Missing Factors** **Find the missing factor.** (3.OA.A.4)

1.

   _____ × 6 = 24

2.

   3 × _____ = 27

▶ **Add Whole Numbers** **Find the sum.** (4.NBT.B.4)

3. 17 + 153 + 67 = _____

4. 8 + 78 + 455 = _____

5. 211 + 52 + 129 + 48 = _____

6. 42 + 9 + 336 + 782 = _____

▶ **Multiply Whole Numbers** **Find the product.** (4.NBT.B.5)

7.   78
  × 6

8.   29
  × 7

9.   42
  × 5

10.   57
  × 9

Math in the Real World

Native Americans once lived near Cartersville, Georgia, in an area that is now a state park. They constructed burial mounds that often contained artifacts, such as beads, feathers, and copper ear ornaments. One of the park's mounds is 63 feet in height. If the top of the mound is rectangular in shape with a perimeter of 322 yards, what could be the side lengths of the rectangle?

Vocabulary Builder

▶ **Visualize It** ●

Sort words with a ✓ using the Venn diagram.

Measurement

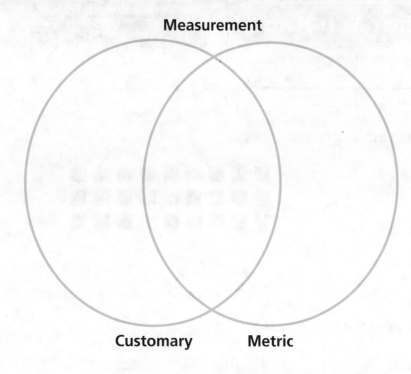

Customary   Metric

Review Words

✓ centimeter
✓ foot
✓ inch
✓ kilometer
✓ meter
✓ mile
✓ yard

Preview Words

✓ area
  base
✓ formula
✓ height
✓ perimeter
  square unit

▶ **Understand Vocabulary** ●

Write the word or term that answers the riddle.

1. I am the measure of the number of unit squares needed to cover a surface.

   _____

2. I am the distance around a shape.

   _____

3. I am a unit of area that measures 1 unit by 1 unit.

   _____

4. I am a set of symbols that expresses a mathematical rule.

   _____

GO DIGITAL
• **Interactive Student Edition**
• **Multimedia eGlossary**

Chapter 13 Vocabulary

area

área

2

base

base

5

centimeter (cm)

centímetro (cm)

7

formula

fórmula

35

height

altura

39

meter (m)

metro (m)

50

perimeter

perímetro

64

square unit

unidad cuadrada

86

A polygon's side or a two-dimensional shape, usually a polygon or circle, by which a three-dimensional shape is measured or named

Examples:

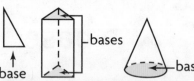

base · bases · base

The measure of the number of unit squares needed to cover a surface

Example:

Area = 9 square units

A set of symbols that expresses a mathematical rule

Example: Area = base × height, or $A = b \times h$

A metric unit used for measuring length or distance
1 meter = 100 centimeters

Example:

1 centimeter

A metric unit for measuring length or distance
1 meter = 100 centimeters

Example:

about 1 meter

The measure of a perpendicular from the base to the top of a two-dimensional shape

Example:

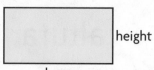

height

base

A unit of area with dimensions of
1 unit × 1 unit

Example:

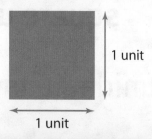

1 unit

1 unit

The distance around a shape

4 cm

2 cm · 2 cm

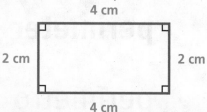

4 cm

Perimeter = 2 cm + 4 cm + 2 cm + 4 cm = 12 cm

Guess the Word

Word Box
area
base, b
centimeter
formula
height, h
meter
perimeter
square unit

For 3 to 4 players

Materials

• timer

How to Play

1. Take turns to play.

2. Choose a math term, but do not say it aloud.

3. Set the timer for 1 minute.

4. Give a one-word clue about your term. Give each player one chance to guess the term.

5. If nobody guesses correctly, repeat Step 4 with a different clue. Repeat until a player guesses the term or time runs out.

6. The player who guesses gets 1 point. If the player can use the word in a sentence, he or she gets 1 more point. Then that player gets a turn choosing a word.

7. The first player to score 10 points wins.

Journal

The Write Way

Reflect

Choose one idea. Write about it in the space below.

- Define *perimeter* and *area* in your own words.
- Explain how to use a formula to find the area of a rectangle.
- Write an area word problem so that the solution is 36 square units.

Name _____

Perimeter

Essential Question How can you use a formula to find the perimeter of a rectangle?

Common Core Measurement and Data—
4.MD.A.3
MATHEMATICAL PRACTICES
MP1, MP7, MP8

Unlock the Problem Real World

Julio is putting a stone border around his rectangular garden. The length of the garden is 7 feet. The width of the garden is 5 feet. How many feet of stone border does Julio need?

Perimeter is the distance around a shape.

To find how many feet of stone border Julio needs, find the perimeter of the garden.

- Circle the numbers you will use.
- What are you asked to find?

_____

_____

🔑 Use addition.

Perimeter of a Rectangle = length + width + length + width

$7 + 5 + 7 + 5 =$ _____

The perimeter is _____ feet.

So, Julio needs _____ feet of stone border.

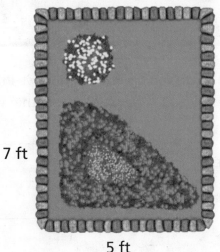

7 ft

5 ft

🔑 Use multiplication.

A Find Perimeter of a Rectangle

Perimeter = (2 × length) + (2 × width)

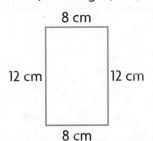

8 cm

12 cm   12 cm

8 cm

Perimeter = (2 × 12) + (2 × 8)

= 24 + 16

= _____

So, the perimeter is _____ centimeters.

B Find Perimeter of a Square

Perimeter = 4 × one side

16 in.

16 in.   16 in.

16 in.

Perimeter = 4 × 16

= _____

So, the perimeter is _____ inches.

 Math Talk

MATHEMATICAL PRACTICES ⑦

Identify Relationships How is using addition and using multiplication to find the perimeter of a rectangle related?

Use a Formula A **formula** is a mathematical rule. You can use a formula to find perimeter.

$$P = (2 \times l) + (2 \times w)$$

↑ perimeter   ↑ length   ↑ width

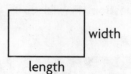
width
length

⚿ Example Find the perimeter of the rectangle.

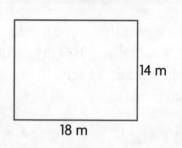
14 m
18 m

$P = (2 \times l) + (2 \times w)$

$= (2 \times \underline{\hspace{1cm}}) + (2 \times \underline{\hspace{1cm}})$ Think: Write the measures you know.

$= \underline{\hspace{1cm}} + \underline{\hspace{1cm}}$ Think: Do what is in parentheses first.

$= \underline{\hspace{1cm}}$

The perimeter of the rectangle is _____.

1. Can you use the Distributive Property to write the formula $P = (2 \times l) + (2 \times w)$ another way? Explain.

_____

_____

_____

_____

Try This! Write a formula for the perimeter of a square.

Use the letter _____ for perimeter.

Use the letter _____ for the length of a side.

Formula: _____

2. Justify the formula you wrote for the perimeter of a square.

_____

_____

_____

_____

Name _____

Formulas for Perimeter

Rectangle:
$P = (2 \times l) + (2 \times w)$ or
$P = 2 \times (l + w)$

Square:
$P = 4 \times s$

1. Find the perimeter of the rectangle.

$P = (\underline{\quad} \times \underline{\quad}) + (\underline{\quad} \times \underline{\quad})$

$= (\underline{\quad} \times \underline{\quad}) + (\underline{\quad} \times \underline{\quad})$

$= \underline{\quad} + \underline{\quad}$

$= \underline{\quad}$

8 ft

4 ft

The perimeter is _____ feet.

Find the perimeter of the rectangle or square.

2.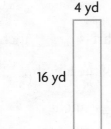
4 yd
16 yd

_____ yards

☑3.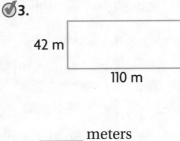
42 m
110 m

_____ meters

☑4.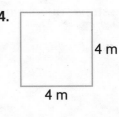
4 m
4 m

_____ meters

Math Talk — MATHEMATICAL PRACTICES ⑧

Draw Conclusions Can you use the formula $P = (2 \times l) + (2 \times w)$ to find the perimeter of a square? Explain.

On Your Own

Find the perimeter of the rectangle or square.

5.
34 in.
20 in.

_____ inches

6.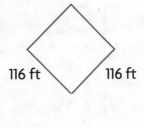
116 ft   116 ft

_____ feet

7.
21 m
42 m

_____ meters

8. **GO DEEPER** Robert wants to put lights around the front of his house. The house is 12 yards long and 7 yards high. How many feet of lights does he need?

_____

9. **MATHEMATICAL PRACTICE ①** **Analyze** What is the side length of a square with a perimeter of 60 meters?

_____

Unlock the Problem

10. **THINK SMARTER**   Alejandra plans to sew fringe on a scarf. The scarf is shaped like a rectangle. The length of the scarf is 48 inches. The width is one half the length. How much fringe does Alejandra need?

Math on the Spot

a. Draw a picture of the scarf, and label the given measurements on your drawing.

b. What do you need to find?

_____

c. What formula will you use?

_____

d. Show the steps you use to solve the problem.

e. Complete.

The length of the scarf is _____ inches.

The width is one half the length,

or _____ ÷ 2 = _____ inches.

So, the perimeter is (_____ × _____) +

(_____ × _____) = _____ inches.

f. Alejandra needs _____ of fringe.

---

11. **GO DEEPER**   Marcia will make a frame for her picture. The picture frame will be three times as long as it is wide. The width of the frame will be 5 inches. How much wood does Marcia need for the frame?

_____

12. **THINK SMARTER**   Maya is building a sandbox that is 36 inches wide. The length is four times the width. What is the perimeter of the sandbox? Show your work. Explain.

Perimeter

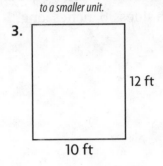
COMMON CORE STANDARD—4.MD.A.3
Solve problems involving measurement and conversion of measurements from a larger unit to a smaller unit.

Find the perimeter of the rectangle or square.

1.

3 in.

9 in.

2.

8 m

8 m

3.

12 ft

10 ft

$9 + 3 + 9 + 3 = 24$

___24___ inches

_____ meters

_____ feet

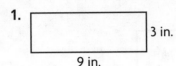

Problem Solving

4. Troy is making a flag shaped like a square. Each side measures 12 inches. He wants to add ribbon along the edges. He has 36 inches of ribbon. Does he have enough ribbon? **Explain.**

_____

5. The width of the Ochoa Community Pool is 20 feet. The length is twice as long as its width. What is the perimeter of the pool?

_____

6. **WRITE** ▸*Math* Imagine you want to put a border around a rectangular room. Summarize the steps you would use to find the length of border needed.

_____

_____

_____

_____

Lesson Check (4.MD.A.3)

1. What is the perimeter of a square window with sides 36 inches long?

2. What is the perimeter of the rectangle below?

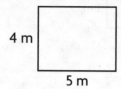

4 m

5 m

_____

_____

Spiral Review (4.NF.C.7, 4.MD.A.1, 4.MD.C.5a, 4.MD.C.5b, 4.G.A.3)

3. Natalie drew the angle below.

What is the most reasonable estimate for the measure of the angle Natalie drew?

4. Ethan has 3 pounds of mixed nuts. How many ounces of mixed nuts does Ethan have?

_____

_____

5. How many lines of symmetry does the shape below appear to have?

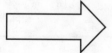

6. Janna drank 0.7 liter of water before soccer practice and 0.70 liter of water after practice. Compare the two decimals using <, =, or >.

_____

_____

FOR MORE PRACTICE GO TO THE Personal Math Trainer

Name _____

Area

Essential Question How can you use a formula to find the area of a rectangle?

Common Core **Measurement and Data—** 4.MD.A.3
MATHEMATICAL PRACTICES
MP2, MP6, MP7

Unlock the Problem

The **base, b,** of a two-dimensional figure can be any side. The **height, h,** is the measure of a perpendicular line segment from the base to the top of the figure.

Area is the measure of the number of unit squares needed to cover a flat surface without gaps or overlaps. A **square unit** is a square that is 1 unit long and 1 unit wide. To find the area of a figure, count the number of unit squares inside the figure.

How are the base, height, and area of a rectangle related?

Remember

Perpendicular lines and perpendicular line segments form right angles.

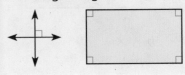

🔑 **Complete the table to find the area.**

Figure	Base	Height	Area
	5 units		

1. What relationship do you see among the base, height, and area?

_____

_____

Math Talk   MATHEMATICAL PRACTICES ⑦

Look for Structure How do you decide which side of a rectangle to use as the base?

2. Write a formula for the area of a rectangle. Use the letter A for area. Use the letter b for base. Use the letter h for height.

Formula: _____

Use a Formula You can use a formula to find the area.

$$A = b \times h$$

↑   ↑   ↑

area   base   height

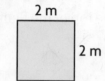

height

base

 Examples Use a formula to find the area of a rectangle and a square.

A

6 ft

2 ft

$A = \quad b \quad \times \quad h$

$= \underline{\hspace{1cm}} \times \underline{\hspace{1cm}}$

$= \underline{\hspace{1cm}}$

The area is _____.

B

2 m

2 m

$A = \quad b \quad \times \quad h$

$= \underline{\hspace{1cm}} \times \underline{\hspace{1cm}}$

$= \underline{\hspace{1cm}}$

The area is _____.

Try This! Write a formula for the area of a square.

Use the letter _____ for area.

Use the letter _____ for the length of a side.

Formula: _____

 **Share and Show** MATH BOARD

1. Find the area of the rectangle.

$A = b \times \underline{\hspace{1cm}}$

$= \underline{\hspace{1cm}} \times \underline{\hspace{1cm}}$

$= \underline{\hspace{1cm}}$

11 cm

13 cm

Formulas for Area

Rectangle:	Square:
$A = b \times h$	$A = s \times s$

Find the area of the rectangle or square.

2.
7 in.
2 in.

☑ **3.**
9 m   9 m

☑ **4.**
8 ft
14 ft

On Your Own

Math Talk

MATHEMATICAL PRACTICES ⑥

Explain how to find the area of a square if you only know the length of one side is 23 feet.

Find the area of the rectangle or square.

5.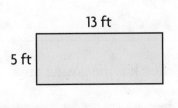
13 ft
5 ft

6.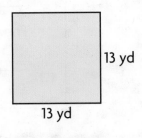
13 yd
13 yd

7.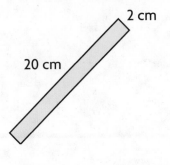
2 cm
20 cm

Practice: Copy and Solve **Find the area of the rectangle.**

8. base: 16 feet

height: 6 feet

9. base: 9 yards

height: 17 yards

10. base: 14 centimeters

height: 11 centimeters

11. **GO DEEPER** Terry's rectangular yard is 15 meters by 18 meters. Todd's rectangular yard is 20 meters by 9 meters. How much greater is the area of Terry's yard than Todd's yard?

12. **MATHEMATICAL PRACTICE ②** **Reason Quantitatively** Carmen sewed a square baby quilt that measures 36 inches on each side. What is the area of the quilt?

Unlock the Problem

13. **THINK SMARTER**   Nancy and Luke are drawing plans for rectangular flower gardens. In Nancy's plan, the garden is 18 feet by 12 feet. In Luke's plan, the garden is 15 feet by 15 feet. Who drew the garden plan with the greater area? What is the area?

a. What do you need to find? _____

_____

b. What formula will you use? _____

c. What units will you use to write the answer? _____

d. Show the steps to solve the problem.

e. Complete the sentences.

The area of Nancy's garden is

_____.

The area of Luke's garden is

_____.

_____ garden has the greater area.

14. **GO DEEPER**   Victor wants to buy fertilizer for his yard. The yard is 35 feet by 55 feet. The directions on the bag of fertilizer say that one bag will cover 1,250 square feet. How many bags of fertilizer should Victor buy to be sure that he covers the entire yard?

15. **THINK SMARTER**   Tuan is an artist. He is painting on a large canvas that is 45 inches wide. The height of the canvas is 9 inches less than the width. What is the area of Tuan's canvas?

_____

_____ square inches

Area

Common Core **COMMON CORE STANDARD—4.MD.A.3**
Solve problems involving measurement and conversion of measurements from a larger unit to a smaller unit.

Find the area of the rectangle or square.

1.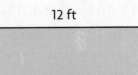

12 ft

9 ft

2.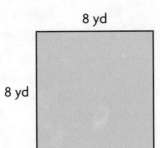

8 yd

8 yd

3.

15 m

3 m

$A = b \times h$

$= 12 \times 9$

108 square feet

 Problem Solving *Real World*

4. Meghan is putting wallpaper on a wall that measures 8 feet by 12 feet. How much wallpaper does Meghan need to cover the wall?

5. Bryson is laying down sod in his yard to grow a new lawn. Each piece of sod is a 1-foot by 1-foot square. How many pieces of sod will Bryson need to cover his yard if his yard measures 30 feet by 14 feet?

6. **WRITE** ▸*Math* Think about what you know about perimeter and area. Describe how to find the perimeter and area of your classroom.

_____

_____

_____

_____

Lesson Check (4.MD.A.3)

1. Ellie and Heather drew floor models of their living rooms. Ellie's model represented 20 feet by 15 feet. Heather's model represented 18 feet by 18 feet. Whose floor model represents the greater area? How much greater?

2. Tyra is laying down square carpet pieces in her photography studio. Each square carpet piece is 1 yard by 1 yard. If Tyra's photography studio is 7 yards long and 4 yards wide, how many pieces of square carpet will Tyra need?

Spiral Review (4.NBT.B.5, 4.NF.B.4c, 4.MD.A.3)

3. Typically, blood fully circulates through the human body 8 times each minute. How many times does blood circulate through the body in 1 hour?

4. Each of the 28 students in Romi's class raised at least $25 during the jump-a-thon. What is the least amount of money the class raised?

5. What is the perimeter of the shape below if each unit is 1 foot?

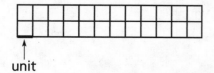

unit

6. Ryan is making small meat loaves. Each small meat loaf uses $\frac{3}{4}$ pound of meat. How much meat does Ryan need to make 8 small meat loaves?

**FOR MORE PRACTICE
GO TO THE
Personal Math Trainer**

Name _____

Area of Combined Rectangles

Essential Question How can you find the area of combined rectangles?

Common Core Measurement and Data—
4.MD.A.3
MATHEMATICAL PRACTICES
MP1, MP6

Unlock the Problem Real World

Jan is visiting a botanical garden with her family. The diagram shows two rectangular sections of the garden. What is the total area of the two sections?

There are different ways to find the area of combined rectangles.

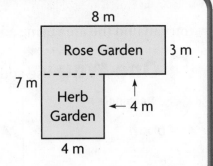

One Way Count unit squares.

Materials ■ grid paper

• Draw the garden on grid paper. Then find the area of each section by counting unit squares inside the shape.

Rose Garden	Herb Garden
Area = _____ square meters	Area = _____ square meters

• Add the areas.

_____ + _____ = _____ square meters

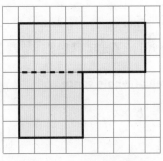

1 square = 1 square meter

Another Way Use the area formula for a rectangle.

Ⓐ Rose Garden

$A = b \times h$

= _____ × _____

= _____ square meters

Ⓑ Herb Garden

$A = b \times h$

= _____ × _____

= _____ square meters

• Add the areas.

_____ + _____ = _____ square meters

So, the total area is _____ square meters.

 Math Talk

MATHEMATICAL PRACTICES ①

Analyze Is there another way you could divide the figure to find the total area? Explain.

Chapter 13 729

🔑 Example

Greg is laying carpet in the space outside his laundry room. The diagram shows where the carpet will be installed. The space is made of combined rectangles. What is the area of the carpeted space?

You can find the area using addition or subtraction.

8 ft   16 ft

9 ft   17 ft

24 ft

🔑 One Way Use addition.

Rectangle A	**Rectangle B**
$A = b \times h$	$A = b \times h$
$= 8 \times \underline{\quad\quad}$	$= \underline{\quad\quad} \times 17$
$= \underline{\quad\quad\quad}$	$= \underline{\quad\quad\quad}$

Sum of the areas:

_____ + _____ = _____ square feet

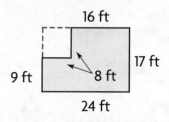

8 ft   16 ft

9 ft   **A**   **B**   17 ft

24 ft

🔑 Another Way Use subtraction.

Area of whole space	**Area of missing section**
$A = b \times h$	$A = b \times h$
$= 24 \times \underline{\quad\quad}$	$= \underline{\quad\quad} \times \underline{\quad\quad}$
$= \underline{\quad\quad\quad}$	$= \underline{\quad\quad\quad}$

Difference between the areas:

_____ – _____ = _____ square feet

16 ft

9 ft   8 ft   17 ft

24 ft

So, the area of the carpeted space is _____ square feet.

• Is there another way you could divide the figure to find the total area? Explain.

_____

_____

_____

_____

Name _____

Share and Show 📓 MATH BOARD

1. Explain how to find the total area of the figure.

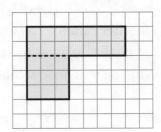

_____

_____

_____

Find the area of the combined rectangles.

2.

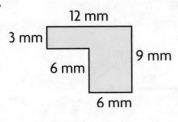

_____

✓ 3.

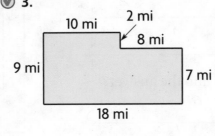

_____

✓ 4.

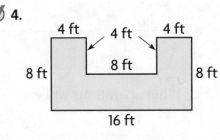

_____

Math Talk

MATHEMATICAL PRACTICES ⑥

Describe the characteristics of combined rectangles.

On Your Own

Find the area of the combined rectangles.

5. **MATHEMATICAL PRACTICE ⑥** **Attend to Precision** Jamie's mom wants to enlarge her rectangular garden by adding a new rectangular section. The garden is now 96 square yards. What will the total area of the garden be after she adds the new section?

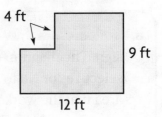

_____

6. **GO DEEPER** Explain how to find the perimeter and area of the combined rectangles at the right.

_____

_____

_____

_____

© Houghton Mifflin Harcourt Publishing Company

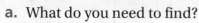 **Unlock the Problem** Real World

7. THINK SMARTER The diagram shows the layout of Mandy's garden. The garden is the shape of combined rectangles. What is the area of the garden?

a. What do you need to find?

_____

b. How can you divide the figure to help you find the total area?

_____

_____

c. What operations will you use to find the answer?

_____

d. Draw a diagram to show how you divided the figure. Then show the steps to solve the problem.

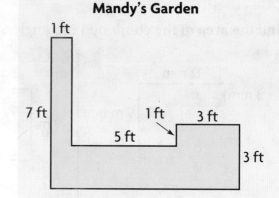

Mandy's Garden

1 ft

7 ft

5 ft   1 ft   3 ft

3 ft

So, the area of the garden is _____.

Personal Math Trainer

8. THINK SMARTER+ Workers are painting a large letter L for an outdoor sign. The diagram shows the dimensions of the L. For numbers 8a–8c, select Yes or No to tell whether you can add the products to find the area that the workers will paint.

8a. 2×8 and 2×4 ○ Yes ○ No

8b. 2×6 and 2×8 ○ Yes ○ No

8c. 2×6 and 6×2 ○ Yes ○ No

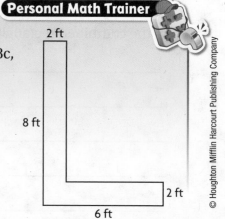

2 ft

8 ft

2 ft

6 ft

Area of Combined Rectangles

COMMON CORE STANDARD—4.MD.A.3
Solve problems involving measurement and conversion of measurements from a larger unit to a smaller unit.

Find the area of the combined rectangles.

1.
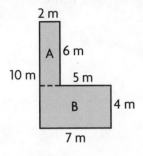

2.
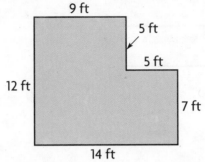

3.
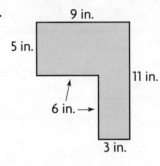

Area A = 2 × 6,

Area B = 7 × 4

12 + 28 = 40

40 square meters

Problem Solving Real World

Use the diagram for 4–5.

Nadia makes the diagram below to represent the counter space she wants to build in her craft room.

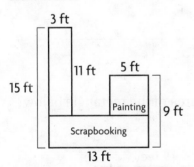

4. What is the area of the space that Nadia has shown for scrapbooking?

_____

5. What is the area of the space she has shown for painting?

_____

6. **WRITE** ▸*Math* Write a word problem that involves combined rectangles. Include a diagram and the solution.

_____

_____

_____

Lesson Check (4.MD.A.3)

1. What is the area of the combined rectangles below?

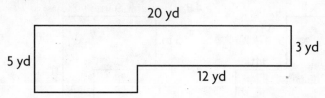

2. Marquis is redecorating his bedroom. What could Marquis use the area formula to find?

Spiral Review (4.OA.B.4, 4.MD.A.1, 4.MD.A.3)

3. Giraffes are the tallest land animals. A male giraffe can grow as tall as 6 yards. How tall would the giraffe be in feet?

4. Drew purchased 3 books each with a different price, for $24. The cost of each book was a multiple of 4. What could be the prices of the 3 books?

5. Esmeralda has a magnet in the shape of a square. Each side of the magnet is 3 inches long. What is the perimeter of her magnet?

6. What is the area of the rectangle below?

9 feet

7 feet

FOR MORE PRACTICE GO TO THE
Personal Math Trainer

✓ Mid-Chapter Checkpoint

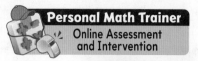

Personal Math Trainer
Online Assessment
and Intervention

▶ **Vocabulary**

Choose the best term from the box.

Vocabulary

area

base

formula

perimeter

square unit (sq un)

1. A square that is 1 unit wide and 1 unit long is a

_____. (p. 723)

2. The _____ of a two-dimensional figure can be
any side. (p. 723)

3. A set of symbols that expresses a mathematical rule is

called a _____. (p. 718)

4. The _____ is the distance around a shape. (p. 717)

▶ **Concepts and Skills**

Find the perimeter and area of the rectangle or square. (4.MD.A.3)

5.

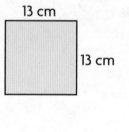

13 cm

13 cm

_____

6.

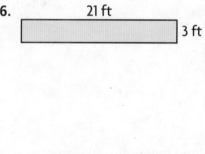

21 ft

3 ft

_____

7.

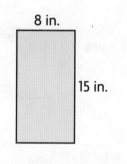

8 in.

15 in.

_____

Find the area of the combined rectangles. (4.MD.A.3)

8.

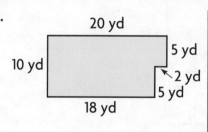

20 yd

10 yd

5 yd

2 yd

5 yd

18 yd

_____

9.

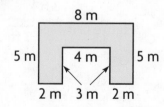

8 m

5 m

4 m

5 m

2 m   3 m   2 m

_____

10.

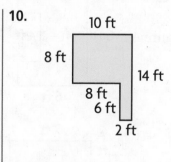

10 ft

8 ft

14 ft

8 ft

6 ft

2 ft

_____

11. Which figure has the greatest perimeter? (4.MD.A.3)

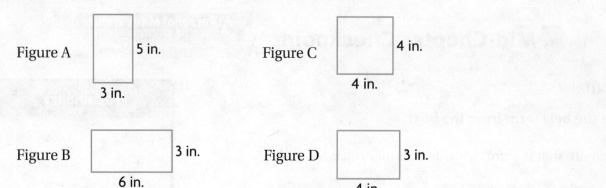

Figure A   5 in.   3 in.

Figure C   4 in.   4 in.

Figure B   3 in.   6 in.

Figure D   3 in.   4 in.

_____

12. Which figure has an area of 108 square centimeters? (4.MD.A.3)

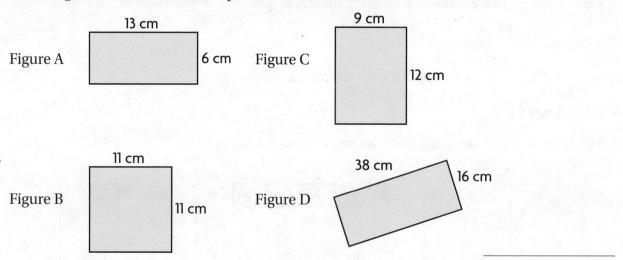

Figure A   13 cm   6 cm

Figure C   9 cm   12 cm

Figure B   11 cm   11 cm

Figure D   38 cm   16 cm

_____

13. **GO DEEPER** Which of the combined rectangles has an area of 40 square feet? (4.MD.A.3)

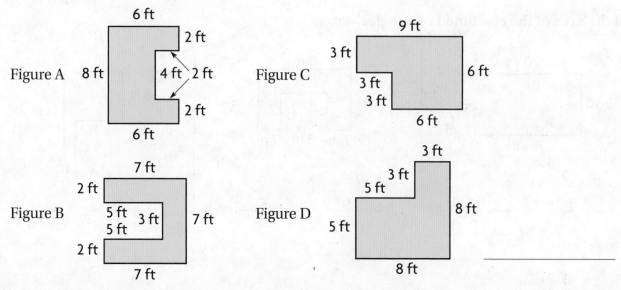

Figure A   6 ft   2 ft   8 ft   4 ft   2 ft   2 ft   6 ft

Figure C   9 ft   3 ft   3 ft   3 ft   6 ft   6 ft

Figure B   7 ft   2 ft   5 ft   3 ft   5 ft   7 ft   2 ft   7 ft

Figure D   3 ft   3 ft   5 ft   8 ft   5 ft   8 ft

_____

Name _____

Find Unknown Measures

Essential Question How can you find an unknown measure of a rectangle given its area or perimeter?

Common Core **Measurement and Data—**
4.MD.A.3
MATHEMATICAL PRACTICES
MP1, MP2, MP7

Unlock the Problem

Tanisha is painting a mural that is in the shape of a rectangle. The mural covers an area of 54 square feet. The base of the mural measures 9 feet. What is its height?

Use a formula for area.

- **What do you need to find?**

  _____

- **What information do you know?**

  _____

Example 1 Find an unknown measure given the area.

MODEL	RECORD

RECORD

Use the model to write an equation and solve.

Think: Label the measures you know. Use *n* for the unknown.

$A =$ _____ $h =$ _____

_____ = _____ _____   Write the formula for area.

_____ = _____ _____   Use the model to write an equation.

54 = 9 × _____   What times 9 equals 54?

The value of *n* is _____.

Think: *n* is the height of the mural.

9

b = _____

So, the height of the mural is _____ feet.

MATHEMATICAL PRACTICES ②

Reason Abstractly How can you use division to find an unknown factor?

1. What if the mural were in the shape of a square with an area of 81 square feet? What would the height of the mural be? Explain.

   _____

   _____

2. Explain how you can find an unknown side length of any square, when given only the area of the square.

   _____

   _____

   _____

Example 2 Find an unknown measure given the perimeter.

Gary is building an outdoor pen in the shape of a rectangle for his dog. He will use 24 meters of fencing. The pen will be 3 meters wide. How long will the pen be?

Use a formula for perimeter.

MODEL

Think: Label the measures you know. Use n for the unknown.

$w =$ _____

$l =$ _____

$P =$ _____

RECORD

Use the model to write an equation and solve.

$$P = (2 \times l) + (2 \times w)$$

_____ = (_____ . _____) + (_____ _____)

_____ = (_____ _____) + _____

Think: $(2 \times n)$ is an unknown addend.

$24 =$ _____ $+ 6$ **Think:** What is $24 - 6$?

The value of $(2 \times n)$ is 18.

To find the value of n, find the unknown factor.

$2 \times$ _____ $= 18$

The value of n is _____.

Think: n is the length of the pen.

So, the pen will be _____ long.

ERROR Alert

Check that you are using the correct formula. Are you given the area or the perimeter?

Try This! The perimeter of a square is 24 feet. Find the side length.

Draw a model.	Write an equation.
	$P = 4 \times s$

Name _____

1. Find the unknown measure. The area of the
rectangle is 36 square feet.

$A = b \times h$

_____ $= b \times$ _____

3 ft [rectangle]

?

The base of the rectangle is _____ .

Find the unknown measure of the rectangle.

2.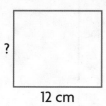

? [square]

12 cm

Perimeter = 44 centimeters

width = _____

3. 9 in.

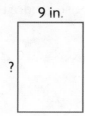

?

Area = 108 square inches

height = _____

4. 5 m [rectangle]

?

Area = 90 square meters

base = _____

Math Talk

MATHEMATICAL PRACTICES ②

Represent a Problem Explain
how using the area formula
helps you find the base of a
rectangle when you know its
area and height.

On Your Own

5.

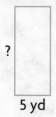

?

5 yd

Perimeter = 34 yards

length = _____

6.

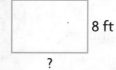

8 ft

?

Area = 96 square feet

base = _____

7.

? [rectangle]

9 cm

Area = 126 square centimeters

height = _____

8. **GO DEEPER** A square has an area of 49 square inches. Explain how to
find the perimeter of the square.

_____

_____

_____

_____

Problem Solving • Applications

9. **MATHEMATICAL PRACTICE 7 Identify Relationships** The area of a swimming pool is 120 square meters. The width of the pool is 8 meters. What is the length of the pool in centimeters?

_____

Personal Math Trainer

10. **THINK SMARTER +** An outdoor deck is 7 feet wide. The perimeter of the deck is 64 feet. What is the length of the deck? Use the numbers to write an equation and solve. A number may be used more than once.

| 7 | 9 | 5 | 14 | 25 | 50 | 64 |

$P = (2 \times l) + (2 \times w)$

$\boxed{} = (2 \times l) + (2 \times \boxed{})$

$\boxed{} = 2 \times l + \boxed{}$

$\boxed{} = 2 \times l$

$\boxed{} = l$

So, the length of the deck is _____ feet.

Connect to Science

Mountain Lions

Mountain lions are also known as cougars, panthers, or pumas. Their range once was from coast to coast in North America and from Argentina to Alaska. Hunting and habitat destruction now restricts their range to mostly mountainous, unpopulated areas.

Mountain lions are solitary animals. A male's territory often overlaps two females' territories but never overlaps another male's. The average size of a male's territory is 108 square miles, but it may be smaller or larger depending on how plentiful food is.

Math on the Spot

11. **THINK SMARTER** A male mountain lion has a rectangular territory with an area of 96 square miles. If his territory is 8 miles wide, what is the length of his territory? _____

Name _____

Find Unknown Measures

Common Core

COMMON CORE STANDARD—4.MD.A.3
Solve problems involving measurement and
conversion of measurements from a larger unit
to a smaller unit.

Find the unknown measure of the rectangle.

1.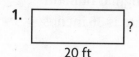
?

20 ft

Perimeter = 54 feet

width = ___7 feet___

Think: $P = (2 \times l) + (2 \times w)$
$54 = (2 \times 20) + (2 \times w)$
$54 = 40 + (2 \times w)$
Since $54 = 40 + 14$, $2 \times w = 14$, and $w = 7$.

2.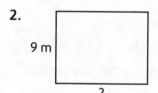
9 m
?

Perimeter = 42 meters

length = _____

3.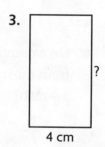
?
4 cm

Area = 28 square centimeters

height = _____

4.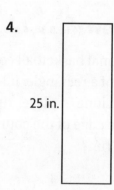
25 in.

Area = 200 square inches

base = _____

Problem Solving Real World

5. Susie is an organic vegetable grower.
The perimeter of her rectangular vegetable
garden is 72 yards. The width of the
vegetable garden is 9 yards. How long is the
vegetable garden?

_____

_____

_____

6. **WRITE** ▸Math Write a problem that
involves finding the unknown measure of a
side of a rectangle. Include the solution.

_____

_____

_____

Lesson Check (4.MD.A.3)

1. The area of a rectangular photograph is 35 square inches. If the width of the photo is 5 inches, how tall is the photo?

2. Natalie used 112 inches of blue yarn as a border around her rectangular bulletin board. If the bulletin board is 36 inches wide, how long is it?

Spiral Review (4.NF.B.3d, 4.MD.A.2, 4.MD.A.3, 4.MD.C.5a, 4.MD.C.5b)

3. A professional basketball court is in the shape of a rectangle. It is 50 feet wide and 94 feet long. A player runs one time around the edge of the court. How far does the player run?

4. On a compass, due east is a $\frac{1}{4}$ turn clockwise from due north. How many degrees are in a $\frac{1}{4}$ turn?

5. Hakeem's frog made three quick jumps. The first was 1 meter. The second jump was 85 centimeters. The third jump was 400 millimeters. What was the total length in centimeters of the frog's three jumps?

6. Karen colors in squares on a grid. She colored $\frac{1}{8}$ of the squares blue and $\frac{5}{8}$ of the squares red. What fraction of the squares are not colored in?

FOR MORE PRACTICE GO TO THE
Personal Math Trainer

Name _____

Problem Solving • Find the Area

Essential Question How can you use the strategy *solve a simpler problem* to solve area problems?

Common Core Measurement and Data—
4.MD.A.3
MATHEMATICAL PRACTICES
MP1, MP4, MP6

Unlock the Problem

A landscaper is laying grass for a rectangular playground. The grass will cover the whole playground except for a square sandbox. The diagram shows the playground and sandbox. How many square yards of grass will the landscaper use?

Use the graphic organizer below to solve the problem.

25 yd
Playground
Sandbox →
15 yd
6 yd

Read the Problem	Solve the Problem
What do I need to find? I need to find how many _____ the landscaper will use.	First, find the area of the playground. $A = b \times h$ = _____ × _____ = _____ square yards Next, find the area of the sandbox. $A = s \times s$ = _____ × _____ = _____ square yards
What information do I need to use? The grass will cover the _____. The grass will not cover the _____. The length and width of the playground are _____ and _____. The side length of the square sandbox is _____.	
	Last, subtract the area of the sandbox from the area of the playground. 375 − 36 _____ square yards So, the landscaper will use _____ _____ of grass to cover the playground.
How will I use the information? I can solve simpler problems. Find the area of the _____. Find the area of the _____. Then _____ the area of the _____ from the area of the _____.	

MATHEMATICAL PRACTICES ①

Make Sense of Problems How did the strategy help you solve the problem?

🔑 Try Another Problem

Zach is laying a rectangular brick patio for a new museum. Brick will cover the whole patio except for a rectangular fountain, as shown in the diagram. How many square meters of brick does Zach need?

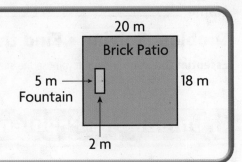

Read the Problem	Solve the Problem
What do I need to find?	
What information do I need to use?	
How will I use this information?	

- How many square meters of brick does Zach need? Explain.

_____

_____

_____

Name _____

Unlock the Problem

✓ Use the Problem Solving MathBoard
✓ Underline important facts.
✓ Choose a strategy you know.

Share and Show MATH BOARD

1. Lila is wallpapering one wall of her bedroom, as shown in the diagram. She will cover the whole wall except for the doorway. How many square feet of wall does Lila need to cover?

   First, find the area of the wall.

   $A = b \times h$

   $= $ _____ × _____

   $= $ _____ square feet

   Next, find the area of the door.

   $A = b \times h$

   $= $ _____ × _____

   $= $ _____ square feet

   Last, subtract the area of the door from the area of the wall.

   _____ – _____ = _____ square feet

   So, Lila needs to cover _____ of wall.

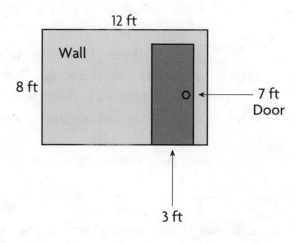

2. What if there was a square window on the wall with a side length of 2 feet? How much wall would Lila need to cover then? Explain.

   _____

   _____

   _____

3. Ed is building a model of a house with a flat roof, as shown in the diagram. There is a chimney through the roof. Ed will cover the roof with square tiles. If the area of each tile is 1 square inch, how many tiles will he need? Explain.

   _____

   _____

   _____

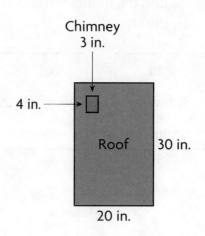

© Houghton Mifflin Harcourt Publishing Company

On Your Own

4. **MATHEMATICAL PRACTICE ① Make Sense of Problems** Lia has a dog and a cat. Together, the pets weigh 28 pounds. The dog weighs 3 times as much as the cat. How much does each pet weigh?

_____

5. **THINK SMARTER** Mr. Foster is covering two rectangular pictures with glass. One is 6 inches by 4 inches and the other one is 5 inches by 5 inches. Does he need the same number of square inches of glass for each picture? Explain.

_____

_____

WRITE ▸ *Math*
Show Your Work

6. **GO DEEPER** Claire says the area of a square with a side length of 100 centimeters is greater than the area of a square with a side length of 1 meter. Is she correct? Explain.

_____

_____

_____

7. **THINK SMARTER** A rectangular floor is 12 feet long and 11 feet wide. Janine places a rug that is 9 feet long and 7 feet wide and covers part of the floor in the room. Select the word(s) to complete the sentence.

To find the number of square feet of the floor that is NOT covered by the rug,

add		area of the rug		from	
subtract	the	length of the rug		by	the area of the floor.
multiply		area of the floor		to	

Problem Solving • Find the Area

 COMMON CORE STANDARD—4.MD.A.3
Solve problems involving measurement and conversion of measurements from a larger unit to a smaller unit.

Solve each problem.

1. A room has a wooden floor. There is a rug in the center of the floor. The diagram shows the room and the rug. How many square feet of the wood floor still show?

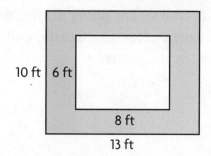

   _____ **82 square feet** _____

   Area of the floor: $13 \times 10 = 130$ square feet
   Area of the rug: $8 \times 6 = 48$ square feet
   Subtract to find the area of the floor still showing: $130 - 48 = 82$ square feet

2. A rectangular wall has a square window, as shown in the diagram.

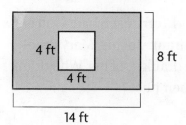

   What is the area of the wall NOT including the window?

   _____

3. Bob wants to put down new sod in his backyard, except for the part set aside for his flower garden. The diagram shows Bob's backyard and the flower garden.

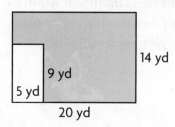

   How much sod will Bob need?

   _____

4. A rectangular painting is 24 inches wide and 20 inches tall without the frame. With the frame, it is 28 inches wide and 24 inches tall. What is the area of the frame not covered by the painting?

   _____

5. **WRITE** ▸*Math* Suppose you painted the walls of your classroom. Describe how to find the area of the walls that are painted.

   _____

   _____

   _____

Lesson Check (4.MD.A.3)

1. One wall in Zoe's bedroom is 5 feet wide and 8 feet tall. Zoe puts up a poster of her favorite athlete. The poster is 2 feet wide and 3 feet tall. How much of the wall is not covered by the poster?

2. A garage door is 15 feet wide and 6 feet high. It is painted white, except for a rectangular panel 1 foot high and 9 feet wide that is brown. How much of the garage door is white?

Spiral Review (4.OA.B.4, 4.NF.A.2, 4.MD.A.2, 4.MD.A.3)

3. Kate made a box to hold her jewelry collection. She used 42 inches of wood to build the sides of the box. If the box was 9 inches wide, how long was the box?

4. Larry, Mary, and Terry each had a full glass of juice. Larry drank $\frac{3}{4}$ of his. Mary drank $\frac{3}{8}$ of hers. Terry drank $\frac{7}{10}$ of his. Who drank less than $\frac{1}{2}$ of their juice?

5. List all of the numbers between 20 and 30 that are prime.

6. Tom and some friends went to a movie. The show started at 2:30 P.M. and ended at 4:15 P.M. How long did the movie last?

FOR MORE PRACTICE
GO TO THE
Personal Math Trainer

Name _____

✓ Chapter 13 Review/Test

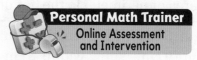

1. For numbers 1a–1e, select Yes or No to indicate if a rectangle with the given dimensions would have a perimeter of 50 inches.

   1a. length: 25 inches   width: 2 inches   ○ Yes   ○ No

   1b. length: 20 inches   width: 5 inches   ○ Yes   ○ No

   1c. length: 17 inches   width: 8 inches   ○ Yes   ○ No

   1d. length: 15 inches   width: 5 inches   ○ Yes   ○ No

   1e. length: 15 inches   width: 10 inches   ○ Yes   ○ No

2. The swimming club's indoor pool is in a rectangular building. Marco is laying tile around the rectangular pool.

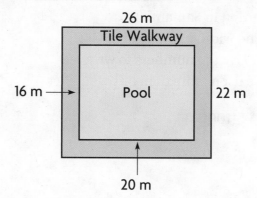

Part A

What is the area of the pool and the area of the pool and the walkway? Show your work.

Part B

How many square meters of tile will Marco need for the walkway? Explain how you found your answer.

 **Assessment Options**
Chapter Test

3. Match the dimensions of the rectangles in the top row with the correct area or perimeter in the bottom row.

length: 5 cm width: 9 cm	length: 6 cm width: 6 cm	length: 6 cm width: 5 cm	length: 9 cm width: 6 cm

• • • •

• • • •

area = 36 sq cm	perimeter = 22 cm	perimeter = 30 cm	area = 45 sq cm

4. Kyleigh put a large rectangular sticker on her notebook. The height of the sticker measures 18 centimeters. The base is half as long as the height. What area of the notebook does the sticker cover?

_____ square centimeters

5. **THINK SMARTER** A rectangular flower garden in Samantha's backyard has 100 feet around its edge. The width of the garden is 20 feet. What is the length of the garden? Use the numbers to write an equation and solve. A number may be used more than once.

| 10 | 20 | 50 | 30 | 40 | 60 | 100 |

$P = (2 \times l) + (2 \times w)$

☐ $= (2 \times l) + (2 \times$ ☐ $)$

☐ $= 2 \times l +$ ☐

☐ $= 2 \times l$

☐ $= l$

So, the length of the garden is ☐ feet.

6. Gary drew a rectangle with a perimeter of 20 inches. Then he tried to draw a square with a perimeter of 20 inches.

Draw 3 different rectangles that Gary could have drawn. Then draw the square, if possible.

© Houghton Mifflin Harcourt Publishing Company

Name _____

7. Ami and Bert are drawing plans for rectangular vegetable gardens. In Ami's plan, the garden is 13 feet by 10 feet. In Bert's plan the garden is 12 feet by 12 feet. For numbers 7a–7d, select True or False for each statement.

7a. The area of Ami's garden is 130 square feet.   ○ True   ○ False

7b. The area of Bert's garden is 48 square feet.   ○ True   ○ False

7c. Ami's garden has a greater area than Bert's garden.   ○ True   ○ False

7d. The area of Bert's garden is 14 square feet greater than Ami's.   ○ True   ○ False

8. A farmer planted corn in a square field. One side of the field measures 32 yards. What is the area of the cornfield? Show your work.

9.  Harvey bought a frame in which he put his family's picture.

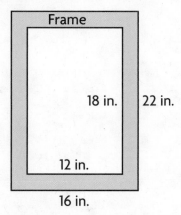

Frame
18 in.   22 in.
12 in.
16 in.

What is the area of the frame?

_____ square inches

10. Kelly has 236 feet of fence to use to enclose a rectangular space for her dog. She wants the width to be 23 feet. Draw a rectangle that could be the space for Kelly's dog. Label the length and the width.

11. The diagram shows the dimensions of a new parking lot at Helen's Health Food store.

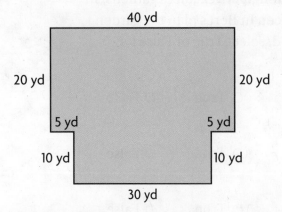

40 yd

20 yd   20 yd

5 yd   5 yd

10 yd   10 yd

30 yd

Use either addition or subtraction to find the area of the parking lot. Show your work.

12. Chad's bedroom floor is 12 feet long and 10 feet wide. He has an area rug on his floor that is 7 feet long and 5 feet wide. Which statement tells how to find the amount of the floor that is not covered by the rug? Mark all that apply.

(A) Add 12×10 and 7×5.

(B) Subtract 35 from 12×10

(C) Subtract 10×5 from 12×7.

(D) Add $12 + 10 + 7 + 5$.

(E) Subtract 7×5 from 12×10.

(F) Subtract 12×10 from 7×5.

13. A row of plaques covers 120 square feet of space along a wall. If the plaques are 3 feet tall, what length of the wall do they cover?

_____ feet

14. Ms. Bennett wants to buy carpeting for her living room and dining room.

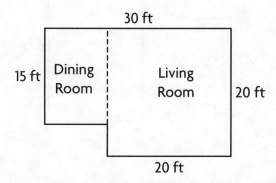

Explain how she can find the amount of carpet she needs to cover the floor in both rooms. Then find the amount of carpet she will need.

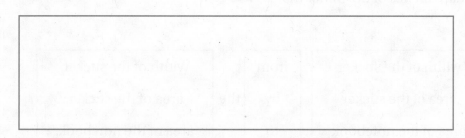

15. Lorenzo built a rectangular brick patio. He is putting a stone border around the edge of the patio. The width of the patio is 12 feet. The length of the patio is two feet longer than the width.

How many feet of stone will Lorenzo need? Explain how you found your answer.

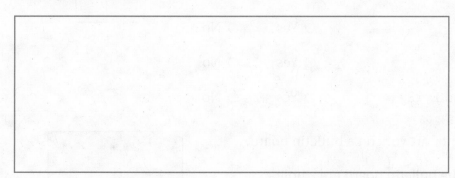

16. Which rectangle has a perimeter of 10 feet? Mark all that apply.

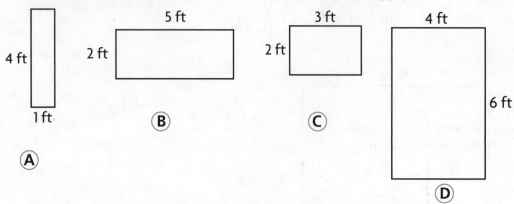

17. A folder is 11 inches long and 8 inches wide. Alyssa places a sticker that is 2 inches long and 1 inch wide on the notebook. Choose the words that correctly complete the sentence.

To find the number of square inches of the folder that is NOT covered by the sticker,

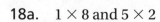

add		width of the sticker	from		width of the sticker.
subtract	the	area of the sticker	by	the	area of the sticker.
multiply		area of the notebook	to		area of the notebook.

18. Tricia is cutting her initial from a piece of felt.

For numbers 18a–18c, select Yes or No to tell whether you can add the products to find the number of square centimeters Tricia needs.

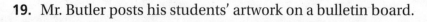

18a. 1×8 and 5×2 ○ Yes   ○ No

18b. 3×5 and 1×8 ○ Yes   ○ No

18c. 2×5 and 1×3 and 1×3 ○ Yes   ○ No

19. Mr. Butler posts his students' artwork on a bulletin board.

The width and length of the bulletin board are whole numbers. What could be the dimensions of the bulletin board Mr. Butler uses?

Area = 15 square feet

Glossary

A

acute angle [ə•kyo͞ot′ ang′gəl] **ángulo agudo**
An angle that measures greater than 0° and less than 90°
Example:

acute triangle [ə•kyo͞ot′ trī′ang•gəl]
triángulo acutángulo A triangle with three acute angles
Example:

addend [a′dend] **sumando** A number that is added to another in an addition problem
Example: 2 + 4 = 6;
          2 and 4 are addends.

addition [ə•di′shən] **suma** The process of finding the total number of items when two or more groups of items are joined; the opposite operation of subtraction

A.M. [ā•em′] **a.m.** The times after midnight and before noon

analog clock [anəl• ôg kläk] **reloj analógico**
A tool for measuring time, in which hands move around a circle to show hours, minutes, and sometimes seconds
Example:

angle [ang′gəl] **ángulo** A shape formed by two line segments or rays that share the same endpoint
Example:

area [âr′ē•ə] **área** The measure of the number of unit squares needed to cover a surface
Example:

Area = 9 square units

array [ə•rā′] **matriz** An arrangement of objects in rows and columns
Example:

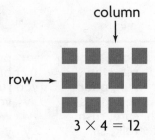

column

row →

$3 \times 4 = 12$

Associative Property of Addition [ə•sō′shē•āt•iv präp′ər•tē əv ə•dish′ən] **propiedad asociativa de la suma** The property that states that you can group addends in different ways and still get the same sum
Example: $3 + (8 + 5) = (3 + 8) + 5$

Associative Property of Multiplication [ə•sō′shē•ə•tiv präp′ər•tē əv mul•tə•pli•kā′shən] **propiedad asociativa de la multiplicación** The property that states that you can group factors in different ways and still get the same product
Example: $3 \times (4 \times 2) = (3 \times 4) \times 2$

bar graph [bär graf] **gráfica de barras** A graph that uses bars to show data
Example:

base [bās] **base** A polygon's side or a two-dimensional shape, usually a polygon or circle, by which a three-dimensional shape is measured or named
Examples:

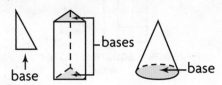

base — bases — base

benchmark [bench′märk] **punto de referencia** A known size or amount that helps you understand a different size or amount

calendar [kal′ən•dər] **calendario** A table that shows the days, weeks, and months of a year

capacity [kə•pas′i•tē] **capacidad** The amount a container can hold when filled

Celsius (°C) [sel′sē•əs] **Celsius** A metric scale for measuring temperature

centimeter (cm) [sen′tə•mēt•ər] **centímetro (cm)** A metric unit for measuring length or distance
1 meter = 100 centimeters
Example:

1 centimeter

cent sign (¢) [sent sīn] **símbolo de centavo** A symbol that stands for *cent* or *cents*
Example: 53¢

clockwise [kläk′wīz] **en el sentido de las manecillas del reloj** In the same direction in which the hands of a clock move

closed shape [klōzd shāp] **figura cerrada** A two-dimensional shape that begins and ends at the same point
Examples:

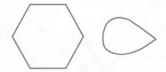

common denominator [käm′ən dē•näm′ə•nāt•ər] **denominador común** A common multiple of two or more denominators
Example: Some common denominators for $\frac{1}{4}$ and $\frac{5}{6}$ are 12, 24, and 36.

common factor [käm′ən fak′tər] **factor común** A number that is a factor of two or more numbers

common multiple [käm′ən mul′tə•pəl] **múltiplo común** A number that is a multiple of two or more numbers

Commutative Property of Addition
[kə•myōōt′ə•tiv präp′ər•tē əv ə•dish′ən] **propiedad conmutativa de la suma** The property that states that when the order of two addends is changed, the sum is the same
Example: 4 + 5 = 5 + 4

Commutative Property of Multiplication
[kə•myōōt′ə•tiv präp′ər•tē əv mul•tə•pli•kā′shən] **propiedad conmutativa de la multiplicación** The property that states that when the order of two factors is changed, the product is the same
Example: 4 × 5 = 5 × 4

compare [kəm•pâr′] **comparar** To describe whether numbers are equal to, less than, or greater than each other

compatible numbers [kəm•pat′ə•bəl num′bərz] **números compatibles** Numbers that are easy to compute mentally

composite number [kəm•päz′it num′bər] **número compuesto** A number having more than two factors
Example: 6 is a composite number, since its factors are 1, 2, 3, and 6.

corner [kôr′nər] **esquina** See *vertex*.

counterclockwise [kount•er•kläk′wīz] **en sentido contrario a las manecillas del reloj** In the opposite direction in which the hands of a clock move

counting number [kount′ing num′bər] **número natural** A whole number that can be used to count a set of objects (1, 2, 3, 4, . . .)

cube [kyōōb] **cubo** A three-dimensional shape with six square faces of the same size
Example:

cup (c) [kup] **taza (tz)** A customary unit used to measure capacity and liquid volume
1 cup = 8 ounces

data [dāt′ə] **datos** Information collected about people or things

decagon [dek′ə•gän] **decágono** A polygon with ten sides and ten angles

decimal [des′ə•məl] **decimal** A number with one or more digits to the right of the decimal point

decimal point [des′ə•məl point] **punto decimal** A symbol used to separate dollars from cents in money amounts, and to separate the ones and the tenths places in a decimal
Example: 6.4
　　　　↑ decimal point

decimeter (dm) [des′i•mēt•ər] **decímetro (dm)** A metric unit for measuring length or distance
1 meter = 10 decimeters

degree (°) [di•grē′] **grado (°)** The unit used for measuring angles and temperatures

denominator [dē•näm′ə•nāt•ər] **denominador** The number below the bar in a fraction that tells how many equal parts are in the whole or in the group
Example: $\frac{3}{4}$ ← denominator

diagonal [dī•ag′ə•nəl] **diagonal** A line segment that connects two vertices of a polygon that are not next to each other
Example:

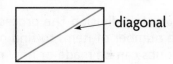

difference [dif′ər•əns] **diferencia** The answer to a subtraction problem

digit [dij′it] **dígito** Any one of the ten symbols 0, 1, 2, 3, 4, 5, 6, 7, 8, or 9 used to write numbers

digital clock [dij′i•təl kläk] **reloj digital** A clock that shows time to the minute, using digits
Example:

dime [dīm] **moneda de 10¢** A coin worth 10 cents and with a value equal to that of 10 pennies; 10¢
Example:

dimension [də•men'shən] **dimensión** A measure in one direction

Distributive Property [di•strib'yōō•tiv präp'ər•tē] **propiedad distributiva** The property that states that multiplying a sum by a number is the same as multiplying each addend by the number and then adding the products
Example: $5 \times (10 + 6) = (5 \times 10) + (5 \times 6)$

divide [də•vīd'] **dividir** To separate into equal groups; the opposite operation of multiplication

dividend [dəv'ə•dend] **dividendo** The number that is to be divided in a division problem
Example: $36 \div 6$; $6)\overline{36}$; the dividend is 36.

divisible [də•viz'ə•bəl] **divisible** A number is divisible by another number if the quotient is a counting number and the remainder is zero
Example: 18 is divisible by 3.

division [də•vi'zhən] **división** The process of sharing a number of items to find how many equal groups can be made or how many items will be in each equal group; the opposite operation of multiplication

divisor [də•vī'zər] **divisor** The number that divides the dividend
Example: $15 \div 3$; $3)\overline{15}$; the divisor is 3.

dollar [däl'ər] **dólar** Paper money worth 100 cents and equal to 100 pennies; $1.00
Example:

 E

elapsed time [ē•lapst' tīm] **tiempo transcurrido** The time that passes from the start of an activity to the end of that activity

endpoint [end'point] **extremo** The point at either end of a line segment or the starting point of a ray

equal groups [ē'kwəl grōōpz] **grupos iguales** Groups that have the same number of objects

equal parts [ē'kwəl pärts] **partes iguales** Parts that are exactly the same size

equal sign (=) [ē'kwəl sīn] **signo de igualdad** A symbol used to show that two numbers have the same value
Example: $384 = 384$

equal to [ē'kwəl tōō] **igual a** Having the same value
Example: $4 + 4$ is equal to $3 + 5$.

equation [ē•kwā'zhən] **ecuación** A number sentence which shows that two quantities are equal
Example: $4 + 5 = 9$

equivalent [ē•kwiv'ə•lənt] **equivalente** Having the same value or naming the same amount

equivalent decimals [ē•kwiv'ə•lənt des'ə•məlz] **decimales equivalentes** Two or more decimals that name the same amount

equivalent fractions [ē•kwiv'ə•lənt frak'shənz] **fracciones equivalentes** Two or more fractions that name the same amount
Example: $\frac{3}{4}$ and $\frac{6}{8}$ name the same amount.

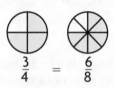

$$\frac{3}{4} = \frac{6}{8}$$

estimate [es'tə•māt] *verb* **estimar** To find an answer that is close to the exact amount

estimate [es'tə•mit] *noun* **estimación** A number that is close to the exact amount

even [ē'vən] **par** A whole number that has a 0, 2, 4, 6, or 8 in the ones place

expanded form [ek•span'did fôrm] **forma desarrollada** A way to write numbers by showing the value of each digit
Example: $253 = 200 + 50 + 3$

expression [ek•spresh'ən] **expresión** A part of a number sentence that has numbers and operation signs but does not have an equal sign

F

fact family [fakt fam′ə•lē] **familia de operaciones**
A set of related multiplication and division
equations, or addition and subtraction
equations
Example: $7 \times 8 = 56 \quad 8 \times 7 = 56$
$56 \div 7 = 8 \quad 56 \div 8 = 7$

factor [fak′tər] **factor** A number that is multiplied
by another number to find a product

Fahrenheit (°F) [fâr′ən•hīt] **Fahrenheit** A customary
scale for measuring temperature

fluid ounce (fl oz) [flo͞o′id ouns] **onza fluida (fl oz)**
A customary unit used to measure liquid
capacity and liquid volume
1 cup = 8 fluid ounces

foot (ft) [fo͝ot] **pie (ft)** A customary unit used for
measuring length or distance
1 foot = 12 inches

formula [fôr′myo͞o•lə] **fórmula** A set of symbols that
expresses a mathematical rule
Example: Area = base × height, or $A = b \times h$

fraction [frak′shən] **fracción** A number that names
a part of a whole or part of a group
Example:

$\frac{1}{3}$

fraction greater than 1 [frak′shən grāt′ər than wun]
fracción mayor que 1 A number which has a
numerator that is greater than its denominator

frequency table [frē′kwən•sē tā′bəl] **tabla de
frecuencia** A table that uses numbers to
record data about how often something
happens
Example:

Favorite Color	
Color	**Frequency**
Blue	10
Red	7
Green	5
Other	3

G

gallon (gal) [gal′ən] **galón (gal)** A customary unit
for measuring capacity and liquid volume
1 gallon = 4 quarts

gram (g) [gram] **gramo (g)** A metric unit for
measuring mass
1 kilogram = 1,000 grams

greater than sign (>) [grāt′ər than sīn] **signo de
mayor que** A symbol used to compare two
quantities, with the greater quantity given first
Example: 6 > 4

grid [grid] **cuadrícula** Evenly divided and equally
spaced squares on a shape or flat surface

H

half gallon [haf gal′ən] **medio galón** A customary
unit for measuring capacity and liquid volume
1 half gallon = 2 quarts

half hour [haf our] **media hora** 30 minutes
Example: 4:00 to 4:30 is one half hour.

half-square unit [haf skwâr yo͞o′nit] **media unidad
cuadrada** Half of a unit of area with dimensions
of 1 unit × 1 unit

height [hīt] **altura** The measure of a perpendicular
from the base to the top of a two-dimensional
shape

hexagon [hek′sə•gän] **hexágono** A polygon with six
sides and six angles
Examples:

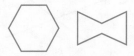

horizontal [hôr•i•zänt′l] **horizontal** In the direction
from left to right

hour (hr) [our] **hora (hr)** A unit used to measure
time
1 hour = 60 minutes

hundredth [hun'drədth] **centésimo** One of one hundred equal parts
Example:

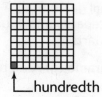

hundredth

Identity Property of Addition [ī•den'tə•tē präp'ər•tē əv ə•dish'ən] **propiedad de identidad de la suma** The property that states that when you add zero to any number, the sum is that number
Example: $16 + 0 = 16$

Identity Property of Multiplication [ī•den'tə•tē präp'ər•tē əv mul•tə•pli•kā'shən] **propiedad de identidad de la multiplicación** The property that states that the product of any number and 1 is that number
Example: $9 \times 1 = 9$

inch (in.) [inch] **pulgada (pulg)** A customary unit used for measuring length or distance
Example:

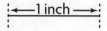

1 inch

intersecting lines [in•tər•sekt'ing līnz] **líneas secantes** Lines that cross each other at exactly one point
Example:

inverse operations [in'vûrs äp•ə•rā'shənz] **operaciones inversas** Operations that undo each other, such as addition and subtraction or multiplication and division
Example: $6 \times 8 = 48$ and $48 \div 6 = 8$

key [kē] **clave** The part of a map or graph that explains the symbols

kilogram (kg) [kil'ō•gram] **kilogramo (kg)** A metric unit for measuring mass
1 kilogram = 1,000 grams

kilometer (km) [kə•läm'ət•ər] **kilómetro (km)** A metric unit for measuring length or distance
1 kilometer = 1,000 meters

length [lengkth] **longitud** The measurement of the distance between two points

less than sign (<) [les <u>th</u>an sīn] **signo de menor que** A symbol used to compare two quantities, with the lesser quantity given first
Example: $3 < 7$

line [līn] **línea** A straight path of points in a plane that continues without end in both directions with no endpoints
Example:

S   T

line graph [līn graf] **gráfica lineal** A graph that uses line segments to show how data change over time

line of symmetry [līn əv sim'ə•trē] **eje de simetría** An imaginary line on a shape about which the shape can be folded so that its two parts match exactly
Example:

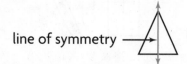

line of symmetry

line plot [līn plöt] **diagrama de puntos** A graph that records each piece of data on a number line
Example:

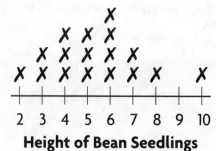

Height of Bean Seedlings

line segment [līn seg′mənt] **segmento** A part of a line that includes two points called endpoints and all the points between them
Example:

A   B

line symmetry [līn sim′ə•trē] **simetría axial** What a shape has if it can be folded about a line so that its two parts match exactly

linear units [lin′ē•ər yoo′nits] **unidades lineales** Units that measure length, width, height, or distance

liquid volume [lik′wid väl′yoom] **volumen de un líquido** The measure of the space a liquid occupies

liter (L) [lēt′ər] **litro (L)** A metric unit for measuring capacity and liquid volume
1 liter = 1,000 milliliters

mass [mas] **masa** The amount of matter in an object

meter (m) [mēt′ər] **metro (m)** A metric unit for measuring length or distance
1 meter = 100 centimeters

midnight [mid′nīt] **medianoche** 12:00 at night

mile (mi) [mīl] **milla (mi)** A customary unit for measuring length or distance
1 mile = 5,280 feet

milliliter (mL) [mil′i•lēt•ər] **mililitro (mL)** A metric unit for measuring capacity and liquid volume
1 liter = 1,000 milliliters

millimeter (mm) [mil′i•mēt•ər] **milímetro (mm)** A metric unit for measuring length or distance
1 centimeter = 10 millimeters

million [mil′yən] **millón** The counting number after 999,999; 1,000 thousands; written as 1,000,000

millions [mil′yənz] **millones** The period after thousands

minute (min) [min′it] **minuto (min)** A unit used to measure short amounts of time
1 minute = 60 seconds

mixed number [mikst num′bər] **número mixto** An amount given as a whole number and a fraction

multiple [mul′tə•pəl] **múltiplo** The product of a number and a counting number is called a multiple of the number
Example:

$$
\begin{array}{cccc}
3 & 3 & 3 & 3 \\
\times\,1 & \times\,2 & \times\,3 & \times\,4 \\
\hline
3 & 6 & 9 & 12
\end{array}
$$
← counting numbers
← multiples of 3

multiplication [mul•tə•pli•kā′shən] **multiplicación** A process to find the total number of items in equal-sized groups, or to find the total number of items in a given number of groups when each group contains the same number of items; multiplication is the inverse of division

multiply [mul′tə•plī] **multiplicar** To combine equal groups to find how many in all; the opposite operation of division

nickel [nik′əl] **moneda de 5¢** A coin worth 5 cents and with a value equal to that of 5 pennies; 5¢
Example:

noon [noon] **mediodía** 12:00 in the day

not equal to sign (≠) [not ē′kwəl too sīn] **signo de no igual a** A symbol that indicates one quantity is not equal to another
Example: $12 \times 3 \neq 38$

number line [num′bər līn] **recta numérica** A line on which numbers can be located
Example:

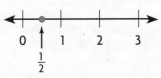

0   1   2   3

$\frac{1}{2}$

number sentence [num′bər sent′ns] **enunciado numérico** A sentence that includes numbers, operation symbols, and a greater than or less than symbol or an equal sign
Example: $5 + 3 = 8$

numerator [n$\overline{oo}$′mər•āt•ər] **numerador** The number above the bar in a fraction that tells how many parts of the whole or group are being considered

Example: $\frac{2}{3}$ ← numerator

obtuse angle [äb•t$\overline{oo}$s′ ang′gəl] **ángulo obtuso** An angle that measures greater than 90° and less than 180°
Example:

obtuse triangle [äb•t$\overline{oo}$s′ trī′ang•gəl] **triángulo obtusángulo** A triangle with one obtuse angle

Example:

octagon [äk′tə•gän] **octágono** A polygon with eight sides and eight angles
Examples:

odd [od] **impar** A whole number that has a 1, 3, 5, 7, or 9 in the ones place

one-dimensional [wun də•men′shə•nəl] **unidimensional** Measured in only one direction, such as length
Examples:

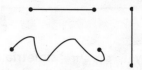

open shape [ō′pən shāp] **figura abierta** A shape that does not begin and end at the same point
Examples:

order [ôr′dər] **orden** A particular arrangement or placement of things one after the other

order of operations [ôr′dər əv äp•ə•rā′shənz] **orden de las operaciones** A special set of rules which gives the order in which calculations are done

ounce (oz) [ouns] **onza (oz)** A customary unit for measuring weight
1 pound = 16 ounces

parallel lines [pâr′ə•lel līnz] **líneas paralelas** Lines in the same plane that never intersect and are always the same distance apart
Example:

parallelogram [pâr•ə•lel'ə•gram] **paralelogramo** A quadrilateral whose opposite sides are parallel and of equal length
Example:

parentheses [pə•ren'thə•sēz] **paréntesis** The symbols used to show which operation or operations in an expression should be done first

partial product [pär'shəl präd'əkt] **producto parcial** A method of multiplying in which the ones, tens, hundreds, and so on are multiplied separately and then the products are added together

partial quotient [pär'shəl kwō'shənt] **cociente parcial** A method of dividing in which multiples of the divisor are subtracted from the dividend and then the quotients are added together

pattern [pat'ərn] **patrón** An ordered set of numbers or objects; the order helps you predict what will come next
Examples: 2, 4, 6, 8, 10

pattern unit [pat'ərn yoo'nit] **unidad de patrón** The part of a pattern that repeats
Example:

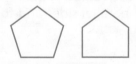
pattern unit

pentagon [pen'tə•gän] **pentágono** A polygon with five sides and five angles
Examples:

perimeter [pə•rim'ə•tər] **perímetro** The distance around a shape

period [pir'ē•əd] **período** Each group of three digits in a multi-digit number; periods are usually separated by commas or spaces.
Example: 85,643,900 has three periods.

perpendicular lines [pər•pən•dik'yoo•lər līnz] **líneas perpendiculares** Two lines that intersect to form four right angles
Example:

picture graph [pik'chər graf] **gráfica con dibujos** A graph that uses symbols to show and compare information
Example:

How We Get To School

Walk	✹ ✹ ✹
Ride a Bike	✹ ✹ ✹ ✹
Ride a Bus	✹ ✹ ✹ ✹ ✹
Ride in a Car	✹ ✹

Key: Each ✹ = 10 students.

pint (pt) [pīnt] **pinta (pt)** A customary unit for measuring capacity and liquid volume
1 pint = 2 cups

place value [plās val'yoo] **valor posicional** The value of a digit in a number, based on the location of the digit

plane [plān] **plano** A flat surface that extends without end in all directions
Example:

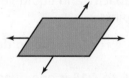

plane shape [plān shāp] **figura plana** See *two-dimensional figure.*

P.M. [pē•em] **p.m.** The times after noon and before midnight

point [point] **punto** An exact location in space

polygon [päl'i•gän] **polígono** A closed two-dimensional shape formed by three or more straight sides that are line segments
Examples:

Polygons   Not Polygons

pound (lb) [pound] **libra (lb)** A customary unit for measuring weight
1 pound = 16 ounces

prime number [prīm num'bər] **número primo** A number that has exactly two factors: 1 and itself
Examples: 2, 3, 5, 7, 11, 13, 17, and 19 are prime numbers. 1 is not a prime number.

prism [priz'əm] **prisma** A solid figure that has two same size, same polygon-shaped bases, and other faces that are all rectangles
Examples:

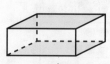

rectangular prism   triangular prism

product [präd'əkt] **producto** The answer to a multiplication problem

protractor [prō'trak·tər] **transportador** A tool for measuring the size of an angle

quadrilateral [kwä·dri·lat'ər·əl] **cuadrilátero** A polygon with four sides and four angles

quart (qt) [kwôrt] **cuarto (ct)** A customary unit for measuring capacity and liquid volume
1 quart = 2 pints

quarter hour [kwôrt'ər our] **cuarto de hora**
15 minutes
Example: 4:00 to 4:15 is one quarter hour

quotient [kwō'shənt] **cociente** The number, not including the remainder, that results from dividing
Example: 8 ÷ 4 = 2; 2 is the quotient.

ray [rā] **semirrecta** A part of a line; it has one endpoint and continues without end in one direction
Example:

rectangle [rek'tang·gəl] **rectángulo** A quadrilateral with two pairs of parallel sides, two pairs of sides of equal length, and four right angles
Example:

rectangular prism [rek·tang'gyə·lər priz'əm] **prisma rectangular** A three-dimensional shape in which all six faces are rectangles
Example:

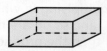

regroup [rē·grōōp'] **reagrupar** To exchange amounts of equal value to rename a number
Example: 5 + 8 = 13 ones or 1 ten 3 ones

regular polygon [reg'yə·lər päl'i·gän] **polígono regular** A polygon that has all sides that are equal in length and all angles equal in measure
Examples:

related facts [ri·lāt'id fakts] **operaciones relacionadas** A set of related addition and subtraction, or multiplication and division, number sentences
Examples: 4 × 7 = 28   28 ÷ 4 = 7
             7 × 4 = 28   28 ÷ 7 = 4

remainder [ri·mān'dər] **residuo** The amount left over when a number cannot be divided equally

rhombus [räm'bəs] **rombo** A quadrilateral with two pairs of parallel sides and four sides of equal length
Example:

right angle [rīt ang'gəl] **ángulo recto** An angle that forms a square corner
Example:

right triangle [rīt trī′ang•gəl] **triángulo rectángulo** A triangle with one right angle
Example:

round [round] **redondear** To replace a number with another number that tells about how many or how much

rule [rool] **regla** A procedure (usually involving arithmetic operations) to determine an output value from an input value

scale [skāl] **escala** A series of numbers placed at fixed distances on a graph to help label the graph

second (sec) [sek′ənd] **segundo (seg)** A small unit of time
1 minute = 60 seconds

simplest form [sim′pləst fôrm] **mínima expresión** A fraction is in simplest form when the numerator and denominator have only 1 as a common factor

solid shape [sä′lid shāp] **cuerpo geométrico** See *three-dimensional figure.*

square [skwâr] **cuadrado** A quadrilateral with two pairs of parallel sides, four sides of equal length, and four right angles
Example:

square unit [skwâr yoo′nit] **unidad cuadrada** A unit of area with dimensions of 1 unit × 1 unit

standard form [stan′dərd fôrm] **forma normal** A way to write numbers by using the digits 0–9, with each digit having a place value *Example:* 3,540 ← standard form

straight angle [strāt ang′gəl] **ángulo llano** An angle whose measure is 180°
Example:

subtraction [səb•trak′shən] **resta** The process of finding how many are left when a number of items are taken away from a group of items; the process of finding the difference when two groups are compared; the opposite operation of addition

sum [sum] **suma o total** The answer to an addition problem

survey [sûr′vā] **encuesta** A method of gathering information

tally table [tal′ē tā′bəl] **tabla de conteo** A table that uses tally marks to record data

> **Word History**
>
> Some people keep score in card games by making marks on paper (IIII). These marks are known as tally marks. The word *tally* is related to *tailor,* from the Latin *talea,* meaning "twig." In early times, a method of keeping count was by cutting marks into a piece of wood or bone.

temperature [tem′pər•ə•chər] **temperatura** The degree of hotness or coldness usually measured in degrees Fahrenheit or degrees Celsius

tenth [tenth] **décimo** One of ten equal parts
Example:

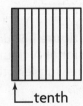
tenth

term [tûrm] **término** A number or object in a pattern

thousands [thou′zəndz] **miles** The period after the ones period in the base-ten number system

Glossary H11

three-dimensional [thrē də•men'shə•nəl] **tridimensional** Measured in three directions, such as length, width, and height
Example:

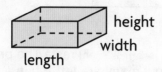

three-dimensional figure [thrē də•men'shə•nəl fig'yər] **figura tridimensional** A figure having length, width, and height

ton (T) [tun] **tonelada (t)** A customary unit used to measure weight
1 ton = 2,000 pounds

trapezoid [trap'i•zoid] **trapecio** A quadrilateral with at least one pair of parallel sides
Examples:

triangle [trī'ang•gəl] **triángulo** A polygon with three sides and three angles
Examples:

two-dimensional [tōō də•men'shə•nəl] **bidimensional** Measured in two directions, such as length and width
Example:

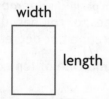

two-dimensional figure [tōō də•men'shə•nəl fig'yər] **figura bidimensional** A figure that lies in a plane; a shape having length and width

unit fraction [yōō'nit frak'shən] **fracción unitaria** A fraction that has a numerator of one

variable [vâr'ē•ə•bəl] **variable** A letter or symbol that stands for a number or numbers

Venn diagram [ven dī'ə•gram] **diagrama de Venn** A diagram that shows relationships among sets of things
Example:

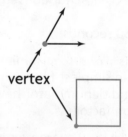

2-Digit Numbers — **Even Numbers**

35 17 29 | 12 10 | 8 6 4

vertex [vûr'teks] **vértice** The point at which two rays of an angle meet or two (or more) line segments meet in a two-dimensional shape
Examples:

vertex

vertical [vûr'ti•kəl] **vertical** In the direction from top to bottom

weight [wāt] **peso** How heavy an object is

whole [hōl] **entero** All of the parts of a shape or group

word form [wûrd fôrm] **en palabras** A way to write numbers by using words
Example: Four hundred fifty-three thousand, two hundred twelve

yard (yd) [yärd] **yarda (yd)** A customary unit for measuring length or distance
1 yard = 3 feet

Z

Zero Property of Multiplication [zē′rō präp′ər•tē əv mul•tə•pli•kā′shən] **propiedad del cero de la multiplicación** The property that states that the product of 0 and any number is 0
Example: $0 \times 8 = 0$

Correlations

 COMMON CORE STATE STANDARDS

Standards You Will Learn

Mathematical Practices		Some examples are:
MP1	Make sense of problems and persevere in solving them.	Lessons 1.8, 2.1, 3.2, 4.6, 5.3, 6.5, 7.4, 9.2, 10.4, 11.5, 12.8, 13.5
MP2	Reason abstractly and quantitatively.	Lessons 1.3, 2.2, 3.3, 4.8, 5.6, 6.2, 7.7, 8.2, 9.5, 10.5, 12.3, 13.4
MP3	Construct viable arguments and critique the reasoning of others.	Lessons 1.7, 2.10, 4.10, 5.2, 6.7, 7.3, 10.5, 11.1,12.2
MP4	Model with mathematics.	Lessons 1.2, 2.5, 3.1, 4.7, 5.1, 6.4, 7.1, 8.3, 9.4, 10.1,12.5
MP5	Use appropriate tools strategically.	Lessons 1.1, 2.3, 4.1, 4.7, 6.1, 9.1, 10.7, 11.3, 12.9
MP6	Attend to precision.	Lessons 1.4, 2.7, 3.6, 4.5, 6.3, 7.5, 8.5, 9.3, 10.2, 11.4, 12.4, 13.3
MP7	Look for and make use of structure.	Lessons 1.5, 2.4, 3.5, 4.4, 5.4, 6.6, 7.6, 8.1, 9.7, 10.3, 11.2, 12.1, 13.2
MP8	Look for and express regularity in repeated reasoning.	Lessons 1.6, 3.4, 4.3, 7.9, 8.4, 9.6, 10.6, 12.10, 13.1

Domain: Operations and Algebraic Thinking		
Use the four operations with whole numbers to solve problems		
4.OA.A.1	Interpret a multiplication equation as a comparison, e.g., interpret $35 = 5 \times 7$ as a statement that 35 is 5 times as many as 7 and 7 times as many as 5. Represent verbal statements of multiplicative comparisons as multiplication equations.	Lesson 2.1
4.OA.A.2	Multiply or divide to solve word problems involving multiplicative comparison, e.g., by using drawings and equations with a symbol for the unknown number to represent the problem, distinguishing multiplicative comparison from additive comparison.	Lessons 2.2, 4.12
4.OA.A.3	Solve multistep word problems posed with whole numbers and having whole-number answers using the four operations, including problems in which remainders must be interpreted. Represent these problems using equations with a letter standing for the unknown quantity. Assess the reasonableness of answers using mental computation and estimation strategies including rounding.	Lessons 2.9, 2.12, 3.7, 4.3
Gain familiarity with factors and multiples.		
4.OA.B.4	Find all factor pairs for a whole number in the range 1–100. Recognize that a whole number is a multiple of each of its factors. Determine whether a given whole number in the range 1–100 is a multiple of a given one-digit number. Determine whether a given whole number in the range 1–100 is prime or composite.	Lessons 5.1, 5.2, 5.3, 5.4, 5.5
Generate and analyze patterns.		
4.OA.C.5	Generate a number or shape pattern that follows a given rule. Identify apparent features of the pattern that were not explicit in the rule itself.	Lessons 5.6, 10.7

Domain: Number and Operations in Base Ten		
Generalize place value understanding for multi-digit whole numbers.		
4.NBT.A.1	Recognize that in a multi-digit whole number, a digit in one place represents ten times what it represents in the place to its right.	Lessons 1.1, 1.5
4.NBT.A.2	Read and write multi-digit whole numbers using base-ten numerals, number names, and expanded form. Compare two multi-digit numbers based on meanings of the digits in each place, using >, =, and < symbols to record the results of comparisons.	Lessons 1.2, 1.3
4.NBT.A.3	Use place value understanding to round multi-digit whole numbers to any place.	Lesson 1.4
Use place value understanding and properties of operations to perform multi-digit arithmetic.		
4.NBT.B.4	Fluently add and subtract multi-digit whole numbers using the standard algorithm.	Lessons 1.6, 1.7, 1.8
4.NBT.B.5	Multiply a whole number of up to four digits by a one-digit whole number, and multiply two two-digit numbers, using strategies based on place value and the properties of operations. Illustrate and explain the calculation by using equations, rectangular arrays, and/or area models.	Lessons 2.3, 2.4, 2.5, 2.6, 2.7, 2.8, 2.10, 2.11, 3.1, 3.2, 3.3, 3.4, 3.5, 3.6
4.NBT.B.6	Find whole-number quotients and remainders with up to four-digit dividends and one-digit divisors, using strategies based on place value, the properties of operations, and/or the relationship between multiplication and division. Illustrate and explain the calculation by using equations, rectangular arrays, and/or area models.	Lessons 4.1, 4.2, 4.4, 4.5, 4.6, 4.7, 4.8, 4.9, 4.10, 4.11

Domain: Number and Operations—Fractions		
Extend understanding of fraction equivalence and ordering.		
4.NF.A.1	Explain why a fraction *a/b* is equivalent to a fraction (*n* × *a*)/(*n* × *b*) by using visual fraction models, with attention to how the number and size of the parts differ even though the two fractions themselves are the same size. Use this principle to recognize and generate equivalent fractions.	Lessons 6.1, 6.2, 6.3, 6.4, 6.5
4.NF.A.2	Compare two fractions with different numerators and different denominators, e.g., by creating common denominators or numerators, or by comparing to a benchmark fraction such as 1/2. Recognize that comparisons are valid only when the two fractions refer to the same whole. Record the results of comparisons with symbols >, =, or <, and justify the conclusions, e.g., by using a visual fraction model.	Lessons 6.6, 6.7, 6.8

Domain: Number and Operations–Fractions

Build fractions from unit fractions by applying and extending previous understandings of operations on whole numbers.

4.NF.B.3	Understand a fraction a/b with $a > 1$ as a sum of fractions $1/b$.	
	a. Understand addition and subtraction of fractions as joining and separating parts referring to the same whole.	Lesson 7.1
	b. Decompose a fraction into a sum of fractions with the same denominator in more than one way, recording each decomposition by an equation. Justify decompositions, e.g., by using a visual fraction model.	Lessons 7.2, 7.6
	c. Add and subtract mixed numbers with like denominators, e.g., by replacing each mixed number with an equivalent fraction, and/or by using properties of operations and the relationship between addition and subtraction.	Lessons 7.7, 7.8, 7.9
	d. Solve word problems involving addition and subtraction of fractions referring to the same whole and having like denominators, e.g., by using visual fraction models and equations to represent the problem.	Lessons 7.3, 7.4, 7.5, 7.10
4.NF.B.4	Apply and extend previous understandings of multiplication to multiply a fraction by a whole number.	
	a. Understand a fraction a/b as a multiple of $1/b$.	Lesson 8.1
	b. Understand a multiple of a/b as a multiple of $1/b$, and use this understanding to multiply a fraction by a whole number.	Lessons 8.2, 8.3
	c. Solve word problems involving multiplication of a fraction by a whole number, e.g., by using visual fraction models and equations to represent the problem.	Lessons 8.4, 8.5

Domain: Number and Operations—Fractions		
Understand decimal notation for fractions, and compare decimal fractions.		
4.NF.C.5	Express a fraction with denominator 10 as an equivalent fraction with denominator 100, and use this technique to add two fractions with respective denominators 10 and 100.	Lessons 9.3, 9.6
4.NF.C.6	Use decimal notation for fractions with denominators 10 or 100.	Lessons 9.1, 9.2, 9.4
4.NF.C.7	Compare two decimals to hundredths by reasoning about their size. Recognize that comparisons are valid only when two decimals refer to the same whole. Record the results of comparisons with the symbols >, =, or <, and justify the conclusions, e.g., by using a visual model.	Lesson 9.7
Domain: Measurement and Data		
Solve problems involving measurement and conversion of measurements from a larger unit to a smaller unit.		
4.MD.A.1	Know relative sizes of measurement units within one system of units including km, m, cm; kg, g; lb, oz.; l, ml; hr, min, sec. Within a single system of measurement, express measurements in a larger unit in terms of a smaller unit. Record measurement equivalents in a two-column table.	Lessons 12.1, 12.2, 12.3, 12.4, 12.6, 12.7, 12.8, 12.11
4.MD.A.2	Use the four operations to solve word problems involving distances, intervals of time, liquid volumes, masses of objects, and money, including problems involving simple fractions or decimals, and problems that require expressing measurements given in a larger unit in terms of a smaller unit. Represent measurement quantities using diagrams such as number line diagrams that feature a measurement scale.	Lessons 9.5, 12.9, 12.10
4.MD.A.3	Apply the area and perimeter formulas for rectangles in real world and mathematical problems.	Lessons 13.1, 13.2, 13.3, 13.4, 13.5

Domain: Measurement and Data		
Represent and interpret data.		
4.MD.B.4	Make a line plot to display a data set of measurements in fractions of a unit (1/2, 1/4, 1/8). Solve problems involving addition and subtraction of fractions by using information presented in line plots.	Lesson 12.5
Geometric measurement: understand concepts of angle and measure angles.		
4.MD.C.5	Recognize angles as geometric shapes that are formed wherever two rays share a common endpoint, and understand concepts of angle measurement:	
	a. An angle is measured with reference to a circle with its center at the common endpoint of the rays, by considering the fraction of the circular arc between the points where the two rays intersect the circle. An angle that turns through 1/360 of a circle is called a "one-degree angle," and can be used to measure angles.	Lessons 11.1, 11.2
	b. An angle that turns through n one-degree angles is said to have an angle measure of n degrees.	Lesson 11.2
4.MD.C.6	Measure angles in whole-number degrees using a protractor. Sketch angles of specified measure.	Lesson 11.3
4.MD.C.7	Recognize angle measure as additive. When an angle is decomposed into non-overlapping parts, the angle measure of the whole is the sum of the angle measures of the parts. Solve addition and subtraction problems to find unknown angles on a diagram in real world and mathematical problems, e.g., by using an equation with a symbol for the unknown angle measure.	Lessons 11.4, 11.5

Domain: Geometry

Draw and identify lines and angles, and classify shapes by properties of their lines and angles.

4.G.A.1	Draw points, lines, line segments, rays, angles (right, acute, obtuse), and perpendicular and parallel lines. Identify these in two-dimensional figures.	Lessons 10.1, 10.3
4.G.A.2	Classify two-dimensional figures based on the presence or absence of parallel or perpendicular lines, or the presence or absence of angles of a specified size. Recognize right triangles as a category, and identify right triangles.	Lessons 10.2, 10.4
4.G.A.3	Recognize a line of symmetry for a two-dimensional figure as a line across the figure such that the figure can be folded along the line into matching parts. Identify line-symmetric figures and draw lines of symmetry.	Lessons 10.5, 10.6

© Houghton Mifflin Harcourt Publishing Company

Index

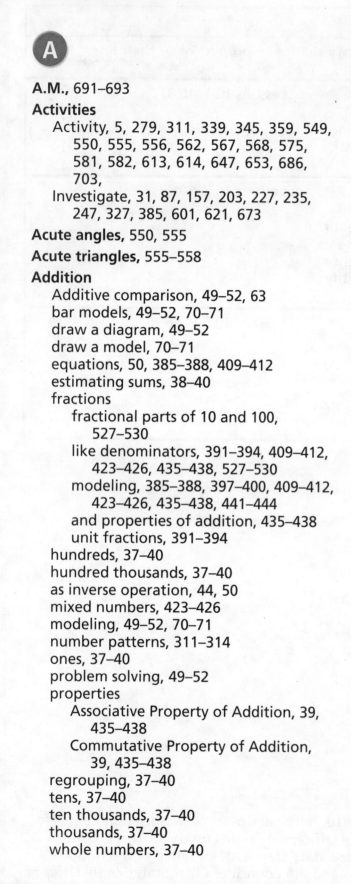

© Houghton Mifflin Harcourt Publishing Company

2. Reason abstractly and quantitatively. In many lessons. Some examples are: 11, 17, 23, 31, 63, 69, 75, 113, 119, 131, 145, 151, 157, 163, 221, 241, 247, 279, 297, 311, 333, 359, 365, 385, 391, 397, 403, 409, 417, 423, 435, 441, 461, 495, 501, 507, 513, 519, 527, 533, 567, 575, 601, 607, 641, 647, 653, 665, 723, 737

3. Construct viable arguments and critique the reasoning of others. In many lessons. Some examples are: 43, 87, 119, 125, 131, 209, 221, 253, 285, 365, 391, 397, 441, 575, 581, 601, 641, 647, 659, 665, 679, 697, 703

4. Model with mathematics. In many lessons. Some examples are: 11, 23, 49, 87, 99, 113, 145, 157, 183, 227, 247, 265, 279, 285, 327, 333, 345, 351, 385, 403, 429, 441, 455, 469, 513, 549, 561, 621, 627, 647, 659, 665, 673, 685, 691, 743

5. Use appropriate tools strategically. In many lessons. Some examples are: 5, 31, 75, 197, 215, 235, 259, 265, 311, 327, 333, 365, 495, 587, 613, 685, 691

6. Attend to precision. In many lessons. Some examples are: 5, 23, 37, 63, 87, 99, 125, 151, 157, 177, 215, 221, 235, 241, 299, 339, 345, 351, 359, 403, 409, 417, 455, 495, 507, 513, 519, 533, 555, 561, 587, 607, 613, 653, 659, 703, 723, 729

7. Look for and make use of structure. In many lessons. Some examples are: 11, 31, 75, 81, 119, 145, 171, 177, 197, 209, 215, 227, 253, 285, 299, 311, 327, 339, 345, 359, 409, 417, 429, 455, 461, 481, 501, 507, 527, 555, 561, 587, 607, 641, 659, 673, 685, 703, 717, 737

8. Look for and express regularity in repeated reasoning. In many lessons. Some examples are: 37, 43, 49, 163, 171, 177, 209, 241, 259, 299, 391, 417, 423, 435, 461, 475, 527, 673, 697, 717

Math Idea, 24, 44, 253, 279, 285, 306, 371, 575, 607, 621, 673, 724

Math in the Real World Activities, 3, 61, 143, 195, 277, 325, 383, 453, 493, 547, 599, 639, 715

Math on the Spot Videos, In every Student Edition lesson. Some examples are: 8, 46, 90, 116, 148, 217, 244, 281, 330, 388, 426, 458, 498, 552, 604, 649, 720

Math Talk, In every Student Edition lesson. Some examples are: 5, 12, 64, 82, 114, 132, 177, 209, 228, 279, 299, 328, 359, 386, 429, 455, 495, 520, 556, 602, 642, 723

Measurement
   angles
      and fractional parts of circle, 601–604
      joining and separating, 621–624
      measuring and drawing, 613–616
      solving for unknown angle measures, 627–630
   area, 723–726, 743–746
      of combined rectangles, 729–732
      concept of, 723–726
      defined, 723
      finding, 723–726, 729–732, 743–746
      finding unknown measures, 737–740
      formula for, 723–726
      perimeter, related to, 731
      of a rectangle, 723–726, 729–732
      square unit, 723
      units of, 723–726
   benchmarks, 641–644
      centimeter, 642–644
      cup, 641
      decimeter, 642
      fluid ounce, 641
      foot, 641, 643
      gallon, 641, 643
      gram, 642–643
      inch, 641, 643
      kilogram, 642–643
      kilometer, 642–643
      liter, 642–643
      meter, 642–643
      mile, 641, 643
      milliliter, 642–644
      millimeter, 642
      ounce, 641, 643
      pint, 641
      pound, 641, 643
      quart, 641
      ton, 641, 643
      yard, 641, 643
   comparing, 642, 647–650, 653–656, 659–662, 685–688

© Houghton Mifflin Harcourt Publishing Company

259–260, 265–266, 279, 282, 285,
291–292, 299, 305, 311, 333–334,
339–340, 345, 351–352, 359–360, 365,
368, 371, 374, 391–392, 394, 397–398,
403–404, 406, 409, 417–418, 423–424,
429–430, 435–436, 455–456, 461–462,
464, 469, 472, 475–476, 481–482,
495–496, 501–502, 507–508, 513,
519–520, 527–528, 533, 536, 549–550,
555–556, 561–562, 567–568, 575–576,
578, 581–582, 587–588, 607–608, 610,
613, 626, 627, 641–642, 647–648,
653–654, 659–660, 665–666, 668, 679,
682, 685–686, 691–692, 697–698, 700,
703, 717–718, 720, 723–724, 726,
729–730, 732, 737–738, 743–744
Reason Abstractly, 387
Sense or Nonsense?, 160, 250, 388, 411,
412, 458, 476, 604, 699
Think Smarter Problems, In every Student
Edition lesson. Some examples are: 8,
25, 63, 88, 122, 154, 211, 228, 262,
281, 328, 386, 426, 457, 498, 552, 610,
644, 720
Try This!, 11, 24, 44, 64, 107, 120, 146,
152, 178, 209, 210, 286, 312, 366,
372, 436, 476, 496, 514, 527, 528,
534, 555, 561, 568, 608, 654, 698,
704, 718, 724, 738
What's the Error?, 13, 46, 96, 134, 330,
409, 706
What's the Question?, 20, 342, 362, 478
Problem-solving strategies
Act It Out, 441–444, 519–522, 587–590
Draw a Diagram, 49–52, 113–116,
183–186, 265–268, 481–484, 627–630,
691–694
Make a List, 291–294
Make a Table, 351–354
Solve a Simpler Problem, 743–746
Products. *See also* Multiplication
estimating, 81–83, 99–102, 151–154
partial, 88, 99–101, 157–160, 163–166
Project, 2, 324, 546
Properties
Associative Property
of Addition, 39, 435–438
of Multiplication, 107–110, 145–148
Commutative Property
of Addition, 39, 435–438
of Multiplication, 63, 107–110, 171

Distributive Property, 87–90, 99–101,
108–109, 227–230, 718
Identity Property of Multiplication, 476

Quadrilaterals, 567–570
defined, 567
parallelogram, 567–570
rectangle, 567–570
rhombus, 567–570
square, 567–570
trapezoid, 567–570
Quart, 641, 659–662
Quarters, 513–516, 519–520
Quick pictures
to model division, 203–206, 248–250
to model multiplication, 75–78
Quotients, 210, 235–238. *See also* Division
estimating, 197–200, 221–224
partial, 241–244
placing the first digit, 253–256

Rays, 549–552
Reading
Connect to Reading, 84, 224
Read Math, 555, 685
Read/Solve the Problem, 49–50, 113–114,
183–184, 265–266, 291–292, 351–352,
441–442, 481–482, 519–520, 587–588,
627–628, 691–692, 743–744
Visualize It, 4, 62, 144, 196, 278, 326, 384,
454, 494, 548, 600, 640, 716
Real World
Problem Solving, In every Student Edition
lesson. Some examples are: 8, 45, 96,
148, 200, 237, 302, 348, 411, 437, 457,
498, 552, 603, 649, 699
Unlock the Problem, In every Student
Edition lesson. Some examples are: 11,
49–50, 93–94, 151–152, 209–210, 279,
345, 394, 429–430, 435–436, 441–442,
455–456, 495–496, 533, 549–550, 578,
647–648, 717–718
Reasonableness of an answer, 23, 43, 82, 93,
99, 119, 151–154, 163, 171, 221, 641

U

V

W

Y

Table of Measures

METRIC

CUSTOMARY

Length

1 centimeter (cm) = 10 millimeters (mm)

1 meter (m) = 1,000 millimeters

1 meter = 100 centimeters

1 meter = 10 decimeters (dm)

1 kilometer (km) = 1,000 meters

1 foot (ft) = 12 inches (in.)

1 yard (yd) = 3 feet, or 36 inches

1 mile (mi) = 1,760 yards, or 5,280 feet

Capacity and Liquid Volume

1 liter (L) = 1,000 milliliters (mL)

1 cup (c) = 8 fluid ounces (fl oz)

1 pint (pt) = 2 cups

1 quart (qt) = 2 pints, or 4 cups

1 half gallon = 2 quarts

1 gallon (gal) = 2 half gallons, or 4 quarts

Mass/Weight

1 kilogram (kg) = 1,000 grams (g)

1 pound (lb) = 16 ounces (oz)

1 ton (T) = 2,000 pounds

TIME

1 minute (min) = 60 seconds (sec)

1 half hour = 30 minutes

1 hour (hr) = 60 minutes

1 day (d) = 24 hours

1 week (wk) = 7 days

1 year (yr) = 12 months (mo), or about 52 weeks

1 year = 365 days

1 leap year = 366 days

1 decade = 10 years

1 century = 100 years

MONEY

1 penny = 1¢, or $0.01

1 nickel = 5¢, or $0.05

1 dime = 10¢, or $0.10

1 quarter = 25¢, or $0.25

1 half dollar = 50¢, or $0.50

1 dollar = 100¢, or $1.00

SYMBOLS

$<$	is less than	$\perp$	is perpendicular to
$>$	is greater than	$\parallel$	is parallel to
$=$	is equal to	$\overleftrightarrow{AB}$	line AB
$\neq$	is not equal to	$\overrightarrow{AB}$	ray AB
¢	cent or cents	$\overline{AB}$	line segment AB
$	dollar or dollars	$\angle ABC$	angle ABC or angle B
°	degree or degrees	$\triangle ABC$	triangle ABC

FORMULAS

	Perimeter		**Area**
Polygon	$P = $ sum of the lengths of sides	Rectangle	$A = b \times h$
Rectangle	$P = (2 \times l) + (2 \times w)$ or $P = 2 \times (l + w)$		$A = l \times w$
Square	$P = 4 \times s$